Interpreting the Theatrical Past

Interpreting the Theatrical Past

Essays in the Historiography of Performance

Theatrical

Edited by
Thomas Postlewait &
Bruce A. McConachie

Past

University of Iowa Press   Iowa City

University of Iowa Press, Iowa City 52242
Printed in the United States of America
Third printing, 2000

Design by Richard Hendel
Typesetting by G&S Typesetters, Austin, Texas
Printing and binding by Edwards Brothers,
Ann Arbor, Michigan

Library of Congress Cataloging-in-Publication Data

Interpreting the theatrical past: essays in the
historiography of performance / edited by Thomas
Postlewait and Bruce A. McConachie. — 1st ed.

    p.   cm.
  Bibliography: p.
  Includes index.
  ISBN 0-87745-228-8, ISBN 0-87745-238-5 (pbk.)
  1. Theater—Historiography.   I. Postlewait, Thomas.
II. McConachie, Bruce A.
PN2115.I54   1989   88-35045
792—dc19   CIP

Contents

Acknowledgments

Herbert Lindenberger's essay was first published in *Idee-Gestalt-Geschichte: Festschrift für Klaus von See,* ed. Gert Wolfgang Weber (Odense: Odense University Press, 1987). We thank Professor Weber for permission to reprint the essay.

Robert Sarlós' essay is a substantially revised and expanded version of an essay first published in *The Drama Review,* volume 28, number 3 (Fall 1984). We thank MIT Press for permission to reprint this essay.

In addition, we appreciate the secretarial help we received from Tracey Roberts and Michelle Henry, Department of Drama, University of Georgia, and Phyllis Leffler and Deborah Buchman, Program in American Studies, College of William and Mary.

Introduction

Thomas Postlewait and
Bruce A. McConachie

The essays in this collection examine the research procedures, practices, problems, and opportunities in the wide field of theatre history. No single methodology or theory dominates this collection; instead, it offers various approaches to the study—that is, the historical interpretation, not just description—of the theatrical past. These essays, though providing information on specific people, events, works, documents, institutions, and social conditions in the history of the theatre, aim primarily to explore theoretical and methodological issues, to review and analyze current research practices and presuppositions, and to identify and apply new theoretical orientations to theatre studies. In addition, some of the essays in the collection highlight specific problems in certain areas of our discipline and suggest new procedures for investigation and analysis.

These essays are not meant to be the final word on research scholarship and interpretation in theatre studies. Nor do they cover, as we well recognize, all areas and aspects of theatre history. We had hoped to present several additional approaches and fields of study, but our choices were limited by the publishing exigencies of deadlines and available space. Still, we feel strongly that the collected essays, within the context of their specific topics, not only identify historiographic problems and issues but also provide interpretative approaches that apply broadly to theatre studies. In this way, they fulfill the basic purpose of this collection, which is to open up topics, to raise issues, to define practices, and to challenge assumptions in theatre history.

Each of our contributors, whatever his or her interpretative viewpoint and rhetorical stance, attempts to contribute to what is becoming an ongoing debate on the methods and purposes of professional training and research in the study of the performing arts. For example, Joseph Donohue looks closely at standards of scholarly research and documentation, including the promise and problems of computer databases. Tracy C. Davis provides a review and a critique of feminist theatre scholarship, an area that deservedly is gaining more attention in theatre studies. James V. Hatch explores the difficulties that continue to hinder the integration of black theatre history and scholarship into curricula and training programs.

Primarily, this collection is directed at theatre scholars and students, especially those who are interested in the professional practices of research, writing, and publishing. But because these essays investigate many of the issues that face all cultural and intellectual historians, this gathering may also serve scholars and students in the related fields of the performing arts, humanities, and social sciences. Scholarship in historiography crosses many disciplines. For this reason, we include a select bibliography that lists not only current studies in theatre historiography but also representative scholarship in cultural studies and general history. Increasingly, theatre scholars are finding that these related fields provide valuable methodologies and theories for grounding theatre scholarship.

Necessarily, then, the essays in this collection relate theatre studies to a number of other academic disciplines, from art history and musicology to sociology and anthropology. Whether discussing specific issues and methodologies or general analytical procedures and problems, these essays show that theatre history does not (or should not) exist as an isolated field of study. Thus, Alan Woods challenges the practice of neatly separating popular and avant-garde cultures, especially as this familiar but problematic distinction functions within formalist histories that study modern theatre as a series of new stylistic movements, occurring apart from social history. Joseph R. Roach investigates a different kind of categorical problem: the difficulty of comprehending the unfamiliar or bizarre in history. By examining the historical conditions and signifying practices of the *castrati* on the eighteenth-century stage, he identifies a discourse of power in the theatre that, in Foucault's terms, shaped action and perception. Leigh Woods, in a study of theatre biography, criticizes our standard ways of recording the exhibitionist life of the actor, whose performances on and off the stage contribute to a narrative mystification, a compulsive mythmaking of the prototypical artist.

Each of the essayists in this collection recognizes that his or her topic could not be fully discussed within the limitations of a single essay. For this reason, the reader should keep in mind that a more complete discussion of the issues can be found in the other publications of the contributors. For instance, R. W. Vince in his essay summarizes the history of theatre historiography, a subject he has investigated in detail in three related volumes that cover the periods from the classical age to the eighteenth century. Robert K. Sarlós studies the possibilities of theatre reconstruction, but this methodological essay is only one of a series that he has published on theatre historiography. Similarly, though Marvin Carlson spells out in his essay some of the important aspects of reception theory and semiotics, his analysis should be placed within the context of a number of wide-ranging and influential essays and books that he has published during the last two decades on theatre history, semiotics, performance spaces, and dramatic theory. Aptly, then, the essays in this collection build upon previous work. Thus, when Erika Fischer-Lichte examines aspects of the history of acting in terms of semiotics and social history, she is drawing upon the work in her well-received *Semiotik des Theaters,* published in three volumes in Germany and forthcoming in translation in a condensed volume from Indiana University Press. Herbert Lindenberger, who discusses how opera functions as a cultural mode of representation, a political act, and a social register of history, has developed his "multiperspectival method" in two major books, *Historical Drama: The Relation of Literature and Reality* and *Opera: The Extravagant Art.* Indeed, each of the essayists has written elsewhere (and continues to write) on the issues analyzed here.

The contributors to this collection were selected because of their current writing on theatre historiography. In this they join a small but significant number of theatre scholars who have attempted to investigate the state of the profession. All of us together, whatever our various methodologies and theories, want to move theatre studies forward as an important field of scholarship and interpretation in cultural history. We hope that at least some of the readers of this collection will want to join in this endeavor, not only by contributing to the needed discussion on theatre historiography but also by applying these ideas on methodology and interpretation to the vital research that awaits good scholars and writers. If, by raising historiographical issues, we can contribute to that research and publishing, we will be satisfied that this collection has fulfilled its purpose.

Interpreting the Theatrical Past

Theatre History as an Academic Discipline

R. W. Vince

As a discipline—certainly as an academic discipline recognized and practiced in colleges and universities—theatre history has seldom had a very high profile; those who profess it have seldom enjoyed a status independent of their academic appointments either in literature departments, where the predominant values and methods are literary, or in departments of theatre, where the primary emphasis often remains on the training of theatre practitioners. For much of the present century, theatre researchers have struggled to distance themselves from literary critics and literary historians, to establish their discipline on the fact of theatrical performance rather than on that of dramatic text; they therefore sought a closer relationship with theatrical practitioners, with directors, actors, and scene designers, and with those who trained them, insisting always on the "living" nature of past theatre.

Ironically, this relationship, too, is breaking down, a fact attested by the declining demand for theatre historians in departments of theatre, by the elimination of Ph.D. programs at major universities,[1] and by the tone of crisis in a recent forum on the state of the profession.[2] In his short history of theatrical research published in 1981, James Arnott found two conceptions of theatre research still current: as a discipline in the service of the theatre practitioner and as "an independent branch of knowledge, emulating the standards established in other fields of scientific investigation."[3] If there is a crisis in theatre research, it lies in our unsure reactions to the necessity—thrust upon us, to be sure—of defining our study as an independent branch of knowledge, of professing a kind of knowledge and a kind of truth intrinsically valuable. In brief, the struggle is for a sense of professional identity.

One way of establishing that identity is to consider the history of theatre research; for although we cling to the notion that we represent a relatively new discipline, the theatre is one of the most ancient of Western institutions and in fact has been studied and written about since antiquity. We must recognize that as modern historians we are part of a long tradition. Just as a sense of personal identity depends upon personal memory, so a sense of professional identity derives in part from the collective and extended memory we call history. Moreover, by considering the theatre historian as the product of a particular time and place, conditioned by current assumptions and ideologies as well as by personal predilections, we keep before us the human face of history. We see it as the product of a human confrontation of data, as dynamic models that are as dependent upon the historian's perceptions as upon the amount and nature of the data that the historian identifies as historical evidence. We are all the inheritors of the past and are influenced by our notions of the past. But historians, above all others, ought to recognize the extent to which that inheritance has formed them. Either consciously or unconsciously, we practice our discipline under the influence of the past. The materials of history, especially for earlier periods, were preserved and identified in the past; many of our traditional attitudes were formed and our common methods developed in the past; the purposes and questions of history together with the parameters of possible answers were formulated in the past. This essay offers a brief sketch of theatrical scholarship, outlines some of the issues that continue to concern us as theatre historians, and concludes with a tentative suggestion for the future.

Theatre historians like to date their discipline from the *Theatriké historia* of King Juba II of Mauretania (ca. 50 B.C.–ca. A.D. 23), a voluminous work reputedly devoted to a discussion of all matters associated with the stage. Unfortunately, we do not have it. As a matter of fact, our knowledge of King Juba's writings, like much of our knowledge of theatre history itself, is based on indirect evidence (in Juba's case, references and citations in later Greek and Latin writers) and on speculation. Only tantalizing tidbits can be gleaned from writers such as Athenaeus in his *Deipnosophistae* or Julius Pollux in his *Onomastikon*. The *Theatriké historia* is not the only document that modern theatre historians wish had been preserved, but the suggestion of a distinct discipline implicit in its title renders its loss particularly painful.

Between Juba's time and the sixteenth century, no one was concerned with the history of the theatre as such. A great deal of scholarly material was, of course, produced, but references to the theatre represent only a minute proportion of what has come down to us. We ought not, nevertheless, discount the scholarly efforts of 1,500 years. If the ultimate task of the historian is to explain, the first task is to preserve and catalogue; and this was the achievement of the Hellenistic, Byzantine, Roman, and medieval scholars as they labored in library, monastery, or school. We might wish that they had gone about their task differently or more thoroughly— principally by adhering to twentieth-century standards of scholarship and by bearing in mind our concerns as well as their own—but, as unreliable as some of the information provided by the various biographers, commentators, encyclopedists, grammarians, transcribers, and historians might be, it represents most of the written information extant concerning the theatres of antiquity.

One result of the kind of labor that characterized scholarship during this extended period was that it became text centered, obsessed with documents, with the written word. The consequences for theatre history were that drama, even if discussed, was treated as literature, and interest in the theatre narrowed to interest in the dramatic text. The most important critical document to survive from antiquity, Aristotle's *Poetics,* which might have provided an appropriate theoretical basis for the study of drama as a performed art, was initially preserved and transmitted via Arabic culture, which officially forbade representational art, including the theatre, after the ninth century. Moreover, the *Poetics* itself has a clear bias in favor of drama as literature. In any event, the document exerted little influence on dramatic theory of any kind until the sixteenth century. Throughout most of the Middle Ages, the terms "tragedy" and "comedy," for instance, were applied to literature rather than to drama. But it is not merely the application of dramatic terminology to nondramatic literature which is significant; rather, it is the treatment of drama as literature.

The Roman playwright Terence, for example, was the subject of many commentaries, but his plays were examined as species of rhetoric, analyzed according to the rules of grammar, or cited as moral exempla. Scholars were aware that Terence had been performed (although they had little idea of the specific conditions), but the nature and effect of any performance were irrelevant to their considerations of Terence's essence, which for them lay in the written text. Certainly, there was no suggestion that the dramatic texts inherited from Greece and Rome bore any relationship to the theatrical performances which from the tenth century had begun to be associated with the Christian church and its festivals. The upshot of this separation of text (important) from performance (unimportant) is that the academic study of drama continued to emphasize the former at the expense of the latter well into the twentieth century.

During the late fifteenth and sixteenth centuries, especially in Italy, scholars were becoming aware that the ancients had staged their plays, and efforts were made to recreate the theatres of Greece and Rome. Classical dramatic forms and genres were imitated, adapted, transformed, or re-created, self-consciously and in defiance of religious and popular practice. Aristotle and Horace were translated, conflated, and transmuted, and neo-classicism was born. Vitruvius' *De Architectura,* translated into Italian in 1521, provided the grounding and the impetus for experiments in theatre architecture and stage effects, culminating in the construction of the Teatro Olimpico (1580–1584). Sixteenth-century conceptions of Greek and Roman theatrical activity might strike us as inaccurate or even bizarre, but these ideas were truly historical in the sense that they resulted from the human interpretation of available data. Not for the first time, historical notions—valid for their own time and place—themselves became the stuff of later history when their explanatory power waned.

The sixteenth century had returned attention to the theatres of Greece and Rome. By 1700, however, the great national theatres of England, Spain, and France had to be accounted for, and eighteenth-century writers were acutely aware of—indeed insisted upon—the merits and achievements of the previous century. Most attention was directed toward the history of dramatic literature, to which was sometimes appended some consideration of theatres and actors. An equally strong tendency to provide biographies—initially of playwrights but eventually of actors as well—also developed during this period. Finally, we find that literary history, of which theatrical or dramatic history was considered a part, began to reflect the idea of independent, individual, national literatures. In some instances, there was an effort to trace dramatic activity from the Middle Ages to the contemporary world, although neoclassical writers in general preferred to see the roots of modern drama in classical forms. In any event, the medieval period usually got short shrift.

The most common form in which theatrical matters were published was the dictionary rather than historical narrative. Dramatic literature, biography, evaluative commentary, and anecdote—these rather than historical concerns of development, influence, or cause and effect were at the center of such compilations. Moreover, without any shaping concept or purpose, the material collected is all too often inaccurate, fragmented, and pointless. These sins continued as well in the innumerable memoirs, biographies, and autobiographies that appeared in the eighteenth and nineteenth centuries. Such work passes almost instantly from history to the materials of history.

On the other hand, the eighteenth century also produced a few theatrical scholars of remarkable industry and insight. The tendency to view theatre as dramatic literature and to emphasize biography continued, but the eighteenth century also saw the beginnings of modern theatre history. We find in the work of Claude and François Parfaict in France,[4] Casiano Pellicer in Spain,[5] and Edmond Malone in England the beginnings of national theatrical histories. Moreover, both Malone and Pellicer introduced serious archival research to the writing of theatre history. Malone especially, in his "Historical Account of the Rise and Progress of the English Stage and of the Economy and Usages of Our Ancient Theatres,"[6] established a continuing reputation for scholarly integrity.

Other writers attempted what might be called "universal history," international in scope and comparative in method. The Italian actor and director Luigi Riccoboni in 1738 turned his attention to a comparative survey of the national theatres of Europe, emphasizing speculation and polemic above historical analysis.[7] On the other hand, the actor and dramatist Charles Dibdin deserves to be treated seriously as a historian. In *A Complete History of the English Stage,*[8] Dibdin stressed the primacy of firsthand experience as a historiographical principle, affirming its superiority to written documents as a basis for history. Dibdin is also among the earliest historians to pay more than cursory attention to the history of the theatre in Europe as well as in England before his own time. He could lay little claim to scholarship in the sense that Malone could, but the only other historian of the period who approached his breadth of scope in the treatment of both contemporary and past theatre was Pietro Napoli Signorelli. Signorelli's *Storia critica dei teatri antichi e moderni* is in fact the first history of Western theatre as an autonomous institution.[9] The theatre, Signorelli believed, expresses the full maturity of a society, but is in the final analysis a self-generating institution. His treatment of the theatre is even more wide-ranging than that of Dibdin.

Eighteenth-century theatre historiography was influenced by the almost universally held idea of historical progress, a notion that underlies the work of theatrical reformers such as Riccoboni and Signorelli, but one that is also reflected in the title of Malone's essay. At the same time, by modern standards at least, Malone's superior scholarship, firmly based on documentary evidence, kept him from the superficialities and speculations of those who sketched on a broader canvas. In fact, the archival searches undertaken by the Parfaicts, by Malone, and by Pellicer mark an important step in the development of a discipline distinct from the study of literature.

On the other hand, speculation can also be justified. It may be that the eighteenth-century attempts at universal history were premature, but the comparative method and chronological analysis that lay behind them

helped to establish an overall conception of a possible history of the theatre. The universal historians pointed to a discernible relationship among
contemporary national theatres, and between those national theatres and
the classical theatres of Greece and Rome. The continuing confusion of
theatre with dramatic literature and the assumptions of neoclassicism
nevertheless made it difficult for most commentators to see any connection
between modern theatre and that of the Middle Ages; and there was little
theoretical underpinning to describe or explain the process that brought
about "progress." Above all, there was as yet no conception of theatre history as a discipline distinct from literary history.

By the early years of the nineteenth century, the way had been prepared
for a fresh examination of the modern theatre, which would go beyond the
limits imposed by neoclassical prejudice and the identification of theatre
with dramatic literature and aim for a more systematic exploitation of
some of the insights tentatively and haphazardly advanced during the previous century. In the eighteenth century, Thomas Percy and Thomas
Hawkins had broken with neoclassical preconception by arguing that the
modern theatre was in fact an indigenous development from the neglected
theatre of the Middle Ages and that the classical influence was secondary.[10]

The nineteenth century went further. In 1838, Charles Magnin employed
the comparative method to draw an analogy between the development of
modern European theatre from the liturgy of the medieval church and the
process by which, a millennium and a half earlier, the ancient Greek theatre had emerged from the worship of Dionysus.[11] In 1869, Louis Leclercq
examined the conditions, methods, and accoutrements of seventeenth-
century performances rather than dramatic literature and paid considerable
attention to such non- or quasi-literary forms as ballet, opera, court entertainments, and machine-plays.[12] The distinction between theatre and
literature was maintained as well in Arthur Pougin's *Dictionnaire du théâtre*
(1885) and Germain Bapst's *Essai sur l'histoire du théâtre* (1893). No longer
would the primary evidence for the history of the theatre consist of dramatic texts, biographical data, collected critical opinion, and anecdote.
Historians were prepared instead to concern themselves with questions of
decor, theatre architecture, lighting, and the logistical and economic aspects of mounting a production and attracting an audience.

An even more rigid separation of theatrical history from dramatic history underlay the efforts in Germany during the early years of the present
century to establish theatre history as an independent university discipline,
centered on the study of scenic space and action and related to social and
art history. Max Herrmann in Berlin is usually credited with founding

Theaterwissenschaft, the historical study of theatrical practice. The German school of theatre history, vigorously championed in the United States by A. M. Nagler, remains rigorously "scientific" in its emphasis on primary documentary evidence and in its reluctance to go beyond demonstrable fact. For them, original research means, in effect, archival research. This "purist's stance" (the phrase is Nagler's) has not been universally accepted, but the insistence on a systematic method for dealing with the materials of theatre history remains a healthy antidote to earlier dilettantism.

Organizations and publications in Germany and elsewhere followed the establishment in 1902 of the Berlin Gesellschaft für Theatergeschichte; and Herrmann's Theaterwissenschaftliches Institut (1923) was the model for similar institutes throughout much of Europe. In 1932, August Rondel, librarian of the Comédie Française, founded the Société d'Histoire du Théâtre. In England, the Society for Theatre Research was established in 1948; in the United States, the American Society for Theatre Research was founded in 1956; in Canada, the Association for Canadian Theatre History/Association d'Histoire du Théâtre au Canada was formed in 1976. These organizations are associated with the International Federation for Theatre Research/Fédération International pour la Recherche Théâtrale, and each publishes a learned journal.

Such a bald account might be taken as evidence that theatre history has come into its own as a specialized discipline with its own purposes, methods, and prestige. Indeed, the first half of the twentieth century saw the publication of numerous scholarly works devoted to the history of the theatre. Even a beginner soon becomes familiar with the names of E. K. Chambers, Gustave Cohen, Allardyce Nicoll, G. C. D. Odell, Wilma Deierkauf-Holsboer, Heinz Kindermann, and A. M. Nagler. However they differ in scope or in their treatment of materials, these scholars were devoted to the conception of theatre history as a discipline separate from the aesthetic consideration of dramatic literature, undertaken with methodological rigor and dedicated to what they thought of as scientific accuracy. Above all, such history was to be based on facts, social and economic as well as theatrical. "Yet from a study of such facts," writes E. K. Chambers, "I am sure, any literary history, which does not confine itself solely to the analysis of genius, must make a start."[13] The notion that history lies in the written and artifactual record is reflected in the "documentary imperative" that continues to characterize most theatre history.

While these scholars were concerning themselves with the national theatres of Europe, quite different factors were stimulating new research into the theatres of Greece and Rome. The nineteenth century was the great age of classical philology and archaeology: Greek and Latin writers of whatever stature were rendered in scholarly and accessible editions; public records and inscriptions were collected and published; statuary and vases depicting theatrical scenes were unearthed and described. The theatre of Dionysus in Athens was excavated in the 1880s by Wilhelm Dörpfeld, a protégé of Heinrich Schliemann. The analysis and synthesis of this new evidence was undertaken, of course, by researchers who considered themselves classical scholars rather than theatre historians. Nevertheless, theatre history was able to add to its honor roll the names of A. W. Pickard-Cambridge, Margarete Bieber, Roy C. Flickinger, and William Beare.

Despite the obvious achievements of such scholars, even by mid-century theatre history had not really succeeded in establishing itself as a reputable academic discipline, particularly in English-speaking countries. Bieber, Beare, and Pickard-Cambridge were associated with departments of classical studies; Chambers was a civil servant who undertook theatre research as an avocation; W. J. Lawrence found no place in the academic community; Gustave Cohen, even as he was publishing the results of his investigations into the medieval theatre, was required to train his students in the techniques of textual explication and literary appreciation. As late as 1959, Glynne Wickham was complaining that "the idea that drama is literature or nothing dies hard: and most faculties of language and literature in our schools and universities seem determined to make a last-ditch stand to defend it."[14] In the United States, the determination of literature departments to consider drama their responsibility led to the anomaly of departments of theatre devoted almost exclusively to the practical training of actors, directors, and scene designers. Under these circumstances, theatre historians found themselves in a no-man's-land: students of literature assumed that the history and literary analysis of drama were identical with the history of the theatre and stage practitioners considered the history of the theatre irrelevant to the immediacy of their own endeavors.

We once again find ourselves considering the crisis noted in the opening paragraphs of this essay. We have too long taken on faith the possibility of the eventual integration of the study of dramatic literature, practical stage work, and theatre history. The question now confronting us is whether or not such an integration is desirable or even possible. The answer will have consequences for academic organization and individual researcher alike.

Four issues are of particular concern: 1. the relationship of theatre history to the study of dramatic literature, 2. the relationship of theatre history to theatre practice, 3. the nature and scope of theatre history as an academic discipline, and 4. the relationship of data and historian.

1. While the theatre has often included nonverbal forms, those interested in drama and the theatre have, for better or worse, traditionally focused their attention on those periods from which dramatic texts have been preserved; the conflict historically has been between those who consider and treat drama as a form of literature analogous to poetry or fiction and those who consider the text a set of incomplete directions for a performance. Thoughtful critics have, of course, long assumed a discernible and explicable relationship between a text and the conditions of its performance and have sought to explain the former in terms of the latter, but dramatic theory and analysis have nevertheless proceeded in general on the assumption that performance is ancillary rather than integral to the drama.

Students of literature have ample justification for their procedure. The world's drama constitutes a significant literature that rewards literary analysis. Moreover, the earliest extant discussion of drama, Aristotle's *Poetics,* is clearly biased in favor of the playwright's art as opposed to the actor's, and it is this document that has provided the analytical method and the terminology familiar to all literary scholars. Aristotle proceeded on the premise that literature, like all art, is a mode of imitation, that drama is a type of literature distinguished by its manner of presentation, and that the object of the imitation is an action. The means by which this imitation is accomplished are for Aristotle (in order of decreasing importance): plot, character, thought, diction, song, and spectacle.

We should note, however, that those means of imitation most strongly stressed by Aristotle—plot, character, thought—are for an audience, or a critic, concepts that must be indirectly inferred from the direct evidence of diction (the text, written or spoken), song, and spectacle. Diction is partially accessible to the literary student (what is spoken but not how it is spoken); melody and spectacle are not. Consequently, there is a temptation to consider the stage representations of a play—the sights and sounds experienced by an audience—external to dramatic form in that their inclusion as differentia for drama would imply that a play exists only in performance. Many literary scholars find this view unacceptable. "Whatever else it may be," writes O. B. Hardison, "this is an extremely limiting view of drama. Discussions of drama are often weakened by ignorance of stagecraft, but acting and staging procedures are certainly not essential elements of the theory of drama."[15] Yet it is precisely these externals that concern theatre historians, and drawing attention to them can result in quite a different theory of drama. If the center of attention becomes what an audience saw and heard at a performance, the aesthetic consideration of the text becomes irrelevant. As J. L. Styan notes: "It may seem that the primary evidence of the play resides in the most stable element in the line of transmission, in the script itself. But the script is not the play."[16]

Admittedly, the difficulties in reconstructing a performance are formidable and the implications of redefining drama in terms of its performance can be disconcerting. Styan, for instance, defines a play as "an historical event, and the focus of the critic's attention is the experience of that play in a particular time."[17] It might well be argued that this experience is simply not accessible, that even a detailed record of a performance is not the equivalent of the performance, and that Styan is asking us to understand every performance, even of the same text, as a different play. Little wonder, then, that literary critics cling to the view that a dramatic text provides all the evidence necessary for its analysis and evaluation. Consequently, a work intended to be experienced collectively and in performance is analyzed and judged through a process of generalization from an experience gained individually through reading.

On the other hand, even theatre historians otherwise quite different in theory and approach agree upon the relevance, even the centrality, of performance to dramatic theory. And, of course, the reason that spectacle, song, and the spoken word are central concerns is that it is these elements that *do* differentiate drama. Meaning and effect are conveyed by those very elements deemed unessential to the study of drama as literature. Moreover, these elements can carry meaning independently of the text, even opposed to the text, as well as simply reinforce its meaning.[18]

In the final analysis, it may very well prove that the study of literature and the study of theatre are completely separate enterprises; but on the face of it, at least, the two disciplines do meet and overlap in the study of drama, whether it be called literature or script. The work of both literary critic and theatre historian is impoverished if there is no attempt to come to terms with one another's perspective.

2. The relationship of theatre history to theatre practice is in some respects even more problematic. The work of theatre historians has unquestionably had an effect on some aspects of modern production. The staging of Shakespeare's plays is an obvious example. Still, we must be cautious in extrapolating from such seeming successes any general principle concerning the necessity of accurate historical knowledge for the successful and effective mounting of plays from the classic repertory. Such a principle has nevertheless often been assumed by theatre historians and historically ori-

ented theorists. In *Drama in Performance,* Raymond Williams argues that the historical relationship between text and performance is the fundamental issue in dramatic theory and concludes that we risk misunderstanding and misrepresenting past drama if we fail to recognize its particular mode of dramatic action.[19] A. M. Nagler is more direct: "A stage director is doomed when, without knowledge of the historical facts, he is called upon to adapt and produce a classical play for a modern audience. In handling the classics the director must be fully informed of the conditions of the original productions and of the cultural background against which the plays initially came to life."[20]

Neither Williams nor Nagler is advocating antiquarianism. We obviously cannot reproduce original conditions of performance in toto. But if the elements of performance carry meaning, an understanding of the original theatrical conventions is essential if they are to be translated or adapted for a modern production. The historical-critical problem is to determine which details of the original performance were accidental or incidental and which make real contributions to the play's meaning and effect. Theatre historians would normally insist that only the former may be varied without distorting the play.

Unhappily, this comforting theory receives little support either from those charged with mounting dramatic productions or, more disconcertingly, from the experience of historians themselves. Few of us have not found ourselves in the awkward position of deriving as theatregoers intense and moving experiences from performances that offended us mightily as historians. Even in those instances where a theatrical producer has consulted historical authorities, it seems to matter little whether or not the scholarship is sound or the information accurate. If there is a principle involved here, it is very likely that noted by James Arnott: "The truth of art is different from the truth of history." Arnott goes on to note that too close an association with contemporary theatre can be detrimental to historical perspective, that "theatrical scholarship in its attempt to reach the truth must necessarily go beyond the ideas . . . current in its own time."[21] In short, theatre historians must remember that, as devoted as they might be to the living contemporary theatre, their prime concern as historians is with past performances and that a revival is a new performance that can become historically significant only through the passage of time.

3. The scope and nature of theatre history as a university discipline remains an unsettled issue. During the first half of this century, as we have seen, the emphasis was to distinguish stage history from dramatic history, to emphasize the collection of facts over aesthetic considerations, and to

insist on a "scientific" approach to these facts. This empirical attitude does not encourage the exercise of the imagination, the speculative interpretation of theatrical phenomena, or the aesthetic appreciation of the art of the theatre. The field is narrowly focused: "We are engaged neither in historical philology nor in the study of literature, neither in folklore nor in sociology. The styles of performance and their more or less plausible reconstructions, these are our primary concern, and I shall be honored if this be called a purist's stance."[22]

Professor Nagler's stance is insufficient for some theatre historians who, synthesizing on the basis of empirical studies, have come to consider their discipline central to a humane education, a subject to be taught in connection with the study of the humanities in general: "Perhaps more than any other area of specialization," writes an American historian, "theatre . . . takes the student into many areas of human knowledge—literature, art, music, politics, economics, philosophy, science, invention—exploring practically all of men's activities and ideas. The study of the theatre can be and ideally *is* the most liberalizing of all the liberal arts."[23] With this enthusiastic advocacy we might compare the argument of a distinguished man of letters at a conference on drama held in Bristol in 1950 that drama, "discontinuous" compared to literature, is insufficient for a university degree since its "entertainment" value makes it more "subjective" than "philosophic" and a "less rigorous intellectual training than literature."[24]

It is difficult to reconcile such disparate estimations of the scope of theatre history and its place in the university curriculum, although in actuality there may be less difference in these extreme positions than at first glance seems to be the case. If we are to reconstruct and explain Nagler's "styles of performance," it seems likely that human activity in many areas will have to be taken into account. At the same time, without a firm focus on performance we run the risk of losing ourselves in cognate fields. (It is worth noting as well that productive research and undergraduate education are not the same thing, nor do they have the same aims.)

4. Just as differences emerge concerning the nature and scope of theatre history, so are there differences concerning evidence and its interpretation. On the face of it, the collection and interpretation of evidence would seem to be a straightforward process requiring two steps: collection followed by interpretation. In a classic critique of the method as used by E. K. Chambers in *The Mediaeval Stage* and Karl Young in *The Drama of the Medieval Church,* however, O. B. Hardison points out that the data were selected on the basis of evolutionary theory and thus naturally illustrated it. The theory, not the evidence, came first.[25] The lesson here, of course, is that his-

tory is written by historians who bring to it habits of mind peculiar to them and their times. It is for this reason that historical evidence must constantly be redefined and history constantly rewritten.

If the collection and the interpretation of historical evidence are inseparable processes, then the conclusions that are drawn are equally dependent on the evidence and the historian. There are two obvious reasons why we cannot limit history to the accurate presentation of data. In the first place, almost by definition, historical data can provide only indirect and incomplete information concerning the past; the most logically rigorous analysis of fragmentary evidence can yield results that are wrong. In the second place, even the most "scientific" of historians, as Hardison's analysis demonstrates, bring to their data assumed patterns of meaning. Moreover, logical reasoning is only one of several attributes that scholars bring to bear. Glynne Wickham refers, for example, to the necessity of resorting to "the imagination, to a process of the spirit rather than of the intellect, at its cheapest a guess, at its best a vision." [26]

The history of human inquiry is replete with discoveries, insights, and truths that depend upon exactly such processes. Guess, intuition, serendipity, vision—call them what we will, they are the products of the human mind, unfettered either by consciousness or by artificial logic. "Logic," writes a psychologist, "is the science of the justification of conclusions we have reached by natural reasoning. . . . The very reason we need logic at all is because most reasoning is not conscious at all." [27] Human knowledge is fundamentally metaphoric in the sense that the patterns of meaning we discern in data are metaphors. [28] Data and metaphor—the interrelationship underlies all intellectual progress. "Revolutionary thinkers are not," notes a historian of science, "primarily gatherers of facts, but weavers of new intellectual structures." [29] This is not to denigrate data, and it is certainly not to recommend pure speculation over the systematic analysis of historical evidence. But if we are to take advantage of the increased access to information in an age of computers, we must pay equal attention to the methods of interpreting it and to the metaphors by which we construct our hypotheses. Of course, a hypothesis, however arrived at, must be subject to validation of some kind. This problem is taken up in the next section.

Various attempts have been made in recent years to define both the object and the subject of theatre studies, but we still appear to be left with the uncertain axiom that the boundaries of the discipline tend to expand in direct ratio to the intensity of the efforts to define and confine it. The num-

ber and variety of activities of a theatrical or paratheatrical nature that theatre historians often find within their purview are multiple: ceremonies
and rituals of many kinds and purposes; pageantry and procession; spectacles and shows of myriad description; folk dances and vaudeville; sports
and athletic events. The list appears endless. But there remains a suspicion
that any attempt to limit the list, to restrict the area of investigation by
defining "theatre" in any particular way as a precondition of study, will
prove both arbitrary and self-defeating.

We might consider instead the possibility of recognizing and elaborating a conceptual framework for our studies that will allow us to include all
of these activities, including the theatre as traditionally conceived, as func-
tionally equivalent. Theatre is, as most of us realize, a sociocultural phenomenon, and its study is in some major aspects a branch of social history.
Recognizing this fact suggests some possibly new procedures. It is usually
assumed—indeed, has become a tenet of faith—that the working theatre
plays a crucial role in the study of the theatre. Several years ago, the UCTA
Standards Committee stated as a matter of course that "the producing theatre is the laboratory for theatre studies and is central to all forms of study
in the discipline." [30] It is undoubtedly true that practical work in the theatre
can provide data important for the theory and history of the theatre as well
as insights useful, even vital, for the interpretation of drama and the understanding of past theatrical conditions. The usefulness of the theatre as
laboratory diminishes, however, as we proceed through the several phases
of historical research and move from a concern with the theatrical event to
a concern with the process underlying a sequence of theatrical events.

It is at this same point that theatre history most closely approximates
social history. It becomes possible to argue that what is being practiced is a
subdiscipline of history. For instance, would not a social historian interested in funeral ceremonies in Victorian England and a theatre historian
who analyzes theatrical events as social rituals analogous to soccer matches
have something to say to one another? [31] Would not both be interested in
an analysis of sport as a transmitter of social and cultural values?

We can explore this idea further. Recall that historical investigation as
normally practiced proceeds in two stages: the collection, organization,
and description of data, selected on the basis of hypotheses or assumptions
either conscious or unconscious; and the interpretation of data at the level
of "cultural-historical integration." [32] That is, the data are explained in
terms of their immediate and contiguous context. For theatre historians,
this second stage involves the analysis and description of the theatrical
conditions affecting the conception and performance of drama in a given

period and the analysis and description of past performances themselves. Such studies are centered on the event or on a series of events. When the events are simply listed and described, we have chronicle; when a hypothesis is postulated that serves as an explanation for those events, we have history. But this history remains fundamentally narrative and descriptive so long as the events and their determining conditions are perceived as unique. There is a third stage in some current historical research, however, in which the focus on process and patterns is intensified and, mainly by means of quantitative methods, an attempt is made to make the specific hypothesis a general rule. This process represents what the archaeologist Richard MacNeish calls the "sciencing" of history, the generating of statements that express "in general terms the conditions under which events of various kinds occur . . . [and serve] as explanations of . . . corresponding happenings."[33]

The sciencing of history, however, involves the validating of hypotheses derived from the analysis of sequentially organized data, and few historians—even among the new social historians—have developed satisfactory validation procedures. Clearly, as theatre historians we cannot approximate the controlled experiments of the physical and biological sciences. The laboratory-theatre has a limited usefulness in establishing limits of interpretation of theatrical events, but it cannot be used to test hypotheses based on historical sequence. We cannot recreate historical process. One possible solution is to test the hypothesis by applying it to a sequence of events from a different time and place. If the hypothesis is confirmed by this comparative method in accord with statistical probability, it becomes the general explanatory statement characteristic of science.[34] What has sometimes been lacking in the historical study of the theatre is precisely the systematic comparison of sequences that might validate the multitude of hypotheses—or at least define the limits of their applicability. In fact, there is a distinct possibility that the procedure would be of more use to theatre historians in a negative sense. For example, the hypothesis that explains the English theatre of the eighteenth century as the product of commercial competition, if applied to the theatre of eighteenth-century France, would very likely fail the test of sciencing. The commercial model is inadequate as a general explanation for theatrical history.

"Sciencing" does not turn history into science, if only because, as Ernest Nagel points out in his chapter on historical inquiry in *The Structure of Science*, "historians are rarely if ever in a position to state the *sufficient* conditions for the occurrence of the events they investigate."[35] We must be satisfied with the *necessary* conditions—and usually only a few of those.

What sciencing can do is point the way to a possible method of hypothesis validation based on comparative historical interpretation. We need to distinguish between hypotheses that explain a unique series of specific events and those admittedly fewer hypotheses that can be validated as generalized explanations in the scientific sense.

Theatre researchers will continue as historians and critics in departments of literature and as historians and theorists in departments of theatre. But it seems likely that there will also be sociocultural historians with a special interest in the theatre who will work to relate "theatre" to ritual, ceremony, sport, pageantry, and so on. Nevertheless, some real issues and some real questions remain. Can the "sciencing" of theatre history and its integration with social history be translated into undergraduate education and graduate training? What academic infrastructure best supports the enterprise—departments of theatre or of history, research institutes, or interdisciplinary programs? What connections can be made and maintained with the traditional functions of criticism and practical training? Should we even attempt such connections, at least on a formal basis? Above all, will theatre history be able to take advantage of new historiographical theories and methods and establish itself as an independent discipline devoted to the historical and theoretical study of the performance event? The empirical tradition in our discipline is very strong; there is no doubt that we will continue to collect and authenticate data and to describe and analyze theatrical events as accurately and in as much detail as we can. But we must undertake such empirical studies within a rational conceptual framework that will promote an awareness of the theoretical bases and an understanding of the fundamental principles of the discipline we profess.

NOTES

1 See Richard Hornby, "The Ph.D. in Theatre: A Vanishing Degree?" *Theatre News* 16 : 3 (1984), 16.

2 Panel on the State of the Profession, Annual Meeting of the American Society for Theatre Research, New York, November 1985.

3 James Arnott, "An Introduction to Theatrical Scholarship," *Theatre Quarterly* 39 (1981), 42.

4 Les frères Parfaict published over twenty-five volumes on the French theatre. The most important is *L'Histoire du théâtre français depuis son origine jusqu'à présent*, 15 vols. (Paris, 1734–1749; rpt. 3 vols., Geneva: Slatkine, 1967).

5 Casiano Pellicer, *Tratado histórico sobre el origen y progresos de la comedia y del histrionismo en España,* 2 vols. (Madrid, 1804).

6 First published in vol. I of Edmond Malone's *Plays and Poems of William Shakespeare* (London, 1790, 1803). A slightly expanded version was published in the posthumous edition of 1821, edited by James Boswell (vol. III).

7 Luigi Riccoboni, *Réflexions historiques et critiques sur les différents théâtres de l'Europe.* The book was translated into English and published as *An Historical and Critical Account of the Theatres of Europe* (London, 1741). The English edition was reissued in 1754 as *A General History of the Stage.*

8 Charles Dibdin, *A Complete History of the English Stage,* 5 vols. (London, 1797–1800; rpt. New York: Garland, 1970).

9 Pietro Napoli Signorelli, *Storia critica dei teatri antichi e moderni,* 6 vols. (Naples, 1787–1790; rpt. 10 vols., Naples, 1813). See Dario Borzacchini, "L'universo del teatro: La prima storia," *Quaderni di Teatro* 4 (1982), 74–83.

10 Thomas Percy, "An Essay on the Origin of the English Stage," in vol. I of his *Reliques of Ancient English Poetry,* 3 vols. (London, 1765); Thomas Hawkins, *Origin of the English Drama,* 3 vols. (Oxford, 1773).

11 Charles Magnin, *Les origines du théâtre moderne* (Paris, 1838); reissued as *Les origines du théâtre antique et du théâtre moderne* (Paris, 1868).

12 Louis Leclercq [Ludovic Cellar], *Les décors, les costumes et la mise en scène au XVIIe siècle 1615–1680* (Paris, 1869).

13 E. K. Chambers, *The Mediaeval Stage,* 2 vols. (London: Oxford University Press, 1923), I, v.

14 Glynne Wickham, *Early English Stages,* 3 vols. in 4 (London: Routledge and Kegan Paul, 1959), I, xxvi.

15 O. B. Hardison, *Christian Rite and Christian Drama in the Middle Ages* (Baltimore: Johns Hopkins University Press, 1965), p. 31.

16 J. L. Styan, *Drama, Stage, and Audience* (Cambridge, England: Cambridge University Press, 1975), pp. 6–7.

17 Ibid., p. 6.

18 Semiology has concerned itself with the study of theatrical performance as a system of signs. See especially Keir Elam, *The Semiotics of Theatre and Drama* (London and New York: Methuen, 1980). For a critique of semiotic analysis, see Bernard Beckerman, "Theatrical Perception," *Theatre Research International,* n.s. 4 (1979), 157–171.

19 Raymond Williams, *Drama in Performance* (London: Chatto and Windus, 1954; rev. 1968).

20 A. M. Nagler, *A Source Book in Theatrical History* (New York: Dover, 1959), p. xxiii.

21 Arnott, "An Introduction to Theatrical Scholarship," p. 42.

22 A. M. Nagler, *The Medieval Religious Stage* (New Haven and London: Yale University Press, 1976), p. xi.

23 Vera Mowbray Roberts, *On Stage: A History of the Theatre*, 2nd ed. (New York: Harper and Row, 1974), p. xi.

24 Nevill Coghill, "The Study of Drama at a University," in *The Universities and the Theatre*, ed. D. G. James (Bristol: Colston Research Society, 1952), p. 47.

25 Hardison, *Christian Rite and Christian Drama*, p. 9.

26 Wickham, *Early English Stages*, I, 307.

27 Julian Jaynes, *The Origin of Consciousness in the Breakdown of the Bicameral Mind* (Boston: Houghton Mifflin, 1976), p. 41.

28 See ibid., pp. 48–66.

29 Stephen Jay Gould, *The Flamingo's Smile* (New York and London: Norton, 1985), p. 151.

30 UCTA Standards Committee, "Minimum Standards for the Accreditation of Theatre Degree Programs in Colleges and Universities," *Educational Theatre Journal* 29 (1977), 546.

31 Cf. Paul S. Fritz, "From 'Public' to 'Private': The Royal Funerals in England, 1500–1830," in *Mirrors of Mortality: Studies in the Social History of Death*, ed. Joachim Whaley (New York: St. Martin's, 1981); Bruce A. McConachie, "Towards a Postpositivist Theatre History," *Theatre Journal* 37 (1985), 465–486; Richard D. Mandell, *Sport: A Cultural History* (New York: Columbia University Press, 1984).

32 The phrase is from Richard S. MacNeish, *The Science of Archaeology?* (Hamilton, Ont.: McMaster University, 1976), p. 7.

33 See ibid., p. 1.

34 See ibid., pp. 1–28; Ernest Nagel, *The Structure of Science: Problems in the Logic of Scientific Explanation* (London: Routledge and Kegan Paul, 1961), pp. 561–563.

35 Nagel, *The Structure of Science*, p. 559.

Theatre and the Civilizing Process
An Approach to the History of Acting

Erika Fischer-Lichte

Theatre is a communal institution, representing and establishing relationships which fulfill social functions. The drama, the production, and the location of the performance all contribute to these functions. Of course, in general terms we recognize this communal condition of theatre. Theatre historians regularly acknowledge that theatre and society are closely related.

The instances of this symbiotic relationship are more or less familiar. Aeschylus' *Oresteia* voiced new social and communal norms that were meant to define, if not control, the ways in which the Athenian citizens of different social strata were supposed to live together. Shakespeare's *Richard III* demonstrated some of the dreadful consequences of Machiavellian politics, a method of stagecraft that in its representation of statecraft both fascinated and terrified the audiences of his time. Calderón's *The Magnanimous Prince* displayed the ideal action of a Christian martyr, thus polemicizing against any kind of apostasy from the true Catholic faith. And Lessing's *Emilia Galotti* confronted the German audiences of the eighteenth century with the bourgeois ideals of a tender, sentimental father and his most virtuous daughter, both representatives of proper emotional and moral behavior.

As far as drama is concerned, it seems to be a truism that in all these cases the stage has proved to be a highly appropriate arena for representing or propagating norms and ideas crucial to the given society. But to phrase the issue in this way may be misleading. We have to recognize that theatre is not just a medium for "transmitting" a play and its themes. Theatre expresses the society in which it occurs through a full range of cultural systems: painting, music, costume, body movement, gestures, language, architecture, commentaries, and so on. All of these systems form an integral

part of the culture as a whole, contributing to its norms and rules, expressing its signs and meanings. Even when transplanted onto the stage, they
never cease to point to their employment and meaning in the general cultural context.

At the most basic level, everything in the theatre and the theatregoing
process has meaning. Especially during the last twenty years, the field of
semiotics has been investigating these theatrical meanings, trying to distinguish the various codes at work in performance. Much valuable work has
been done, but unfortunately semioticians of the theatre, with a few exceptions, have separated theatre from history. In the process of breaking theatre into its many codes, semioticians have sometimes lost sight of a primary condition of signs on the stage. A theatrical costume of a medieval
king, for example, tells us that the person wearing this costume is meant to
represent the historical and cultural conditions of a medieval king. The
gestures and body movements of the actor have their cultural, not just theatrical, meanings. To a large extent, theatre depends upon the specific
functions and developments of the cultural systems which it employs. So
we may say that not only the drama, which expresses in words and actions
certain ideas and values of the society, but all of the various cultural systems in the theatre contribute to its social functions. The challenge for a
theatre historian is to understand these interpretative cultural systems, to
assess how the theatre shapes and is shaped by the fundamental ways of
being and doing which constitute historical cultures.

Admittedly, in the case of drama itself, most scholars are aware that
plays express a social perspective or "world view." Thus, we find books
with titles such as *The Elizabethan World Picture, Shakespeare in His Own
Age, Shakespeare and the Renaissance Image of Man,* and *The Artist and Society in Shakespearean England.* Sometimes they are too reductive in defining what the supposed world view is, but at least drama is placed within a
social picture. When we turn, however, to the other aspects of the theatre,
we find almost nothing written on how theatrical systems point to, embody, or influence certain cultural systems. For instance, we need to investigate at the level of these systems how decoration relates to architecture
and painting, how costume relates to clothing (not just "expresses a period
style"), how acting represents and affects social and personal gestures, fa-
cial expressions, and body movements.

With respect to acting, it is true that we can find books on *Acting Shakespeare, Elizabethan Acting,* or *The Performance Practice of Acting: The Eighteenth Century.* Up to a point, they explain to the reader certain aspects of
historical acting, but they say little on how and why types of acting are

related to or derived from any historically determined cultural context. Usually, the social context is merely taken as a given, a series of choice phrases and metaphors that are quite problematic. In turn, the historical changes in acting styles seem to be caused by very general aesthetic principles that guide the production of artworks within a given epoch, but to have little or nothing in common with the historical and social situation in which they occur.

Let us consider, at least in a preliminary way, the history of acting in order to illustrate some of the issues involved in a cultural history of theatre. At first sight, it seems appropriate to define acting as the ways in which the human body is shaped and presented on the stage. We say that the human body belongs to the realm of nature. It has organic traits; it has physical and physiological functions, needs, and purposes. It is a part of nature. Not surprisingly, all actor training puts great emphasis on these physical characteristics. The common aim is to strip away the superfluous or outer aspects (that inhibit expression) in order to discover the real, natural body.

Consequently, we would hardly be astonished to find, insofar as the human body is defined in these terms, that acting—the presentation of the body on the stage—is not primarily described or considered in historical terms. In fact, acting is taught and learned primarily in physical ways; cultural history, if taught and studied, is something quite divorced from this idea of acting (and thus is perhaps not very significant or relevant, as many actors believe). Acting teachers, for example, seldom know (or are prepared to teach) cultural history; they do not understand how to situate their acting training in the cultural practices of history. Even history teachers, when and if they consider acting, tend to define it as a formal style (natural or artificial) rather than a cultural practice. History is but the overlay of "period styles," which a costume, a few gestures, and some quickly learned methods of walking and sitting take care of.

Yet the human body never exists as pure nature, apart from history. From the very beginning of life, culture starts to shape, restructure, and regulate the body and its physical needs and functions. The instinctual drives and the special modes of their articulation are formed by culture. Culture even has an effect on the shaping of the body's developmental and adult form, insofar as culturally determined factors, such as nutrition, hygiene, and public health, assert themselves. And, obviously, each culture's ideas on valid, desirable, and ideal body types exert amazing influence on the "natural" body. Thus, any human body should be seen as the result of a reciprocal process of the organic and the cultural, an interaction between individual nature and cultural context. The process begins at the moment of birth and continues until the moment of death. As a result, each individual body participates not only in the natural order but also in the symbolic order of culture. The body, like any other cultural phenomenon, is historically determined.

In his pioneering study *The Civilizing Process*, Norbert Elias has described and analyzed the history of the "European body" from the Middle Ages onward as a "structural change in people towards an increased consolidation of their affect controls, and therefore both of their experience (e.g., in the form of an advance in the threshold of shame and revulsion) and of their behaviour (e.g., in the differentiation of the implements used at table)."[1] He notes, for example, that in the Middle Ages people often walked and ran naked through the streets to the public bathhouse, where men and women alike had their weekly baths without any separation of the sexes. Medieval people ate from one common bowl, using their fingers not forks (which did not even exist yet as eating implements). The process of eating was accompanied by sniffing, belching, spitting, and farting. But from the Renaissance onward, the threshold of shame and revulsion constantly advanced, through the early twentieth century, and people became more and more "civilized." Thus, the civilizing process transformed not only social practices but the very operation and manifestation of the body within society. As Elias points out, in great historical detail and subtle analysis, this process was closely connected with a "long-term change in the social structure towards a higher level of differentiation and integration—for example, towards a differentiation and prolongation of the chains of interdependence and a consolidation of 'state controls.'"[2]

It seems plausible that these long-term changes in the structure and behavior of human personality were necessary prerequisites to certain cultural rearrangements and achievements in European history that promoted the general progress of culture. But Elias emphasizes that these changes cannot be esteemed or classified as the progressive march of history—at least not in the sense in which the nineteenth century understood and defined progress. Rather, this spread of "civilization" should be seen as the price, within elaborate conditions of order and control, that the European cultures had to pay for their technological, scientific, economic, and social changes. This is an argument, from a different perspective, that Michel Foucault also makes in his series of historical studies.

If we describe the European history of the human body in terms of the civilizing process, the question arises whether the history of acting might not also be investigated and explained in like terms. For the actors' bodies, as presented on the stage, are likewise culturally conditioned in accordance with the actual state of the civilizing process. Moreover, the particular mode of their presentation onstage may contribute to this ongoing process by representing and propagating new models of self-presence and self-presentation for audience imitation. The actor promotes and ridicules modes of behavior both uncommon and common for the time. In such cases, acting not only mirrors but partakes in and contributes to the historical process of civilization and thus fulfills important social functions.

Possible illustrations of the connections between the art of acting and the social process of civilization can be seen by referring to the theatre of three different epochs marked by important social changes: the Baroque theatre; the bourgeois, illusionistic stage of the eighteenth century; and the avant-garde theatre at the beginning of the twentieth century.

In examining some of the acting conventions of these three epochs, I draw upon handbooks and theories of acting instead of detailed descriptions or pictures of actual performances. I do not use these sources because they are especially privileged; nor do I rule out in any manner the value of detailed research on actual daily practices, from theatre to theatre, actor to actor. But for the convenience of quickly illustrating the issues here, these prescriptive materials provide us with clear definitions of the new norms and rules that were put forward and instituted in one manner or another. Needless to say, there is often a gap between theory and practice. It is true that sufficient descriptive sources demonstrate that the prescriptions were not always followed or fulfilled. Still, the use of key theoretical works can tell us much about an epoch and its cultural ideas. These works grant us a deeper insight into the intended general impact of acting and thus enable us to formulate a theory concerning possible connections between the art of acting and the civilizing process in European history of the last three centuries.

The Body as a "Text" Composed of Artificial Signs

The theory of acting in the Baroque period proceeded from the assumption that strong emotional impact was its primary aim. Emotional responses were excited by the representation of emotion onstage, and it follows that the representation of emotion was the most important task and function of acting.

In *Dissertatio de actione scenica* (Munich, 1727), the Jesuit priest Franciscus

Lang summarized the rules to be observed in order to guarantee the most effective representation of emotions:

1. Admiration: Both hands outstretched above the chest and palms towards the audience.
2. Shame: The face turned away over the left shoulder and the hands calmly joined behind the back. This same result can be achieved by just the right hand when it is clenched and unclenched repetitively.
3. Entreating: Both hands upraised with the palms turned to the listener again and again. Also with the arms hanging down. Also with the hands clenched together.
4. Weeping and Melancholy: Both hands joined in the middle of the chest, either high on the chest or lower about the belt. Also accomplished by extending the right hand gently and motioning towards the chest. . . .
5. Reproach: Three fingers folded and the forefinger extended. . . .
6. Imploring: Both hands extended towards the one being spoken to as if about to embrace him. . . .
7. Repentance: Pressing the hands to the breast.
8. Fear: The right hand reaching towards the breast with the four digits visible while the rest of the body is bent, relaxed and bowed.[3]

Performing such gestures, the actor had to take care not to give up the so-called *crux scenica,* an angle of 90 degrees formed by his feet. Such a stance was interpreted as the adequate representation of a firm ego which may be attacked by strong emotions but never overwhelmed, as, for example, in the case of the Christian martyr or the ideal courtier. The gestures are rather complicated and required long and thorough training, and the actors who mastered them became living examples of emotional and physical control. Imitating these models, members of the audience could exhibit approved behavior and complete self-discipline in their everyday lives.

When we look at the rules of acting laid down by Lang in the context of the sociogenesis of such a seventeenth-century court society, as described by Norbert Elias, some striking parallels reveal themselves. Elias notes that, for the formation of this new society, the individual was required to learn self-discipline, calculation of future aims and purposes, and control of not only the emotions but the whole body:

> In tracing the sociogenesis of the court, we find ourselves at the centre of a civilizing transformation that is both particularly pro-

nounced and an indispensable precondition for all subsequent spurts and counter-spurts in the civilizing process. We see how, step by step, a warrior nobility is replaced by a tamed nobility with more muted affects, a courtly nobility. Not only within the Western civilizing process, but as far as we can see within every major civilizing process, one of the most decisive transitions is that of *warriors to courtiers*.[4]

It need scarcely be said, as Elias notes, that "there are widely differing stages and degrees of this transition, this inner pacification of a society," but gradually a more complex social order for expressing power and controlling behavior develops:

> Competition for prestige and royal favour is intense. "Affaires," disputes over rank and favour, do not cease. If the sword no longer plays so great a role as the means of decision, it is replaced by intrigue, conflicts in which careers and social success are contested with words. They demand and produce other qualities than did the armed struggles that had to be fought out with weapons in one's hand. Continuous reflection, foresight, and calculation, self-control, precise and articulate regulation of one's own effects, knowledge of the whole terrain, human and nonhuman, in which one acts, become more and more indispensable preconditions of social success.[5]

The qualities and proprieties of the required social behavior exactly coincided with those promoted by the contemporary art of acting. Thus, the comportment of the actor could be presented and perceived as a generally acknowledged model that should be copied.

In turn, the actor responded to the ideal versions of this behavior in the court society. Accordingly, the character presented by the actor who followed the rules was clearly marked as an ideal. Should the actor break the rules by running across the stage, falling down and rolling on the floor, lowering his hands below the waist, or keeping his feet parallel, he indicated to the audience that the character he embodied had a weak identity, as in the case of a fool, madman, or tyrant. Undoubtedly, the tyrant and the madman acted as negative examples, not to be copied; the fool served to grant the spectators a feeling of superiority, to relieve them—at least temporarily—of the enormous pressures caused by the rigorous demands of self-control. The theatre, thus, assumed the cultural function of conveying an ideal behavior pattern which individuals had then to internalize and practice in order to adapt to the challenges of everyday court life.

The Body as a "Text" Composed in the "Natural Language of the Emotions"

The formation of middle-class society in the eighteenth century was paralleled by the formulation of a new concept of art in general, and of theatre in particular. Art was expected to become an imitation of nature (*imitatio naturae*) in accordance with the development of materialistic culture. The new ideal of life and art was "naturalness." The behavior of aristocrats was criticized and reproached as being artificial and even unnatural. Increasingly, if not exclusively of course, the task, function, and aim of the theatre were to be redefined: the stage should imitate nature and so create an illusion or semblance of reality. Accordingly, the greatest German actor of this epoch, Conrad Ekhof, defined the task of acting thus: "The art of acting is to imitate nature through art and to approach it so closely that probabilities must be taken for truth, or to present events as naturally as if they were taking place right now."[6]

The development of a new art of acting was closely related to the contemporary discussion of an original or primitive language. Since Condillac had stated that the first human language had been a *langage d'action,* consisting of gestures and movements, it was a common and widespread idea that gestural language had been a universal human language. Accordingly, most theoreticians of the period agreed that acting should be an imitation of this natural language. For instance, Georg Christoph Lichtenberg argued that actors should take as a model the "involuntary language of gesture, which passion in all gradations uses throughout the world. Man learns to understand it completely, usually before he is twenty-five. He is taught to speak it by nature and this so emphatically that it has become an art to make faults."[7] Nature's language had to be transferred to the stage in order to provide actors with the desired patterns of natural behavior.

But in which ways could this be accomplished? Rémond de Sainte Albine suggested in *Le Comédien* (1747) that the actor had to identify with the dramatic character he enacted. For, as Sainte Albine argued, the actor, sensing the emotion the dramatic character was supposed to feel, would bring forward the appropriate gestural signs for this emotion quite automatically. Lessing, however, objected to this argument:

Mr. Rémond de Sainte Albine, in his whole book, proceeds from the implied assumption that the external movements of the body occur as natural consequences of the internal condition of the soul, and thus follow spontaneously. Admittedly, it is true that everyone without special training is able to express to some extent the state of his soul by means of signs which can be perceived through the senses—in one way or another. Onstage, however, we want to see sentiments and passions expressed not just in a partial manner, not just in the imperfect way in which an individual would express himself in the same circumstances. We want rather to see them expressed as perfectly as possible, leaving no room for further improvement.[8]

As Lessing—and, along with him, Diderot—concluded, empathy could not be taken as a method for creating the natural signs of emotion onstage. Nor could the observation of people's gestures in everyday life serve as a method, because education spoils man by teaching him either to hide or to exaggerate his true emotions. Where then should actors find the natural language of emotions which was to be imitated? Two possible solutions were offered. The actor should search for them where they preserve their original expressiveness, as in savages, children, and the common people. And the natural language of emotions might be reconstructed with reference to the "Law of Analogy": anything that occurs in the mind has its analogue in the body.

On the basis of the Law of Analogy, Johann Jakob Engel in his *Ideen zu einer Mimik* (1785–1786) attempted to make an exhaustive list and detailed description of all possible gestural signs which might represent character and emotion. He deduced and described the perfect representation of a sluggard as follows:

> Very significant is a head not carried erectly on the shoulders; parted lips leaving the chin drooping; eyes with half of the eyeball hidden behind the eyelid; tottering knees; a belly stretched forward; feet turned inward; hands reaching straight into the pockets of the jacket or even arms swinging freely. Who will not, at first sight, recognize there a limp and inactive soul, incapable of any attention, any interest, a soul, not really awake, without even enough energy to flex the muscles necessary to carry the body properly and to hold its limbs properly? Only a sluggard, being extremely dull and lazy, can present a posture so meaningless and soulless.[9]

In deducing and describing the gestural representations of different emotions, Engel proceeds in like manner. Since, for example, happiness opens the soul widely, a person experiencing happiness will open the mouth with a smile and accelerate every movement. The body in this view serves as a perfect and natural means for expressing psychic experience.

The actor who observes the Law of Analogy transforms the human body into a perfect natural sign which expresses each emotion and psychic state of the dramatic character. In being so employed, however, the body ceases to be perceived as sensual nature. The actor's body is thus presented as a cultural system which nature itself has created and defined as such: it becomes a composition of signs constituted by nature as a "text" which is "written" in the "natural language of emotion." While attempting to "read" and understand this text, the spectators supposedly forget that the actor's body is sensual nature and perceive and interpret it as a texture of signs which represent most adequately the emotions of a dramatic character.

Such treatment of the human body on the stage of the bourgeois illusionistic theatre corresponded very closely with certain tendencies which were fundamental to the formation and establishment of middle-class society, in part because this society of the eighteenth century claimed to restore the lost naturalness which court society had despised and neglected. Thus, middle-class society reestablished the "original" parallelism between nature and society. Insofar as the theatre aimed to restore the original language of gestures in the art of acting, it served as a corrective force in the civilizing process, which under the influence of court society had spoilt and deformed this language to the point that it had been almost completely lost in European culture. In turn, this claim for naturalness, though paying homage to the child and the savage, served as a pretext for pushing ahead the civilizing process: the repression of instinctual drives (of the "animal" nature of man) in order to assert a rigorous concept of virtue.

Thus, certain values that were basic and vital to middle-class society were passed off as demands made by nature itself. The theatre not only adopted this concept of nature but also propagated it overtly: the positive dramatic characters—mostly the daughters, as in Lillo's *The London Merchant* or Lessing's *Emilia Galotti*—were shaped as models for virtuous behavior and self-denial and the actors who embodied them were supposed to present their bodies not as sensual nature but as a text composed of "natural signs" of goodness. The spectators would identify with the dramatic characters, copy their behavior, and thereby develop the individual sensibilities and the required new standards of virtue and renunciation that were the prerequisites to the progress of bourgeois society.

The Body as Raw Material for Sign Processes

At the beginning of the present century, the representatives of avant-garde theatre all over Europe unanimously negated the principles underlying the bourgeois illusionistic stage, as formulated in the eighteenth century and then realized in the nineteenth century, culminating in the realist and naturalist movements. Although one line of modernist theatre, from Chekhov and Stanislavski to Pinter and Peter Hall, continued to carry forward this realist tradition (usually treated ironically), much of the modern theatre turned away from it. The actor's body was no longer perceived as a text composed of natural signs for emotions but as raw material for sign processing with a wider field of reference than the emotions of a dramatic character. In order to realize their particular aims, the avant-gardists turned to the art of acting as developed and employed in the theatre of the Far East, in Japan, China, Bali, and India. Instead of creating an illusion of reality, they intended to lay open the conventional nature of the theatrical process, to foreground and theatricalize it, as Meyerhold explains:

> Neither the antique stage nor the popular stage of Shakespeare's time had any need for the scenery which the striving for illusion demands nowadays; nor was the actor merely a unit of illusion in those days. It was the same in medieval Japan. From descriptions of Japanese theatrical performances, we know that special stage-assistants, known as "kurogo" and clad in special black costumes resembling cassocks, used to prompt the actors in full view of the audience. When the costume of an actor playing a woman's part became disarranged at a tense moment in the drama, one of the kurogo would quickly restore the graceful folds of the actor's train and attend to his coiffure. In addition, they had the task of removing from the stage any objects dropped or forgotten by the actors. After a battle, the kurogos would remove fallen helmets, weapons and cloaks. If the hero died on the stage, the kurogo would quickly cover the corpse with a black cloth and under the cover of the cloth the "dead actor" would run off the stage. When the course of the action required darkness on stage, the kurogo would squat down at the hero's feet and illuminate his face with a candle on the end of a long stick. To this day the Japanese preserve the acting style of the days of the creators of Japanese drama.[10]

As can be gathered from this statement, which reveals the fascination of the avant-gardists with the theatre of non-European cultures, the interest mainly was based on the abundance of nonrealistic modes and conventions to be found there. These theatres provided an art of acting and production which was not meant to express the emotions of an individual—let alone of a European middle-class individual—a point strongly emphasized by Artaud, who denied, both completely and uncompromisingly, that the individual was of any relevance for the theatre:

> The theatre must side with life, not with the individual life, that aspect of life where the CHARACTERS triumph, but with a kind of liberated life in which human individuality is brushed aside and man is no more than a reflection. The true object of the theatre is the creation of myths, the translation of life under its universal and immense aspect, and the extraction of images from life, in which we desire to find ourselves again.[11]

Avant-gardists assumed that the acting in Japanese and Chinese theatre did not promote any kind of identification between the spectator and the embodied character onstage in the manner of the realistic acting in the European theatre. According to Brecht, for example, the Chinese art of acting seemed to be a perfect model of a form of acting that brings forth the effects of alienation:

> The peculiarity of the artist watching himself, which is an artistic and ingenious act of self-alienation, prevents the total identification of the spectator—that is to say, an identification bordering on self-abandonment—and brings forth a wonderful distance from the events. . . . The artist presents processes of great passion, but his performance does not become heated. In moments of intensity for the portrayed person, the artist puts a lock of hair between his lips and bites it. But that is like a rite, there is nothing eruptive in it. . . . The artist shows that this character is beside himself, and he does this by indicating the signs of the emotional condition. . . . The controlled effect is due to the fact that the artist in this manner keeps his distance from the character he portrays.[12]

The fascination with non-European cultures was not limited to theatre people. It was common to the avant-gardists in all the arts: in poetry and the novel as in theatre, in painting as in sculpture. This condition begs for additional explanation. In 1890, for instance, James George Frazer published in two volumes his pioneer study *The Golden Bough: A Study in Comparative Religion*. By 1936, it had enlarged to thirteen volumes. Frazer had compiled an enormous amount of material taken from different cultures in order to demonstrate striking analogies between the thoughts and customs of the so-called primitives and the manners and institutions of the European culture, similarities that are supposedly rooted in the collective unconscious. Thereby, he paved the way for giving up the idea of Europe as the center of the world, so typically assumed in Western culture. In this light, then, the devotion of the European avant-gardists to non-European cultures can be seen as an attempt to escape or revolt against the European civilization which had repressed human nature, to return to unspoilt, "original" states of culture.

It follows, then, that the approach to the Asian and African cultures entailed a certain ambiguity. On the one hand, it expressed the desire for an escape from Western civilization. On the other hand, it promoted the ongoing process of civilization. For there is no doubt that such highly codified alien forms of acting had an enormous appeal for the avant-gardists, resulting in a high degree of stylization in the modern theatre. No gesture pretended to be a natural expression; instead, it openly declared itself to be an abstract articulation. The body no longer functioned as a natural sign for human emotions and psychic states but rather as material to be shaped and used in order to signify other things. The actor presented his body not as a natural expression of the mind or soul of a dramatic character but as raw material by means of which he formed a sign that represented whatever he wanted it to express. Formulating these tendencies in his essay "The Actor of the Future" (1922), Meyerhold wrote: "The actor must train his material [his body], so that it is capable of executing instantaneously those tasks which are dictated externally [by the actor, the director]."[13]

Although the avant-gardists often differed in their particular aims and styles, sometimes considerably so, they all understood the actor's body to be raw material that could be reshaped according to artistic intentions. Proceeding from this assumption, they elaborated new techniques of acting such as Meyerhold's biomechanics, Artaud's theatre of cruelty, and Brecht's alienation effect. It is interesting to note that in spite of their appraisal of Far Eastern acting, they did not copy either its particular techniques or its repertory of theatrical signs, although they sometimes borrowed single elements for special purposes (as did Tairov, who used elements of the Indian theatre when staging *Sakontala* by Kalidasa).

When formulating and elaborating his theory of biomechanics, Meyerhold referred to working processes:

. . . apart from the correct utilization of rest periods, it is equally essential to discover those movements in work which facilitate the maximum use of work time. If we observe a skilled worker in action, we notice the following in his movements: (1) an absence of superfluous, unproductive movements; (2) rhythm; (3) the correct positioning of the body's center of gravity; (4) stability. Movements based on these principles are distinguished by their dance-like quality; a skilled worker at work invariably reminds one of a dancer; thus work borders on art.[14]

Accordingly, Meyerhold defined the actor as being equivalent to the constructor:

$N = A_1 + A_2$
where N = the actor
A_1 = the artist who conceives the idea and issues the instructions necessary for its execution
A_2 = the executant who executes the conception of A_1.

The actor became an engineer and his body a machine or part of a machine. This tendency is even more obvious and dominant in the theatre of the Russian constructivists. Nicolai Foregger was particularly successful with his so-called machine-dances based on a special technique of acting called *tafia-trenage*. The technique was acquired by using "acting machines" which were at the disposal of the spectators during the breaks. Foregger proclaimed: "Actors! Directors! Don't look for inspiration. There is but one teacher: The Machine!"[15] Thus, the mechanization of movement which could be reproduced at any time and without depending on the individuality of the actor became the new ideal for acting (not just, we might note, in the case of certain avant-garde theorists but perhaps most tellingly in the widespread practice of film, which made all movement a machine dance of signs).

Regardless of the differences in programs and styles, the avant-gardists employed mechanical motion in order to place the actor's body in the more comprehensive context of not only the surrounding space and the—often technical—objects structuring it but also the totality of movement (i.e., the movement of all bodies, objects, and, just as significantly, light). The body of the actor was no longer considered and exploited as a natural sign pointing exclusively to psychic states and processes of an individual but as an arbitrary sign. It was presented as a machine which functioned according to mechanical laws (as with the constructivists and cubofuturists) or as constituent of a ritual which was performed according to a determined pattern (as with Artaud and, partly, Schlemmer).

By means of the increasing semiotization of his body, the actor produced movements in the modern theatre which pointed to the total integration of the once-natural human organism into a nonhuman, nonnatural "superior" order: either into a world of technique—an everlasting process made possible by the second industrial revolution—or into a metaphysical order formed by transindividual, rather mysterious forces. That is to say, the treatment of the human body by the avant-gardists was marked by ambiguity. On the one hand, they employed the actor's body as raw material, as a precise and easily moldable instrument. In this respect, their acting techniques both supported and promoted the civilizing process by rigorously repressing or distancing the immediate sensual nature of the body. Onstage and in film the body became objectified (even in the service of the sexual appeal of the actor's body). On the other hand, by remaking (and defamiliarizing) the actor's body, the avant-gardists aimed at creating a "new man" beyond the limits of contemporary Western civilization: man as "producer of new meanings" (Meyerhold) or "man in harmony with the universe" (Artaud).

So we can conclude that the avant-gardists are to be seen as both the culmination of the civilizing process and the expression of the revolt against it. They were contradictory, ironic, and "grotesque" (Meyerhold's key word and idea for yoking unexpected opposites). They stood against bourgeois individualism, yet as revolutionary artists they asserted the artistic integrity of the individual artist who operates as the defining and controlling producer or director of meaning. This dynamic of both fulfilling and necessarily revolting against the civilizing process is an integral part of the ambiguity in the way the avant-gardists treated the actor's body.

Before drawing any methodological conclusions regarding the consequences of a possible connection between the art of acting and the civilizing process, let us summarize.

Each of the three theatre periods and formal modes under consideration came into being in times of social upheaval or fundamental transformations. Each negated the aims and purposes of the preceding theatrical form. Each developed a new style of acting which paralleled the formation of new behavior patterns in society.

From the seventeenth century onward, there was a growing tendency on the stages of Europe to repress the body as sensual nature. During the

Baroque period, the human was presented both as a text of artificial signs (when the actor followed the rules) and as a representation of disordered sensual nature (when the actor broke the rules, particularly when enacting uncivilized or fitful behavior, as in the case of the fool). On the bourgeois stage of the Enlightenment, however, the body ceased to be represented and perceived by means of this codified system of sensual nature. It was, rather, employed as a natural sign system organized for the expression of individual emotions. Subsequently, in the avant-garde theatre the human body was understood and employed as raw material which the actor might reorganize and transform into a well-functioning mechanism or work of art. In fact, the tendency to repress the body as sensual nature, as un-problematic physical presence, is manifested in an ever-increasing semi-otization of the actor's body.

As a consequence of these results, it may be argued that theatre has con-tributed to the civilizing process by employing and interpreting the actor's body as a sign system. By gradually transforming the human body from an image of sensual nature into a system of arbitrary signs, Western theatre has continually confronted actors and spectators alike with changing cul-tural systems that express, interpret, and control human nature—and this is exactly what characterizes the civilizing process.

More recently, in the contemporary theatre of the neo-avant-garde (or postmodern) movements which arose in Europe and in the United States during the 1960s, the connection between the art of acting and the civiliz-ing process has been reinterpreted. Although having different presupposi-tions and aiming at different ends, all these movements have agreed in attacking the body concept inherent in the Western theatre of the last cen-tury: "What we have tried to liberate was the actor's body!"[16] While, for example, Robert Wilson "liberated" the actor's body from meaning and accomplished its desemiotization, the Living Theatre "revived" the sensual nature of the actor's body. Thus, the neo-avant-garde theatre can be seen as an attempt to free the human body from the pressures brought about by the Western civilizing process.

If there is such a close connection between the art of acting and the civi-lizing process, as this brief overview suggests, we have to consider some methodological consequences. In any case, the history of theatre has to be related to social history. This does not mean that one will be reduced to a mere result of the other, to the status of an effect. It is impossible to prove decisively that acting initiated the social conventions or, contrariwise, that social conventions influenced acting. There is only evidence of congruences between acting and social behavior, between theatre and other aspects of social life. But this connection is sufficient reason to argue that theatre history in all its aspects cannot be explored without regarding social history. Theatre historians should strive for a precise, detailed, and exhaustive description of all theatrical signs that are elaborated and employed by the theatre of a certain epoch—or, at least, of the general principles guiding their elaboration and usage. The functioning of these signs—that is, the constituted processes of meaning which were performed onstage and initiated in the audiences—can only be explained and understood when they are related both to the cultural context and to the social situation in which the theatre took place. The theory of the civilizing process, as developed in the analysis of Norbert Elias, is just one such attempt. Theatre history as social history still remains an undercultivated but certainly fertile field of research and interpretation.

NOTES

1 Norbert Elias, *The History of Manners: The Civilizing Process,* vol. I, trans. Edmund Jephcott (New York: Pantheon Books, 1982), 224. This study was originally published in Switzerland in 1939 under the title *Über den Prozess der Zivilisation.* The German edition (Frankfurt am Main: Suhrkamp) was published in 1976.

2 Elias, *Manners,* p. 223.

3 Ronald Gene Engle, "Franz Lang and the Jesuit Stage" (Ph.D. dissertation, University of Illinois, 1968; Ann Arbor: University Microfilms), p. 107.

4 Norbert Elias, *Power and Civility: The Civilizing Process,* vol. II, trans. Edmund Jephcott with some notes and revisions by the author (New York: Pantheon Books, 1982), 259.

5 Ibid., 259, 271.

6 Heinz Kindermann, *Conrad Ekhofs Schauspieler-Akademie* (Vienna: R. M. Rohrer, 1956), p. 12.

7 Georg Christoph Lichtenberg, *Schriften und Briefe,* ed. Wolfgang Promies (Munich: Hauser, 1972), p. 278.

8 Gotthold Ephraim Lessing, *Lessings Werke,* ed. Robert Boxberger (Berlin/Stuttgart: Spemann, 1883–1890), pp. 158–159.

9 Johann Jakob Engel, *Ideen zu einer Mimik,* 2 vols. (Berlin, 1785–1786; rpt. Frankfurt am Main: Athenäum, 1971), II, 11–12.

10 Vsevolod Meyerhold, *Meyerhold on Theatre,* trans. and ed. Edward Braun (London: Methuen, 1969), pp. 99–100.

11 Antonin Artaud, "Le théâtre et son double," in *Oeuvres complètes,* 23 vols. in 25 (Paris: Gallimard, 1978), IV, 125.

12 Bertold Brecht, *Schriften zum Theater 2. Gesammelte Werke,* 20 vols. (Frankfurt am Main: Suhrkamp, 1967), XVI, 622.

13 Meyerhold, *On Theatre,* p. 198.

14 Ibid., pp. 197–198.

15 Nicolai Foregger, "Experiments in the Art of Drama," *The Drama Review* 19 (1975), 76.

16 Herbert Blau, *Blooded Thought* (New York: Performing Arts Journal Publications, 1982), p. 2.

Using the Concept of Cultural Hegemony to Write Theatre History

Bruce A. McConachie

ontemporary historians with varying methods and commitments have been using notions of cultural hegemony for some time now to structure their historical explanations. Marxist historian Raymond Williams notes that Antonio Gramsci's concept of cultural hegemony has broadened his and others' ideas of the function of ideology in shaping culture. T. J. Jackson Lears, historian of American consumer culture, adds, however, that "the impression that Gramsci's work is relevant only to self-consciously Marxist scholars" is incorrect. Actually, states Lears,

> Gramsci can inspire fresh thought in historians from a variety of intellectual traditions. By clarifying the political functions of cultural symbols, the concept of cultural hegemony can aid intellectual historians trying to understand how ideas reinforce or undermine existing social structures and social historians seeking to reconcile the apparent contradiction between the power wielded by dominant groups and the relative cultural autonomy of subordinate groups whom they victimize.[1]

As if to substantiate Lears' claim, intellectual historian Giles Gunn, a committed pragmatist and no friend to Marxism, urges that the concept of cultural hegemony be placed at the center of American Studies scholarship:

> The real subject of American Studies should be the structure of experience within culture by means of which certain relations of dominance and subordination are socially maintained in the name of meanings and values that are at least emotionally, if not cognitively, acknowledged

as alternatives within a distinctive but always developing range of possibilities.[2]

Indeed, the notion that upper-class hegemony limited the widespread expression of radical dissent is central to theatre historian Walter Cohen's explanation of the conservatism of "popular" theatre in Elizabethan England: "Gramsci's notion of hegemony—broadly speaking, domination by consent—nicely captures the structured complex of ruling-class power and popular opposition, specifying both the limits and the possibilities of insurgency from below." In short, the concept of cultural hegemony as a useful tool of historical analysis has even gained a foothold in the discourse of theatre history.[3]

Detailing the widespread interest in centering historical explanations on a notion of cultural hegemony is not meant to transform Gramsci into "the Marxist you can take home to mother."[4] But it is meant to suggest that historians concerned with unraveling the cloth of culture to understand how symbolic expression becomes stitched to political power are finding the insights of this Italian Communist increasingly helpful. Nevertheless, theatre historians will encounter difficulties swallowing Gramsci whole, more for the fragmentary nature of his writing than for his ideological commitments. Gramsci wrote his *Prison Notebooks,* the chief repository of his thinking, while he languished in Mussolini's jails in the late 1920s and early 1930s, bereft of a good library and more concerned to jot down discrete observations than to develop his ideas systematically.

Compounding these shortcomings for theatre historians is the fact that Gramsci, despite his interest in Pirandello, never articulated the specific ways in which play performances might function to influence the political views of their audiences. Gramsci had no doubt that such influence occurred; but as to exactly how, he remained vague and overly rationalistic. Although committed to changing people's minds and actions, Gramsci never developed an understanding of rhetoric, the use of symbols to effect persuasion. To be applicable to problems of theatre history, Gramsci's notion of cultural hegemony consequently requires elaboration and expansion.

Kenneth Burke's ideas on rhetoric provide the necessary complement. As critic Frank Lentricchia states, Burke "was doing Gramsci's work before anyone but Gramsci (and his censors) could read what would be called the *Prison Notebooks.*"[5] Indeed, as I hope to make clear, Burke and Gramsci share a congruent philosophical orientation as well as a desire to effect progressive social change. By piggybacking Burke on Gramsci, the theatre historian can avoid some of the shortcomings of Gramsci's Marxism and devise strategies for investigating how past performances helped to reinforce or to undermine existing social relations.

The following essay is divided into three parts. The first section sketches the major themes and processes of cultural hegemony as Gramsci understood them. Next, I dovetail this concept with Burke's explication of rhetoric, first demonstrating that both thinkers stand on the same ground of philosophical realism. In a final section, I use this Gramsci-Burkean synthesis to understand and explain the popularity of three of Dion Boucicault's melodramas for New York audiences in the late 1850s. Curiously, *The Poor of New York, The Octoroon,* and *The Colleen Bawn* appealed to working-class as well as middle-class spectators—an apparent anomaly not only because these audiences had been enjoying very different kinds of theatre a few years before, but also because Boucicault's plays relegated workers to the status of a permanent underclass. Gramsci and Burke can help us to understand what workers may have found to applaud in these shows. They can also assist in revealing some of the ideological contradictions which Boucicault's plays helped his American audiences to ignore.

Gramsci's *Prison Notebooks,* unlike most Marxist writing, are put together more like an intricate garden than a well-built house. Rather than establishing a firm foundation of definitions and assumptions and erecting his structure through logic and selected historical examples, Gramsci deploys his arguments and copious examples along several winding paths which intersect at significant points to create a complex network of insights. There is, for example, no clear definition of cultural hegemony in the *Prison Notebooks*.

Nevertheless, certain major patterns emerge from Gramsci's topiary: his distinction between cultural hegemony and domination by force, his emphasis on language as the chief propagator of cultural hegemony, and his conviction that hegemonic culture, however pervasive, is always contradictory and open to change. Behind these attributes of hegemonic culture are dynamic forces which set various "historical blocs" in conflict with one another. These blocs, especially those enmeshed in the ideology of ruling elites, influence subordinate groups and subcultures to accept a world view which can facilitate the unintended participation of the oppressed in their own victimization. Overall, then, cultural hegemony works primarily through legitimation, the half-conscious acceptance of the norms of behavior and the categories of knowledge generated by social institutions, public activities, and popular rituals viewed as "natural" by the people whose actions they shape.

Noting the variety of ways in which groups have exercised power over others, Gramsci distinguishes between domination by force and hegemonic legitimation: "The supremacy of a social group manifests itself in two ways, as 'domination' and as 'intellectual and moral leadership.'"[6] Few groups maintain their power through "domination" alone. Indeed, even after gaining control of the means of coercion, nearly all ruling groups seek to win consent through "intellectual and moral leadership." The Athenian elite in classical Greece legitimated power and influence, in part, by sponsoring play productions in religious festivals. In modern times, ruling elites broadcast their conception of the world through the press, the schools, the entertainment media, and other institutions in the private sphere. These institutions cooperate with dominant groups not only because of self-interest, but because many people in these institutions share the same or similar beliefs. Hence, cultural hegemony involves no conspiracy of the "classes against the masses" and little overt social control.

As Raymond Williams asserts:

> The processes of education; the processes of a much wider social training within institutions like the family; the practical definitions and organizations of work; the selective tradition at an intellectual and theoretical level; all these forces are involved in a continual making and remaking of an effective dominant culture, and on them, as experienced, as built into our living, its reality depends. If what we learn there were merely an imposed ideology, or if it were only the isolable meanings and practices of the ruling class, or of a section of the ruling class, which gets imposed on others, occupying merely the top of our minds, it would be—and one would be glad—a very much easier thing to overthrow.[7]

Hegemonic culture both educates and mystifies its adherents, including those in dominant as well as those in subordinate groups. Subordinate consent, however, is often as much a matter of resignation as of persuasion.

Ordinary people acquiesce to the legitimacy of ruling groups primarily because hegemonic culture works its way into their "spontaneous philosophy." According to Gramsci, all people are "philosophers," their thinking being contained by:

1. Language itself, which is a totality of determined notions and concepts and not just of words grammatically devoid of content;
2. "Common Sense" and "good sense";
3. Popular religion and, therefore, also the entire system of beliefs, superstitions, opinions, ways of seeing things and of acting, which are collectively bundled together under the name of "folklore."[8]

Gramsci's interest in the political influence of language and belief derives, in part, from his graduate work in historical linguistics. Language, he believes, massively shapes a social group's ideology and culture, a term which he loosely defines as "a way of feeling and seeing reality."[9] Within any language group, folkloric belief and "common sense" further limit the possibilities of progressive, counterhegemonic action. Historically, then, certain tendencies grounded in the language and customs of specific groups will predispose (but not, Gramsci would insist, predetermine) them to acquiesce in the rule of others. For Gramsci, the first step toward a revolution of the people would be to change their "common sense" to "good sense," another potential in language which would allow ordinary folks to discover their true needs and interests. The dialogue and songs of many of Brecht's plays attempt this transformation, inducing "good sense" by exposing the contradictions of "common sense." Language is consequently Janus-faced for Gramsci: even as it pulls people back to an oppressive past, it also creates opportunities for political activists (theatre practitioners among them) to motivate people to shape a progressive future.

Reform and radical change are possible, thinks Gramsci, because hegemonic cultures are historically dynamic and incomplete. While some dominant cultures are more open to counterhegemonic alternatives than others, all of them can be changed. Hegemony is "a process of continuous creation which, given its massive scale, is bound to be uneven in the degree of legitimacy it commands and to leave some room for antagonistic cultural expressions to develop," according to one of Gramsci's critics.[10] A given sociohistorical moment "is never homogeneous," states Gramsci; "on the contrary, it is rich in contradictions."[11] In affirming the possibility of exposing and building upon these contradictions, notes Jackson Lears, Gramsci deepens the question "who has power" at "both ends":

The "who" includes parents, preachers, teachers, journalists, literati, "experts" of all sorts, as well as advertising executives, entertainment promoters, popular musicians, sports figures, and "celebrities"—all of whom are involved (albeit often unwittingly) in shaping the values and attitudes of a society. The "power" includes cultural as well as economic and political power—the power to help define the boundaries of common sense "reality" either by ignoring views outside those boundaries or by labeling deviant opinions "tasteless" or "irresponsible."[12]

To suppose, then, that the theatre merely reflected larger political or economic realities—that it had no efficacy of its own—would be a serious misjudgment, according to Gramsci. Because dominant cultures have always been dynamic and contradictory, theatre may have had more potential power than its practitioners may have wished to acknowledge.

To bring about genuine change, however, individuals or small groups would need to join with others into a historical bloc. Unlike most Marxists, Gramsci focuses on heterogeneous groups, loosely aligned through ideological belief as well as economic self-interest, rather than social classes and an elite cadre of intellectuals as the makers of history. An economically based social class such as the bourgeoisie or proletariat is normally at the heart of a historical bloc, but its values and practices must be widely shared by others before its culture can attain hegemony. Indeed, it is primarily through "intellectual and moral leadership" rather than through political or class alliances that one "way of feeling and seeing reality" gains dominance, first over those within the bloc and eventually, if the historical moment is right and the bloc persuades enough others, over an entire nation. The notion of historical blocs explains how some oppressed social groups may have helped to shape and end up participating in a cultural order which victimizes them. What may at one point in history appear to a class or group as a path toward social and economic liberation may eventuate in more modern forms of oppression. Gramsci's theoretical framework allows for and even encourages the perception of such complex historical ironies.

In this and other ways, Gramsci's *Prison Notebooks* expanded orthodox Marxist notions of economically based power and the dynamics of historical change. Yet, in other areas, the conventional Marxism of the 1920s and 1930s hobbled the reach and usefulness of his theories even as it energized his political commitments. Gramsci, for instance, never fully revised the received Marxist concept of ideology as "false consciousness" in the light of his insights concerning the centrality of language to culture beliefs. Further, despite his understanding of hegemonic culture as political education, Gramsci paid little attention to the nonrational means through which political orientations are often promulgated in a culture. Perhaps the biggest stumbling block in Gramsci for contemporary historians is his conviction that economic relationships fundamentally shape the forms of cultural consciousness dominant in any historical period.

To be sure, as Raymond Williams and others have noted, Gramsci loosened the mechanistically causal relationship in orthodox Marxism whereby the "base" of any social order (i.e., the forces and relations of production) "determines" the "superstructure" of that society (i.e., its culture). Gramsci's notions of hegemony and historical bloc do indeed blur the conventional distinctions and linkages between base and superstructure, but they do not eliminate them. The problem here is Gramsci's *a priori* reduction of culture to a function of economic experience. Such essentialism closes the door on historical inquiry instead of opening it. What should be a debatable question—the historical relations between cultural expressions such as theatre and nonsymbolic aspects of human behavior—becomes an unfalsifiable hypothesis, leaving the historian to argue in a circle. Rejecting Gramsci's base/superstructure assumption, however, cuts out a substantial portion of his cultural theory.

Yet Gramsci, unlike most later Marxists, was no materialist. The "base" of culture for him may have been economic action, but it was not material conditions or forces. "Matter as such therefore is not our subject, but how it is socially and historically organized for production . . . ," he asserts.[13] Like several other Italian Marxists of his generation, Gramsci did not believe that Marx was a materialist. Rather, as historian Thomas Nemeth affirms, he derived his ontology and epistemology from Marx's notion of *praxis,* man's ability to alter the material and cultural world through conscious action. Likewise, states Nemeth, "Gramsci absolutely rejected the notion of objective social laws independent of human will. In his eyes such laws condemned man to historical passivity."[14] Despite some of Gramsci's theoretical baggage, then, his insights provide broadly applicable analytical tools for examining the historical intersections of theatre and power. Further, his emphasis on action and his rejection of materialism and determinism map out substantial common ground with Kenneth Burke upon which to elaborate the rhetoric of cultural hegemony.

After praising Gramsci's concept of hegemony as "one of his most original and suggestive" ideas, political theorist Walter Adamson notes several difficulties in using it as an "analytical guide" to discerning the politics of cultural history:

> How exactly does hegemony function as a set of concrete linkages between the political and cultural spheres? Are there patterns in

these linkages which seem to lead predictably to the formation of counterhegemonies? Moreover, if counterhegemonies cohere because of the symbols they evoke and manipulate and because of the values they carry, how might one adequately comprehend this process at the level of political psychology? [15]

What Adamson misses in Gramsci is an understanding of the rhetoric of culture, the means whereby any social group persuades itself and attempts to persuade others that its own values and patterns of symbolic action are natural and right. Kenneth Burke's understanding of the pervasiveness and power of cultural rhetoric is well equipped to fill this lacuna in Gramsci's thinking.

On the face of it, Burke and Gramsci have much in common, especially with regard to the dynamics of cultural hegemony. Like Gramsci, Burke understands that cultural symbols legitimating the power of the dominant class are distributed among most of the "rules, courts, parliaments, laws, educators, constabulary, and the moral slogans linked with each." The "priests" (Burke's term) of the schools, churches, popular arts, and communication media educate the common man to believe "that he 'has a stake' in the authoritative structure that dispossesses him; for the influence exerted upon the policies of education by the authoritative structure encourages the dispossessed to feel that his only hope of repossession lies in his allegiance to the structure that had dispossessed him." [16] Further, hegemonic culture works its way into the habits, rituals, and language of a people such that radical possibilities become "bureaucratized," says Burke, when they are translated and embodied "in the realities of social texture, in all the complexities of language and habits, in the property relationships, the methods of government, production and distribution, and in the development of rituals that reinforce the same emphasis." Because people view everything through a "fog of symbols," he cautions, "one must watch the mind as you would eye a mean dog." [17]

Nevertheless, Burke joins Gramsci in affirming that any hegemonic culture, despite its massiveness and persistence, is not immutable. This is so not only because oppression and ideological contradiction tend to generate opposition but also, according to Burke, because of the paradoxical, undecidable nature of language itself. Consequently, counterhegemonic groups as well as dominant historical blocs can lay claim to such loaded terms as "the people," and "freedom"—terms whose definition can never be completely appropriated and finally fixed by any group or class, no matter how powerful. The success of antiwar theatre groups in the late

1960s and early 1970s in the United States partly hinged on such fundamental ambiguities in the national discourse of patriotism.

Moreover, Burke and Gramsci stand upon the same general philosophical ground; both are realists in the tradition of Aristotle. Unlike most phe-
nomenologists and others committed to subjective views of reality, realists
take as their task the explanation of objects, processes, and experiences
which exist independently of thinking. They differ from positivists, however, in their concern to ground their explanations not only in observable
and recurrent phenomena (beyond which positivists refuse to go), but also
in the "generative mechanisms" that produced the observable facts.[18] To
reveal the layers of causality leading to any discrete event, realists engage in
constructing probable theories as well as in accumulating, clustering, and
synthesizing appropriate data. Among historians and culture critics, nearly
all Marxists are realists; but realism embraces modified notions of empiri-
cism and many approaches of historicism as well as dialectical materialism.

As philosophical realists, Burke and Gramsci recognize that ascertaining
valid truths about reality can only be accomplished through forms of symbolic communication inescapably shaped by culture and history. "Does it
seem that there can exist an extra-historical and extra-human objectivity?"
asks Gramsci rhetorically. "But who will be the judge of such objectivity?
Who can put himself in this kind of 'standpoint of the cosmos in itself' and
what will such a standpoint mean?"[19] For Burke, too, truth is culture-
bound, in his case because of the "undecidable" nature of discourse itself.
Since discourse shapes historical and scientific explanations of reality, the
real can never be completely and finally comprehended through communicable symbols. In their epistemologies, Burke and Gramsci implicitly
posit an ongoing dialectic between tentative explanations and perceived
realities, with historians gradually narrowing the gap in the correspondence between the two. Hence, knowledge is gained partly through the
"hermeneutic circle," a version of the historicist method of validating truths
first explored in depth by Wilhelm Dilthey. Or rather, historians arrive at
valid explanations through a "hermeneutic spiral," Donald Polkinghorne's
useful emendation of Dilthey's term to suggest the transcendence of weaker
explanations which occurs as historians narrow their search for knowledge
of past realities.[20]

Assuming, then, a general congruence between the thinking of Burke
and Gramsci, how may some of the notions of rhetoric of the former be
used to sharpen the cutting edge of the ideas of the latter to write theatre
history? Rhetoric is ubiquitous and irreducible for Burke: "Wherever
there is 'meaning' there is 'persuasion.'" Rhetoric, states Burke, is the

"symbolic means of inducing cooperation in beings that by nature respond to symbols."[21] Hence, rhetoric is the primary means whereby social groups construct, legitimate, and gradually alter their culture. Burke extends the much narrower classical definition of rhetoric into the realm of the sociology of knowledge. No longer is rhetoric merely the occasional conscious embellishment of oratory to manipulate and persuade an audience; in Burke's hands, rhetoric works mostly at subconscious levels to persuade entire groups throughout an era of their common bonds.

Rhetoric fosters social norms and knowledge through identification. Burke believes that people will always need to identify with others because of their fear of alienation and estrangement: "identification is affirmed with earnestness precisely because there is division. Identification is compensatory to division. If men were not apart from one another, there would be no need for the rhetorician to proclaim their unity." Although a permanent need of symbol-using animals, identification can take (and has taken) a bewildering variety of historical forms. Rhetorical identification commonly occurs in three ways, says Burke:

> The first is quite dull. It flows in such usages as that of a politician who, though rich, tells humble constituents of his humble origins. The second kind of identification involves the working of anti-thesis, as when allies who would otherwise dispute among themselves join forces against a common enemy. This application can also serve to deflect criticism, as a politician can call any criticism of his policies "unpatriotic," on the grounds of the nation's enemies. But the major power of "identification" derives from situations in which it goes unnoticed. My prime example is the word "we," as when the statement that "we" are at war includes under the same head soldiers who are getting killed and speculators who hope to make a killing in war stocks.[22]

Commentators have glossed Burke's three types of rhetorical identification as common ground, identification by antithesis, and the "assumed we." To bring Burke closer to Gramsci, however, the third and most powerful type might better be termed the "hegemonic we."[23]

In theatrical performance, Burke's range of identifications includes all the primary means playwrights, directors, designers, and actors use to involve and persuade their audiences of the legitimacy of certain kinds of actions. *Oedipus Tyrannos* and most other Greek tragedies, for example, relied extensively on a "common ground" strategy. The audience of male citizens was invited to empathize with the chorus and to share in the role of a leader, with the result that both identifications generally reinforced group allegiance. Performances of Renaissance comedies and melodramas hinged primarily on "identification by antithesis," the singling out of specific types of foolishness or villainy to be laughed at or denigrated. In such "rituals of victimage," as Burke calls them, the audience's sense of itself as a social congregation was effected primarily through segregation. Identification through the "hegemonic we" is involved in each of the above examples, but may perhaps best be seen in early Restoration comedy where the "fun" depended upon members of a mostly male aristocratic audience taking their sexual prowess and social superiority for granted. Identifying with the action of a character on the basis of taken-for-granted values—situations which have recurred in performances ranging from *The Brothers Menaechmus* to *Death of a Salesman*—is the hallmark of the "hegemonic we." Most theatrical performances involve three types of rhetorical identification, giving release, as theorist Bruce Wilshire states, "to our primal mimetic absorptions in types of doing and being. These absorptions are constitutive . . . of our identity as persons." [24]

A shared system of symbols, chief among them a common language, is a prerequisite for effective rhetorical identification. Indeed, language in rhetorical situations can act like a fond embrace or a loaded gun. "The spontaneous speech of a people," states Burke (echoing Gramsci), "is intensely moral—its names for objects contain the emotional overtones which give us the cues as to how we should act toward these objects." In the theatre, auditory and visual signs, constituted by music, scenery, an actor's line reading, stage movement, and so forth, merge with the words of the playwright to create a metalanguage or, more specifically, a semiotics of the stage charged with "emotional overtones" for the audience. Like a written language, this vocabulary for the theatre contains "a scheme of the appropriate" developed historically by its cultural groups. In effect, then, even as historical blocs manipulate language and other signs in the theatre and elsewhere to enhance their dominance, every system of signs sets limits on the reach of a bloc's cultural hegemony. [25]

Rhetorical identification leads individuals in a social group to accept an "orientation," a term Burke uses to denote a complex of feelings, values, and cognitions corresponding roughly to the world view of a culture. The need to identify with others—a need energized by rhetoric—also helps to create and sustain social institutions such as families, governments, and economic systems, each with its own roles, hierarchies, and persuasions.

During most historical eras, orientations and social institutions reinforce one another, the orientation itself becoming institutionalized. As Burke states:

> An orientation, once it is entrenched, tends to uphold itself, our ethical and legal standards upholding the structure of our institutions, our institutions shaping the nature of our interests, our interests dictating our educational patterns, our educational patterns calling into play specific kinds of imaginative emphasis, such imaginative emphasis corroborating the ethical standards, etc., etc.[26]

In his *Attitudes toward History,* Burke uses the "medieval synthesis" as an example of this hegemonic process conjoining orientation with social institutions. The mutually reinforcing action of medieval Christianity and feudalism created a dominant culture which took centuries to change.[27] Artisan production of mystery plays on pageant wagons may be seen as generally reinforcing the hegemony of the Catholic church and the feudal hierarchy in England. Little wonder, then, that a Protestant Renaissance queen, Elizabeth I, outlawed these performances in England.

Gramsci and Burke point the theatre historian toward an agenda of questions which can open up possible explanations for the popularity of Boucicault's plays among middle- and working-class spectators in the late 1850s. Indeed, the foregoing understanding of cultural hegemony and of the means of its persuasiveness holds potential explanatory power for the social function of any performance popular with any historical audience.

Given the precepts of Gramsci and Burke, the theatre historian might begin by looking at the kinds of identifications imbedded in the historical performances of popular plays. Rather than expecting a single orientation to emerge from a "reading" of these performances, the historian should anticipate tensions and even contradictions, especially if the shows appealed to various groups and classes. Next, he or she must analyze the audiences, examining their historical circumstances and their psycho-social needs—the hopes, fears, and desires that may half-consciously have motivated them to identify with certain actions on the stage. At this point, the theatre historian may wish to investigate the persuasive force of various extratheatrical activities on the lives of these audience groups, since what they were reading, the social groups they were joining, or the other rituals in which they were participating probably answered needs similar to the ones aroused and satisfied when these same groups went to the theatre.

Finally, having followed the hermeneutic spiral toward ever-narrower explanations, the historian can arrive at a probable interpretation of the general social-political effects of these performances on their viewers. Did these shows help to enfold most of their auditors in the values and practices of the dominant culture? Did they encourage modes of perception and action that were counterhegemonic? Or did they do both? How might these performances have worked differently on various audience groups, and might these differences have facilitated the partial formation or destruction of a historical bloc? Interpreting the popularity of *The Poor of New York* (1857), *The Octoroon* (1859), and *The Colleen Bawn* (1860) in the light of these questions can demonstrate the utility of Gramsci's and Burke's approach, even though the summary nature of the following discussion cannot validate my insights with conclusiveness.[28]

Boucicault and his performers used the "common ground" strategy of rhetorical identification to induce the audience to empathize with genteel characters seeking to secure their social respectability. In *The Poor of New York,* these are members of the Fairweather family, initially paupered by the financial panic of 1837 but eventually helped to middle-class happiness by the end of the play. Similarly, the audience was induced to find common ground with George Peyton and his poor-but-honorable Louisiana family in *The Octoroon.* George struggles to keep the family plantation and to gain freedom and respectability for Zoë, his octoroon fiancée, thrown back into slavery because of a legal loophole which nullified her emancipation. A parallel situation structures *The Colleen Bawn,* with Hardress Cregan trying to save his family's estate in Ireland and to elevate his brogue-laden peasant wife without sacrificing his social standing. In all three plays, Boucicault invited his audience to empathize with the chance-ridden circumstances and heartwarming struggles of these families and encouraged audience relief and inner rejoicing when they gained their well-deserved rewards.

A secondary and less pervasive identification on the basis of common ground aligned the audience with working-class "detectives" in these shows. Myles-na-Coppaleen, a whimsical, tippling peasant, solves the mystery of the Colleen Bawn, for instance. *The Octoroon* and *The Poor of New York* also feature a working-class friend of the protagonist who doubles as a detective of sorts. Significantly, the actors cast in each of these roles—the young Joseph Jefferson III in *The Octoroon,* Lester Wallack in *The Poor of New York,* and Boucicault himself in *The Colleen Bawn*—won critical and popular acclaim for their performances in these parts. The importance of good detective work in these melodramas is tied to the centrality of chance in their plots. With misunderstandings and accidents as well as occasional acts of villainy shaping the action, it takes a keen mind to distinguish chance from malign intent and to deduce the overall situation from the fragmentary evidence at hand. Boucicault's plays, then, coupled traditional melodramatic techniques with the convention of early detective fiction, a genre whose popularity with American readers of all classes had just arrived by the 1850s.[29]

Also, because of the importance of chance in his fictitious world, Boucicault and his performers relied less on "identification by antithesis" to hold their audience than had melodramatists earlier in the century. Although he kept a villain among his cast of characters in these plays—thus occasionally encouraging his audience to join forces against this common enemy—Boucicault just as frequently used withheld secrets, central misunderstandings, and lost receipts to motivate misfortune. (He had mastered these Scribean techniques during his apprenticeship months as a playwright in the Paris theatres of the mid-1840s.) Consequently, only one of the three Boucicault villains, M'Closky in *The Octoroon,* is as wicked as his traditional counterparts. The other two are merely guilty of social indiscretions and minor crimes, with the result that one can reform in the last act and the other gets off with a simple dunking in the horsepond. In effect, Boucicault shifted the center of gravity of traditional melodrama, affirming for his late 1850s audience that random chance was more to be feared than willful villainy.

What taken-for-granted values shaped the rhetorical "we" of these popular plays, limiting the probable kinds of identifications audiences might make with the actions of any of the characters? At this mostly subconscious level, an interesting contradiction arose. On the one hand, economic success for any major character was seen mostly as a matter of chance. On the other hand, these plays endorsed a nearly static social order which sharply distinguishes a respectable upper and middle class from a lower class of unrespectables.

Language and race or ethnicity rather than money provide the primary marks of distinctiveness. In *The Poor of New York,* the Puffys, a lower-class Irish family temporarily wealthier than the Fairweathers, keep the middle-class family as boarders. Nevertheless, when the Fairweathers invite a friend to dinner, Mrs. Puffy acknowledges her social inferiority by waiting table for them and taking her own meal in the kitchen. Clearly, Boucicault expected the "we" in his audience to define certain groups of people—immigrant Irish in *The Poor of New York,* black slaves in *The Octoroon,* and peasant Irish in *The Colleen Bawn*—as permanent members of a servant class. That occasional exceptions to this social definition of respectability, motivated in *The Octoroon* and *The Colleen Bawn* by a romantic attachment between a respectable man and unrespectable girl, may occur only strengthened the class division. By suggesting that romantic love can lower social barriers (even, in both plays, as it leads to intense psychological conflicts), Boucicault and his actors gave sentimental flexibility to their notion of respectability.

Despite Boucicault's yearning for a clear social distinction between respectables and unrespectables, the chance-ridden nature of economic life as portrayed in his plays continually undercut his proffered stability. The audience was induced to take competitive laissez-faire capitalism for granted in these shows: a boom-and-bust urban economy causes two financial panics in *The Poor of New York;* the precarious finances of the cotton market force the Peytons to sell their slaves in *The Octoroon;* modern changes in the land tenancy system of Ireland leave the Cregans financially embarrassed in *The Colleen Bawn.* Although Boucicault acknowledged that modern capitalism wreaks havoc on the lives of good people, his plays never encouraged the audience to suppose that the injustices of a chance-ridden economy could be changed. Unlike some earlier melodramatists, Boucicault kept such a tight focus on individual pathos that larger issues of economic justice and self-determination never arose. "I'm an unclean thing, forbidden by the laws—I'm an Octoroon," wails Zoë helplessly (*Octoroon,* p. 266), never questioning the legitimacy of laws supporting a capitalistic slave system in the first place. The situation of the octoroon or the Irish peasant girl yearning for respectability is potentially "tragic," as Boucicault would persuade his audience to believe, only if the economic system enforcing such definitions and causing such hardships is accepted unquestioningly.

The result is a significant contradiction in the "hegemonic we" of Boucicault's shows. Socially, Boucicault sought to assure his audience that respectability is a matter of birth and early socialization; once race, ethnicity, and language place you on either side of the class line, you will probably remain there throughout your life. Economically, however, success is mostly a matter of chance, one's fortune having very little to do with one's respectability. To be sure, Boucicault's plays reward the respectable with riches in the end, but he persuaded his audience that no providence watches over worthy characters to ensure that economic and social success join together by the final tableau.

This disjuncture between economic and social realms reveals gaps in the ideological armor projected by these shows. These gaps, in turn, raise at least two divisive questions within the discourse of this ideology—how can respectable people be assured of economic well-being? and what is to prevent unrespectable people from gaining economic power?—and many more once the focus is broadened. Clearly, Boucicault did not encourage the kinds of identifications which might lead audiences to ask such questions. Indeed, the plays may be seen as unwitting attempts to channel audience interests and desires so as to avoid the contradictions implicit in their hegemonic ambitions. As with symbolic actions in most cultures, the persuasive power of these plays lay in their ability to encompass and smooth over ambiguities troublesome to their audience.

What kinds of spectators applauded these successful shows? *The Poor of New York, The Octoroon,* and *The Colleen Bawn* achieved their greatest popularity in New York at middle-class theatres, accumulating over two hundred performances between 1857 and 1862, a period when long runs were rare.[30] Their appeal to a mid-century bourgeois audience is not difficult to fathom. Most middle-class men and women in the 1850s believed that their economic success was due as much to chance as to their innate morality. As social historian Richard Sennett points out, "The businessmen and bureaucrats of the last century had little sense of participating in an orderly system. The new principles of making money and directing large organizations were a mystery even to those who were very successful. . . . [Most pictured] their activities in terms of the gamble, the game of chance—and the appropriate scene was the stock exchange."[31]

The 1850s also witnessed the hardening of social divisions as the new middle class strove to distance itself from "unrespectable" immigrants, day laborers, and the poor. "Above the class line lay the paths of progress that adults could choose if they would. Here, it was claimed, no one enjoyed privileges that others could not share, and everyone achieved a success equivalent to merit. . . . Below the class line the poor were expected to stay in rags, and most of them did. Barred from the opportunities to advance, they fulfilled the prophecies of doom that respectable citizens hurled at them," states historian Robert Wiebe.[32] Aware, then, that economic success was partly a matter of chance, middle-class Americans were nevertheless under enormous pressure to demonstrate their respectability.

One response to this situation was a rapid increase in the 1850s in the sale of books and pamphlets offering practical advice for business success. Another was the proliferation of novels and magazines elucidating codes of fashion and etiquette by which the middle class might preserve its respectability, regardless of occasional business reversals. The success of these three Boucicault plays among urban middle-class auditors may consequently be understood as a palliative, in part, to ease middle-class fears about securing respectability in the midst of economic chance. "Maintain your respectability," these performances assured them, "and you will eventually gain economic security whatever financial embarrassments you may suffer along the way." For their middle-class spectators, then, these shows functioned to legitimate significant beliefs centering on class and money. By bolstering confidence in the social justice of the emerging status quo, these performances underwrote bourgeois hegemony in the antebellum United States.

Middle-class audiences were not the only ones enjoying these shows, however. Theatre companies in working-class playhouses in New York staged Boucicault's plays for more than a hundred performances between 1857 and 1862, fewer than those for middle-class auditors but still a sizable quantity by mid-century standards. Why did workers applaud plays which, in hindsight, ran counter to their social and economic interests? To simplify the matter greatly, an increasing percentage of working-class New Yorkers were accepting the tenets of the "new industrial morality." As historians Alan Dawley and Paul Faler describe it, the values of self-control, competitiveness, and self-reliance were replacing a more traditional orientation founded on casual camaraderie, republican virtues, and artisan solidarity. The regimen of the clock and the steam engine, the economic levers of power in the 1850s, socialized some workers into accepting beliefs in accord with these historical realities. Others were gradually won over to the new industrial morality by revivalists, temperance reformers, the new common schools, and other agencies of the emerging bourgeois hegemony in the 1850s.[33]

Workers valuing abstinence, individualism, and competition found much to applaud in *The Poor of New York, The Octoroon*, and *The Colleen Bawn*. These qualities, after all, were the prime ingredients of good "character," a necessary (though not a sufficient) part of the definition of respectability in these plays. Recognition of these qualities in the respectable families at the center of these melodramas probably would have led such workers to identify with the actions of these middle-class characters, despite the class disparity. Workers may have identified more closely with the actions of characters near the edge of the class divide, however. The plight of an Irish lass afflicted with a brogue and the success of a marginally respectable detective figure would have been appealing to audience members barely able to claim respectability for themselves.

In this era of early industrialization, few native-born workers had accepted definitions of themselves as wage-earning proletarians, permanently shut out of property-owning self-sufficiency. At the same time, they saw evidence all around them of immigrants, the shiftless poor, and probably a few of their boyhood friends who had sunken into the "dangerous classes" of the urban swamp. Consequently, many native American workers in the 1850s internalized middle-class standards of respectability, more often out of fear than hope. Notes Wiebe, "The interior drive to meet those standards—and to convince others that they met them—shaped lives all along the urban class margin."[34] Boucicault's plays educated working-class audiences in the niceties of the class line, assuring them that they, too, could aspire to secure respectability.

Working-class plays had not always persuaded their audiences to accept bourgeois hegemony. From the mid-1830s through the 1840s, apocalyptic melodramas pitting a working-class avenger against aristocratic villainy had urged artisan solidarity to maintain traditional rights. Though lacking a modern sense of class consciousness and proposing a religious solution to worldly evil, these popular plays nevertheless pointed to clear differences between the status quo and social justice. Beginning in the mid-1840s, temperance melodramas made some inroads into traditional working-class belief, shifting it toward an accommodation with the new industrial morality. The success of *Uncle Tom's Cabin* in 1852 and 1853 on working-class stages spawned numerous sentimental spin-offs in the mid- and late 1850s which effectively altered the center of melodramatic discourse for workers away from an apocalyptic definition of their hopes and fears toward a sentimental one. Apocalyptic plays had depicted the powerless artisan against the powerful aristocrat. The new sentimental plays, such as *Orion, the Gold Beater* and *The Gun-Maker of Moscow* (both 1857), generally ignored problems of power to focus on a respectable working-class hero saving the deserving poor from petty villains of their own class. For the most part, they reinforced the values of the new industrial morality: self-reliance, self-control, and individual competition.[35]

Boucicault's plays took working-class admirers a step further into compliance with the strictures of bourgeois hegemony. Now a respectable family, not a competitive artisan, was placed at the center of these plays for audience identification. Class lines, relatively permeable in *Orion* and *The Gun-Maker,* had hardened with the recognition that some groups of people were meant to be servants. Workers might maintain their respectability if they could do detective work in Boucicault's shows, but otherwise they had little to offer except service and comic relief.

This is not to say that all or even most urban workers accepted the constraints of the emerging hegemony as natural and just. Some were co-opted and did join with most of the moral and intellectual leaders, much of the traditionally minded elite, and nearly the entire middle class to form a historical bloc in the northern United States that would fight the Civil War and ensure its own cultural dominance through the Gilded Age of American life. Other workers were persuaded neither by Boucicault's plays nor by the similar rhetoric of sermons, editorials, and school lessons to put their trust in the respectable and successful.

Further research into urban working-class persuasions in the late 1850s, however, would likely demonstrate that many were divided in their thoughts and loyalties. Gramsci notes that many workers exhibit "contradictory consciousness"—pulled one way by the class constraints of their everyday lives and in the opposite direction by the hegemonic culture of the dominant class. Despite the "good sense" taught the worker by his social situation, the dominant culture "binds him to a certain social group, influences his moral behavior and the direction of his will in a more or less powerful way; and it can reach the point where the contradiction of his conscience will not permit any action, any decision, any choice, and produces a state of moral and political passivity." Even though cultural hegemony may produce whole eras of general working-class passivity, as occurred in the entire industrializing world from the 1850s through the mid-1870s, Gramsci cautions that political inaction cannot be equated with agreement or even acquiescence to dominant cultural norms. Recurrent strikes, capitalist violence, union organizing, and the memory of traditional ways of living and working broadcast a very different message to American workers during these years, a message which kept many of them alienated from bourgeois capitalism even if it did not speed their acceptance of radical alternatives.[36]

NOTES

1 Raymond Williams, "Base and Superstructure in Marxist Cultural Theory," in *Problems in Materialism and Culture: Selected Essays* (London: NLB, 1980), p. 37; T. J. Jackson Lears, "The Concept of Cultural Hegemony: Problems and Possibilities," *American Historical Review* 90 (June 1985), 568.

2 Giles Gunn, *The Culture of Criticism and the Criticism of Culture* (New York: Oxford, 1987), p. 166.

3 Walter Cohen, *Drama of a Nation: Public Theatre in Renaissance England and Spain* (Ithaca, N.Y.: Cornell University Press, 1985), pp. 28–29.

4 Quoted in Lears, "The Concept of Cultural Hegemony," p. 568.

5 Frank Lentricchia, *Criticism and Social Change* (Chicago: University of Chicago Press, 1983), p. 37.

6 Antonio Gramsci, *Selections from the Prison Notebooks of Antonio Gramsci,* ed. Quintin Hoare and Geoffrey Nowell-Smith (New York: International Publishers, 1971), pp. 57–58.

7 Williams, "Base and Superstructure," p. 39.

8 Gramsci, *Selections from the Prison Notebooks,* p. 373.

9 Antonio Gramsci, *Selections from Cultural Writings,* ed. David Forgacs and Geoffrey Nowell-Smith (Cambridge, Mass.: Harvard University Press, 1985), p. 98.

10 Walter Adamson, *Hegemony and Revolution: A Study of Antonio Gramsci's Political and Cultural Theory* (Berkeley and Los Angeles: University of California Press, 1980), p. 174.

11 Gramsci, *Selections from Cultural Writings,* p. 93.

12 Lears, "The Concept of Cultural Hegemony," p. 572.

13 Gramsci, *Selections from the Prison Notebooks,* p. 465.

14 Thomas Nemeth, *Gramsci's Philosophy: A Critical Study* (Sussex, England: Harvester Press, 1980), p. 187. Several of the contributors to *Marxism and the Interpretation of Culture,* ed. Cary Nelson and Lawrence Grossberg (Urbana and Chicago: University of Illinois Press, 1988), disregard Gramsci's generally orthodox notions of ideology, base-superstructure relations, and rationalistic psychology to extend and reformulate his thinking so as to bring it closer to contemporary theories of democratic socialism, feminism, and film theory. See especially Stuart Hall, "The Toad in the Garden: Thatcherism among the Theorists," pp. 58–74; Chantel Mouffe, "Hegemony and New Political Subjects: Toward a New Concept of Democracy," pp. 89–104; Michael Ryan, "The Politics of Film: Discourse, Psychoanalysis, Ideology," pp. 477–486. These neo-Marxist writers retain the general concept of cultural hegemony but emphasize the relative autonomy of culture vis-à-vis economic forces, assume that all types of social relations—race, gender, as well as class—may result in historically significant conflict, and explore various notions of social psychology for their potential explanatory power within a loosely Marxist framework.

15 Adamson, *Hegemony and Revolution,* pp. 244–245.

16 Kenneth Burke, *Attitudes toward History* (1937; rpt. Boston: Beacon Press, 1961), pp. 329–330. Burke's later work builds upon these insights and incorporates them into larger conceptual frameworks.

17 Ibid., p. 225; Kenneth Burke, *The Philosophy of Literary Form,* 3rd ed. (1941; rpt. Berkeley and Los Angeles: University of California Press, 1973), p. 65.

18 See Gregor McLennan, *Marxism and the Methodologies of History* (London: Verso Books, 1981), especially chapters 2 and 4. See also Anthony Giddens, *The Constitution of Society: Introduction to the Theory of Structuration* (Berkeley: University of California Press, 1984).

19 Gramsci, *Selections from the Prison Notebooks,* p. 445.

20 Donald Polkinghorne, *Methodology for the Human Sciences: Systems of Inquiry* (Albany: State University of New York Press, 1983), p. 227.

21 Kenneth Burke, *A Rhetoric of Motives* (1950; rpt. Berkeley and Los Angeles: University of California Press, 1969), pp. 172, 43.

22 Ibid., p. 22.

23 Kenneth Burke, *Dramatism and Development* (Barre, Mass.: Clark University Press, 1972), p. 28.

24 Bruce Wilshire, *Role Playing and Identity: The Limits of Theatre as Metaphor* (Bloomington: Indiana University Press, 1982), p. 23.

25 Kenneth Burke, *Permanence and Change* (1935; rpt. Indianapolis: Bobbs-Merrill, 1965), p. 177; Kenneth Burke, "My Approach to Communism," *New Masses* 10 (March 20, 1934), 19.

26 Kenneth Burke, "On Interpretation," *Plowshare* 10 (February 1934), 39–40.

27 Burke, *Attitudes toward History,* pp. 94–134.

28 *The Poor of New York,* French's Standard Drama, Acting Edition, no. 189 (New York: Samuel French, 1857); *The Octoroon, or Life in Louisiana,* in *The Black Crook and Other Nineteenth-Century American Plays,* ed. Myron Matlaw (New York: E. P. Dutton, 1967), pp. 206–256; *The Colleen Bawn, or The Brides of Garry Owen,* in *Nineteenth-Century Plays,* ed. George Rowell (1953; rpt. London: Oxford University Press, 1960), pp. 173–232. In analyzing the historical relation between audiences and performances, I proceed along the same lines as Tony Bennett's understanding of the relation between readers and texts, which he terms a "reading formation." This Bennett defines as "a set of discursive and inter-textual determinations which organize and animate the practice of reading, connecting texts and readers in specific relations to one another in constituting readers as reading-subjects of particular types and texts as objects-to-be-read in particular ways. This entails that texts have and can have no existence independently of such reading formations . . ." ("Texts in History: The Determinations of Readings and Their Texts," in *Poststructuralism and the Question of History,* ed. Derek Attridge et al. [Cambridge: Cambridge University Press, 1987], p. 70). Likewise, performances and spectators are mutually dependent and mutually defining. The rhetorical power of the theatre only works within an "audience formation," to adapt Bennett's phrasing.

29 See Dennis Porter, *The Pursuit of Crime: Art and Ideology in Detective Fiction* (New Haven: Yale University Press, 1981).

30 I arrived at the approximate figure of over two hundred performances in this five-year period by estimating the number of performances for each show at each middle-class theatre as reported by Odell. These estimates are as follows: *Poor of New York* (Wallack's), 48; *Octoroon* (Winter Garden), 63; *Colleen Bawn* (Laura Keene's, Winter Garden, Wallack's, Niblo's), 96. See *Annals of the New York Stage,* 15 vols. (New York: Columbia University Press, 1927–1949), vols. 6 and 7.

31 Richard Sennett, *The Fall of Public Man: On the Social Psychology of Capitalism* (New York: Random House, 1976), pp. 138–139.

32 Robert Wiebe, *The Opening of American Society: From the Adoption of the Constitution to the Eve of Disunion* (New York: Knopf, 1984), p. 322.

33 I also used Odell to tabulate estimates for these performances in predominantly working-class playhouses: *Poor of New York* (National), 7; *Octoroon* (Barnum's, Bowery, New Bowery), 49; *Colleen Bawn* (Barnum's, New Bowery), 58. On the new industrial morality, see Alan Dawley and Paul Faler, "Working-Class Culture and Politics in the Industrial Revolution: Sources of Loyalism and Rebellion," *Journal of Social History* 9 (June 1976), 466–480.

34 Wiebe, *The Opening of American Society*, p. 333.

35 On apocalyptic melodrama, see my essay, "'The Theatre of the Mob': Apocalyptic Melodrama and Preindustrial Riots in Antebellum New York," in *Theatre for Working-Class Audiences in the United States, 1830–1980*, ed. Bruce McConachie and Daniel Friedman (Westport, Conn.: Greenwood Press, 1985), pp. 1–46; G. L. Aiken, *Orion, the Gold Beater, or True Hearts and False*, MS, Players Library, New York [1857]; John Brougham, *The Gun-Maker of Moscow*, French's Standard Drama, Acting Edition, no. 164 (New York: Samuel French, n.d.).

36 Antonio Gramsci, *The Modern Prince and Other Writings* (New York: International Publishers, 1967), pp. 66–67. On working-class passivity in the industrializing world in the 1850s and 1860s, see Eric J. Hobsbawm, *The Age of Capital, 1848–1875* (New York: Scribner's, 1979), pp. 228–252.

Questions for a Feminist Methodology in Theatre History

Tracy C. Davis

In almost all areas of the humanities and social sciences, feminist research has become an immutable component of scholarly discussion. In some disciplines, such as psychology and sociology, feminists' critique of mainstream scholarship has been embraced, while in others, such as modern languages and history, the theoretical critique and canonical revisions feminists propose are less widely accepted. The following remarks on a feminist methodology for theatre history incorporate some of the questions posed by sociologists, literary critics, historians of women, and semioticians but do not imitate any one group. While the informing conception is interdisciplinary, the approach avoids mere eclecticism by its fidelity to a coherent political ideology, namely, feminism. The proposals are based partly on examples of feminist historical writing on theatre (the stream of articles and books that became noticeable about 1972), partly on methodological writing about women's history *qua* history and its intellectual challenges (excellently précised in Lerner),[1] and partly on a personal preference for the way the field is to take form.

Most wings of the feminist movement claim that ideology is formed by activists, at the grass-roots level, and that application should antedate theoretical musings. Considerable tension exists between feminist activists and feminist academics, though the distrust that commonly exists between theatre practitioners and theatre academics is minimized in the feminist realm because most feminist academics and theorists are involved in theatre production or social activism, or a combination of both. Whether because of political conviction, coincidence, or lethargy, feminist theatre historians have yet seriously to attempt an all-embracing manifesto or methodological design for research.

This may account for the fact that much current research focuses on feminist theatre groups and attempts to recognize feminist methodology in the production and performance of plays—essentially a descriptive rather than an analytical endeavor that does not redesign the historian's craft. In an academic community curious but skeptical about feminism, we feel some pressure for our conclusions to be miraculously correct on the first attempt. Consequently, we usually employ conventional research models spiced by feminist literary theory and philosophy. Given that the theatre has been used as a feminist agitational and educative tool for most of this century (first in suffrage campaigns, and continuously since the mid-1960s), that feminist discussion rings throughout the academy, and that a large number of theatre practitioners and historians are interested in the subject, it does not seem premature to begin to undertake a discussion of methodological concerns. The grass roots are well enough established to undergo some heavier treading.

Identifying the Subject

The fear of "segregating" women is acute in theatre studies, even among editors who designate special issues (hence Michael Kirby's apologetic and uninformative introduction to *The Drama Review* T86).[2] Feminist critics working with sophisticated gynocritical models are more advanced in their applications of feminist theory, but neither drama nor the performance of texts is usually investigated by these writers.[3] Consequently, most sophisticated critical pursuits are as yet rooted in language studies rather than theatre studies, though recent work by Janelle Reinelt on Brechtian theory and British playwriting and articles such as Phyllis Rackin's on various theatrical reflections of the androgyne (boys portraying heroines) on the Renaissance stage suggest that this discrepancy is being addressed.[4]

As in film studies, art history, and dance anthropology, the representation of the female body and women's socialization are of considerable concern to all feminists. Interpretations of meanings and significance differ greatly, but there seems to be agreement that representations of sexuality and gender are and have been male constructions (representations *of,* but not *by,* women) and that eroticism is an indispensable concern of feminist performance history. Dance historian Frank Aschengreen, for example, argues that after 200 years of domination by male dancers, the French Romantic ballet almost eliminated the masculine, replacing it with a new aesthetic that combined demonism and eroticism in ballerinas who appealed directly to the senses.[5] Ann Daly argues in a similar way about George Balanchine's choreography, which glorifies a passive, manipulated image of womanhood.[6] Jill Dolan writes about how women's experiments in performance art and lesbian cabaret reveal the rigidity of ideas about representation and how women's erotic performances might break the mold.[7] Elsewhere, I have discussed the language shared by Victorian pornography and the stage, arguing that pornography's preoccupation with actresses (fictional and real) both influenced and reflected the way men viewed performance.[8] Therefore, the material eligible for consideration as a model for feminist theatre history methodology is limited, but growing.

Nancy Reinhardt and Claudia Johnson have demonstrated the importance of class and gender in the drama and the theatre building,[9] but in general the so-called cultural histories of popular (usually nonlegitimate) performers and genres form the most methodologically sophisticated field in theatre studies. Issues of class permeate the work of Peter Bailey, Penny Summerfield, and Eileen and Stephen Yeo: class distinctions in the auditoriums, dressing rooms, and songs of Victorian music halls are variously interpreted as persuasive or affirmative. Most feminists would agree that distinctions of class are interactive components of the presentation and reception of performance and an indispensable consideration in the writing of history. Sheila Rowbotham argues, however, that "we are not just sex-beings in the family and class-beings in the community, the state and at work": capitalism and patriarchy interlock, affecting women's "ideas of themselves and other people, their work, habits and sexuality, their participation in organization, their responses to authority, religion and the state, and the expression of their creativity in art and culture."[10]

In an essay on Jenny Hill, a late Victorian seriocomic singer and dancer, J. S. Bratton demonstrates how this insight can be incorporated into music hall history. She reexamines the contemporaneous and posthumous myths about Hill in the light of economic, material, social, and professional considerations of her status as a woman, an advocate for the working classes (especially women), an outspoken orator in a profession where women rarely spoke up, and a highly successful artiste whose attempts to manage her own career and channel earnings into career-enhancing investments faltered in part because of externally imposed limitations on members of her sex. According to Bratton, the mythologizers present Hill as an exploited youngster whose excellence at her art eventually led her into alliances with capable men and then meteoric professional success. Bratton's revision is substantial, for she presents Hill as a highly successful artiste whose fortune was won by hard work and talent, and whose career was continually molded by factors beyond her control—factors deliberately rendered invisible by show business, time, and Hill herself. To the public gaze, Jenny Hill was the "Vital Spark" (the vital glamour, display, energy, and expertise of popular entertainment), but she was at once both limited and sustained by the patriarchal control of late nineteenth-century halls that kept her, like so many other women, from attaining and holding her place in the pantheon of male performer-managers. Indeed, she was the perpetual employee, though an honored one, who received diamonds from admirers and colleagues. Bratton astutely analyzes the sign of the be-jeweled actress as a mark of a possessed rather than of a possessing nature: "She wears the badge of her dishonourable honours, which impresses women less well found, while warning off men whose wealth does not match that of her present protectors." Even when, as in the case of Hill, the jewels are bestowed by managers and audiences rather than by lovers, "the sign remains powerful, enabling the patriarchy to perceive her wealth as the gift of men rather than the earning-power of the woman."[11] In no case is the gift an investment compensation for the *de facto* disadvantages of being a female performer: male control of management, hiring, wages, repertoire, and women's sexual reputation.

Rina Fraticelli, Kay Carney, and Julianne Boyd (all theatre professionals) draw similar conclusions about patronage and the socio-sexual infrastruc-ture of the profession in their studies of the underrepresentation of women administrators, directors, designers, and playwrights in desirable posts in present-day Canada and America.[12] They argue that women's career pat-terns should be studied in conjunction with the cultural and professional forces that channel the sexes into different occupations. Judith Lynne Hanna takes the notion of occupational ghettoizing further by asserting that career choices relate to gender-determined prestige categories that relegate women and homosexual men into the symbolically "low-status" and economically precarious employments of fields like dance. In such cases, sex, sexual preference, and cultural constructions of "the body, emotion, and gender" are all shown to have a bearing on employment patterns.[13]

Feminists are not just interested in women as a biological category, but are united by the conviction that gender is socially constructed and that this should be the primary component of analysis. Some historians of women in theatre, such as Rosamond Gilder, Albert Auster, Claudia Johnson, and Katharina Wilson, make the sexual (biological) distinctions without necessarily making a gender (social) distinction. Therefore, an in-forming political perspective resulting from their subjects' existence as so-cial beings in a specific time and place with particular consequences for women and men is lacking.[14] Marxist anthropologists such as Sherry Ortner and Harriet Whitehead, who view culture as ideology that justifies the status quo by systematically mystifying and distorting the sources of oppression and exploitation, provide a more fruitful lead.[15] In the *Annales* tradition, S. E. Amussen documents this cultural process for early-modern England by demonstrating the informal enforcement of gender expectations through gossip and the manipulation of reputations, which affects courtship, marriage, and marital breakdown.[16] The importance of these factors in theatre history—particularly actress biography—is generally recognized but underestimated by theatre historians.

Approaches

Most of the published work on women and theatre fits comfortably in one of two categories:

1. Endeavors to recover data about women and fill in the "female blanks" of history. This leads to discussion of the gendered asymmetry of society and culture, and then to revisionist history, particularly in the form of biographies and collective biographies (though so far usually of the very successful, famous, and therefore atypical elite of the art). Recovery and revision also take the form of histories of overtly feminist action, especially actresses' involvement in suffrage agitation and feminist theatre groups, which highlights women's activities in contrast or opposition to dominant traditions.[17]

2. Feminist literary criticism complementing historians' work by reclaiming "lost" plays and uncanonized playwrights, providing an alternate reading of texts, and reprinting or publishing modern plays by women.[18]

REVISIONIST HISTORY

Recovery is probably an indispensable first step of feminist scholarship, but, as Lynda Nead points out with reference to art history, the effort must not stop at rediscovering names and integrating them into the discipline, but must go on to challenge the terms, periodization, and categories of the scholarly tradition.[19] As yet, the canon of works and panoply of notable figures inherited from traditional history have not been substantially revised, so work like Nancy Cotton's on women playwrights of fifteenth- to eighteenth-century England, which is exceptional in its attention to minor and overlooked figures, is commendable but not the final word.[20] If feminist historians are going to rewrite history, the revisions must cut deeply. Not only lives have been left "blank." The importance of theatre as a medium of culture, the social context of performers and performance, and assumptions inherent in the "unrevised" versions of history are all issues central to the study of public figures (particularly women) whose livelihoods depended on the observation and approval of private individuals (particularly men).

Greater attention to period-based histories of women's lives and culture would undoubtedly enhance most theatre research in contemporary and distant eras and may inspire researchers to locate and tap unusual types of evidence. Performers' itinerant, eccentric lives are not conducive to the collection and subsequent deposition of manuscript correspondence, diaries, and professional records (such as contracts and résumés), and this compounds the elitist record of theatre history. Music hall historians are helped by the volume of song sheets published in the nineteenth century, but again there are acute difficulties in interpretation, and the material is haphazardly preserved. As Thomas Postlewait argues in this collection, the interpretation of published autobiographies is also problematic, in part due to women's reluctance to discuss the machinations of invisible professional forces (such as patriarchal exclusion and sexual coercion) and to mention delicate personal matters relating to romantic liaisons and the female life cycle. Sometimes the sources of feminist history, imaginatively interpreted, will fill in blanks and sometimes they will add whole new chapters and volumes.

Little has yet appeared that offers a means to reevaluate women's experiences of theatre except as outstanding performers, exceptional producers, or privileged critics, but feminist revisionism is not limited to women in these roles. Marie-Claire Pasquier dares to ask "who is theatre for?" and then "who makes it and defines its terms?"—both disturbing and provocative questions about women's love of theatre and their peripheral participation both as spectators and as professionals.[21] Helen Chinoy and Linda Jenkins conscientiously avoid the chronicle-of-stars approach in their American anthology and suggest several intriguing new directions:

> We need research that considers the visual image/icon on stage as it is shaped by director/performer/designer: What gender values are being reinforced or created by the "stage picture" alone? We need more study of audience response to the apparent experience of the theatre event: How closely will they allow it to approximate their perception

of actual experience and how much challenge will they allow? Is there a gender differentiation with respect to who really censors stage images that challenge socially institutionalized images?[22]

Some of these challenges have begun to be taken up. The appropriateness to women of theatre structures and production methods has been questioned by Roberta Sklar, just as gender as a category of analysis in production and reception has been taken up by Linda Jenkins and Susan Ogden-Malouf with respect to actor training and "maleness" in the compositional language of the mise-en-scène.[23]

Neither feminism as a political theory nor feminism as a methodological practice of history is a fully formed, unitary vision: both are emergent and multifaceted, and consequently innumerable and irreconcilable theoretical variations are discernible. What is consistently shown, however, is that feminist theatre history is incompatible with positivist methodology. Positivism may result in a viable history of women but it is incompatible with the deeper questioning of feminist studies; observable facts do not necessarily reflect the cultural and political context of artistic pursuits and rarely spark a concern for causation. A theatre history that assembles primary sources (textual, visual, and tactile) to describe but not to analyze performance results in what Vesna Pistotnik calls "the *archaeology* of theatrical forms and the assessment of how they have been used to serve the needs of the dramatic text on stage."[24] Feminist theatre historians are rarely satisfied with "recreative" approaches because the meaning of productions is always paramount among our concerns. The interplay of performance with psychological, sociological, biological, and economic factors contributes to the challenge of recent historiography; feminists add the importance of the personal dimension of social activity to this list and insist on the political significance of everything. The types of questions asked in the collection of oral history by Kathleen Betsko and Rachel Koenig, for example, validate the importance of the female life cycle in the artist's life and invite commentary from the women playwrights on how their personal experience relates to a world view, and how both are rendered into playtexts and productions.[25]

In common with the original aims of the Ruskin College History Workshops, feminist theatre historians seem to be determined to give credence to informal modes of resistance and limited revolution, to draw on participant observation and oral history (testaments and interviews), and often to write locally or regionally focused histories.[26] The basic idea is to give voice to what would otherwise be silenced by individuals, cultures, and history itself. Because silence is not absence, it is not only a plausible but also a valid and verifiable subject of historical inquiry. By historicizing the silence (and silencing) of racial minorities, ethnic subcultures, and classes in any culture, we articulate what is known by women to exist but is unspoken or unspeakable in the dominant tradition. When interviewing women playwrights, for example, Koenig discovered that "the censor, operant in the self and in society, was both attracted to and compelled to silence those elements of the work which were most deeply connected to female sentience and experience, those elements which either criticized or questioned male power and authority, or those elements which truthfully revealed male vulnerability."[27] The feminist historian's task is to address the censoring impulse, to validate the experience, and to connect the woman with the work and the work with the world at large.

FEMINIST LITERARY CRITICISM

The ontology that distinguishes theatre from written drama is a central point: just as the personal is political (integrative and reactive), the theatrical is rhetorical (persuasive and enacted). While feminist poetics of the dramatic text may in time prove essential to theatre history methodology, consideration of the conditions of theatrical production and the many forces that shape artistic decisions and social reception of theatre needs to be combined with the present hermeneutic and exegetic emphasis in criticism.[28] Feminist theatre history necessarily incorporates literary history by asking how art (or nonart) is related to the tastes of its audience and to the predominant styles of its time and place, as in Lisa Jardine's extraordinary study of women and drama in Renaissance England.[29]

The conservatism of mainstream theatre studies derives from an enduring preoccupation (after 2,300 years) with Aristotelian poetical terminology: Aristotle's classification of poetic and theatrical types and his division of the structure of dramatic incidents may have very little to do with the "common" woman's (or even the exceptional woman's) experience of theatre whether as a spectator, performer, or playwright. By revealing gendered concepts of form, content, and excellence in drama, Reinhardt and Carol Gelderman have addressed some of the issues for literary critics (including linear structuring, the manly debate of *agon*, and masculine individualism); by validating what women choose to do in contravention of regular practice, Dinah Leavitt, Karen Malpede, and special issues of *The Drama Review* and *Canadian Theatre Review* have given the issues historical particularity.[30] The Magdalena Project's explorations into women's creative processes and expressive language undertake an analogous project in a "laboratory" setting.[31] This deep questioning by cultural feminists of the basic tenets of dramatic and performance theory may have profound effects on the conceptualization of theatre and the hierarchical valuations of art.

The theory of difference, which holds that women and men have innate biological differences that result in a typology of cultural characteristics and bodily awareness distinct for each sex, may also have significance for dramatic and performance theory and, subsequently, for historical thinking.[32] Generalizations about women's "horizontal" rather than "linear" thinking and the genetically justified delineation of a separate social sphere for women may have had an effect on women's theatre-making and the assertion of men's cultural hegemonic prerogative in every historical era. High culture's choice of particular motifs, myths, legends, and historical incidents *is* dramatic literature, and the accepted canon of dramatic literature sets out roles and a hierarchy of career specialties that may have little or nothing to do with what excites women to pity and fear, or with what women honor in lieu of the catharsis of high tragedy and the fatal downfall of highborn characters who are distinctly lacking in perspicacity, intuition, and plain common sense. This does not simply imply a Marxian view of poetics from the underside of culture, or an alternate tradition among an oppressed and marginalized subculture, and certainly does not require a psychoanalytic theory of spontaneous generic female experience.

However, as Gramsci points out, imagined form can become genuine content: "if the cultural world for which one is fighting is a living and necessary fact [in the minds of its advocates], its expansiveness will be irresistible and it will find its artists."[33] This certainly seems true of feminist drama of the second wave. Like much feminist literary criticism rooted in the novel and poetry, Gramsci's insight suggests a starting point for questioning traditions of dramatic form, the possession of power by those in command of the approved form, and the valuation of certain traditions amid a silent but living imaginative alternative. Feminist art history has come a long way since Linda Nochlin debunked the question "Why have there been no great women artists?"[34] Theatre historians can also learn much from the debates in fine art about traditions of art practice, culturally partisan appraisals of "greatness," and a reoriented focus that permits women to become visible in their own right and not just in the shadow of men.

Toward a Feminist Methodology

The following proposals for a feminist methodology for theatre history do not advocate a technical or mechanical procedure, but offer a theoretical framework translated into organizational principles. These principles are contained in three procedural questions phrased in as broadly applicable a manner as possible without limitations to a particular historical period. The result, I hope, might lead to research that cannot be comfortably apportioned as a "historical" or a "literary" endeavor because a marriage, however uneasy, has been achieved between these two complementary practices. For the time being, until more research has been done, many of the following remarks are necessarily speculative. They are intended to consolidate the contributions of recent research (theoretical and substantive) in feminist theory and theatre studies and to suggest hypotheses for additional work in theatre history.

Each question relates to professional concerns for workers in the theatre. The point is not just to study the phenomenon of women working in the theatre, or to identify what is definitively "feminist" in theatre, but to examine the work process and its allotment of control and privilege to various artists and social groups, always seeking the consequences for performance. Making the invisible visible in female *and* male experience is the route of insight into all culture—not because it addresses an imbalance, but because it is more all-encompassing.

HOW DOES THE IDEOLOGY OF THE DOMINANT CULTURE AFFECT WOMEN'S STATUS?

Socialist feminists note the gendered separation of experience into the home (which is private) and the work place (which is public). This separation was violated every time an actress stepped onto a stage. Actresses' coexistence in both spheres and their social construction as "honorary males" to mitigate this transgression are significant. Female performers (and to some extent female dramatists and technicians) personify women living within the boundaries of male society and culture. This suggests that in some respects theatrical women are better off than their counterparts outside the theatre, but social judgments and ostracism typically negate the advantages.

Once actresses' participation in the public arena was officially sanctioned by law and society (from 1587 in Spain and 1660 in England) or otherwise permitted by practice (certainly from the 1530s in Italy and the 1540s in

France), they held exclusive rights to their professions (denoted by the feminized terms of their work: *actriz,* ballet-girl, *comediante, cantatrice,* etc.). In contrast to the majority of women, actresses found it *necessary* to acquire formalized learning in their trades—learning which often included the liberal arts of music, languages, and grammar—which was sanctioned and applauded by the society that harbored them. Once they were established in the theatre, actresses neither encroached on a male labor market nor affected the scale of wages for men in the same trade and so were immune to pressure to give over their livelihood to principal (male) breadwinners.

Another advantage in the past was that they had a good chance of receiving equal pay for work of equal value (as assessed by box office appeal) and appeared to enjoy limited ingress to the highest ranks of management, though this may need qualification. An impressive number of Victorian actresses controlled theatres, but few remained as lessees for longer than a couple of years; those whose tenancy was long-lived often had a male business partner (such as Eliza Vincent and David Osbaldiston at the Old Vic, and Marie Wilton and Squire Bancroft at the Prince of Wales Theatre), or succeeded to control as widows (Sara Lane at the Britannia, Ellen Poole at the South London Palace of Varieties, and Mrs. Nye Chart at the Theatre Royal, Brighton). In other cases, membership in a theatrical family may have been important to the accession of lesseeship—further research is necessary on Louisa and Mary Ann Swanborough of the Strand Theatre, as well as countless manageresses whose biographies were not written up in contemporaneous who's whos or theatrical obituaries and thus escaped J. P. Wearing's guide to sources in theatrical biography.[35]

By engaging in an insecure, itinerant, and bohemian occupation, female performers pushed beyond the traditional consciousness of home-centered women and engaged in an active struggle with the ideology of the dominant (masculine) culture. When the official religious and legal institutions of masculine culture did not formally preclude women from appearing onstage, the cultural context determined the social meaning of actresses' public lives and generically fixed all aspects of their status in the community at large without respect to actual personal conduct. Actresses' co-sexual work place meant that they enjoyed freedoms unknown to women of other socially sanctioned occupations. They were symbols of women's self-sufficiency and independence, but although their independence, education, allure, and constant flouting of sexual mores gave them access to the male ruling elite, it was also a grave transgression of gender taboo and similar enough to prostitution to raise objections.

The ambiguous status of Restoration actresses such as Hester Davenport, Elizabeth Barry, and Peg Hughes came from their sexual liaisons, which, in turn, arose from being set up as erotic commodities.[36] Like prostitutes, actresses confronted the sexual double standard daily, in public. They contravened traditional family structures, the balance of economic power, and gender-based restrictions of association, movement, dress, education, influence, and sexual choice. Their sexual expatriation from the domestic sphere, challenge to patriarchal supremacy in the public sphere, and disturbance of masculine prerogative in the sexual sphere often led to social ostracism and vilification.[37] While they might be feminists' heroic prototypes, their independence, courage, and transcendence turned sourly into dependence, compromise, and barely tolerated survival.

HOW DO SOCIAL, CLASS, AND ECONOMIC FACTORS AFFECT PRIVILEGE?

Since the theatre was traditionally a family-based enterprise, it seems entirely logical that kin (or lack of kin) affected actresses' ease of access to the stage, likelihood of success, financial rewards, management openings, and job security.[38] Although the nuclear family rarely delineated the actual unit of production, the theatre kept the realms of production and reproduction together longer and more equitably than most other sectors of the economy following industrialization. Whether through a system of shares usual in the Renaissance or through the waged work of the nineteenth century, employment for every family member regardless of sex, age, and skill was built into the traditions of the dramatis personae, including apprenticeship into the acting craft. Time after time, among the Andreinis, Kembles, and Terry-Lewises, the nuclear and extended family wage was earned collectively through the actual labor of all members or the superior popularity of a few, resulting in increased advantages for all. In biographies, therefore, women's involvement in the extended family and roles in the nuclear family (including marriage, maternity, and child rearing—as applicable) need to be examined in tandem with women's apprenticeship, career development, retirement, and professional-kin relationships.

Like women, theatre practitioners did not form a single economic or social class.[39] It is less obvious, however, that, unlike most women, actresses' economic class was rarely congruent with their social status. No matter how materially successful a Roman dancer or a Victorian Gaiety Girl became, her earnings were believed to be of illegitimate origin (through performing as well as sexual adventuring) and she remained a demimondaine.

Eminence in a "serious" specialty (particularly tragedy) enhanced social credibility and tended to narrow the gap between salary and status, but comediennes and acrobats could be just as distinguished among fellow professionals and as highly paid as tragediennes, yet never achieve social acceptance. Society and the profession each structured hierarchies of performers, but the hierarchies did not necessarily resemble one another.

The notion that ascription to a class is a lifelong condition is also inappropriate among actresses. Marriage into and out of the profession could radically change a woman's rank (even to empress, in the case of Theodora), and a break from a bourgeois or strict Protestant background could disinherit a stage aspirant (such as Carolina Neuber) who, as a woman, was not reinstated by the laws of primogeniture. Socioeconomic measures of actresses' privilege, based on ownership and control of property, are more quantifiable indicators of rank but are still not entirely reliable marks: analysis is complicated by the practice of wearing rented or paste jewelry, by kinship (one person's—particularly a woman's—share in collective assets is difficult to surmise), and by the deceptive "advancement to management" as widows but never as wives (an inheritance common among modestly scaled Victorian music hall operations).[40] Female performers' social and artistic status was partly determined by their access to education, types and frequency of employment, and freely owned property, but familial and sexual relationships were generally connected—overtly or covertly—to that status.

HOW IS THE STATUS QUO MAINTAINED OR CHALLENGED IN ARTISTIC MEDIA?

Feminists regard literature as a social institution: the theatre puts literature inside another social institution for the mutual delectation of spectators in a communal act of viewing and hearing. Nancy Reinhardt describes theatre as a conservative art and postulates that its conservative content and form may make its sexism less glaring than in a medium like the cinema. If that is true, the theatre's cultural role as image-relayer and image-definer in shaping society's outlook is particularly tied to the dominant culture's ideology and particularly liable to reinforce it. The response to women's participation in this unconventional occupational sphere can be interpreted as a natural extension of legal, medical, and artistic treatment of womankind as a whole, which explains the female in sets of antitheses, none of which are positive: thus, women are debased or heavenly, primally sexual or procreatively moribund, mentally shallow or intellectually subversive, decorative or hideous, and socially peripheral or highly dangerous. Just as theatre practitioners tend to consider production as a collective process involving various specialists, historians tend to consider spectatorship as a communal activity by and for a specific community, but the "neutrality" of the image-makers and the images made demand careful scrutiny. Historians should consider just how "communal" production and reception really are in any culture: perhaps conservatism actually belies a more (not less) glaring sexism.

This sexism may be painfully evident to the women who work in the theatre. The concentration of contemporary women's employment in regional theatre, children's theatre, theatre in education, and public relations jobs may owe more to professional practice and institutionalized sexism than to personal inclination. Michelene Wandor outlines a range of women's responses to a variety of working conditions:

> A feminist working in a very traditional theatre situation, where attitudes are very reactionary, is likely to find herself experiencing strong, gut, radical-feminist angers; a woman in a position of power . . . has to face and deal with both her desires for power, and her actual objective power at work. And a feminist who is in a position to work democratically with others . . . is more likely to be exploring ways of sharing power and control over work with others, with taking responsibility for herself and her work as a woman.[41]

All of these scenarios have been described in testimonial writings by artists like Liane Aukin and Ann Jellicoe.[42] The consequences for women's careers have also been noted by Chinoy, who observes that opting for dignity and the democratization of work by and for workers has led American women to associate with or form regional, institutional, little, art, and alternative theatres rather than spending their lives trying to be on Broadway or the commercial stage.[43] According to Chinoy, the work of Eva Le Gallienne, Susan Glaspell, Minnie Maddern Fiske, and Hallie Flanagan Davis takes on particular resonances because they were women. An alternative interpretation of their career paths (along with the work of Joan Holden, Ellen Stewart, Megan Terry, Joan Littlewood, and perhaps Eliza Vestris) is that as women in positions of artistic control or financial and administrative decision making they reversed the customary power structures in society as well as theatre. Unless they are segregationists, such women must require that power be surrendered to them by male performers and technicians who are accustomed to male authority; this may simply be more feasible and rewarding for all concerned when carried out in smaller alternative ventures. Women have certainly made an impact on theatre administration, and continue to do so, for empirical research shows that women who attain authoritative positions tend to hire women and men in more equal measures.[44] It remains to be shown, however, whether women's different social reality and inner experience find their way to performance in sympathetic mixed-sex companies (unlike the Magdalena Project) or to reception in mixed-sex audiences (unlike some of Leavitt's examples) which challenge the status quo on every level.

For historians of an art practice or cultural medium, questions about the status quo are essential for understanding the social process of relaying and reforming ideas about sexuality. Whereas literature is a private act of the imagination (for writer and reader), theatre happens in the present tense (fleetingly) before the eyes of an audience. In order to be theatre, it must have witnesses; their response is necessarily authoritative, not the elite critics' or historians' postfactual record.

Theatre communicates through highly representational means, with deeply encoded systems not only of language but of speech, not only of configuration but of action, and not only of selected events but of events lit, dressed, arranged, and performed—sometimes over and over again. A text rendered with all the resources of stage expression and pragmatically received by the public in performance may be termed a mise-en-scène. If it were possible to "score" a theatrical performance the way music is scored, and to account for all the components of stage expression (costume, decor, music, lighting, furnishings, action, words, line, color, intonation, rhythm, etc.), the experience of reading the mise-en-scène could be the same experience as being in the audience. But this is not possible, for however complete the score is, it is only a partial rendering of a real and immediate experience. Inseparable from the mise-en-scène (and essential to the unreality/reality of performance) are the elaborate encodings of gender. As something that is readable according to social conventions, gender is infinitely subject to redefinition.[45]

The mise-en-scène is affected by casting, costume, allocation of stage space in narrative configuration, decor, and speech acts; social valuations of gender can change the apparent meaning of any of these elements, and vice versa. Cross-dressing provides an interesting example of how social values are manifest in casting traditions and how costume and gesture are related to gendered theatricality. When, for example, women were prohibited by law or custom from appearing on the occidental and oriental stages, men played the female roles.[46] The attitude taken by an actor to his conveyance of "femaleness" affects reception, which in the Renaissance may have been complicated by homoeroticism in male spectators and gender narcissism in female spectators.[47] The audience's ability to interpret this transvestism was determined by conventions of signification, but more than acting style is involved in the conveyance of gender.

Therefore, feminist historians may wonder: when women were excluded from the public forum of the stage and males played female roles, was this necessarily an act of obliteration of women, usurpation of womanhood, misogyny, silencing, or ridicule? Were women's gestures, words, and gowns taken over by men to ridicule what the gowns, words, gestures, and women stood for? Was it like blacking up (as in minstrelsy)? Sue-Ellen Case identifies the mythical invention of acting as a male construct; Arion gave (male) dithyramb singers the costume of the (male) satyrs:

> The power of representation was given only to the male celebrants. The invention of acting was gender-specific—the actor was the satyr. The gender-specific quality of the actor in the satyr play was even underscored by his wearing of the leather phallus. Yet in order to dramatize the battle of the genders, the female must somehow be represented. . . . In considering this portrayal, it is important to remember that the notion of the female derived from the male point of view, which remained alien to female experience and reflected the perspective of her gendered opposite. This vocabulary of gestures initiated the image of "Woman" as she is seen on the stage—institutionalized through patriarchal culture and represented by male-originated signs of her appropriate gender behavior.[48]

If, as Case argues from evidence in Aristotle's *Poetics* and *Politics,* the institutionalization was antiwoman, what could it mean when women were subsequently permitted on the stage and performed the same texts that were written for males to play? Were they still blacking up, or were they whiting up? When do the words, gowns, gestures, and gender become those of the women characters and performers? Do they always remain male, even when spoken by women? Irrespective of the original performer's sex, is acting a masculine art—immutably dressed in the satyr's costume—and can it be feminized?

Since the Restoration, convention has permitted the cross-dressed actress—a woman in a male role—liberation into a quasi-masculinity that permitted her character to *do* things and not be a villain, harpy, or sexual adventurer. She could take romantic initiative (as Romeo, or a pantomime boy), comic liberties (as Falstaff, or in burlesque), and even satirize men and masculinity (as a music hall swell). This is not an entirely positive development: the sexual identity of the cross-dressed actress was never ambiguous; cross-dressing was often employed to reveal her figure and suffuse her presence with eroticism, rendering her an exhibitionist for public (male) scrutiny. The spectator's erotic rewards from watching Charlotte Cushman as Romeo or Mrs. Webb as Falstaff may have been minimal, but the principle is proved by Peg Woffington, Dora Jordan, Charlotte Clarke, Priscilla Horton, and Fanny Wallack.[49] The cross-dressed actress did not have the opportunity to impersonate the other sex, but could only indicate her own. The political act of her cross-dressing is substantively different from the boy-actress, for in her case maleness was not substituted for femaleness.

The allocation of stage space and its plotting in the mise-en-scène have been discussed as functions of gender. Feminist historians have shown that the placement of characters onstage (by dramatists and stage manager/directors) carries meaning. According to Reinhardt, center stage is the locus of male protagonists, whereas "the sides, background, niches and balconies function as the inner domestic space where the woman are [*sic*] usually kept. . . . If, as a character on the stage, she defies convention and invades the male central stage area, she is often exaggerated or distorted as 'an angel or a monster.'"[50] In this case, the stage picture realizes the social division of two spheres and any female transgressors are instantly discernible by their position onstage. Jenkins suggests that settings perform a similar function: "[In plays by men] males claim and name space and territory. Note that males claim spaces in the domestic sphere. They have honored places in the living room and dining room . . . they even have their own studies and workshops. While the kitchen is the woman's sphere, males have their places at the table and have access to everything in the room (who has access to his study, his shop?)."[51] These depictions of social roles are perceived, if only unconsciously, by the audience. Western culture reads the center as power. It reads periphery as silence. It reads confinement as imprisonment for men and proper socialization for women.

It is readily accepted that playwrights' allocation of words to characters reflects power balances in the drama, as well as power in the acting company. Performers' ability to command privilege depended on their access to education, artistic cultivation, capital, and outside patronage; for men, there were social clubs, public inns, secret societies, and political parties through which to garner allies, but for women sexuality was preeminent; except for rare actresses, compliance with the gender system of display and attraction was necessary for professional advancement. The theatre offers two principal means to attract—words and pictures—both of which backfire on the actress. Whereas monologue is regarded as eloquence in men, it is usually received as verbosity in women. Whereas ostentation in costume has generally indicated power in men, it signals sexual advertisement in women whether or not it is logical within the dramatic fiction and consistent with the mise-en-scène.

Finally, women spectators had a role in the maintenance of the status quo. If women attended in fewer numbers than men in a given period, why did they stay away? What might this suggest about society, the theatrical neighborhood, the social significance of the theatre event, male hegemony over culture, the distribution of income, and spending patterns? Dagmar Höher discovered that whereas working women with one child still attended music halls, two or more children kept women at home, which lowered the family income and relegated the leisure of music hall attendance to a male prerogative until the family grew up, household expenses dropped, and women could resume their youthful pleasures.[52] The importance of class patronage and its reflections of and about repertoire are widely acknowledged, but the interrelatedness of repertoire and the class and gender of spectators is a promising field. Similarly, the social or kin combinations of women's attendance in every period, including the present, are a feminist issue that involves cultural bonding, sexual rites, women's public safety, and the perpetual redefinition of woman through the theatrical microcosm of society.

Although there is a great deal to be learned from recent feminist and social history, the theatre historian's concern with a theatrical event which is only real on some levels suggests that different analytical tools and source materials are required in theatre history than in nonart histories. The eclectic nature of theatre (and hence of theatre history) is complemented by the pluralistic approach of feminist history, which constantly seeks to question the traditions by which knowledge becomes accredited, often rejecting both the traditions and the knowledge thus generated. By delineating a new range of questions for historical consideration, feminist scholarship can tap a new range of sources, broaden the intellectual base, and identify hitherto ignored or undervalued data as well as reexamining the familiar. As Lynda Nead asserts, "feminism redefines the objects and aims of study. . . . and reworks the discipline itself."[53] To that end, everything bearing on the operation of gender difference and sexuality in the theatre is appropriate to the endeavor.

NOTES

1 Gerda Lernelt, *The Majority Finds Its Past* (New York and Oxford: Oxford University Press, 1979) esp. pp. 168–180; and *Teaching Women's History* (Washington, D.C.: American Historical Association, 1981).

2 Michelene Wandor, of all critics, argues that "a dualistic approach negates and forecloses discussion," in *Look Back in Gender* (London and New York: Methuen, 1987), p. xvi.

3 Representative collections are assembled in Elaine Showalter, ed., *The New Feminist Criticism: Essays on Women, Literature, and Theory* (London: Virago, 1986); and Gayle Green and Coppelia Kahn, eds., *Making a Difference: Feminist Literary Criticism* (London and New York: Methuen, 1985). Toril Moi's critical overview of trends in feminist criticism provides a useful review, full of insights, but also ignores drama and theatre: *Sexual/Textual Politics: Feminist Literary Theory* (London and New York: Methuen, 1985).

4 Janelle Reinelt, "Beyond Brecht: Britain's New Feminist Drama," *Theatre Journal* 38:2 (May 1986), 154–163; and Phyllis Rackin, "Androgyny, Mimesis, and the Marriage of the Boy Heroine on the English Renaissance Stage," *PMLA* 102:1 (January 1987), 29–41.

5 Frank Aschengreen, "The Beautiful Dancer: Facets of the Romantic Ballet," *Dance Perspectives* 58 (Summer 1974).

6 Ann Daly, "The Balanchine Woman: Of Hummingbirds and Channel Swimmers," *The Drama Review* 31:T113 (Spring 1987), 8–21.

7 Jill Dolan, "The Dynamics of Desire: Sexuality and Gender in Pornography and Performance," *Theatre Journal* 39:2 (May 1987), 156–174.

8 Tracy C. Davis, "Sexual Language in Victorian Society and Theatre," *American Journal of Semiotics* 6:1 (1989).

9 Nancy S. Reinhardt, "New Directions for Feminist Criticism in Theatre and the Related Arts," in *A Feminist Perspective in the Academy: The Difference It Makes,* ed. Elizabeth Langland and Walter Gove (Chicago: University of Chicago Press, 1981), pp. 25–26; and Claudia D. Johnson, "That Guilty Third Tier: Prostitution in Nineteenth-Century American Theaters," in *Victorian America,* ed. David Walker Howe (Philadelphia: University of Pennsylvania Press, 1976), pp. 111–120.

10 Sheila Rowbotham, "The Trouble with Patriarchy," in *People's History and Socialist Theory,* ed. Raphael Samuel (London: Routledge and Kegan Paul, 1981), pp. 367, 366.

11 J. S. Bratton, "Jenny Hill: Sex and Sexism in the Victorian Music Hall," in *Music Hall Performance and Style,* ed. J. S. Bratton (Milton Keynes: Open University Press, 1986), p. 103.

12 Rina Fraticelli, "The Invisibility Factor: Status of Women in Canadian Theatre," *Fuse* 6 : 3 (September 1982), 112–124; and Kay Carney and Julianne Boyd, "Directors and Designers Report on Sex Discrimination in the Theatre," *Women and Performance* 1 : 2 (Winter 1984), 46–54.

13 Judith Lynne Hanna, "Patterns of Dominance: Men, Women, and Homosexuality in Dance," *The Drama Review* 31 : 1/T113 (Spring 1987), 23.

14 Rosamond Gilder, *Enter the Actress: The First Women in the Theatre* (1931; rpt. New York: Theatre Art Books, 1960); Albert Auster, *Actresses and Suffragists: Women in American Theatre, 1890–1920* (New York: Praeger, 1984); Claudia D. Johnson, *American Actress: Perspective on the Nineteenth Century* (Chicago: Nelson-Hall, 1984); and Katharina M. Wilson, ed., *Medieval Women Writers* (Manchester: Manchester University Press, 1984).

15 Sherry B. Ortner and Harriet Whitehead, eds., *Sexual Meanings: The Cultural Construction of Gender and Sexuality* (Cambridge: Cambridge University Press, 1981).

16 S. E. Amussen, "Féminin/masculin: Le genre dans l'Angleterre de l'époque moderne," *Annales ESC* (March–April 1985), 269–287.

17 Claire Hirshfield, "The Actresses' Franchise League and the Campaign for Women's Suffrage 1908–1914," *Theatre Research International* 10 : 2 (Summer 1985), 129–153; and Julie Holledge, *Innocent Flowers: Women in the Edwardian Theatre* (London: Virago, 1981); Charlotte Rea, "Women's Theatre Groups," *The Drama Review* 16 : 2 (June 1972), 79–89; Catherine Itzin, *Stages in the Revolution: Political Theatre in Britain since 1968* (London: Methuen, 1980); Dinah Luise Leavitt, *Feminist Theatre Groups* (Jefferson, N.C.: McFarland, 1980); Marie-Claire Rouyer and Ann Cipriani, "Women's Theatre in Great Britain," *Fireweed* 7 (Summer 1980), 46–61; and Susan E. Bassnett, "Towards a Theory of Women's Theatre," in *Semiotics of Drama and Theatre,* ed. Herta Schmid and Aloysius Van Kesteren (Amsterdam and Philadelphia: John Benjamins, 1984), pp. 445–466.

18 Fidelis Morgan, *The Female Wits* (London: Virago, 1981); Dale Spender and Carole Hyman, eds., *"How the Vote Was Won" and Other Suffragette Plays* (London and New York: Methuen, 1985); Viv Gardner, ed., *Sketches from the Actresses' Franchise League* (Nottingham: Nottingham Drama Texts, 1985); and C. W. E. Bigsby, ed., *Susan Glaspell* (Cambridge: Cambridge University Press, 1987); Wandor, *Look Back in Gender;* Honor Moore, ed., *The New Women's Theatre: Ten Plays by Contemporary American Women* (New York: Vintage, 1977); Julia Miles, ed., *The Women's Project,* 2 vols. (New York: Performing Arts Journal and American Place Theatre, 1980 and 1984); Judith E. Barlow, ed., *Plays by American Women: 1900–1930* (New York: Applause, 1981); Michelene Wandor,

ed., *"Strike While the Iron Is Hot": Three Plays on Sexual Politics* (London and West Nyack: Journeyman Press, 1980); Michelene Wandor, ed., *Plays by Women*, 6 vols. (London: Methuen, 1982, 1983, 1984, 1985, 1987, 1988); and Kate McDermott, ed., *Places, Please! The First Anthology of Lesbian Plays* (Iowa City: Aunt Lute, 1985).

19 Lynda Nead, "Feminism, Art History and Cultural Politics," in *The New Art History*, ed. A. L. Rees and Frances Borzello (London: Camden Press, 1986), pp. 120–124.

20 Nancy Cotton, *Women Playwrights in England c. 1363–1750* (Lewisburg, Bucknell University Press, 1980).

21 Marie-Claire Pasquier, "Women in the Theatre of Men: What Price Freedom?" in *Women in Culture and Politics: A Century of Change*, ed. Judith Friedlander et al. (Bloomington: Indiana University Press, 1986), pp. 194–206.

22 Linda Walsh Jenkins, *Women in American Theatre: Careers, Images, Movements, An Illustrated Anthology and Sourcebook*, ed. Helen Crich Chinoy and Linda Walsh Jenkins (New York: Crown, 1981), p. 237.

23 Robert Sklar, "Toward Creating a Women's Theatre," *The Drama Review* T86 (June 1980), 35–39; Linda Walsh Jenkins, "Locating the Language of Gender Experience," *Women and Performance* 2:1 (1984), 5–17; and Linda Walsh Jenkins and Susan Ogden-Malouf, "The (Female) Actor Prepares," *Theatre* 17:1 (Winter 1985), 66–69.

24 Vesna Pistotnik, "Towards a Redefinition of Dramatic Genre and Stage History," *Modern Drama* 28:4 (December 1985), 681.

25 Kathleen Betsko and Rachel Koenig, eds., *Interviews with Contemporary Women Playwrights* (New York: William Morrow, 1987).

26 Raphael Samuel, ed., *People's History and Socialist Theory* (London: Routledge and Kegan Paul, 1981).

27 Koenig, "Introduction," *Interviews*, p. 12.

28 Elizabeth J. Natalle succeeds in this by insisting on the rhetorical function of recent women's work, in *Feminist Theatre: A Study in Persuasion* (Metuchen, N.J., and London: Scarecrow, 1985).

29 Lisa Jardine, *Still Harping on Daughters* (Sussex: Harvester, 1983).

30 Carol W. Gelderman, "The Male Nature of Tragedy," *Prairie Schooner* (Fall 1975), 220–236; Leavitt, *Feminist Theatre Groups*; Karen Malpede, ed., *Women in Theatre: Compassion and Hope* (New York: Limelight, 1983); *The Drama Review* 24:2 (June 1980); and *Canadian Theatre Review* 43 (Summer 1985).

31 Susan Bassnett, "Women Experiment with Theatre: Magdalena 86," *New Theatre Quarterly* 3:1 (August 1987), 224–234.

32 This is denied by Eugenio Barba, "The Actor's Energy: Male/Female versus Animus/Anima," *New Theatre Quarterly* 3:1 (August 1987), 237–240, who insists that "pre-expressivity" is asexual, and discussed by Bassnett, "Perceptions of the Female Role: The ISTA Congress," 234–236.

33 Antonio Gramsci, *Selections from Cultural Writings,* ed. David Frogacs and Geoffrey Nowell-Smith (Cambridge, Mass.: Harvard University Press, 1935), p. 109.

34 Linda Nochlin, "Why Have There Been No Great Women Artists?" in *Art and Sexual Politics: Women's Liberation, Women Artists, and Art History,* ed. Thomas B. Hess and Elizabeth C. Baker (New York: Macmillan; London: Collier Macmillan, 1973).

35 See Diana Howard, *London Theatres and Music Halls, 1850–1950* (London: Library Association, 1970); and J. P. Wearing, *American and British Theatrical Biography: A Directory* (Metuchen, N.J., and London: Scarecrow, 1979).

36 Antonia Fraser, "The Actress as Honey-Pot," *The Weaker Vessel* (London: Methuen, 1984), pp. 473–496.

37 Tracy C. Davis, "Does the Theatre Make for Good?: Actresses' Purity and Temptation in the Victorian Era," *Queen's Quarterly* 93 : 1 (Spring 1986), 33–49.

38 Michael Baker, *The Rise of the Victorian Actor* (London: Croom Helm, 1978), pp. 62–94.

39 Joan Kelly, *Women, History, and Theory: The Essays of Joan Kelly* (Chicago: University of Chicago Press, 1984), p. 5.

40 Howard, *London Theatres.*

41 Michelene Wandor, *Carry On, Understudies: Theatre and Sexual Politics,* 2nd ed. (London: Routledge and Kegan Paul, 1985), p. 138.

42 Susan Todd, ed., *Women and Theatre: Calling the Shots* (London: Faber and Faber, 1984).

43 Helen Crich Chinoy, "Art Versus Business," *The Drama Review* 24 : 2 (1980), 3–10.

44 Fraticelli, "The Invisibility Factor."

45 For a few reinterpretations, see Rackin, "Androgyny"; Dolan, "The Dynamics of Desire"; and Sande Zeig, "The Actor as Activator: Deconstructing Gender Through Gesture," *Women and Performance* 2 : 2 (1985), 12–17.

46 Based on observation of Kabuki *onnagata,* Peter Hyland suggests that mature men may have "played the more mature female roles of, for example, Gertrude, Cleopatra, and Volumnia." For a full explanation, see "'A Kind of Woman': The Elizabethan Boy-Actor and the Kabuki *Onnagata,*" *Theatre Research International* 12 : 1 (Spring 1987), 1–8.

47 Jardine, *Still Harping,* pp. 9–26. This view is disputed by Kathleen McLuskie, "The Act, the Role, and the Actor: Boy Actresses on the Elizabethan Stage," *New Theatre Quarterly* 3 : 10 (May 1987), 120–130.

48 Sue-Ellen Case, "Classic Drag: The Greek Creation of Female Parts," *Theatre Journal* (October 1985), 321.

49 Emma Stebbins, *Charlotte Cushman: Her Letters and Memories of Her Life* (Boston: Houghton, Osgood, 1879), p. 60; Lyman Horace Weeks, "Some Women in Doublet and Hose," *Lippincott's Monthly Magazine* 57 (1896), 88–94; and Kathy Fletcher, "Planche, Vestris, and the Transvestite Role: Sexuality and

Gender in Victorian Popular Theatre," *Nineteenth Century Theatre* 15 : 1 (Summer 1987), 9–33.

50 Reinhardt, "New Directions," pp. 42–43.

51 Jenkins, "Locating the Language," p. 15.

52 Dagmar Höher, "The Composition of Music Hall Audiences, 1850–1900," in *Music Hall: The Business of Pleasure,* ed. Peter Bailey (Milton Keynes: Open University Press, 1986), pp. 73–92.

53 Nead, "Feminism," p. 124.

Theatre Audiences and the Reading of Performance

Marvin Carlson

R eader-response and reception theory has become a thriving new area in the crowded field of contemporary literary speculation, but so far its strategies and concerns have stimulated comparatively little work in the area of theatre study in general and in historical theatre study in particular.[1] This somewhat surprising situation is unfortunate for both theatre study and reception theory, since theatrical performance, as a unique event structure for a circumscribed and often identifiable body of receivers, presents a controlled field of study quite different from the usual literary concerns of reception theory and since this theory may offer to theatre research a different way of considering traditional material, leading to new insights.

Despite the much more obvious participation and contribution of the "reader" to the theatrical event than to the novel or poem, much theatre theory still regards the theatre performance as something created and set before an essentially passive audience. Our histories speak of plays or parts of plays directed toward certain audiences or parts of audiences (Shakespeare's jokes to amuse the groundlings or Lillo's morality lesson for London apprentices), or of conventions that historical audiences somehow learned to accept (masks in the Greek theatre, the invisible Japanese propman, the Elizabethan boy-actresses), but these are almost invariably presented as features of the performance or play, to which an audience passively responds. Little is said about how that audience learns to respond to such matters or what demands and contributions it brings to the event.

The rather extensive reader-response and reception bibliography of the past decade or so suggests a number of potentially useful strategies for analyzing contemporary and historical theatre experience. We might consider, for example, the process of concretization as discussed by Wolfgang Iser— the process by which, according to Iser, a reader serves as coproducer of the meaning of a text by creatively filling gaps (*Leerstellen*) left in that text by the author.[2] Those familiar with recent semiotic theory may recall that Anne Ubersfeld has described the dramatic text in particular as *troué,* that is containing gaps, in this case to be filled by staging.[3]

An interesting parallel is suggested by this convergence of metaphor. The theatrical production itself is a kind of reading, very much in the sense described by Iser: "an act of defining the oscillating structure of the text through meanings, which as a rule are created in the process of reading itself."[4] This process of definition between dramatic text and audience, a central feature of theatre, makes the reading process here particularly complicated. We might explore how the concretization of the dramatic text by a reader (in the traditional sense) relates to the concretization by a group of theatre artists and to the concretization by the audience-reader who witnesses their performance, asking whether performance in fact "fills or rejects" the same gaps as Iser suggests a normal reader does, or whether it fills some and leaves others or creates new ones of its own.

A central concern for the scholar of theatre history is the dynamic involved in the changing interpretations (or readings) of works in different historical periods, a concern of more central interest to Hans Robert Jauss, another pioneer in reception theory. Like Iser, Jauss wishes to emphasize the importance of the reader without giving way to total subjectivism and for this purpose emphasizes a "specific disposition" of an audience, "which can be empirically determined and which precedes the psychological reaction as well as the subjective understanding of the individual reader." The empirical disposition is provided, according to Jauss, by a "horizon of expectations," itself based upon three factors—"the familiar norms or the immanent poetics of the genre," the "implicit relationships to familiar works of the literary-historical surroundings," and "the opposition between fiction and reality."[5] A number of useful directions for theatre studies are suggested here, some of which I return to below. Generic expectations and relationship to other works (intertextuality) are clearly as relevant to theatre reception as to reading, and the juxtaposition of fiction and reality perhaps even more relevant, given the particularly central role played by mimesis and iconicity in the theatre.

Umberto Eco has approached the subject of reader response from a somewhat different perspective, that of semiotics; since an important part of modern theatre theory shares this orientation, it is not surprising that the theory which has most recently appeared on this subject has had much closer ties to Eco than to Iser or Jauss. Two of Eco's ideas have already proven particularly stimulating (though more in general theatre studies than in studies with a particular historical orientation)—that of the model reader and of open and closed texts. The model reader (a concept found, in various articulations, in much reading theory) is the possible reader assumed by the author to whom the book is imaginatively directed, a reader "supposedly able to deal interpretively with the expressions in the same way as the author deals generatively with them."[6] Any text, Eco suggests, postulates its own receiver as an indispensable condition of its potential for meaning.

Marco de Marinis, following the lead of Eco, has spoken of the "Model Spectator," anticipated by theatrical performance.[7] One might, of course, apply this concept to any historical period, but the modern theatre provides a striking example of the embodiment of this hypothetical construct in an actual person, the director, who watches the development of a performance from the seat of a presumed spectator and orchestrates the effects for spectator reception. De Marinis has also applied Eco's distinction of open and closed texts to theatrical performance, with certain qualifications. Texts that aim at generating a precise response from a more or less precise group of empirical readers Eco characterizes as closed, while texts that give fewer and fewer specific response indications are increasingly open.[8] De Marinis suggests that theatre productions may also tend toward the closed (as in didactic theatre) or the open (as in much modern avant-garde work), but he also notes Eco's observation that open works are paradoxically often less accessible than closed ones. Their very lack of specific direction for readers may restrict their audiences to a very few "super-competent readers" willing to undertake the complex response task put before them. De Marinis suggests, however, another possibility for open texts in theatre, as in some traditional Indian performance, where a wide variety of response is encouraged by an event which attempts to be as inclusionary as possible.[9]

Even in open texts, the emphasis in Eco remains upon the text as the primary determinant of the reading situation, and this emphasis is generally to be found in the more recent work in semiotically oriented response theory as well. This tendency is, however, not entirely avoided in Iser or Jauss, a situation which Stanley Fish has attempted to escape by focusing, like Jauss, upon changing interpretations, but more particularly on the social dynamics by which varying interpretations are advanced and legitimized rather than on the mechanisms in the text which permit or seek to channel such interpretations. This has led Fish from the "informed reader" of Jauss or the "model reader" of Eco ("informed" and "model" both suggesting authentication by the text) to a "community of readers," socially defined, which shares common values and determines collectively the norms and conventions according to which individual readings take place. A particularly self-conscious model of such communities may be found in the world of academic criticism in America, where new interpretations are tested against the norms of various reading communities and are given objective validity by the acceptance of those communities. Readings are thus ultimately authenticated empirically not by the text but by the institution of the community.

Fish's approach also provides stimulating possibilities for historical theatre research. The social organization of theatre as created and experienced makes its institutional structure more apparent than that of the book. Its communities, by the active choice of assembling to attend plays, are more apparent as groups to themselves and to others than are the more abstract literary communities. Moreover, one can consider theatre communities on a number of levels, all involved in the formation and authentication of reading strategies, from the rather abstract and scattered communities and subcommunities which would correspond in the world of theatre to those described by Fish in the literary world to the specific and unique community assembled for a particular performance.

There is no question that even these unique communities function as a group in the reading process. The social occasion in which theatre is embedded obviously conditions in a major way both the experience and its interpretation. A *New Yorker* cartoon some years ago showed a theatre audience member, having paused to wipe tears from his cheeks, looking around in some consternation to see everyone laughing uproariously. "Hey, wait a minute," he says. "Is this satire?" Certainly, in just this way the pressure of audience response can coerce individual members to structure and interpret their experience in a way which might well not have occurred to them as solitary readers and, further, which might not have been within the interpretive boundaries planned by the creators of the performance text.

Theatre history provides many examples of audiences that have not at all responded to a performed work in the expected manner, and the frequency of such disjunctures demonstrates clearly that the community of readers assembled for a theatre event may be applying very different strategies from those of the model readers assumed by the performance. Problems are particularly likely to arise when an experimental work resists the reading strategies of an audience expecting something more conventional. In a regular reading situation, a frustrated reader may simply put the book aside and turn to something else. The theatre, as a social event, encourages more active resistance; not a few demonstrations and even riots have arisen from performances (like *Hernani* or *Ubu Roi*) failing to play the game according to the rules many in the audience expected. Every actor or director can recall instances when an audience created a meaning for a line or action not at all intended by the producers—and audiences have been known to wrest interpretive control entirely and openly from expected patterns, treating a presumedly serious work, for example, as a stimulus to laughter.

Such occasions, if we wish really to deal with the pragmatics of historical performance, give particular importance to the efforts of scholars like Fish to find a theory of reading response which would not ultimately lead back to the text as the ultimate determinant of meaning. A useful definition of reading provided by Tony Bennett looks in this direction, and I would like to utilize it as the basis for the following specific explorations in this area: "the means and mechanisms whereby all texts—literary, filmic and televisual, fictional or otherwise—may be 'productively activated' during what is traditionally, and inadequately, thought of as the process of their consumption or reception." [10]

When we are dealing not with the sort of recorded texts listed by Bennett but with the text of theatrical performance, what de Marinis has called the "spectacle text," we are really speaking, as has already been noted, of two readings and thus of two simultaneous "productive activations"—that of the performance itself and that of the audience. The means and mechanisms by which the first of these readings takes place—that is, the conversion of a literary text into a spectacle text—have been given frequent attention in the study of theatre history; but very little attention has been paid to the other reading, the contribution of the audience, and still less to the factors which contribute to the formation of that reading. This is of course more closely analogous to what concerns Bennett in the process of reading traditional texts.

Some general indications of the way theatre historians might make use of the insights of theorists like Iser, Jauss, Eco, Fish, and Bennett have already been suggested, but it might be useful to illustrate how such procedures might be undertaken with some specific examples. I would like to suggest four historical means and mechanisms which have provided audiences with strategies for organizing and interpreting their involvement with the theatre event, some of them closely analogous to means available to readers of written text, others based upon the particular characteristics of theatre as performance. The first relates directly to Jauss' remarks on the response orientation of the phenomenon of genre, and here we deal most closely with the written script. The next, lines of business, looks at a related strategy in the performance itself. The other two are more related to the views of Fish and of the work of social institutions, including that of the theatre itself, in the formation or guiding of reading. First we consider briefly the phenomenon of publicity and programs, then the effects of institutionalized "readers"—dramaturgs and reviewers.

Throughout much of the history of Western theatre, a strong conservatism in subject matter and genre organization has provided spectators with highly predictable psychic models to apply in the reading of new dramatic pieces (or in revivals of older ones). From the Greeks until fairly recent times, the designation of a play as a comedy or a tragedy alerted the spectator to seek a certain emotional tone, certain types of characters, even certain themes and a certain structure of action.

The Greeks established the practice of taking the plots of their tragedies from familiar stories of legend, myth, and history; as Tadeusz Kowzan has pointed out,[11] the drama since classic times has been the literary mode particularly open to reworkings of previously treated character relationships and configurations of action. The spectators who attended the original performance of the classic Greek tragedies also attended a *proagon* opening the dramatic festival during which the authors and actors were introduced and the names of the plays to be performed were announced.[12] Since the general structure of tragedy was given and the stories were drawn from the cultural storehouse, these spectators arrived at the theatre with a good deal of their reading strategy already in place, even when the play had never been presented before. In later times, as the classic works were revived, previous acquaintance with a particular dramatic action added further preparation for audience members. Classic comedy did not, like tragedy, deal with material from history and legend; but, by Roman times, a remarkably consistent narrative structure involving trickery and love intrigues had been developed for this genre, with an attendant character configuration which reemerged in both the learned and popular comedy of the Renaissance and which has strongly influenced comedic structure and thus audience anticipation ever since.

Toward the end of the eighteenth century, the traditional generic divisions of comedy and tragedy were increasingly attacked; Romantic theorists like Hugo called in the name of freedom and liberty for the destruction of all rules and traditions which might hinder the free play of artistic imagination.[13] The particular targets of Romantic attack—traditional neoclassic comedy and tragedy, already largely exhausted—were in the long run not difficult to overcome, but the idea of genre itself was too central to the dynamic of audience response to be so easily put aside. The popular theatre in particular found, as always, that audiences were more comfortable with plays they could experience in generally predictable ways; the post-Romantic theatre, far from freeing itself from the restrictions of genre, developed instead a great variety of more particularized genres, each of which tended to be supported by its own public, familiar with its rules.

The old theatrical monopolies in London and Paris were now no longer in effect, and a large number of theatres competed for a public. Many of these gained and held a public by specializing in certain types of play, often written especially for that theatre by house dramatists. Thus, even if nineteenth-century spectators did not know what specific play was being performed at a certain theatre, they could predict with reasonable assurance the *type* of play offered there, with all the attendant generic expectations—whether it be a nautical melodrama, a vaudeville, a burletta, a domestic comedy, or a fairy spectacle. Participation at that theatre was likely to be very similar to previous experiences at the same locale.

The public attending such theatres may be considered to constitute one of Fish's "interpretive communities," parallel in many respects to the literary subcommunities Fish locates in present-day America: "Within the literary community there are sub-communities (what would excite the editors of *Diacritics* is likely to distress the editors of *Studies in Philology*)."[14] Similarly, one might say that what would excite nineteenth-century audiences of the London Adelphi or the Bouffés-Parisiens would be likely to distress the audiences of Covent Garden or the Comédie Française.

The traditional high predictability of genre organization in the theatre is very closely related to a high degree of predictability in dramatic characters, and so from genre we move naturally to the practice of lines of business. Researchers into narrative codes such as Propp and Greimas have found certain basic patterns of character relationships and their actantial patterns in many narrative structures, but actantial patterns in theatre, like genre definitions, have throughout much of theatre history been more highly codified and more predictable than those in other narrative traditions. In the *commedia dell'arte,* for example, the traditional comic structure of frustrated young lovers, an elderly blocking agent, and a wily servant was filled by a very specific and highly detailed set of characters, largely unchanged through thousands of performances and generations of audiences. The *commedia* spectator could expect Pantalone, identifiable by mask, costume, and dialect, to be the stubborn father or jealous older husband, Il Capitano to be the foolish rival, Harlequin the clever if mercurial servant, and so on.

Further, the same actors would portray these characters in scenario after scenario, so that audiences could expect certain actions, even certain gestures, from particular actors. This close relationship between actor and specific role or type of role was especially marked in the highly codified theatre of the Renaissance and early Baroque period; but even though some subsequent eras and some actors have emphasized versatility in interpretation, there has never been a period in theatre history without a rather high correlation between certain actors and specific types of roles. We are perhaps most familiar with this custom in connection with the stock roles in nineteenth-century melodrama, but long before the rise of melodrama actors specialized in noble fathers, male romantic leads, tyrants, soubrettes, and ingenues. Nor is this a peculiarly European phenomenon. The classic Sanskrit theatre manual, the *Natyasastra,* contains lengthy descriptions of a great array of traditional stock character types, and Japanese Kabuki contains carefully delineated traditional role categories. Actors perform in the same category throughout their lives, the few who change (such as Ichinatsu Sanokama I in the eighteenth century, who began playing young women and changed to villains in later life) causing considerable amazement.[15]

There are many reasons for this widespread tendency in theatre. Most basic, surely, is the fact that an actor is always to some extent limited by the appearance and capabilities of his/her own body. In the course of theatre history, men have played women and women men, youths played age and the aged youth, physically unprepossessing actors created dashing heroes and magnificent physical specimens hidden their endowments as grotesques and clowns, but there is always a strong tendency pressing actors or actresses toward certain roles for which they seem especially suited physically or emotionally. Not surprisingly, there is a high degree of correlation between the ideal of masculine and feminine beauty at different periods and the actors and actresses displayed in the theatre as objects of that period's desire. One of the earliest extended treatises on the art of acting, Sainte-Albine's *Le Comédien* in 1749, remarked that although many physical types were acceptable on the stage, actors, whatever their ability, could not depart far from audience expectations of the type of roles they were playing—heroes must have imposing bodies and lovers attractive ones, actors must look the proper age for their roles and have the natural vocal qualities suitable for their characters.[16]

The commercial theatre has always been especially involved with a certain predictability in casting, not only on the grounds of Sainte-Albine's concern with verisimilitude, but also from a desire to repeat a proven success. If the public has enjoyed a certain actor in a particular role, there has always been strong commercial pressure to repeat that same character in other plays or to create other characters so similar that the actor can essentially present the same persona. Contemporary television and popular films provide overwhelming evidence of the continuing appeal of this kind of predictable characterization and plotting, and theatre history abounds in instances of audiences bitterly protesting a popular actor unexpectedly appearing in a role out of harmony with a previously established persona. Clearly, these audiences came to the theatre with certain strategies already in place for their own contribution to the performance event and were angered by being offered material that resisted the play they were attempting to see.

Since theatre analysis in the past has emphasized the study of the text and of the performance over the study of reception, it has given almost no attention to those elements of the event structure aside from text and performance or of the larger social milieu, which may be as important to the formation of the reading of the experience as anything actually presented on the stage. To a few such elements—publicity, programs, and reviews—we now turn. The neglect so far of such matters by theatre semioticians interested in reading formations is perhaps even more surprising than their neglect by theatre historians, since message-bearing constructs of this sort constitute for most audiences the most obvious first exposure to the possible world of the performance they are going to see. Moreover, these elements are consciously produced by the institution which also produces the performance as devices for stimulating and channeling the desires and the interpretive strategies of the spectator.

Theatre programs in the modern sense appeared during the latter part of the nineteenth century, often in a form somewhat suggestive of the printed bill of fare at an elegant dinner. The basic form is still widely used today—the name of the theatre followed by the title and author of the play, next a listing of the characters (often with a brief indication of their relationships) and the actors portraying them, and then information on the time and place of the action. Even this relatively modest body of information provides a certain orientation for the audiences, and unquestionably affects their reading, as was strikingly illustrated in the recent play *Sleuth,* which achieved part of its surprise effect by providing the audience with false information in the program.

The typical program in the American professional theatre today provides the names of other participating creators such as costume and lighting designers and, if the play is a musical, a chronological listing of the songs, which may be considered in part an orienting device for the audience. The most substantial addition to this basic material is normally a brief biography of the participating actors, director, and designers, encouraging a kind of intertextuality peculiar to theatre and film—the remembrance of actors in previous roles.

Programs in many of the American regional and university theatres and in many European countries are far more involved in the process of affecting reading formations. Most obvious are the plot summaries often provided for plays in foreign languages or for plays of particularly difficult or complex action (Shakespearean history plays, for example, which often also stimulate a genealogical table in the program). The plot summaries provided by Peter Sellars for his highly innovative interpretations of traditional operatic works are often more iconoclastic than anything he places onstage and clearly are created to prepare the audience, violently if necessary, for his new reading of familiar texts. Interpretive essays by a director or dramaturg often seek to condition audience response in an even more programmatic way, and such conditioning need not even take the form of discursive analysis. Programs often include sketches, literary quotations, or photographs not directly related to the play, but suggesting a preferred interpretive strategy. Even a single image can have a profound effect upon interpretation. Consider the differences in reading encouraged in two audiences attending Shakespeare's *Henry V:* one given a program with a British flag on the cover or a soldier in heroic pose, sword uplifted; another given a program depicting a broken corpse on the field of battle.

Many modern productions use a specific image or logo not only on the program but, more importantly, on posters and in newspaper advertising, so that an audience member's first important impression of the production may well arise from this source. Where the theatre production is offered as a commercial product, the logo clearly bears an institutional relationship to commercial symbols used in the advertising of many contemporary products, though theatre logos avoid the abstract geometrical designs and calligraphic fancies favored by many products and corporations. Their logos, like the theatre itself, are primarily iconic and are often drawn from a particular visual image within the production, thus foregrounding that image when the production is experienced (the masked figure in *Amadeus,* for example, or the tableau of the prostrate nuns in the Metropolitan Opera's *Dialogues of the Carmelites*).

The use of the logo is one example of how publicity, primarily designed to attract an audience to a specific production, also inevitably affects the reception of that production. Even the composition of the community of readers which makes up the theatre audience is closely related to the institutional organization of publicity, since modern audiences, faced with a bewildering selection of possible activities, are extremely dependent upon publicity to discover what these alternatives are and to select among them. Well aware of this dynamic, theatres attempt to conceive and to distribute their publicity so that it will be most effective in reaching the audience considered most likely to support this particular production. The response theory concept of the "model reader" or "implied reader" has particular relevance here—before ever entering the theatre, or even buying a ticket, that reader must be targeted and sought by appropriate publicity. Thus, large musicals seeking a mass audience from an entire region may purchase spots on television, while small theatres seeking to develop a local audience may rely upon notices in supermarkets, banks, laundromats, and neighborhood newspapers. In New York, the two major outlets for theatrical newspaper advertising are the *New York Times* and the *Village Voice,* associated with reading communities so different that the same production rarely advertises in both papers. Obviously, large Broadway productions advertise in the *Times,* but so do productions (especially musical) which would normally be classified as off-Broadway but which seek the patronage of an uptown audience. Experimental productions of more limited and specialized appeal seek their audiences in the more congenial *Voice.*

The two invariable elements of the newspaper advertisement (and of its eighteenth- and nineteenth-century predecessor, the playbill) are the name of the production and its location. Other elements included inevitably provide information about the desired self-image of the production and thus, like the logo, provide anticipatory suggestions for the public's reading strategies. English playbills of the late eighteenth century normally included only the name of the playhouse, the play, and the actors and their roles. In the course of the nineteenth century, when many productions were created whose major focus was visual spectacle, this orientation was reflected in playbills which listed the sequence of scenic effects, often devoting to them more space and more impressive typeface than given to the actors.

An 1870 playbill from the Queen's Theatre, Longacre, for *A Midsummer Night's Dream* leaves little doubt as to how this particular performance is intended to be read. Immediately under the title of the play comes the name of the scenic designer, then the props master, then the designers of machinery and costumes, then the choreographer and conductor, then the actors. Next, occupying the largest and most ornate section of the playbill, comes a scene-by-scene listing of visual effects. The first three scenes give an idea of the whole: "Act I, scene I. PERISTYLE OF THESEUS' PALACE, OVERLOOKING ATHENS. Scene 2. QUINCE, the Joiner's Workshop, COPIED FROM THE DISCOVERIES OF HERCULÆNEUM. Act 2, scene I. A WOOD NEAR ATHENS! MEETING OF OBERON AND TITANIA, AND 150 ELVES AND FAIRIES." Obviously advertising of this sort, especially for productions of Shakespeare, disappeared with the end of scenically oriented revivals in the early twentieth century, but advertising today still suggests when some element in the production apparatus is being foregrounded, such as the director ("The Peter Brook production of A MIDSUMMER NIGHT'S DREAM") or a leading actor ("The RSC presents Anthony Sher in RICHARD III").

So important has advance publicity become in the modern theatre, and so institutionally remote is it from most of those involved in the creation of the production itself, that there is often a danger that the community of readers or the horizons of expectation of one may be quite different from those assumed by the other, resulting in serious reading difficulties during the performance. Alan Schneider considered the audience's determination to see a different play than the one he was presenting the paramount reason for the disastrous American premiere of *Waiting for Godot* in Miami—clearly, advance publicity contributed importantly to this. "The Miami audience," reports Schneider, "was being informed, in large type, that Bert Lahr, 'Star of *Harvey* and *Burlesque*,' and Tom Ewell, 'Star of *The Seven Year Itch*,' were about to appear in their midst in 'The Laugh *Sensation* of Two Continents,' *Waiting for Godot*. The name of the author appeared only in very small print. My name, luckily, hardly appeared at all."

The result was a memorable example of an audience's frustration at attempting to create a particular, expected theatre experience out of extremely recalcitrant material:

> Instead of *The Seven Year Itch* or *Harvey*, the audience got *Waiting for Godot*, not the "laugh sensation of two continents," but a very strange sensation indeed. At first they laughed—at Bert trying to take off his shoe, at Tommy realizing his fly was unbuttoned; but as soon as they realized that the actors were on to more serious matters, they stopped. By the time they got to the Bible and the Thieves, they were laughless. . . . Whole groups started to sneak out. Then droves. . . .[17]

Fifteen years later, in an off-Broadway theatre in New York, with audiences aware that the author of this unconventional play was a major experimental writer, winner of the Nobel Prize, and prepared by publicity calling the work "a cornerstone of the modern theatre" and "a timeless classic," the play, again directed by Schneider, received a warm and enthusiastic welcome.

This sort of radical disjuncture between the horizon of expectations assumed by the production and that actually brought to the theatre by a community of readers may be encouraged, as it clearly was in Miami, by an institutional disjuncture between publicity and production, but larger structural concerns lie behind this specific manifestation. Toward the end of the eighteenth century and at the beginning of the nineteenth, a number of major changes, artistic and political, significantly altered both the creation and staging of plays and the audiences attending them. Out of this crisis emerged a new figure in the theatre—the dramaturg, along with his near relative, the reviewer. Their function was in general to mediate between performance and spectator, suggesting to the latter possible strategies and mechanisms to be employed in reading performance. Their influence on reading, like the publicity in Miami, has often been able to outweigh or to negate the reading guides of the performance itself.

Although their relationship to reading formations has been historically very similar, the dramaturg and the reviewer come to this function from opposite directions, one from the theatre, the other from the audience. The position of dramaturg is usually considered to have begun in the theatre with the appointment of Gotthold Lessing to this position in Hamburg in 1767. The Hamburg theatre was the first attempt at establishing a German national theatre, and its founders realized that it would not be enough to create an original German repertoire, establish a state-supported cultural institution, and elevate the public image of both stage and actors, difficult as all these tasks were, unless they could at the same time develop an audience, not yet in existence, that could actively and intelligently participate in this new venture. Thus, an important element in those essays Lessing wrote for Hamburg was guiding and developing proper response skills in the new audience.

The first modern reviews appeared in France somewhat later, but in response to a similar need. Here the Revolution separated the post-1800 tradition even more radically than had the search for a new drama devoid of French influence in eighteenth-century Germany. The community of readers which for generations had supported the theatre in France disappeared with the Revolution; the community which appeared subsequently, eager to participate in the cultural life of novels and theatre, often lacked the knowledge of how to do so. Thus, a new community of readers had to be created.

In response to this need appeared the first modern reviews, the feuilletons of Geoffroy in the *Journal des Débats,* beginning in 1800. The previous century had seen journalistic reports on the theatre, but these were directed toward a public already familiar with the conventions of the traditional system. Geoffroy's public required from him something quite different—a guide not only to meaningful participation in the theatre event, but, perhaps equally important, to subsequent intelligent discussions of that event in the drawing rooms and salons of polite society.[18] For this public, Geoffroy provided much of the sort of material brought to the theatre in earlier times by the audience itself—intertextual relationships with other works, an acquaintance with the tradition, the author, the actors. He took upon himself the role of model reader and was unquestionably powerfully influential in the training of responses of a whole generation of theatregoers in Paris.

After Geoffroy, the reviewer became a regular feature of the French theatre world, as influential in theatrical life as any actor, director, or playwright. The popular impression today of a reviewer is that of a journal writer who advises audiences whether they should attend a play or not; certainly, this function has been a powerful one, especially when such reviews are widely read or quoted and major financial and artistic ventures are at stake. Equally important for the functioning of the theatre, however, is a less generally acknowledged function—providing audiences with strategies for the reading of performances. In countries such as the United States, where dramaturgs related to specific companies are rare, it is often the case that the comments of reviewers, especially regarding unusual or experimental works, are more powerful than any other single source in structuring the way that audiences will receive the performance within the theatre.

Reviewers still commonly follow the example of Geoffroy in not only providing judgments on productions, but making intertextual connections, suggesting interpretations, ordering elements, proposing relationships and emphases by citing particular passages as effective or ineffective. An excellent and by no means unusual example of this dynamic at work may be seen in Walter Kerr's review of the highly innovative 1977 production by Andrei Servan of *The Cherry Orchard*. The review begins with a powerful and specific claim for a certain reading of the production: "There are at least five images I shan't forget as long as I live in Andrei Servan's mounting of *The Cherry Orchard*." A large part of the remaining rather lengthy article is devoted to a vivid and evocative description of each of these five images, complete in each case with an interpretation. The review then continues with other reading aids, such as this guide to certain relevant intertextuality: "some of these instances have the smell of the circus about them, some of vaudeville, some of chamber music, some of a thumping brass band, some of Peter Brook, and some of Robert Wilson, and some of Samuel Beckett, transformed into a high-wire mountebank. . . ."[19]

So striking and specific a review could hardly fail to condition the subsequent reception of this play by any spectator who read it; the position of the review, on the front page of the "Arts and Leisure" section of the Sunday *New York Times,* guaranteed that it would be noticed by an important percentage of the likely public. For many viewers, this review surely provided an important structuring framework of the production ("Ah, here is the third unforgettable image—thus there are still two to come"); as a member of that public, I can bear witness that the review foregrounded these images for me in a manner that I found rather troublesome.

The contribution of reviews to reading formations is reinforced in the modern theatre by the frequent recycling of reviews by the theatre institutions themselves. In the absence of dramaturgs, particularly in the American theatre, both theatre organizations and the public have come to accept reviewers as "official" readers of productions, giving their reactions a particular authority. Short citations from reviews, selected for their presumed ability to stimulate audience interest, have become an almost invariable component in newspaper advertisements and in New York are often also displayed on special signboards at the entrance to the theatre. The frequent hyperbole of such phrases and the fact that they are necessarily taken out of context obviously erodes their authority for many, but does not remove their power to condition reception. Even a reader who does not believe that a new play is "the wittiest comedy since Noel Coward" is unlikely, having read such a comment, to see the play without Coward becoming a fairly conscious intertextual element in the reception.

More detailed and more specific guidance is given when theatres display on their premises entire reviews or newspaper stories, to be read by prospective patrons or, even more significantly, by those actually attending the performance. The lobbies of many theatres in London, Paris, and New York today regularly display such reviews, and they are invariably eagerly read by patrons before and after the performance and, perhaps most importantly, during the intermissions. The on-site availability of such authorized readings ostended but not created by the organization producing the performance itself provides a contribution to reading formation highly unusual in the history of the theatre, and one which would surely repay closer study.

The comparatively small amount of reception research carried out in the theatre to date has been developed almost entirely through interviews and questionnaires seeking to establish what an audience thought or felt about a performance after its completion. Almost no organized work has been done on the other end of this process—what an audience brings to the theatre in the way of expectations, assumptions, and strategies which will creatively interact with the stimuli of the theatre event to produce whatever effect the performance has on an audience and what effect the audience has upon it. This essay has attempted to suggest, at least in brief form, some of the kinds of material available for such research and how it might be pursued. A clearer understanding of how spectators today and at other historical periods have learned and applied the rules of the game they play with the performance event in the theatre will provide us with a far richer and more interesting picture of that complex event than has the traditional model which treated the spectator as an essentially passive recipient of the stage's projected stimuli.

NOTES

1 The work that has appeared has been largely semiotic in orientation and so far has dealt very little with specifically historical questions. A leading representative of this approach is Marco de Marinis, most recently in "Dramaturgy of the Spectator," *The Drama Review* 31:2 (Summer 1987), 100–114, and earlier in "L'esperienza dello spettatore: Fondamenti per una semiotica della ricezione teatrale," *Documenti di lavoro* (Urbino: Centro di Semiotica e Linguistica di Urbino, 1984), pp. 138–139, and "Theatrical Comprehension: A Socio-Semiotic Approach," *Theater* 15:1 (Winter 1983), 12–17. A special issue of *VS* (41 [May–August 1985]) was devoted to "Semiotica della ricezione teatrale." See also Darko Suvin, "The Performance Text as Audience-Stage Dialog Inducing a Possible World," *VS* 42 (October 1985), 3–20.

2 Wolfgang Iser, *Die Appellstruktur der Texte* (Constance: Druckerei und Verlagsanstalt Konstanz, 1970), p. 15.

3 Anne Ubersfeld, *Lire le théâtre* (Paris: Editions Sociales, 1977), p. 24.

4 Iser, *Appellstruktur,* p. 11.

5 Hans Robert Jauss, *Toward an Aesthetic of Reception,* trans. Timothy Bahti (Minneapolis: University of Minnesota Press, 1982), pp. 22–23, 25.

6 Umberto Eco, *The Role of the Reader* (Bloomington: Indiana University Press, 1979), p. 7.

7 Marco de Marinis, *Semiotica del teatro* (Milan: Bompiani, 1982), pp. 198–199, and "Dramaturgy," pp. 102–103.

8 Eco, *Role,* pp. 7–8.

9 De Marinis, "Dramaturgy," pp. 103–104.

10 Tony Bennett, "Text, Readers, Reading Formations," *Literature and History* 9 (1983), 214.

11 Tadeusz Kowzan, *Littérature et spectacle dans leurs rapports esthétiques, thématiques et sémiologiques* (The Hague: Mouton, 1975), p. 25.

12 Arthur Pickard-Cambridge, *The Dramatic Festivals of Athens* (Oxford: Oxford University Press, 1968), p. 67.

13 Perhaps most famously in the preface to *Cromwell*, which calls for "the liberty of art against the despotism of systems, codes, and rules" (Victor Hugo, *Oeuvres complètes,* 18 vols. [Paris: Librairie Ollendorff, 1967], III, 77).

14 Stanley Fish, *Is There a Text in This Class?* (Cambridge: Harvard University Press, 1980), p. 349.

15 Earle Ernst, *The Kabuki Theatre* (New York: Oxford University Press, 1956), p. 200.

16 Pierre Rémond de Sainte-Albine, *Le Comédien* (Paris, 1749), p. 228.

17 Alan Schneider, *Entrances* (New York: Viking, 1986), p. 232.

18 Charles Marc des Granges, *Geoffroy et la critique dramatique* (Paris: Hachette, 1897), pp. 120–121.

19 Walter Kerr, *New York Times,* Sunday, February 27, 1977, II, 1, 5. This sort of authoritative reading may be seen in film reviewing as well. A recent review by David Denby (*New York Magazine,* June 22, 1987, 71) begins: "There are exactly two good scenes in *The Witches of Eastwick.*"

Power's Body
The Inscription of Morality as Style

Joseph R. Roach

> We must cease once and for all to describe the effects of power in
> negative terms: it "excludes," it "represses," it "abstracts," it
> "masks," it "conceals." In fact, power produces; it produces real-
> ity; it produces domains of objects and rituals of truth.
> —*Michel Foucault,* Discipline and Punish

> [Balanchine] halted class and approached me for a kind of
> physical inspection. With his knuckles, he thumped on my ster-
> num and down my rib cage clucking his tongue and remark-
> ing, "Must see the bones."
> —*Gelsey Kirkland,* Dancing on My Grave

In his popular study of the great cat massacre in the
Rue Saint-Séverin, Robert Darnton argues the historiographic utility of the bizarre. Knowing that time
empties meaning from once vital rituals, Darnton, historian of eighteenth-century France, adopts the methods of his colleague,
anthropologist Clifford Geertz: "When you realize that you are not getting something—a joke, a proverb, a ceremony—that is particularly meaningful to the natives, you can see where to grasp a foreign system of meaning in order to unravel it." In the 1730s, the apprentices in a Parisian print
shop made a joke out of the mock trial and elaborate execution of all the
cats they could catch. More mysterious still, they reenacted these scenes
of condemnation and torture in pantomime to the delight and hilarity of
their brethren. Why felines? What Darnton sees in cats generally—in the
eerie intelligence of their eyes or in the horripilating quasi-human timbre
of their night screams—is "an ambiguous ontological position, a strad-
dling of conceptual categories," which has always given them special "ritual value."[1] Why the Rue Saint-Séverin? Examining the records of the
French printing business of the period, reaching back to the mocking fes-

tivals of the charivaris, Darnton plumbs the deep structure and gets the joke: it would seem that the cats were better fed, better housed, and better loved than the apprentices; they were more honored in the households of the master-printers and their egregious wives; in sum, the cats were in every way more bourgeois than the boys, who, though literate and highly skilled, lacked advancement. The felines thus satisfied the apprentices' vengeful need for victims in a carnival of ritual surrogation and slapstick sacrifice. The ceremony of their pseudo-judicial liquidation dramatized through gestures and actions the otherwise unutterable verdict of the disenfranchised upon the lives and fortunes of the privileged.

Prescient theatre historians have recognized the ideological power of secular ritual in performances of many diverse kinds.[2] The performative structures of ritualized discourse, however, remain only partially explored, especially in well-documented relationship to theatrical style. Style and ritual share a common structure. Each consists of a formalized network of surrogations whereby doubles stand in for originals. Actors, for example, serve necessarily as double signs, referring at once to themselves and to the characters they represent. Their duality poignantly recalls the liminality of the cats of the Rue Saint-Séverin. Acting styles regulate the intelligibility of performances by authorizing certain substitutions as appropriate and proscribing others as meaningless or false. When critics agree that an actor has been miscast in a role, they implicitly refer to an error of substitution within a generally intelligible stylistic code. Theatre historians might be prepared to explain how such modes of surrogation operate in what they call period style, for within those ritualized gestures and strange formal conventions of historic performance the ideological and the aesthetic converge.

The eighteenth century offers the historian perhaps the widest range of materials pertaining to the study of performance styles of any period. Theatre scholarship has only begun to assess the remarkable proliferation of choreographic handbooks, singers' guides, elocutionary texts, and treatises on the expression of the Passions from this period. The rise of "how-to" manuals on the mastery of bodily expression for the stage has yet to be adequately taxonomized or even collected.[3] One impediment remains the needlessly parochial separation of theatre history, dance history, and musicology into discrete fields. The study of historic performance could be a unified discipline with very stimulating conferences at some future time. Meanwhile, I would like to propose here a method for studying period style across genres by considering parallel representations of the body in several kinds of performance, noting ideologically significant trends among the substitutions that audiences expected and applauded.

Self-evidently, the signifying body is central to theatrical representation in any form. The techniques whereby the body is prepared for performance, the particular bodily expressions whereby the public accepts the truth of performance, and the imagery whereby the body is eroticized in performance illuminate at any given cultural moment the relationships between sexuality and power. The eighteenth-century theatre seems to contain the most vivid uses of the sexually expressive body of the actor to stand in for the aesthetic and ideological significance of the character, a suggestion to which the practice of castrating its most popular performers lends both factual support and symbolic illustration.

In considering the preeminence of the operatic *castrati* in eighteenth-century performance, I have been guided by the analysis of power relations and the signifying body in two works of Michel Foucault, *Discipline and Punish: The Birth of the Prison* (1975) and the first volume of *The History of Sexuality* (1976). Each book features the eighteenth century as the crucial moment in the development of the modern relationships of knowledge and power that Foucault, following Nietzsche, terms "genealogies."[4] These relationships constitute the interstices of cognitive discourses and historical practices. Foucault argues that power touches people's lives through social and cultural practices more than through centralized state organizations or systems of belief. Power is diffused at the "capillary" level in the micropolitics of daily life.[5]

The emergence of this modern form of power in the eighteenth century was unlike any previous historical manifestations in that it rendered power productive at every locality; it was no longer centralized inefficiently and symbolically in the body of the sovereign, but rather universally disseminated by pervasive new "technologies." These included the modern conceptions of surveillance and punishment embodied in the spatial designs of prisons, for instance, and the "incitement to discourse" in medicine, political science, and bio-science on the subject of sexuality. The body unifies *Discipline and Punish* and *The History of Sexuality* as the dominant problem and the best evidence. As histories of the body and of discourses on the body, both books ought to be of extraordinary interest to theatre historians, who necessarily chronicle the observances of the fleshly shrine where the body is represented nightly as the principal medium and the chief attraction.

Moreover, the history of performance since the eighteenth century is the history of the ever more rigorous subjection of the body to forms of internalized control. The goal of such systems is the attainment of a self-mastery so perfect that the exhaustive methods of its acquisition become invisible to the spectators and even to the performers themselves. This conforms to Foucault's model of a modern power so deeply embodied at disparate sites that no agent need be present to apply its force. It is omnipresent through training and drill in the bodies of the subjects who have obligingly mastered themselves through their routinized submission to diverse technical controls from the calisthenic to the confessional. "What I want to show," Foucault notes in summarizing *The History of Sexuality,* "is how power relations can materially penetrate the body in depth."[6]

As time has drained the obscure rituals of the Rue Saint-Séverin of their meanings, marooning those performances in the archives of the French printing trade, so it seems to have relegated many common eighteenth-century theatrical practices to the repository of the bizarre. Castration to preserve the male soprano voice is obviously one such superannuated practice, but I believe that it is emblematic of many more, including the sequences of gestures obligatory in the performance of sentimental drama such as Richard Steele's *The Conscious Lovers.* Such practices Foucault calls "rituals of truth." He argues that they are alive in us, not dead in the archive like Darnton's cats. To unravel their mystery is to plumb not alien systems of meaning but invisible commonplaces in the political unconscious of the present. These practices, mentalities, and discourses, Foucault writes, center "in the body as machine: its disciplining, the optimization of its capabilities, the extortion of its forces, the parallel increase of its usefulness and its docility, its integration into systems of efficient economic controls, all this was insured by the procedures of power that characterize the *disciplines:* an *anatomo-politics* of the *human body.*"[7] For Foucault, then, power is productive and diffuse.

Like Foucault's genealogies, Darnton's history of the cat massacres demonstrates that power is a constantly changing field, a set of contending practices, of relationships, not a property completely owned by some and denied to others. But unlike Foucault, Darnton argues the extreme periodization and localization of the practices he unearths in the archive: they pertain only to their time and place; the cat massacres are even discrete from the September Massacres of the French Revolution. It is this contradictory experience of historical distance—the oscillation between Darnton's sense of the remoteness and uniqueness of past practices and Foucault's sense of their tangible and pervasive presence—that I want to probe here by looking at the technologies of the body available to the eighteenth-century theatre. I want to explore the dual nature of their distance from us, at once alien and familiar, by distinguishing as far as possible between the discontinuities and the continuities of their styles. Foucault would have us recognize what he calls a history of the present. Tug persistently at the odd, loose threads, Darnton counters, and only then will the fabric of the alien culture of the past begin to unravel, yielding up its perplexities to our auto-ethnographic gaze.

Among the loose threads extruding from the theatrical history of the eighteenth century is the sex appeal of the *castrati*. Musicology has documented their dominance as international superstars.[8] But theatre history, usually supine before the lurid charms of anecdote, has generally ignored their notoriety as performers onstage and off.[9] Neutered before puberty to preserve their soprano voices, popular in both male and female roles, the *musici* or *virtuosi,* as they were euphemistically known, occasioned the ornate erotic complications chronicled in works from Casanova's *Mémoires* to Balzac's *Sarrasine*. Their gender hovered in suspense, transcended by the astonishing power and silvery sweetness of their voices. Their mysterious bodies reanimated the disputations on the sex of the angels, and some of them, trained to standards of physical execution hitherto unimagined, made music-drama with the precision of machines.

Casanova, nerves finely spun and alert to each nuance of sensation, left us an account of his visit to the Roman opera in 1761, which might be read, following Darnton, as a cultural-anthropological field report on the exotic practices of the natives. Observing that the "Holy City drives the whole human race to become pederasts," Casanova recalled his complicated response to Giovanni Osti, scandalously nicknamed Giovannino di Borghese:

> We went to the Teatro Aliberti, to which the *castrato* who was playing the leading woman's part was drawing the entire city. He was the favorite of Cardinal Borghese, with whom he was invited to sup alone every evening.
>
> The *virtuoso* sang very well, but his principal attraction was his beauty. I had seen him strolling at the Villa Medici, dressed in men's clothes, and though his face was handsome enough he had not made an impression on me, for one saw at once that he was not a whole man; but on the stage, dressed as a woman, he was a firebrand.
>
> It would seem that a man dressed as a woman could not but be known for what he was if he let too much of his chest be seen; but it was precisely by so doing that the little monster bewitched everyone in the audience. Tightly laced in a very well-fitting corset, he had the

figure of a nymph, and few women could show a firmer and more enticing bosom than his. The illusion he created was such that it was impossible to resist it. One looked, the spell acted, and one had either to fall in love or be the most stolid of Germans. When he walked across the stage waiting for the *ritornello* of the aria he was singing his gait was imposing, and when he swept his gaze over the boxes his black eyes revolved so tenderly and modestly that they ravished the soul.[10]

The very ambiguity of the *castrato*'s body intensifies its sexual meanings for Casanova. Its cancellation of gender opens up a resonant space for the amplification of sexuality, a hollowness at the center which is an incitement to talk about sex. The *castrato*'s body tempts Casanova to particularize his descriptions as if he were writing a manual to ensure that such a performance could be repeated. In fact, his formulaic narrations of sexual encounters throughout his notorious autobiography have much in common with the actors' handbooks of the time. They share repetitiveness, elaborated descriptions of the precise movement of separate appendages, and the implicit physiological premise that the body is a machine exhibited in time and space for the measured production of sensational effect. Foucault argues in *The History of Sexuality* that sexuality itself is a discursive construct geared to the production of the docile body, the body whose mechanized movements conform to an internalized dressage created by precise habits of physical self-surveillance and exhibition.

In his account of the *castrato*'s body, Casanova responds to more than the individual illusion created by the substituted body of the performer. He also warms to the generalized theatrical convention of the balletic *ritornelli*. These long instrumental passages preceding the arias required the calculated display of the singer's body, its various parts and appendages featured sequentially in a fetishistic promenade. This convention challenges the modern stage director who vainly seeks to "motivate" the dramatic action invented to fill the moments vacated by the disappearance of the original posturing occasioned by this High Baroque striptease. Filling the *ritornelli* with graceful action and poses drawn from ancient statuary was an important element of the eighteenth-century singer's art, emphasizing Casanova's point that the body as well as the voice of the *castrato* created sensational effects.

Goethe, German but by no means stolid, equally smitten, wanted to replace actresses with travestied *castrati* because he found them more feminine.[11] But the Protean *musici* played it both ways. More often than not, they took the ultramasculine roles of heroes, conquerors, and irresistible lovers. In this guise their erotic authority reigned supreme among the ladies: duchesses made fools of themselves, virgins ran mad. The libretti of the *opera seria*, designed around the star attraction of the *musici*, served up plenty of what we would call strong sexual situations.

In act III of *Hydaspes*, for instance, which premiered in London in 1710, the seminude *castrato* Nicolo Grimaldi (called Nicolino or Nicolini) hero-ically fought and killed a lion with his bare hands. "I was last Thursday at the New opera," Lady Mary Wortley Montagu recounts in a letter, "and saw Nicolini strangle a lion with great gallantry. But he represented naked-ness so naturally, I was surprised to see those ladies stare at him without any confusion, that pretend to be so violently shocked at a poor *double entendre* or two in a comedy."[12] The intensity of their gaze, unwavering even at a time of self-conscious moral renovation of the theatre in the wake of the Jeremy Collier controversy, suggests the power of this weird spec-tacle to ritualize and perhaps legitimize urges that could not be spoken in the hearts of those who could not silence them. *Spectator* called for the scene to be encored and the cat massacred a second time for the satisfac-tion of the house.

Some contemporary verses presage Casanova's ambivalent longings, but from a woman's point of view:

> 'Tis too much! she cryes, and I can hear no more,
> How sweet's his Voice, how tender is his Air?
> But oh! They cost th' Unhappy Youth too dear.
> The gentle Beau, that Ever-dying Swain,
> Beats the slow time, and Sighs with pleasing Pain;
> And lisps the tender Accents back again.
> Ev'n the rough Soldiers mov'd, the dusty Field,
> And the big War to softer Pleasures yield;
> Such is the Force of the enchanting Strains,
> Where Caesar listens, but Grimaldi reigns.[13]

The castrated body exculpates the desire it awakens, but its seductive ambi-guity provides a site for the representation of contending sexualities and powers. As the warlike Caesar surrenders to the lisping swain, as Eros un-mans Mars (a favorite eighteenth-century operatic theme), so the lion, which doubles for the physical impulses that typical operatic heroes struggle to master, succumbs in the epicene embrace of the disarmed gladiator. Joseph Addison thought that Nicolino's triumph could be explained by the datum of natural history that a lion would never hurt a virgin.[14] The outcome of the combat and its encore, however, suggest that the ladies were applauding with emphasis the symbolic conquest of a violently untamed nature by a suavely docile one.

Theatre historians typically approach the problem of style by asking how *natural* a performance was. That question seems even more than usually sterile in this instance. Historians might more profitably ask by what methods the performance signified, how its meanings came to be shared with its audience, and why its success or failure seemed to be rooted in the particular ideological and aesthetic contingencies of the moment. Specifically, how did the style of castration signify and what needs could it have fulfilled?

Like Darnton's cats, the *castrati* clearly straddled conceptual categories, occupying an ontologically ambiguous position. Can they be said to have had "ritual value" as well? The dual nature of Casanova's "little monster" holds Casanova transfixed, poised between loathing and desire, his senses ravished by the illusion, his mind unsettled by the monstrosity of the substitution that creates the illusion. Nicolino inspires a comparable ambivalence by substituting for the hero's character a bodily instrument that continuously deflects the desire it compels, replacing the sexual object with the sexual symbol, a hollow signifier.

In *Violence and the Sacred,* René Girard draws our attention to the efficacy of the "monstrous double" in ritualized practices. The double translates the real into the unreal by an act of surrogation. It defers violent desire to an ordered agenda of disguises. Girard delineates the contradictory impulses that create the "monstrous double": the sacrificial victim must be neither divisive nor trivial, neither fully a part of the community nor fully outside it; he or she must rather be distanced by a special identity that specifies isolation while simultaneously allowing plausible surrogation for a member of the community. This occurs in a two-stage process: the community finds a surrogate victim for itself from within itself; then it finds an alien substitute for the surrogate. This is the "monstrous double." [15]

Prizing their special distance from women, Goethe would have substituted the *castrati* for the Italian female impersonators who filled in for the actresses: their double nature makes such surrogation all the more satisfying, especially where the erotic representation of chastity is concerned. The extreme artifice of the performance, the substitution of this special kind of monstrous double, physically contains sexuality within a being whose essence is defined by what it does not have, whose actions are predicated by what it cannot do, whose most powerful presence exists as an absence.

As surrogation exerts its force on style, the actor stands in for the character, the character for the members of the audience, who project their desires on the fictive life of their onstage doubles. The actor is not there *for* us, but *instead of* us. The higher the level of stylization, the greater the perceived distance of the substitute from the original it represents, and the wider the range of possible representations of apparently remote objects. This made life hard on cats, but it empowered the performances of the *castrati* by ensnaring the audience in their seductive liminality.

Roger North, an eighteenth-century historian of music, commented upon Nicolino's performance of a lament-aria from *Hydaspes* ("Unhappy Prisoner," act III): "Besides all this, the soft and loud hath a reall representation, whereby part of the subject may be conceived . . . and in like manner the state of a person solitary or unfortunate, as when Nicholini sings— *Infelice prigionero*. And the swelling and dying of musicall notes, with *tremolo* not impeaching the tone, wonderfully represents the waiving of the air, and pleasant gales moving, and sinking away." The technical stylization of the voice, *tremolo* substituting for a sigh, expands the frame of reference outward, touching North deeply, creating in his mind's eye pathetic images of all nature suspiring for the hero's plight. Nicolino as the surrogate victim, the unhappy prisoner, embodies his sacrifice in his own voice, drawing North into the empathetic vortex, even against his better judgment, compelling him to identify with his double: "Musik . . . being applycable to each pathetick sence, makes the passion sublime and noble, so that in such sweetness wee envy even the miserable, and would rejoyce to enter their condition." [16]

Liminality intensifies signification. The semiotician Roland Barthes devotes sizable portions of *S/Z* to the analysis of the character of La Zambinella, the exquisitely cross-dressed *castrato* who inspires the sculptor Sarrasine's desperate passion in Balzac's story. Barthes characteristically privileges "double signs," those that gesture to their own material existence even as they convey other meanings. This task the *castrato* must perform, like all other actors, but with the singular properties of the disembodied voice to ensure its inimitable self-reference.

For Barthes, La Zambinella performs as an unstable signifier, a gap, a hollowness, a blank space wherein Sarrasine will inscribe his own urgent meanings. The *castrato* is the neutral surface upon which the spectator projects his fantasies, not unlike the automata in pornographic films, who are purposively neutralized to invite the imaginative participation of the beholders. The "sadistic configuration" of the sculptor's response to her "weak [speaking] voice, her manner, her movements," fulfills "the sense of violence, aggressiveness, assigned to Sarrasine at the outset."[17] Hatred interpenetrates desire, and the "monstrous double" as the symbolic woman serves as the convenient receptacle for the violence of everybody's ambivalent urges—the *Story of O*. The extreme case in the archive is probably that of the *castrato* Torcchino, who, captured by Don Cossacks, first melted their hearts with his singing before they fed him to the wolves.[18]

Such ritualized violence applied to the flesh of surrogated victims illuminates a general structural principle that mediates between performers and spectators in any period. What historical conditions prompted the singular international success of the style of castration in the early eighteenth-century theatre? Notoriously, torture and execution in the eighteenth century remained public rituals, subjecting the victim, of course, but also the spectator to their intense theatricality. One of the deliciously self-referential ironies of *The Beggar's Opera* (1728), for example, requires the climactic scene at the gibbet to be played as a morally instructive opera at prices the people can afford. Torture and execution compelled the suffering body of the victim to signify. It signified both the guilt of the condemned and the ideological potency of the sovereign power that could inscribe such vivid lessons on living flesh.

Foucault's *Discipline and Punish,* however, traces through the course of the century the increasing diffusions of power to newly organized and more diverse, but no less potent, institutional structures of subjection. Power is no longer centralized in the body of the sovereign, and punishments eventually disappear from public view. The new spatial extension of power includes prisons, schools, hospitals, factories, military formations, and even classes in penmanship. Foucault explores the training of the body, its conditioning, its movement in time and space, the regulation of even its most subtle gestures, and the provisions for the surveillance of its every activity. Foucault also demonstrates the necessary cooperation of the docile body in its own subjection. Indeed, he reiterates the positive effects of self-control on the growing efficiency, dispersion, and productivity of power.

Discipline and Punish and *The History of Sexuality,* therefore, in addition to their history of the public representation of the body, offer an analysis of the technology of self-mastery. This implies a control over the body so deeply inscribed that it seems to originate spontaneously from within, which is precisely how Diderot and others described the automization of the performer's art in light of such exhibitions as David Garrick's mechanical Passions and Jacques Vaucanson's robotic ducks and flutes.

The most accessible model of discipline available to the eighteenth-century public, the most spectacular forum in which it could see its body doubled, short of the increasingly passé hangings al fresco, was theatrical virtuosity. Virtuosity, the physical mastery of a particular style, means subjection. In its name, the appropriate expressions and trills, the correct sequences and spatial designs, must be deeply inscribed upon the body. The virtuoso's muscles and nerves must remember at speeds often exceeding consciousness which procedures the style authorizes and which it proscribes.

Castration exemplifies the rigors of such inscriptions, but it does not begin to exhaust their regulative possibilities. The operation itself, harrowing as it is for us to contemplate, actually involved the most subtle of incisions, the simple ligature of certain ducts, performed on a patient anesthetized by opium, by soothing baths, and by the momentary pressure of the skillful physician's finger on his jugular. Compared to the ritual of eighteenth-century executions or even to tooth extractions, this procedure, which had its own medical specialists, seems a relatively progressive subjection. In any event, there was never a shortage of willing candidates. Authorized by the express consent of the boy and his parents, the operation was a precise initiation, a rite of passage to be elaborated upon by the priestly disciplines that followed in the regulated curriculum of the *conservatori*. These included ten hours of instruction per day in theory, counterpoint, and the execution of difficult passages, as well as exercises in front of a mirror, as in ballet class, to practice deportment, posture, and gesture.[19] The goal remained mastery of the flesh affirmed by the deep inscription of virtuosity.

The governance of the body and its Passions had long been an imperative of moral philosophy and a theatrical cliché, but the techniques of inculcating self-mastery in the eighteenth century were revolutionized by advances in notation. The manufacture of a legible record of appropriate physical behavior developed to a high degree of technical elaboration in this period. Notation of movement is simultaneously an inscription and a discipline. Like ritual, notation aims at authentic repetition. And like ritual, it offers an array of fixed points through which the body must progress, by which its efficacy may be measured, against which its deficiencies may be rendered visible, and within which its mastery may be displayed. Notation confers the power to write movement, to authorize and control the activities of the body, and to expose each of its appendages to a precise surveillance.

Amidst the profusion of inscribed movements in the Diderot/

D'Alembert *Encyclopedia,* for example, the contemporaneous emergence of ballet choreography and close-order drill is most striking. The command over bodies individually and in ensembles constitutes a technology of power of the utmost importance in military and theatrical history: the deployment of moving bodies in exactly the right places at exactly the right times, and in the right relationships to one another, at once defines the art of Jean-Georges Noverre and the strategy of Frederick of Prussia. "What is a ballet," Noverre asked, "but a more or less complicated piece of machinery?"[20] Among the indispensable provisions for Napoleon's Egyptian campaign was his corps de ballet, whose highly disciplined motion the great tactician found edifying—and rightly so.[21]

Napoleon realized that style of performance may be controlled, manipulated, and reconfigured to represent the regularities of a larger order. Style readily disseminates those regularities, operating powerfully on the decorums of everyday life. The theatre tests behaviors on the bodies of exceptional practitioners, but it does so in the process of a wider distribution. Generalities that govern conduct and establish priorities of value—Taste, Duty, Beauty, Honor—gain from the theatre an otherwise unattainable specificity under conditions of precise selection and control. As ritualized discourse, the theatre plays a part in what Foucault calls the "capillary form" of the diffusion of power. Theatrical performance provides a "point where power reaches into the very grain of individuals, touches their bodies and inserts itself into their actions and attitudes, their discourses, learning processes and everyday lives."[22] In their reductive mechanisms, what are generally called period styles seem alien or merely quaint. In their ambition to promulgate self-mastery and to implant particular behaviors in the body, however, they seem to have far greater contemporary resonance.

Among various inscriptions of movement in eighteenth-century aesthetics, the textbooks regularizing the theatrical Passions most fully elaborate this technology of self-control. These treatises, proliferating in the wake of Descartes' mechanical physiology and Le Brun's systematic illustrations, shape the discourse of theatrical representation into a fixed taxonomy of morally universal types—astonishment, terror, pity, rage, and so forth. The earliest texts, unsurprisingly on reflection, emerge from the Jesuit theatre-schools. Franciscus Lang's *Dissertatio de Actione Scenica* (1727), illustrated by figures of bodies in correct and incorrect postures, shows the derivation of aesthetic subjections of the theatre from the spiritual exercise of confession, which Foucault calls in *The History of Sexuality* "a ritual in which the expression alone . . . produces intrinsic modification in the person who articulates it."[23] The secular descendants of these manuals also externalize the Passions, opening them to the domain of public surveillance where their activity may be regulated by the meticulous enumerations of their expressive signs. They promulgate the circumscriptions of style by subjecting the body to ordered sequences of behavior. They transform Passions into manners, for if Passions may not be controlled, style can.

The entries for *Authority, Gravity,* and *Command* from the lexicon of the Passions in James Burgh's *The Art of Speaking* (1761) exemplify the genre:

> *Authority* opens the countenance; but draws down the eyebrows a little, so far as to give the look of *Gravity.* See *Gravity.* . . . *Gravity,* or seriousness, the mind fixed upon some important subject, draws down the *eyebrows* a little; casts down, or shuts or raises the eye to heaven, shuts the mouth and pinches the lips close. The posture of the body and limbs is composed, and without much motion. The speech, if any, slow and solemn; the tone unvarying. . . . Commanding requires an air a little more peremptory, with a look a little severe or stern. The hand is held out, and moved toward the person, to whom the order is given, with the palm upwards, and the head nods toward him.[24]

Burgh's treatise goes on to apply these and other behaviors from his taxonomy of the Passions to scenes from popular plays. He writes a subtext or score in the margins of each scene. The performer is invited to study Burgh's marginalia and embody the Passions sequentially as elaborated in his glossary. These notations shape behavior toward the virtuosic ideal of self-mastery, a goal shared by both the self-consciously moralizing dramas of the eighteenth century and the contemporaneous operas in which the *castrati* appeared. This mutually supportive relationship can be seen most clearly in Richard Steele's exemplary comedy *The Conscious Lovers* (1722), produced at the height of the popularity of the Italian opera on the London stage.

Of the eighteenth-century plays most likely to qualify as alien to our understanding and sympathy, as alien perhaps as the cat massacres, *The Conscious Lovers* takes pride of place. It has been blamed for the oft-bemoaned displacement of wit comedy by sentimental comedy. Steele professedly wrote the play to reform the stage, to induce in his public "a joy too exquisite for laughter," offering an exemplary hero in place of the negative rake-hero of Etherege.[25] Steele sought nothing less than the renovation of morals through the transformation of theatrical style. A synopsis reveals his strategy. Bevil Jr. selflessly loves Indiana, an apparent orphan he has rescued from an attempted rape. He maintains her at his own very considerable expense but asks for nothing in return. He cannot marry her because his father intends him for Lucinda, the daughter of a wealthy merchant. Bevil Jr. makes his father's word law, even to the docile acceptance of Lucinda's hand. His friend Myrtle, the foil, is in love with Lucinda and insanely jealous. In act IV he challenges Bevil Jr. to a duel, which the hero manfully struggles to decline.

James Burgh glosses this famous scene in *The Art of Speaking*. His inscriptions of morality as style, very much in the spirit of Steele's reform drama, are marked "Lessons." Burgh recognizes that style is intensified behavior predicated on surrogation, and he offers a carefully notated menu of substitutions of manners for Passions:

Anger roused.	*Bev.* You have *touched* me beyond the *patience* of a *man:* and the defence of *spotless innocence,* will, I hope, excuse my *accepting* your *challenge,* or to at least my *obliging* you to retract your *infamous aspersions.* I *will not,* if I can avoid it *shed your blood,* nor shall *you mine.*
Authority.	But *Indiana's purity,* I *will defend.* Who *waits?*
Submission.	*Serv.* Did you *call,* Sir?
Command.	*Bev. Yes,* go call a *coach.*
Trep[ida- tion] with submission.	*Serv. Sir,*—Mr. *Myrtle*—*Gentlemen*—You are *friends*— I am but a *Servant*—But—
* Anger.	*Bev.* * *Call* a *coach.*
	[Exit Serv.]
Recollect.	[A *long pause; they walk sullenly about the room.*] [*Aside.*] Shall I (though provoked beyond *sufferance*) *recover* myself at the entrance of a *third person,* and that my *servant* too; and shall I not have a due *respect* for the dictates of my own *conscience;*

[To be spoken with the *right hand* on the *breast.*] [26]

Steele claimed to have written the play for the sake of this scene—and as a trope of self-mastery under extreme provocation, it would be hard to excel. In it the old chivalric code of honor retreats before modern behavioral constraints. Burgh's marginal Passions show the reader how to act the scene line by line. The jealous lover taunts the exemplary hero with several categories of insult, each more inflammatory than the last, culminating in a slur on the virtue of the heroine. This would seem to be more than flesh can bear, but Bevil's is no ordinary flesh. Flaring up momentarily ("Anger roused"), he orders a servant to send a carriage to carry the two antagonists to a dueling place (*"Authority. . . . See Gravity"*). The exertion of his authority, the subjection of his servant ("Trep[idation] with submission"), the long silence that follows, bring him to his senses ("Recollect[ion]").

This sequence recapitulates in miniature the action of the entire play, which is a narrative of denial and self-mastery. This displacement of Young Bevil's anger in his order to a submissive menial is a characteristic and effective touch. By commanding his servant, he recollects and is able to command himself. Myrtle doubles his friend here, permitting the externalized representation of a violence of feeling over which Bevil can eventually triumph. The physical contrasts highlight both the dangerously antisocial consequences of Passions unleashed and the utility of their confinement within limits defined by gestures that can be inscribed as style. The exchange ends with a line that Burgh scores with "Admiration": "O Bevil! You are capable of all that is great, all that is *heroic.*"[27] Myrtle's Passion is mastered by Bevil after a fierce struggle (much as Nicolino slew the lion with great gallantry) as the dramatic embodiment of the subjection of his own nature.

Steele recognized that only performance could effect the embodiment of morality as style: "a play is to be seen and is made to be represented with the advantage of action" (p. 5). What has not been adequately appreciated is the dramaturgical thoroughness with which he created opportunities for the performers to realize his goals. *The Conscious Lovers* does not set out to reform the stage by repressing sex; rather, it makes the power of sexuality the main subject that the lovers are conscious of, an emphasis Steele deferred to gesture and corporeal expression. Of one character the text promises: "in one motion she speaks and describes herself better than all the words in the world can" (I.i.247–249). The sophistication of Steele's deployment of sexuality onstage makes Etherege's libertine posturing seem adolescent by comparison. *The Conscious Lovers,* long thought part of a reform movement directed at prohibition and censorship, actually takes a part in the immensely productive discursive network defined by Foucault in *The History of Sexuality:* "Toward the beginning of the eighteenth century, there emerged a political, economic, and technical incitement to talk about sex."[28]

Steele's principal stratagem, following the example of the contemporary opera, turns on the sexual neutralization, the effective castration of the hero. Asked why he does not confess his love to Indiana, Bevil Jr. replies: "My tender obligations to my father have laid so inviolable a restraint upon my conduct that, till I have his consent to speak, I am determined on that subject to be dumb forever" (I.ii.225–227). As the father authors the son's bodily self-discipline, Indiana's very existence, such as it is, depends on her circumscribed hero: "All the rest of my life is but waiting till he comes. I live only when I'm with him" (II.ii.118–119). Even the actors' silences enunciate this acute awareness—the lovers' consciousness of the power that flows from their ability to control their own and one another's bodies. "Alas, what machines are we!" as Bevil Jr. wistfully puts it (IV.i.196).

The interview in act II, scene ii, between Bevil Jr. and Indiana, her name redolent of the charms of colonization, features a discussion of the sensual appeal of two recent operas of Bononcini, a way for the lovers to talk of love and its constraints by talking about another kind of performance that demands the utmost physical control. A musical interlude follows. Steele originally intended a song depicting the "distress of a lovesick maid" (p. 6). The words were cut for want of a singer, but the languid tune was played by Signior Carbonelli on the violin. The lovers respond in silence, but with great expressiveness. Their inhibitions are pressed to the limit here, as the implied stage direction subsequently given by Indiana's duenna suggests: "I saw the respectful downcast of his eye when you catcht him gazing at you during the music. He, I warrant, was surprised, as if he had been taken stealing your watch. Oh, the undissembled guilty look" (II.ii.308–312). This unsung interlude had the effect of operatic *ritornello*, and it was clearly meant to remind the audience of the kind of business that went on during one. Bevil Jr. is a virtuoso of self-denial.

It will be recalled that Casanova was inflamed by the modest revolution of the black eyes of the travestied *castrato*. Like Casanova, Steele would particularize the physical movements of the various parts of the body as it emotes in silence. The kind of stage business Steele imagined for his actors in *The Conscious Lovers* may be further amplified by the business he most admired in all the *Tatler* essays, the *ritornelli* of the *castrato* Nicolino in the role of Pyrrhus. Here he provides an eyewitness summary even more alert than Casanova's to the style of castration and its powers of signification on the eighteenth-century stage:

> For my own part I was fully satisfied with the sight of an actor, who, by the grace and propriety of his action and gesture, does honour to the human figure. Every one will imagine I mean Signior Nicolini, who sets off the character he bears in an opera by his action, as much as he does the words of it by his voice. Every limb and every finger

contributes to the part he acts, inasmuch that a deaf man may go along with him in the sense of it. There is scarce a beautiful posture in an old statue which he does not plant himself in, as the different circumstances of the story give occasion for it. He performs the most ordinary action in a manner suitable to the greatness of his character, and shows the prince even in the giving of a letter, or dispatching of a messenger. Our best actors are somewhat at a loss to support themselves with proper gesture, as they move from any considerable distance to the front of the stage; but I have seen the person of whom I am now speaking enter alone at the remotest part of it, and advance from it with such greatness of air and mien as seemed to fill the stage, and, at the same time, commanded the attention of the audience with the majesty of his appearance.[29]

The central motive in Steele's admiration of the *castrato* is self-mastery. The body becomes the site for a theatre of subjection. It is defined completely by the external ideals it imitates: the human figure is honored to the extent it aspires to the condition of statuary. It gives a letter or dispatches a messenger with an authority that dramatizes the technical efficiency of its self-control. This is the technology of power as embodied in eighteenth-century theatrical performance. No gesture need be wasted when morality is so perfectly inscribed. "In fact, power produces," Foucault observes; "it produces reality."[30] Style is social order as lived in the body.

But to what extent is eighteenth-century performance a period style, a discontinuity, a superannuated ritual like the massacre of cats? It is tempting to retrace the triumph of organicism in the style of modern acting, its wholesomeness shaming the perversities of the long ago and far away. But the mortifications of the flesh imposed by the technologies of castration place more contemporary theatrical disciplines, particularly the ascetic rigors of ballet, in an illuminating context. The ballerina's body might be interpreted as the focus of both desire and subjection.[31] Like the secular rituals of eighteenth-century performance, her discipline at the *barre* and before the studio mirror translates ideology into precisely elaborated exemplary behavior. Hers is an art of the most rigorous placement. It mediates between the discursive strategies of "sexuality" and the micropolitical practices of denial and exhibition. A sacrifice to virtuosity, the ballerina's body, like the singer's larynx of yesteryear, is tortured into shapes and launched into trajectories that are not in nature. Liminal, feline, poised between worlds, she provides a whitened surface upon which the contemporary audience beholds the contradictory projections of its own idealizing, self-reflexive, and dismembering gaze.

Reading Gelsey Kirkland's autobiography, as she describes the neo-*castrati* of Lincoln Center, gives the theatre historian a sense of déjà vu. The distortions of exaggerated turnout and *pointe,* the misalignments working their way up through the spine, the overprescription of Butazolidin (an anti-inflammatory drug used to treat tendonitis in racehorses and ballerinas), the stressed ligaments and joints, the slow anorexic diminution of the flesh—all these combine to produce a body of a highly specialized type, powerfully charged with dual meanings. It is the body of a child of larger growth, linear, breastless, neutralized by starvation and hyperextension, its startling movements as denatured as its invisible processes, normalized neither by gravity nor by menstruation. Yet *normally* every little girl learns to dream of becoming one. Her parents validate her longing to be styled to skeletal concision by techniques that do not exclude bulimia, to imagine herself infinitely supple before the tyrannies of a certain perfect line, and to suffer herself to be supported weightlessly aloft, pliant limbs unresisting in the grasp of strong, shaping hands. The ballerina's solo affirms the moral efficacy of her aesthetic self-immolation. The duet inscribes the ideal of submissiveness on whatever is left of her flesh. We cannot really hide in history our complicit knowledge of the kind of social relationships she doubles. In our rituals of truth, there can be no innocent beauty and no motiveless style.

NOTES

1 Robert Darnton, "Workers' Revolt: The Great Cat Massacre of the Rue Saint-Séverin," in *The Great Cat Massacre and Other Episodes in French Cultural History* (1984; New York: Vintage Books, 1985), pp. 78, 89–90.

2 See especially Bruce A. McConachie, "Towards a Postpositivist Theatre History," *Theatre Journal* 37 (1985), 465–486.

3 The most useful work to date is the anthology of excerpts collected and translated by Dene Barnett, "The Performance Practice of Acting: The Eighteenth Century," *Theatre Research International* 2–6 (1977–1981), parts I–V, 157–186, 1–19, 79–93, 1–36, 1–32.

4 Foucault first came to the attention of readers in several disciplines with the publication of the astringent *Madness and Civilization: A History of Insanity in the Age of Reason,* trans. Richard Howard (1961; rpt. New York: Vintage Books, 1973) and *The Birth of the Clinic: An Archaeology of Medical Perception,* trans.

A. M. Sheridan Smith (1963; rpt. New York: Vintage Books, 1975). Far less fiercely preoccupied than many historians with the autonomy of the peculiar, Foucault with his "archaeologies" excavates the juxtaposition of spaces, statements, and practices, reaching out to encompass relationships he calls "discursive formations" in those broad frames of historical reference he articulated in *The Order of Things: An Archaeology of the Human Sciences* (1966; rpt. New York: Vintage Books, 1973) and *The Archaeology of Knowledge and the Discourse on Language,* trans. A. M. Sheridan Smith (1969; New York: Pantheon Books, 1972). These studies analyze disciplines such as natural history, political economy, general grammar, and clinical medicine as discursive networks, characterized by the sorts of statements and practices they will admit or exclude. For generally helpful commentary, see *Foucault: A Critical Reader,* ed. David Couzens Hoy (New York: Basil Blackwell, 1986).

5 See Nancy Fraser, "Foucault's Body Language: A Post-Humanist Political Rhetoric?" *Salmagundi* 61 (1983), 55–70. Cf. Harry Berger, Jr., "Bodies and Texts," *Representations* 17 (1987), 144–166.

6 Michel Foucault, "The History of Sexuality," in *Power/Knowledge: Selected Interviews and Other Writings, 1972–1977,* trans. Colin Gordon et al., ed. Colin Gordon (1972; rpt. New York: Pantheon Books, 1980), p. 186.

7 Michel Foucault, *The History of Sexuality,* trans. Robert Hurley (1976; rpt. New York: Vintage Books, 1980), I, 139.

8 Angus Heriot, *The Castrati in Opera* (1956; rpt. New York: Da Capo, 1975).

9 A notable exception is the urbanely magisterial *Biographical Dictionary of Actors, Actresses, Musicians, Dancers, Managers, and Other Stage Personnel in London, 1660–1800,* ed. Philip Highfill, Kalman Burnim, and Edward Langhans (Carbondale and Edwardsville: Southern Illinois University Press, 1973–), s.v. "Nicolini" and "Farinelli." See also Jill Campbell's important essay, "'When Men Women Turn': Gender Reversals in Fielding's Plays," in *The New Eighteenth Century: Theory, Politics, English Literature,* ed. Felicity Nussbaum and Laura Brown (New York and London: Methuen, 1987), pp. 62–83.

10 Giacomo Girolamo Casanova de Seingalt, *History of My Life,* trans. Willard R. Trask (New York: Harcourt, Brace Jovanovich, 1966–1971), VII, 250–251.

11 *Goethe's Travels in Italy,* trans. J. W. Morrison and Charles Nisbet (London: George Bell and Sons, 1892), pp. 567–568.

12 *The Complete Letters of Lady Mary Wortley Montagu,* ed. Robert Halsband (Oxford: Clarendon Press, 1965), I, 22–23.

13 "The Signior in Fashion: or the Fair Maid's Conveniency; A Poem on Nicolini's Musick-Meeting," in T. J. Walsh, *Opera in Dublin* (Dublin: Allen Figgis, 1973), p. 314.

14 *Spectator,* March 15, 1711.

15 René Girard, *Violence and the Sacred,* trans. Patrick Gregory (1972; rpt. Baltimore: Johns Hopkins University Press, 1977), pp. 160–164, 251–252, 272–273.

16 *Roger North on Music,* ed. John Wilson (London: Novello, 1959), pp. 128, 129n.

17 Roland Barthes, *S/Z*, trans. Richard Miller (1970; rpt. New York: Hill and Wang, 1974), p. 170.

18 Heriot, *The Castrati*, p. 61n.

19 Ibid., pp. 44, 48.

20 *The Works of Monsieur Noverre* (1782–1783; rpt. New York: AMS, 1978), I, 59.

21 Lincoln Kirstein, *Dance: A Short History of Classic Theatrical Dancing* (1935; rpt. New York: Dance Horizons, 1969), p. 251.

22 Foucault, "Prison Talk," in *Power/Knowledge*, p. 39.

23 Foucault, *History of Sexuality*, I, 62. See Ronald G. Engle, "Lang's *Discourse on Stage Movement*," *Educational Theatre Journal* 22 (1970), 179–187.

24 James Burgh, *The Art of Speaking* (1761; rpt. Baltimore: John W. Butler, 1804), pp. 19–23.

25 Richard Steele, *The Conscious Lovers*, ed. Shirley Strum Kenney (Lincoln: University of Nebraska Press, 1968), p. 5. Subsequent citations from this edition are given in the text.

26 Burgh, *The Art of Speaking*, p. 118.

27 Ibid., p. 119.

28 Foucault, *The History of Sexuality*, I, 23. For the place of *The Conscious Lovers* in the reform movement, see John Loftis, *Steele at Drury Lane* (Berkeley and Los Angeles: University of California Press, 1952), pp. 183–213.

29 *Tatler*, January 3, 1709/1710. For the connections between Barton Booth, the actor who created the role of Bevil Jr., and Nicolino, see my "Cavaliere Nicolini: London's First Opera Star," *Educational Theatre Journal* 28 (1976), 189–205.

30 Foucault, *Discipline and Punish: The Birth of the Prison*, trans. Alan Sheridan (1975; rpt. New York: Vintage Books, 1979), p. 194.

31 See Judith Lynne Hanna, *Dance, Sex and Gender: Signs of Identity, Dominance, Defiance and Desire* (Chicago: University of Chicago Press, 1988), pp. 122–136.

Opera as Historical Drama
La Clemenza di Tito, Khovanshchina, Moses und Aron

Herbert Lindenberger

The title of these remarks brings together two generic categories—opera and historical drama—that are not precisely parallel to or commensurate with one another. We can define opera, after all, by its formal properties, as in its use of music to represent human speech. Historical drama, by contrast, tends to be defined by its subject matter—for example, its use of such materials from public history as conspiracies or the rise and fall of rulers. As a form, historical drama remains a subcategory within spoken drama—and by no means one that, like tragedy or comedy, has been easy to classify, for it can coexist with either of these dramatic forms—indeed, sometimes partake of both at once.

Yet opera and historical drama, however different the criteria by which we define each, have exhibited a natural affinity to one another ever since the composition of the first operas on historical themes early in the seventeenth century.[1] Except for comic operas, Italian opera until well into the nineteenth century drew its plots chiefly from historical, or purportedly historical, narratives. Even when opera composers turned to private domestic life, as Verdi did in *La traviata*, they found it necessary to retain the costumes and decor of earlier periods to keep a temporal distance between the audience and the events onstage. History, or at least the semblance of history, has proved a particularly convenient way of establishing that distance between a real and a represented world that opera has traditionally cultivated.

If opera has shown a continuing penchant for representing history, historical drama has often displayed features that we can characterize as operatic in nature. The strongly ceremonial elements in many historical plays—for example, the pageantry marking shows of royal power or the rituals accompanying a character's path to martyrdom—often seem to cry out for musical realization. To audiences acclimated to the full sonorities of operatic style, a historical drama may well seem like an opera manqué. Moreover, within historical plays a feature such as a crowd of citizens venting its anger or praising its leaders rarely lends itself to satisfactory treatment—at least not since the Greeks, who after all had their own, now lost, musical forms to accompany choral speeches. While Shakespeare in *Coriolanus* or Goethe in *Egmont* presented stage directors with challenges they have often struggled in vain to meet, the massive choral forces we find in many nineteenth-century operas allow crowds to function dramatically in much the way that individual characters do.[2]

Despite the fact that music often offers history plays a means of transcending the limits of words alone, the operatic versions of many famous historical dramas and novels have all too often struck their auditors as less substantive in serious historical content than their originals. For example, the auto-da-fé scene that Verdi's librettists added to Schiller's *Don Carlos* in turning the play into a French grand opera, though it extended the play's ceremonial dimensions, is a reminder that opera is less historically reflective than spoken drama. Moreover, the reflectiveness about history that we praise today in works such as Scott's *Old Mortality* and *The Bride of Lammermoor* is notably missing in those celebrated operas, Bellini's *I puritani* and Donizetti's *Lucia di Lammermoor*, that are based on these novels. Among major historical works that have been turned into great operas, perhaps only Musorgsky's *Boris Godunov* elicits praise for its historical seriousness commensurate with that accorded the Pushkin play from which it is derived.

This paper demonstrates that opera over the centuries has cultivated its own ways of articulating history—and in a manner quite distinct from that of nonmusical theatre. I propose to look at three operas widely dispersed in time—Mozart's *La clemenza di Tito,* composed in 1791; Musorgsky's *Khovanshchina,* begun in 1872 and left unfinished at the composer's death in 1881; and Arnold Schönberg's *Moses und Aron,* the first two acts of which were set to music between 1930 and 1932, with the final act left uncomposed, except for some musical sketches, when Schönberg died in 1951. A study of simply the librettos to these works would give only a partial, sometimes even a misleading, indication of how operas function as historical drama. To understand these operas as historical drama, I treat them as works deeply embedded in their own historical worlds—works that themselves embody, often unconsciously, notions about history we now see as peculiar to and representative of their time.

To start with, let me suggest four distinct layers of history within which historical operas participate. First, one can cite that earlier historical period which the opera purportedly tells us about. The three operas I am discussing draw their materials from three of the major areas that historical operas have traditionally been "about": *La clemenza di Tito* derives from classical history, *Khovanshchina* from the composer's national history, *Moses und Aron* from biblical history. A second historical level encompasses events and attitudes of the composer's own time that, from our present point of view, seem relevant to an understanding of each work. *La clemenza di Tito*, for example, was commissioned to celebrate the coronation of Holy Roman Emperor Leopold II as king of Bohemia; *Khovanshchina* voices not only the nationalist impulses common in Musorgsky's generation, but above all the sympathies toward the common people and the desire for social change shared by the Russian intelligentsia during the 1860s and 1870s; *Moses und Aron* was composed soon after Schönberg's return to Judaism at a time when the composer, while witnessing the rise of Nazism and reflecting upon the course of recent Jewish—and in particular Zionist—history, asked himself some fundamental questions about the nature of political leadership.

A third historical level, closely related to the second, consists of those larger ideas about historical change and the uses of history that we, with our own hindsight, can discern underlying each opera. Thus, *La clemenza di Tito* embodies the Enlightenment view that human nature is everywhere and at all times the same, that an incident supposedly from Roman history can serve as an exemplum to enlighten a modern ruler on the virtues of pardoning rather than punishing those who threaten his life. *Khovanshchina*, by contrast, embodies that nineteenth-century view of history we associate with Hegel whereby an older order encumbered by traditional cultural forms gives way to a new order, in this instance the radically new dispensation of Peter the Great. *Moses und Aron*, in a way characteristic of many early modernist writings, treats a crisis drawn from earlier history as at once real and archetypal, and it does not shy away from placing its insights in an explicitly religious and metaphysical framework.

A fourth level of historical meaning is evident in the significations that have accumulated for these works since the composer's time through the interpretive efforts of stage directors, performers, and critics. When *La clemenza di Tito* began to be revived during our time it received a variety of interpretations, for, having been virtually forgotten for a century and a half, it lacked a continuing interpretive history against which new approaches were forced to contend. Thus, a 1970 San Francisco production in modern dress could assert the applicability of the opera to the politics of the Nixon administration, while Jean-Pierre Ponnelle's television production, filmed in the actual ruins of Hadrian's villa with the characters clothed in Roman costumes, in effect asserted the temporal distance separating the ancient Roman setting from the cult of ruins that flourished at the time the opera was composed. A relatively realistic production of *Khovanshchina,* like that designed by Nicola Benois and used in a number of opera houses, works to confirm the late nineteenth century view of history originally propagated by the opera; a less realistic, more stylized production such as those in London and Geneva during the early 1980s would—to judge by photographs of the stage sets—distance the audience from this view, perhaps even make the audience question it.[3] Similarly, a director's choice of a realistic or an abstract approach to *Moses und Aron* would readjust the particular balance of real and archetypal that Schönberg attempted to achieve.[4]

However different the approaches to history one can locate in each of these works, all three show certain striking similarities. All of them, for instance, are structured around conspiracies; as in most historical plays, political plotting becomes a means for organizing dramatic plotting.[5] Thus, *La clemenza di Tito* is built around a frustrated attempt against Emperor Titus by his friend Sextus, who, in the fashion of neoclassical historical plays, is motivated to commit the deed through his attachment to a woman, in this instance the fierce Vitellia, herself motivated at once by private and political concerns; the imperial act of clemency that gives the opera its title works both to resolve the political tensions generated by the conspiracy and to make a didactic statement about the conduct proper to an absolute ruler.

Although Musorgsky eschews the tight classical plotting of Mozart's opera, *Khovanshchina* is built around the struggles that took place during the 1680s among at least three competing political factions who either conspire against one another or accuse one another of conspiring; most of the action consists of plotting and counterplotting until, by the end, all factions go to their defeat in the face of the new order represented by Peter the Great. Of all three operas, *Moses und Aron* contains the most simplified conspiratorial plot—namely, that between Aron and the populace to institute idol worship against the austere strictures pronounced by Moses as spokesman for a jealous Hebrew God.

If operas based on history employ conspiratorial plots in much the same way as nonmusical historical plays, music encourages them to realize another feature common to historical plays—the ceremonial and ritual element latent within their subjects. Indeed, opera can exploit this element in ways that dramatic speech alone could never command. As a recent study of the overture to *La clemenza di Tito* points out, "Trumpets and drums, fanfares, and majestic dotted rhythms betoken the imperial ambience in *Titus*"; as this study goes on to show, the original audience would have associated the elaborate contrapuntal development in the overture with the House of Hapsburg, which, as heir to the Holy Roman Empire, would, by implication, have suggested its connection with the grandeur of ancient Rome.[6] In the course of the opera, Mozart interrupts the succession of arias and small ensemble groups with a march and several choral numbers that work at once to represent and to celebrate imperial power.

The huge historical panorama that Musorgsky created in *Khovanshchina* allowed him to introduce a variety of ceremonial scenes—for example, the oriental exoticism of the opera's most familiar music, the dance of the Persian maidens, or the choruses sung in an archaic mode by the Old Believers as they prepare for their martyrdom. Music, in fact, often allows opera to suggest a certain religious dimension that most historical plays generally touch on lightly, if at all. Thus, the martyrdom of the Old Believers before the triumph of Peter the Great's new order achieves a power and a pathos impossible within nonmusical drama by means of the traditional liturgical forms in which they voice their plight. Among the most gripping musical and dramatic scenes in Musorgsky's opera is the prophecy aria, in which the Old Believer Marfa, the opera's major female character, predicts the downfall of one of the opposing factions; as in much historical drama, prophecy provides a naturalistic means of suggesting a supernatural dimension.[7]

The strongly ceremonial character of *Moses und Aron* manifests itself right from the start, for biblical precedent allows Schönberg to introduce the supernatural through the voice of God emanating from the Burning Bush.[8] By mixing a chorus intoning in *Sprechstimme* with a traditional chorus of singers, Schönberg creates a mysterious divine voice that sounds like nothing anybody has ever heard before in opera or spoken drama. If divinity seems to speak more authentically in musical form than it would as straight dramatic speech, the "negative" ceremony of the Golden Calf scene achieves an orgiastic fury attainable only by the strange rhythms and the unconventional combination of instruments Schönberg uses to accompany the wild doings onstage.

The three works I have chosen to demonstrate the means by which opera becomes historical drama provide compelling examples for several reasons. For one thing, unlike *Don Carlos* and *Boris Godunov*, none derives from a famous play against which one is forced to compare it and to argue for the virtues of one medium in respect to the other—or to debate which version is more "faithful" to history. *La clemenza di Tito* is based on a text that the preeminent eighteenth-century librettist Pietro Metastasio had composed nearly sixty years before and that innumerable composers had set in the meantime;[9] the Metastasio text had, in turn, been based on a few lines from Suetonius. The libretto of *Khovanshchina,* by the composer himself with the help of his advisor Vladimir Stasov, derives from memoirs and scholarly accounts. For *Moses und Aron* Schönberg took a few brief passages from the Old Testament but omitted most of the biblical material about the two brothers.

Moreover, all three of these operas are relatively recent rediscoveries and thus, unlike works with long and continuing interpretive traditions, allow us to approach them with fresh perceptions. To be sure, *La clemenza di Tito* was once one of Mozart's most popular operas and for the first quarter of a century after its composition shared this popularity only with *Don Giovanni* and *Die Zauberflöte*.[10] Largely because the *opera seria* genre came to seem archaic, *Tito* went out of favor early in the nineteenth century, and it remained virtually forgotten until its recent revivals beginning in the 1960s. Although *Khovanshchina,* doubtless because of its relevance to Soviet political concerns, has remained part of the Russian repertory throughout most of this century, it has excited interest in Europe and North America only since the 1960s.[11]

The staging of *Moses und Aron* was delayed during the last two decades of Schönberg's life while he sought—unsuccessfully as it turned out—to compose the text he had prepared for the last act. Even so, despite a concert performance of the first two acts in Hamburg in 1954 and a first staging in Zurich in 1957, the opera did not excite much attention outside avant-garde circles until the London and Paris productions during the 1960s and 1970s demonstrated that what had long been thought a forbidding work could communicate with the larger public. Even though none of these three operas has as yet created a secure place for itself in the international repertory, each has had distinguished and much-publicized productions in a number of major opera houses.

Although *Moses und Aron* retains the status of a fragmentary work—despite frequent assertions that the first two acts constitute a rounded whole—neither of the other two operas was actually completed by its composer. The hurry to which Mozart was subjected in fulfilling his commission for the coronation ceremonies presumably caused him to leave the composition of the recitatives to a student, traditionally thought to be

Süssmayr, who accompanied him to Prague for the rehearsals and the first performance.[12]

The textual status of *Khovanshchina*, like that of all Musorgsky's operas, remains problematic. In this instance, except for the orchestration of two brief passages, only a piano score of the opera was left behind after the composer's death. Musorgsky's friend Rimsky-Korsakov, whose musical aesthetic we now recognize as alien to that of the composer, orchestrated and radically cut the opera; it is Rimsky's version that is still most frequently performed today despite the superiority of Shostakovich's version, which not only restores the cuts but, unlike Rimsky's, attempts to preserve the composer's bold harmonies. To complicate matters further, Musorgsky failed to bring the second act to conclusion and also left the opera's final scene in unconnected fragments—with the result that each arranger has had to decide on the closure appropriate to two uncompleted acts. Both Rimsky and Shostakovich, as it turned out, near the end of the opera reintroduce an earlier martial theme associated with Peter the Great and thus present a view of history, whether or not consonant with the composer's view, that stresses the triumph of the new order.[13]

If Schönberg had been able to complete his last act, audiences might have been left with a somewhat different interpretation of biblical history, for the spiritual triumph that Moses voices over Aron in the words of the uncomposed third act contrasts strikingly with the sense of defeat that Moses admits at the end of the second act, at the very point where performances must perforce break off.

If I have stressed Schönberg's ability to manipulate historical meanings, different though the resolutions may seem at the end of his second and third acts, this is also a consequence of the relative freedom that a modernist composer enjoys. Quite in contrast to Mozart, who composed *Tito* in response to a commission whose political purposes he could not control, Schönberg, who made his living teaching music, did not have to take commercial matters into consideration. Even if he had finished *Moses und Aron* in 1932, he could have hoped at best for occasional productions applauded by a few champions of avant-garde music and derided by most of the operagoing public.

The degree of autonomy that Musorgsky enjoyed in determining the historical statements emerging from his opera was surely closer to that of Schönberg than of Mozart. As author of his own libretto, he could shape the historical events from his sources to suit the notions that he and his populist friends embraced. Although it was long believed that the substantial revisions to which he subjected *Boris Godunov* derived from a fear of censorship and a need to conform to the conventions imposed by the imperial theatre, the Maryinsky, recent scholarship has affirmed the artistic independence and rigorously experimental attitude that characterizes both versions of the opera.[14] When the vocal score of *Khovanshchina* was submitted to the Maryinsky, the unconventionality of *Boris* remained so strongly imprinted in the officials' minds that they rejected the new opera; even after Rimsky's orchestration had been completed, *Khovanshchina* was performed not by the Maryinsky but by an amateur group, and it did not become a part of the Russian repertory until well into our own century.[15] Since the Russian theatres had little tolerance for experimentation and since Musorgsky depended on his job in a government office for his income, he was, in effect, free to treat his theme in as uncompromising a way as he had in *Boris Godunov*—even though this meant, as it would later for Schönberg, that his chances for immediate public performance were meager.

The autonomy that an opera composer can exercise in matching character with voice has often been a register of the freedom he has enjoyed. The relative lack of artistic freedom within the musical world inhabited by Mozart is evident from the fact that the tenor voice that the composer originally intended for the frustrated assassin Sextus gave way to a *castrato,* the voice that was called for in the contract that Mozart's impresario, Domenico Guardasoni, had earlier signed with the Bohemian authorities sponsoring the coronation ceremonies.[16] It would never have occurred to Mozart to compose an opera that had little chance of performance—or of remuneration, for that matter. In contrast, Musorgsky and Schönberg did not work under contract, nor with any immediate plans for performance. Musorgsky could let his musical imagination create the massive choral forces that dominate the opera regardless of whether these would soon be realized on the stage. Since Schönberg did not need to consider the biases of audiences, critics, or donors—only those of his peers and disciples—he could refuse to set his character Moses for any voice that did not suit his aesthetic program; thus, with telling dramatic effect, he could allow Moses to express himself in the conspicuously nonoperatic *Sprechstimme* with which he had experimented in *Pierrot Lunaire* two decades before.[17]

The difficulties that all three of these works experienced before they could be understood and absorbed by the operagoing public may well have to do with the fact that each of them combines what at the time of composition seemed an advanced compositional style with a larger dramatic structure that was distinctly old-style. Although some of the arias of *La clemenza di*

Tito, notably Sextus' "Parto, parto" and Vitellia's rondo "Non più di fiori," sustain a musical interest commensurate with the major arias of the three great comic operas immediately preceding the composition of *Tito,* the *opera seria* form, which went back to the start of the eighteenth century, did not allow those complex dramatic ensembles associated with *opera buffa;* indeed, it is on these ensembles that Mozart's stature as a great musical dramatist rests today. To be sure, the librettist Caterino Mazzolà, who was assigned to work with Mozart on *Tito,* revised Metastasio's clearly old-fashioned dramatic structure through the substitution of several duets and trios, even a quintet, for the long succession of individual arias that marked the *seria* form.[18]

Yet even these revisions were insufficient, after the first quarter of the nineteenth century, to keep the opera from seeming too archaic to hold its place in the repertory with the other late Mozart operas. Wagner's dismissal of *La clemenza di Tito* as "stiff and dry" is a comment at once on the relative backwardness of its dramatic organization and, by implication, on the world of the *ancien régime* for which Metastasio was a famed spokesman and whose prolongation the opera, through the occasion for which it was commissioned, sought to celebrate.[19] Not that Mozart was even appreciated by the objects of his compliments: at the first performance the empress, who was of Spanish Bourbon extraction and who had lived most of her life in Tuscany, was reported to have labeled the opera *porcheria tedesca* (German garbage),[20] perhaps a comment that a local Austrian boy could not possibly beat the Italians at their own game. This negative attitude was not, however, shared by the whole audience, for a contemporary account describes the first-act finale as "lovely enough to lure the gods down to earth."[21]

The notions of musico-dramatic progress that Wagner propagated and that stood behind his rejection of *La clemenza di Tito* have also worked to the detriment of Musorgsky's reputation. Although Musorgsky composed *Khovanshchina* at a time that Wagner's conception of music-drama as a continuous musical flow was fast becoming doctrine in progressive musical circles throughout the rest of Europe, he fiercely resisted the Wagnerian model and constructed his opera according to the more traditional structure that divided a work into a series of discrete numbers. Despite this traditional structure, *Khovanshchina* is innovative in some fundamental ways—for instance, in Musorgsky's attempt here (though less so than in his earlier work) to accommodate the voice line to Russian speech intonations rather than to seek melodic beauty regardless of the words being sung. In *Khovanshchina,* which attempts to make history concrete in the realistic spirit that also motivated Russian prose fiction and painting at the time, the musical imitation of speech intonations in the recitative passages helps create an illusion of verisimilitude by means of which the national past seems to come directly to life.[22] Yet this illusion is, of course, possible only among Slavophone audiences; in Western Europe and America, *Khovanshchina* has communicated mainly with a small elite willing to take the authenticity of its intonations on faith.

Doubtless Musorgsky's most daring musical experimentation lay in his harmonies, which, as it turns out, still remain little known to the public, which has heard his two major operas—as well as his orchestral songs—mainly in the instrumentation of Rimsky-Korsakov; as part of his heroic effort to preserve his friend's name, Rimsky worked assiduously to conventionalize what he viewed as Musorgsky's untutored musical style. Since stylistic progress has been defined largely through the example of Wagner and his followers—an example that Musorgsky strongly resisted—music historians are only now beginning to recognize that Musorgsky's style has its own uniqueness and integrity.

Although Schönberg's use of the twelve-tone system to sustain an extended operatic work would count as progressive according to the prevailing post-Wagnerian model of music history, in its dramatic organization and its employment of large-scale visual and sonic effects *Moses und Aron* remains firmly within the tradition of the Wagnerian *Gesamtkunstwerk*. Despite the overwhelming image that Schönberg presented to the world as an innovator, one might recall that the aesthetic behind the *Gesamtkunstwerk* goes back eighty years before the composition of *Moses und Aron* to Wagner's tract *Oper und Drama,* directly after which Wagner put his theories into practice by composing the *Ring*.[23] Certainly the economics of performing a grand-scale *Gesamtkunstwerk*, even if it does not deter the production of the Wagnerian music-dramas, which audiences have now quite assimilated, must make any impresario think twice about mounting a work with as difficult a musical texture as *Moses und Aron*.

As I have tried to demonstrate thus far, our understanding of how an opera embodies history must go considerably beyond a study of its words and music alone. *La clemenza di Tito* serves as a particularly striking example, not only because the historical occasion for which the opera was composed helps us understand why it differs as greatly as it does from Mozart's other later operas, but also because the text that Mozart set resonates with meanings associated with earlier historical occasions widely separated in time. Metastasio, who served as official poet—*poeta cesareo*—at the imperial court in Vienna, originally wrote the libretto (first set by the composer Antonio Caldara) to celebrate the name day of Charles VI in 1734. In the compliments that the text metes out to rulers who practice clemency, Metastasio, like other court-appointed poets during the age of absolute monarchy, succeeded at once in pleasing his employer and in making a didactic statement that anybody could call morally impeccable.

It is significant that Voltaire, while arguing the superiority of Italian to French recitative in 1748, picked the two most memorable moments from Metastasio's libretto—Titus' confrontation with the guilt-ridden Sextus and the subsequent monologue in which the emperor deliberates whether to grant him clemency—as worthy of Corneille, Racine, and the Greek tragedians at their best. Voltaire's singling out of these passages is far more than an aesthetic judgment—moving though the lines he quotes are, even without any musical setting—it is also a political recommendation, as Voltaire makes quite clear in pointing out that Titus' monologue "should serve as an eternal lesson for all kings."[24] The real-life emperor for whom Metastasio had written his libretto was in fact known for humane qualities similar to those of Titus, though it is also thought that Metastasio's compliments were intended to soothe him for losses he had recently suffered on the battlefield.[25] Certainly, Voltaire would not have viewed a Baroque-style ruler such as Charles VI as an embodiment of Enlightenment ideas. Moreover, the ruler for whom Mozart composed his opera undid some of the famous reforms of his late brother, Joseph II,[26] who has provided the model of the enlightened despot that every schoolchild learns.

Nor would anybody have used the term "enlightened" in its eighteenth-century sense to characterize Cardinal Richelieu, who, nearly a century before Metastasio's text, was the original recipient of the political message intended by the lines that Voltaire praised. As Voltaire well knew, Metastasio's libretto derives much of its plot and above all its treatment of clemency from Corneille's great play *Cinna,* which, although ostensibly about the Emperor Augustus' clemency toward the conspirator Cinna, would have been viewed by its audiences in the early 1640s as a political statement directed to Cardinal Richelieu in his efforts to stabilize the French monarchy against various conspiratorial threats.[27] Metastasio's libretto, one might add, also manages to incorporate elements from two of Racine's tragedies, *Andromaque* and *Bérénice;* the latter, like the libretto, presents a benign portrait of Emperor Titus.[28] I mention these many intertextual connections in order to stress how strongly Mozart's opera, composed as it was 150 years after Corneille's play, creates the illusion of an ahistorical, timeless world in which rulers from widely different periods are interchangeable with one another and in which absolute rule is made to seem noble if it is sufficiently tempered by magnanimity—and in which artists earn their places in the hierarchy, or at least their livelihoods, through the moral sentiments that they praise and recommend to their employers.

From our post-Hegelian vantage point, the timelessness that radiates from *La clemenza di Tito* is radically undercut by the historical realities that lurk beneath the noble images it offers of how rulers rule. Indeed, it would be tempting to note that the 150-year span of the dramatic theme initiated by Corneille is coexistent with what history books call the age of absolute monarchy on the Continent. If Cardinal Richelieu stands at the beginning of a historical development, the reigning monarchs of Mozart's time stand quite conspicuously at its end.

Note, for example, the political events that we can now view as backdrops to the opera. Three months before its first performance, Marie-Antoinette, sister of the monarch whom Mozart was honoring, lost her final opportunity to escape from France through her capture at Varennes—though she was not to be executed for another two years. Certainly, Emperor Leopold's sister by 1791 was in no position to disburse clemency or even the cake she had supposedly once recommended to a rebellious populace. Moreover, in late August, while Mozart was composing the opera, Leopold, together with the king of Prussia, issued the Declaration of Pillnitz; this turned out to be an ambiguous document, for although it intended to leave open the question of whether Austria would attack the French revolutionary government, it actually rallied the revolutionists to the point that, in the following year, they began the war that was to change the political structure of Europe for all time. Leopold himself died a natural death before the war started, only half a year after the operatic performance that had honored him; Mozart died only three months after this performance, though not before completing *Die Zauberflöte,* a work that we now praise as an embodiment of Enlightenment humanitarianism.

In view of our own quite self-conscious way of interpreting history, it is tempting to ask if Mozart could have been aware of the historical ironies surrounding the composition of *La clemenza di Tito* and the earlier uses of its text. I for one doubt that he concerned himself much with these matters—though he must have awed his contemporaries to the point that one observer at the coronation ceremonies declared he would prefer being Mozart to being the new emperor himself.[29] Although we have romanticized Mozart with the label "genius"—a term that his own example helped define for the Romantic generation—it is difficult to assign him the prescience by which he could have understood the historical meanings of *La clemenza di Tito* in the way we are likely to construe them. Surely

Mozart was too much a functionary of the social and economic system of the *ancien régime* to have reflected unduly about the political resonances of his operas as, say, Verdi and Musorgsky were to do during the next century. Certainly, the revival of *La clemenza di Tito* in Prague to celebrate the accession of the young emperor Franz Josef during the revolutionary tensions of the year 1848 displayed a typically nineteenth-century reflectiveness, indeed pugnaciousness, about how art can make its political points.[30]

The historical ironies to which Mozart doubtless remained oblivious at the opera's performance in 1791 are, of course, discernible only to those whose view of the past was shaped by that historical consciousness which first developed during the nineteenth century. From our present vantage point, it seems particularly striking—and also ironical—that a theme originating at the beginnings of absolute monarchy in France should be invoked once again in the revolutionary year 1848 to celebrate the coronation of an emperor who, as it turned out, was to continue ruling (though with considerably less than absolute power) until a year before the Russian Revolution.

The historical consciousness largely missing in *La clemenza di Tito* is, of course, central to *Khovanshchina*. This consciousness is, in fact, built into the musical style, not only, as I indicated earlier, in Musorgsky's attempt to imitate the intonation of everyday Russian speech, but above all in his ability to differentiate musically between political factions representing different moments in the historical process. For example, the brisk rhythm of the theme associated with the forces of Peter the Great provides a musical embodiment of the militant new order that will bring an end both to the factionalism of the past and to the traditional religious values represented by the Old Believers.[31]

Contrasting with this theme are the wild choruses in act III sung by the Streltsy, the unruly and boisterous Moscow urban guard that Ivan Khovansky succeeds in bringing under his control and that must ultimately make way for the new order. But Musorgsky provides an additional musical distinction in his depiction of the Old Believers. Shortly before they burn to death in a mass suicide at the end of the opera, they chant a theme in the Phrygian mode, which any Russian listener would associate with the ancient liturgy used during the early centuries of Christianity in Russia. In a letter Musorgsky voiced his conviction that this chorus would create an impression "of old times and truth."[32] To provide this impression Musorgsky researched both liturgical and folk music. The actual folksong that he inserts for his heroine, Marfa, in act III was quite familiar during Musorgsky's time and would probably have suggested a simple, timeless realm to contrast with the rapidly shifting worlds that clash with one another during the course of the opera.

Like a historical novelist such as Walter Scott, Musorgsky treats the outgoing order with a special pathos that is linked to a recognition of its inevitable defeat. It seems no accident that the parts of the opera most moving to listeners are those sung by the Old Believers as a group and by Marfa in particular. Music, of course, can communicate this pathos with an immediacy impossible within narrative prose or even in spoken drama, though the latter form in the nineteenth century often introduced folksongs such as Marfa's to achieve this immediacy. Above all, the varying musical forms in which the warring factions in *Khovanshchina* express themselves enable Musorgsky to represent historical process in a way uniquely different from—and far more economical than—that of the historical novelists and philosophers of history of his century.

If I have implied that *Khovanshchina* propounds a Hegelian view of history,[33] I should add that, by emphasizing the centrality of the populace rather than that of rulers and heroic individuals, it represents a peculiarly late nineteenth century conception of historical process. In preparing the libretto for *Boris Godunov*, Musorgsky had given the populace an even larger role than it had occupied in Pushkin's drama, which is itself regarded as a turning point in the formation of Russian historical consciousness.[34] In *Khovanshchina*, he went still further—to the point that no royalty appears onstage in the later opera.[35] We know Peter the Great only obliquely through his soldiers, while the regent appears only by means of a letter recited by her minister and lover Golitsin. The most powerful individual roles in the opera, except for Marfa, who voices the plight of the Old Believers, are not rulers but political figures such as Ivan Khovansky and Dosifei, whom we witness actively controlling and attempting to lead their forces.

Through the opportunity it gives for the display of large choral forces, opera can characterize the populace to a degree impossible in any other aesthetic form. But Musorgsky's attempt to center his opera around the masses represents far more than the exploitation of an artistic opportunity, as it did for the many nineteenth-century composers who used large choruses to sensationalize history. Rather, his concentration on the masses was an expression of political convictions dominant among the Russian intelligentsia during the 1860s and 1870s—convictions that resulted, moreover, in a radical reinterpretation of the Russian past for which *Khovanshchina* provides a major example. The fact that the composer subtitled the opera "a folk music-drama" and did much of his own research into primary documents such as memoirs, letters, and sermons, not to speak of the ancient music he sought out, is a testament to the power exerted by these convictions. The period that Musorgsky researched was of particular interest to historians of his time, for the composer's generation viewed the years just before the ascendancy of Peter the Great as the end of an authentically Russian culture that Peter was to transform irrevocably into an appendage to Western European culture.[36]

The years during which Musorgsky worked at the opera were also the period in which the so-called populist movement reached its height among the younger members of the intelligentsia; during 1873–1874, for example, many educated young people dressed up in peasant garb and traveled to backward villages to raise peasant consciousness and at the same time to savor the spirit of ancient Russian customs.[37] If *Khovanshchina* had been available to them, they might well have thought they could hear the song of the earth in the folksongs and choral outpourings. "*The finest traits in man's nature* and in the *mass of humanity*," Musorgsky wrote as he began work on the opera, "tirelessly digging through these little-known regions and conquering them—that is the true mission of the artist."[38] But the populist nationalism of *Khovanshchina* was something more than a local Russian phenomenon, for, as Isaiah Berlin puts it in his essay on this opera, the work shares "some of the ideas of William Morris, Ruskin, and Tolstoy: it was part of the opposition to commercialism on the one hand and timeless, contemplative aestheticism on the other." Berlin goes on to place *Khovanshchina* within an intellectual ambience that "looks at history and anthropology for the unique, the individual, the quintessential—the authentic core of a people, a movement, a period, a historic outlook."[39] What in one sense seems a wholly local enterprise is, as Berlin reminds us, part of an international movement that sought to grant universal significance to local particularities.

The panoramic scope that Musorgsky gave his national music-drama is distinctly missing in *Moses und Aron*. Although the forces that Schönberg employs are overwhelming in their massiveness, Schönberg's populace of Hebrews wandering through the Sinai desert is treated with none of the compassion Musorgsky grants his various factions. The crowd in Schönberg functions as the willing participant in Aron's plot to exercise charismatic leadership over the masses. The central dramatic conflict within the opera is not between leader and followers, but between the two brothers, Moses and Aron, who represent contrasting attitudes both about the nature of God's word and about the means by which this word should be transmitted. Whereas Moses is inarticulate and unable to communicate

God's word adequately to the people, Aron communicates with them all too easily—to the point that he can manipulate them like children through playing on their desire to worship tangible images such as the Golden Calf.

Schönberg uses two sharply divergent forms of expression to distinguish the two brothers. By communicating in *Sprechstimme* within an otherwise operatic context, Moses in effect communicates his difficulty in reaching out to others. Boldly contrasting with his way of speaking is the sinuous, even mellifluous tenor line of Aron, who expresses his trickiness in what is virtually a parody of traditional operatic discourse. At many points, Schönberg, by allowing the two brothers to speak simultaneously in their contrasting vocal forms, demonstrates how the range of expressive forms possible in opera allows him to characterize his figures with a directness impossible within nonmusical drama.[40]

It may seem ironic that the *Sprechstimme* Schönberg employs for the speeches of Moses and for the divine voice emanating from the Burning Bush should so powerfully express and represent what we are intended to view as inarticulate or inexpressible. Yet Schönberg, like other modernist artists of his generation, is explicitly concerned with the nature of representation. Whereas a nineteenth-century composer such as Musorgsky could conceive himself representing historical events and processes in all their concreteness, Schönberg in this opera provides not so much a representation of history as a representation of a problem. To put it another way, his thematic concern with the representability of God and with the inarticulateness of Moses becomes a way of foregrounding his formal concern with representation as an aesthetic problem.[41]

Despite the fact that *Moses und Aron* adopts the external form of Wagnerian music-drama, Schönberg has shied away from the often chaotic variety of events that fill a nineteenth-century historical opera such as *Khovanshchina* or *Die Meistersinger,* and he has concentrated instead on working out the implications of the conflict between his two characters. To do so, he has designed his drama with a mathematical precision analogous to that he employed in creating the opera's musical structure out of a single twelve-tone row. A nineteenth-century composer surely would have drawn a greater variety of material than Schönberg did from the biblical source, in which the conflict between Moses and Aron alternates with episodes that depict their collaboration.

The rigor with which Schönberg reduced and manipulated the narrative elements of his source did not allow for a rich and broad historical panorama.[42] It is significant, for instance, that Schönberg originally planned the work as an oratorio that, to judge from the libretto of this early version (never, as it turned out, set to music), would have been dramatically even more austere than the opera.[43] The music of the Golden Calf scene, which Schönberg considered the most "operatic" part of *Moses und Aron*,[44] does not, moreover, attempt to represent a recognizable Near Eastern world as do the many orientalist purple patches to be found in late nineteenth century operas. One need only recall the Near Eastern intervals and rhythms of Musorgsky's Persian dance and compare these with those strange sounds from the Golden Calf scene, which by themselves would not tell audiences what historical milieu they are meant to evoke. Musorgsky calls upon his audiences' associations with what they take to be Near Eastern music, just as he elsewhere claims to represent Russian speech patterns musically; as a result, he creates the illusion that *Khovanshchina* allows a "real" world to unfold before us. By contrast, Schönberg, like other modernist artists, questions the very basis by which we attribute reality to his representations.

Although Schönberg radically narrows the field of action that characterized historical operas during the preceding century, the fraternal conflict around which *Moses und Aron* is centered invites its audience to propose an extraordinarily wide range of meanings. As its origins in oratorio form suggest, *Moses und Aron* can be viewed foremost as a statement of religious faith—above all, faith in the monotheistic God who reveals himself to Moses and whose nature Aron perversely chooses to misread. In a letter written to Alban Berg during the composition of the opera, Schönberg also admits the autobiographical nature of the work.[45] As a religious testament, *Moses und Aron* is deeply embedded in history—on one level, the personal history of its composer, who in the 1920s returned to Judaism after an early conversion to Christianity.[46]

As a narrative concerned with the return of the Jews to Palestine after long exile, the opera refers by implication to public history, above all to certain political and ideological controversies that Schönberg had observed within the Zionist movement. Shortly before starting *Moses und Aron*, Schönberg had, in fact, written a play, *Der biblische Weg* (1926–1927), which speculates on what might have happened if Theodor Herzl, the founder of the Zionist movement, had succeeded in implementing the so-called Uganda project. This project, espoused by Herzl, but rejected by the Zionist Congress in 1903 in favor of holding out until Palestine should become available, would have created an autonomous Jewish state in East Africa.

Although Schönberg's Herzl-like hero, named Max Aruns in the play, succeeds in founding his East African colony, he is later martyred as a result of a conspiracy instigated by Zionists who are opposed to any settlement except for Palestine itself. Just before Max Aruns undergoes martyr-dom, a prophetic figure tells the hero that, as his name implies, he has successfully sought to combine two opposing types of leaders—on one hand, the visionary Moses; on the other, the pragmatic and cunning Aaron.[47] In moving from this play to the opera, Schönberg took two de-cisive steps: first, he shifted from a contemporary to an ancient biblical set-ting; second, he separated the two leadership types that had been uncom-fortably fused within Max Aruns and returned to the biblical archetypes themselves.

Behind the particularities of personal and Jewish history in *Moses und Aron,* one can locate a larger, if also quite implicit, area of significance—namely, the coming to power of the Nazis. Schönberg, one might remem-ber, was living in Berlin at the time. The political atmosphere surrounding the composition of the opera was that of the last years of the Weimar Re-public, during which Hitler was demonstrating how powerfully rhetoric could work to command the devotion of a restless, dissatisfied populace.[48] In view of the fascination felt at the time with the role of an individual leader in effecting change or creating stability within a culture, it is scarcely surprising to find a music-drama obsessed with a crisis in leadership, above all with the vulnerability of the masses to a charismatic leader such as Aron.

Beyond these religious and political levels, one is also tempted to read *Moses und Aron* as an allegory of the avant-garde artist who, like Schönberg himself in the guise of Moses, is too uncompromising and austere a figure to appeal readily to the public. In describing his conception of Moses to a correspondent, Schönberg compared his figure to that of Michelangelo, adding, "He is not at all human."[49] His unbending refusal to allow idol worship, like Schönberg's break with the tonal system, thus becomes an act of visionary leadership against which the masses react with hostility and ingratitude, little recognizing the necessity of this art for the benefit of future generations. By contrast, Aron, like those artists who have con-tinued to pursue the tonal system in music and traditional modes of repre-sentation in fiction and painting, pursues leadership with a slickness of manner that sacrifices later recognition in favor of immediate popularity. As an allegory about the fate of the artist, *Moses und Aron* stands as a pecu-liarly modern type of historical drama, for in our own century the political actions within the aesthetic realm have achieved the status of public history analogous to those that take place in that area we have traditionally labeled political.

What holds together these seemingly diverse areas of significance—the religious, the political, and the aesthetic—is Schönberg's concern for the way a leader can translate his visions effectively within the practical world. "A Four-Point Program for Jewry," a document that Schönberg wrote in English in 1938 but that was not published until 1979, explicitly links the political and the aesthetic realms to indicate what the composer considers the proper conduct of a leader. For example, he criticizes Herzl for refusing to play a dictatorial role and instead allowing the Zionist Congress to overrule him on the Uganda issue. By contrast, he points to his own conduct as leader of an avant-garde musical society, the Society for Private Musical Performances: "I was a kind of dictator, 1920, in a musical society erected by myself in my ideas." When a dissident group within the society sought to oppose his principles, Schönberg tells us with pride that he clamped down ruthlessly: "I did something which under other circumstances could be called illegal: I dissolved the whole society, built a new one, accepted only such members who were in perfect agreement with my artistic principles and excluded the entire opposition."[50]

If the political power that Schönberg exercised within the aesthetic realm seems a small matter in comparison with the exercise of power over masses of people, one might note that in this same document Schönberg briefly refers to certain ambitions that he himself entertained to exercising leadership over a large Jewish movement.[51] In 1933, he had in fact written a letter to several Jewish musicians expressing these ambitions: "Therefore, I wish to create a movement that will bring the Jews together again as a people and unite them as a state within an enclosed territory."[52] Schönberg's political aspirations, though they never became translated into real-life actions, were scarcely a whim of the moment; some fifteen years later, he drafted a document (still unpublished) announcing the formation of a Jewish government in exile, of which, in words that betray a confidence in his right to lead similar to that of his character Moses, he declares himself president: "Here I am, Arn Sch, the president of the Government in Exile of the Jewish Nation on a ship which we have received through the generosity of Pr. Tr. [President Truman], the Am. Government and the Am. People."[53]

One suspects that the dictatorial powers that Schönberg had managed to wield successfully over a small group of avant-garde musicians would likely have had disastrous consequences if exercised in the larger world and that, like his character Max Aruns, the composer might have headed toward a martyr's death. In view of Schönberg's own will to power, one can view *Moses und Aron* as a battleground between the more lofty aspects of power represented by Moses and those meaner aspects represented by Aron. By separating these two aspects of power and placing them within an explicitly religious context, the opera succeeds in idealizing the role of the leader and providing a transcendental authorization for the power he attempts to exercise. The defeat that Moses encounters as a result of Aron's machinations and of the people's fickleness comes to seem a victory, for the providential perspective through which we are asked to view the work makes us recognize the ultimate vindication of Moses' unbending stance on monotheism and representation. The autobiographical and the "religious-philosophical" meanings of the opera that Schönberg suggests at separate points in his correspondence are thus brought together by means of the composer's attempt to find a divine sanction for the calling he felt to exercise leadership.

In the course of this paper, I have tried to show that depictions of history in opera are themselves very much implicated in what we take to be history itself. Schönberg's obsession with power and leadership within both the musical community and the larger world; Musorgsky's coupling of his generation's populist sentiments with a Hegelian view of historical process in his picture of seventeenth-century political conflicts; Mozart's celebration of the next-to-last Holy Roman emperor by means of a text celebrating an earlier emperor and itself echoing a text that praises a founder of absolute monarchy in France—and all these texts purportedly about the first and tenth ancient Roman emperors—such entanglements are typical of the engagements between opera and the public realm throughout the history of the form.

Similar entanglements mark those other art forms that seek to represent history—history plays, historical novels, historical paintings, and also, as we have come to recognize in recent years, those historical narratives that disclaim fictiveness in favor of telling as it really was. What separates historical operas from these other historical forms is the essential lack of seriousness that has traditionally been attributed to opera in comparison with the other genres that make claims on history. We tend to think of opera as "sensuous" rather than intellectual, as a mode of entertainment rather than of enlightenment. Even though historical narratives that claim to be telling the truth have been taken more seriously than the more overtly fictive forms, at particular times—for example, the historical novel and historical painting during the early nineteenth century—these fictive forms have achieved a high degree of prestige for their ability to represent aspects of the past that elude the more truth-directed modes of historical narration. Opera has rarely been accorded such prestige:[54] indeed, the phrase "historical opera" itself sounds awkward—partly because of the lack of seriousness generally ascribed to opera, partly also because for a long stretch of operatic history all noncomic operas pretended to draw their materials from history.

Throughout this paper, I have tried to show that the seriousness of an opera's engagement with history can be understood not simply by examining the work itself, but by asking precisely how it speaks out as history. The history we see in opera exists at once inside and outside the work—above all, in that interplay between what we ordinarily call a work of art and its context. The history we experience in Mozart's coronation opera derives, on one level, from its celebration of an idealized ruler's power to reconcile dissident factions and, on another level, from our awareness of the gap that separates Mozart's idealization from a rapidly changing world that would soon develop new images—for example, those of *Fidelio* little more than a decade later—to make sense of its political life. The history voiced in *Khovanshchina* is the clash of forces that speak in diverse musical styles to represent diverse stages within the historical process. The history that emanates from *Moses und Aron* reveals the composer's despair at the difficulties of political leadership in the modern world: after having represented these difficulties in the two irreconcilable sides of his dramatic hero Max Aruns, Schönberg in the opera divided his hero into two figures who speak in distinct vocal styles that themselves define distinct types of leadership.

The ceremonial elements that opera can exploit, together with its use of musical styles to define conflicting attitudes, allow the form to create images of history uniquely different from those we find in other forms of historical representation. Like historical drama and the historical novel, opera thrives on the conflicts of history—yet the very sensuousness that prevents its being taken as seriously as these other genres also allows it to represent these conflicts with an intensity and a transformative power impossible to achieve without musical means. Through its peculiar mode of representation, opera tests and expands our notion of what properly belongs to that domain we label history.

NOTES

1 For some brief discussions of opera as a branch of historical drama, as well as of the operatic nature of much historical drama, see my study *Historical Drama: The Relation of Literature and Reality* (Chicago: University of Chicago Press, 1975), pp. 48, 50, 60–63, 66, 68, 80–81, 124. For discussions of historical drama as a branch of opera, see my study *Opera: The Extravagant Art* (Ithaca: Cornell University Press, 1984), pp. 68, 256–284. The title of the present essay deliber-

ately plays on the titles of both these studies, for it attempts to relate the two concepts without treating either as simply a branch or subtype of the other.

2 On crowd scenes in history plays, see *Historical Drama*, pp. 4, 146–153, 161–162. For crowd scenes in opera, see *Opera*, pp. 34–36.

3 Photographs of these productions are reproduced in the issue of *L'Avant-Scène* devoted largely to *Khovanshchina* (57/58 [November/December 1983]), pp. 84, 92, 108, 160–161, 164–165. For photographs of the traditionally realistic Benois production, see pp. 56, 65, 72, 97, 102.

4 Although he never witnessed the staging of his opera during his lifetime, Schönberg left detailed instructions for the work's scenic embodiment that show a desire for both realism, as in the scenic backdrop and the depiction of the miracles, and abstraction, as in the ritualistic approach he takes to the configuration of characters on the stage and the attitudes they display to one another. See *Moses und Aron* in *Sämtliche Werke*, section III, series A, ed. Christian Martin Schmidt (Mainz: B. Schott's Söhne; and Vienna: Universal Edition, 1977), VIII/I, 5–6.

5 On the relation of conspiracies to the structure of history plays, see *Historical Drama*, pp. 30–38.

6 See Daniel Heartz, "Mozart's Overture to *Titus* as Dramatic Argument," *Musical Quarterly* 64 (1978), 32, 49. On the festiveness that permeates the overture, see Stefan Kunze, *Mozarts Opern* (Stuttgart: Reclam, 1984), pp. 552–553.

7 On Marfa's priestesslike function not only in this scene but throughout the opera, see Marie-François Vieulle, "Marfa ou la flamme à la question," in *L'Avant-Scène*, pp. 124–131. On the composer's intention to present Marfa as a realistically motivated character who uses prophecy for political ends, see his letter of August 6, 1873, to Vladimir Stasov in *The Musorgsky Reader*, ed. and trans. Jay Leyda and Sergei Bertensson (New York: Norton, 1947), pp. 239–241.

8 For a superb analysis of the ceremonial nature of this opera, see Theodor W. Adorno, "Sakrales Fragment: Über Schönberg's *Moses und Aron*," *Gesammelte Schriften*, ed. Rolf Tiedemann (Frankfurt: Suhrkamp, 1978), XVI, 454–475.

9 Well over thirty composers had set the libretto before Mozart got to it, while at least five settings, the last in 1839, were completed after Mozart's. For a list of these settings, see Pietro Metastasio, *Tutte le opere*, 2nd ed., ed. Bruno Brunelli (Milan: Mondadori, 1953), I, 1498–1499.

10 On the early reception of *La clemenza di Tito*, see A. Hyatt King, *Mozart in Retrospect: Studies in Criticism and Bibliography* (London: Oxford University Press, 1955), pp. 11–13, and Karl Gustav Fellerer, "Zur Rezeption von Mozarts Oper um die Wende des 18./19. Jahrhunderts," *Mozart-Jahrbuch 1965–1966* (Salzburg: Zentralinstitut für Mozartforschung, 1967), pp. 39–49. Both sources provide statistics on the frequency of early performances and the publication of scores; in addition, Fellerer charts transcriptions and the publication of segments of the operas. All these findings attest to the great popularity of *La clemenza di Tito* around 1800.

11 For the reception of *Khovanshchina,* see the lists of productions in *L'Avant-Scène,* pp. 173–189.

12 For a discussion of the problems in attributing the composition of the recitatives, see Franz Giegling, "Zu den Rezitativen von Mozarts Oper 'Titus,'" *Mozart-Jahrbuch 1967* (Salzburg: Zentralinstitut für Mozartforschung, 1968), pp. 121–126. The *secco* recitatives in Mozart's autograph of the opera are neither in Mozart's handwriting nor in Süssmayr's. Giegling argues against the possibility of Mozart's authorship of the recitatives by demonstrating a considerably greater musical sophistication in the recitatives that Mozart composed for two of his two earlier *opere serie, Mitridate* and *Idomeneo.*

13 For comparisons of the various realizations of Musorgsky's piano score, see André Lischke, "Les versions de la Khovantchina," in *L'Avant-Scène,* pp. 110–119, and Edward R. Reilly, *The Music of Mussorgsky: A Guide to the Editions* (New York: Musical Newsletter, 1980), pp. 19–21. A critical edition of Musorgsky's piano score is available in Modest Mussorgsky, *Complete Works,* ed. Paul Lamm (New York: Edwin F. Kalmus, n.d.), IV.

14 See Richard Taruskin, "Musorgsky *vs.* Musorgsky: The Versions of *Boris Godunov,*" *Nineteenth Century Music* 8 (1984–1985), 91–118, 245–272.

15 On the early difficulties in getting the work performed, see the program note, "*Khovanshchina,*" written by Isaiah Berlin for a Covent Garden production and reprinted in the *Khovanshchina* program issued by the San Francisco opera, fall season, 1984, p. 40.

16 Mozart's original intention to make a tenor out of Sextus, a part that in earlier settings of the opera had customarily been set for *castrato,* is evident from early sketches. See R. B. Moberly, "The Influence of French Classical Drama on Mozart's 'La clemenza di Tito,'" *Music and Letters* 55 (1974), 291–292. The contract between the Bohemian authorities and Guardasoni is reproduced by Tomislav Volek, "Über den Ursprung von Mozarts Oper 'La clemenza di Tito,'" *Mozart Jahrbuch 1959* (Salzburg: Zentralinstitut für Mozartforschung, 1960), pp. 281–282. The first Sextus was the *castrato* Domenico Bedini. Early studies of the opera, through a misunderstanding of the documents at hand, assumed that Bedini sang Annius. The misunderstanding was cleared up by J. A. Westrup in his article "Two First Performances: Monteverdi's 'Orfeo' and Mozart's 'La clemenza di Tito,'" *Music and Letters* 39 (1958), 333–335.

17 On the history of Schönberg's experiments with *Sprechstimme,* above all the difficulties he encountered getting performers to realize his intentions, see Peter Stadlen, "Schönberg's Speech-song," *Music and Letters* 62 (1981), 1–11.

18 For an analysis of Mazzolà's revisions to Metastasio's libretto, see Franz Giegling, "Metastasios Oper 'La clemenza di Tito' in der Bearbeitung durch Mazzolà," *Mozart-Jahrbuch 1968–1970* (Salzburg: Zentralinstitut für Mozartforschung, 1970), pp. 88–94. The dramatic and ceremonial elements that give Mozart's opera its peculiar character could not have manifested themselves if Mozart simply had set Metastasio's original text without Mazzolà's revisions; for ex-

ample, the interchanges between the soloists and the chorus with which Mazzolà ended each act enabled Mozart to create climactic ensembles quite alien to both the letter and the spirit of the older *opera seria*. Daniel Heartz, through a demonstration of how closely the opera reflects changes in *opera seria* style among Italian composers of the 1780s, has challenged the long-standing notion that *Tito* is a "backward" work in its dramatic organization and musical style. See "Mozart and His Italian Contemporaries: 'La clemenza di Tito,'" *Mozart-Jahrbuch 1978–1979* (Kassel: Bärenreiter, 1979), pp. 275–293. Note especially his assertion that Tito "was the most modishly up-to-date work that he [Mozart] left" (p. 292). However, "up-to-date" Mozart's upgrading of the *opera seria* form may have seemed during the 1790s, by the mid-nineteenth century, once the work of his Italian contemporaries had been forgotten, *La clemenza di Tito*, like Mozart's earlier *opere serie*, was automatically associated with a genre that had not only died out but was bound to an extinct social order.

19 "Mozart knew [the tragic muse] only behind the mask of the Metastasian *opera seria*: stiff and dry—*Clemenza di Tito*" ("Über die Anwendung der Musik auf das Drama," in *Gesammelte Schriften*, ed. Julius Kapp [Leipzig: Hesse und Becker, n.d.], XIII, 285). The statement dates from 1879.

20 Reported in Oscar Teuber, *Geschichte des Prager Theaters* (Prague: A. Haase), II (1885), 267.

21 According to Teuber, these words appeared in the diary of a Professor G. A. Meissner (see ibid., p. 268). The same words appear in the anonymously published memoir *Fantasien auf einer Reise nach Prag* (Dresden and Leipzig: Richtersche Buchhandlung, 1792), p. 119. If Teuber is correct in his attribution, for which he provides no documentation, the author of this memoir is Meissner. According to the Österreichische Nationalbibliothek, a photograph of whose copy I have examined, the author is Franz von Kleist, uncle of the dramatist.

22 On the history of Musorgsky's experiments with speech rhythms, above all in his early fragment *The Marriage*, see Richard Taruskin, *Opera and Drama in Russia: As Preached and Practiced in the 1860's* (Ann Arbor: UMI Research Press, 1981), pp. 307–325. Nowhere in his later work was Musorgsky as radically experimental with speech intonations as he had been in his early fragment *The Marriage*, which could be described as totally recitative in style without any lyrical relief whatsoever. For a trenchant analysis of Musorgsky's innovativeness in general, see Carl Dahlhaus, "Musorgskij in der Musikgeschichte des 19. Jahrhunderts," in "Modest Musorgskij: Aspekte des Opernwerks," ed. Heinz-Klaus Metzger and Rainer Riehn, *Musik-Konzepte* 21 (September 1981), 7–22. On the relationship of *Khovanshchina* to earlier operatic form, see the article "*Chovanscina*" by Mario Baroni in the same volume, pp. 69–94.

23 For the continuity of the Wagnerian aesthetic down to Schönberg, see Joseph Kerman, "Wagner: Thoughts Out of Season," *Hudson Review* 13 (1960), 329–349. Adorno analyzes *Moses und Aron* as a Wagnerian music-drama in "Sakrales Fragment," pp. 466–470. For some detailed descriptions of how *Moses und Aron*

builds upon nineteenth-century musical style and organization, see Pamela C. White, *Schoenberg and the God-Idea: The Opera Moses und Aron* (Ann Arbor: UMI Research Press, 1985), pp. 118–129, 138–150, 160–234. White stresses, for instance, Schönberg's development of Wagnerian *Leitmotive* as a means of musical narration as well as his way of finding "equivalents" for modulation outside the tonal system.

24 " . . . these other lines should serve as an eternal lesson for all kings and as a spell for all mankind. . . . These two scenes, comparable, if not superior, to all that was most beautiful in ancient Greece; these two scenes, worthy of Corneille when he is not declaiming, and of Racine when he is not thin" ("Dissertation sur la tragèdie," in *Oeuvres complètes* [Paris: Garnier, 1877], IV, 491–492). Since the two passages praised by Voltaire appear as recitatives, they were evidently not set to music by Mozart, but by whichever assistant composed the recitatives; one might note that Giegling, in his article on the recitatives to the opera, singles out the setting of these very two passages as examples of inferior musical writing ("Zu den Rezitativen von Mozarts Oper 'Titus,'" pp. 123–124).

25 For the historical circumstances surrounding Metastasio's libretto, see Adam Wandruszka, "Die 'Clementia Austriaca' und der aufgeklärte Absolutismus: Zum politischen und ideelen Hintergrund von 'La clemenza di Tito,'" *Österreichische Musikzeitschrift* 31 (1976), 187–188.

26 Wandruszka mentions analogies made between Leopold and Titus during the former's lifetime (ibid., p. 191); he also presents a more positive portrait of Leopold, especially in relation to Joseph II, than historians generally accept.

27 The particular conspiracy that stands behind *Cinna* has long been a matter of scholarly conjecture; it has sometimes been thought that Corneille used the play as a means of asking Richelieu's clemency toward those responsible for a rebellion in the playwright's native city of Rouen. For a review of several theories, see Henry Carrington Lancaster, *A History of French Dramatic Literature in the Seventeenth Century* (Baltimore: Johns Hopkins University Press, 1932), III/II, 312–314. For a discussion of Corneille's relationship to French politics and political theory of his time, see Paul Bénichou, *Morales du Grand Siècle* (Paris: Gallimard, 1948), pp. 52–76.

28 For the complex mixture of earlier French sources in Metastasio's libretto, see Moberly, "The Influence of French Classical Drama on Mozart's "La clemenza di Tito,'" pp. 288–289, 295–297.

29 "Wer möchte nicht heute lieber Mozart als Leopold, der eben Gekrönte, sein?" (Today who wouldn't rather be Mozart than Leopold, the just-crowned monarch?)—attributed by Teuber to the diary of the same Meissner who had praised the finale of the first act (*Geschichte des Prager Theaters,* II, 268), as noted above. The same statement, though in slightly different wording—"genug, ich wünschte in diesen Augenblicken lieber Mozart als Leopold zu seyn" (enough, at these moments I should rather be Mozart than Leopold)—occurs in the

anonymous *Fantasien auf einer Reise nach Prag,* p. 91. It is probably an allusion to Mozart's comic song "Ich möchte wohl der Kaiser sein" (K. 539), composed three years before.

30 For a brief description of the 1848 performance, see Teuber, *Geschichte des Prager Theaters,* III (1888). After a detailed chronicle of the difficulties that the revolutionary activities of 1848 had created for the theatrical life of the city, Teuber describes the return to political stability that coincided with the coronation and the performance of the opera: "They performed Mozart's coronation opera *Titus,* and the occasion for this performance was the coronation of the youthful Emperor Franz Josef. A festival play by Hickl, *Austria's Stars,* opened the celebration; the grand *Sextus* of Fehringer and the sympathetic *Vitellia* of Grosser were worthy of the festive presentation with which the theatre season of 1848, one of the most significant and precarious years in the history of the Prague theatre, to a certain degree achieved a happy conclusion. The venerable institution had averted catastrophe" (pp. 387–388).

31 The theme associated with Peter the Great appears near the end of act IV and was used by both Rimsky-Korsakov and Shostakovitch to provide an ending for the uncompleted last act. The fragmentary last act as printed in Lamm's critical edition gives no evidence that Musorgsky intended to end the opera with this theme.

32 Letter of July 23, 1874, to Lubov Karmalina, in *The Musorgsky Reader,* p. 277.

33 This conception is evident in the conventionally Hegelian language used by Stasov when he described proposing the *Khovanshchina* theme to Musorgsky in mid-1872: "It seemed to me that the fight between old and new Russia, the exit of the former and the entrance of the latter, would provide rich soil for drama and opera. . . . 'Old Russia' is passing away and a new age beginning" (*The Musorgsky Reader,* p. 187). Although Musorgsky retains this conception of "old" and "new" and distinguishes between them in his musical style, he by no means implies that the coming of the new represents progress in the Hegelian sense. The idea of history that emerges from this opera, as from *Boris Godunov,* suggests a strong skepticism and gloom about historical change, inevitable though the latter may be.

34 In his painstaking recent study of the differences between the first and second versions of *Boris Godunov,* Taruskin claims that the strong populist sentiments we note in Musorgsky's treatment of the populace did not enter the opera until the latter version (1871) and that—whereas the first version (1869) deviated relatively little from Pushkin's text—the new version, above all in the Kromy scene that the composer added to the end of the opera, deviates from Pushkin at the same time that it postulates a more positive view of the populace than before; Taruskin attributes this new view to the influence of Musorgsky's contemporary Nikolai Kostomarov (Taruskin, "Musorgsky *vs.* Musorgsky," p. 256). For a study of the generic changes that both Pushkin and Musorgsky worked on the Boris theme, see Caryl Emerson, "Bakhtin and Intergeneric Shift: The Case of

Boris Godunov," *Studies in Twentieth Century Literature* 9 (1984), 145–167. I am grateful to Professor Emerson for sharing her not yet published research on *Khovanshchina* with me.

35 In a letter Musorgsky indicates his need to keep Peter and the regent offstage: "(But Peter and Sofia are kept off stage—this is decided; better without them), and I am eager to do a people's drama—*I am so eager*" (letter of July 23, 1873, to Polyxena Stasova, in *The Musorgsky Reader,* p. 224).

36 See Ruth Volpé, "L'intérêt du XIX siècle russe pour la culture nationale," *L'Avant-Scène,* pp. 135–137; Eugène Ternovsky, "Le Raskol, composant historique d'une querelle idéologique," *L'Avant-Scène,* pp. 148–151; and James H. Billington, *The Icon and the Axe: An Interpretive History of Russian Culture* (New York: Knopf, 1966), pp. 412–414. As Volpé and Ternovsky point out, within the new populist historiography the Old Believers were seen as models for resistance against the centralized state. Ternovsky mentions the popularity of the Old Believers in other forms such as historical fiction and painting during Musorgsky's time (p. 151). For a history of the Old Believer schism from its origins in the religious reform of the 1650s through the revival of interest in the schism that took place during Musorgsky's time, see Michael Cherniavsky, "The Old Believers and the New Religion," *Slavic Review* 25 (1966), 1–39.

37 For the historical background, see Franco Venturi, *Roots of Revolution: A History of the Populist and Socialist Movements in Nineteenth Century Russia,* trans. Francis Haskell (New York: Knopf, 1964), pp. 501–506, and Andrzej Walicki, *A History of Russian Thought from the Enlightenment to Marxism,* trans. Hilda Andrews-Rusiecka (Stanford: Stanford University Press, 1979), pp. 222–235.

38 Letter of October 18, 1872, to Stasov, in *The Musorgsky Reader,* p. 199.

39 Berlin, "*Khovanshchina,*" p. 34.

40 For a musical analysis of these contrasting vocal forms, see White, *Schoenberg and the God-Idea,* pp. 152–153, 214–215, 224–225.

41 On the relation of representation to the divine prohibition against concrete images, see Adorno, "Sakrales Fragment," pp. 458–459.

42 For a detailed study of how Schönberg compressed and altered his biblical materials, see Odil Hannes Steck, *Moses und Aron: Die Oper Arnold Schönbergs und ihr biblischer Stoff* (Munich: Kaiser, 1981).

43 On the oratorio version and its relation to the opera, see White, *Schoenberg and the God-Idea,* pp. 21, 92–112.

44 "In the realization of this scene, since it affects the center of my conception, I went quite far, and at this spot my piece is probably also most 'opera'—which indeed it should be" (*Briefe,* ed. Erwin Stein [Mainz: B. Schott's Söhne, 1958], p. 188). The "operatic" nature of this scene was a cause of some embarrassment to Schönberg, as we note in the apologetic tone with which he describes the scene to Anton von Webern: "You know that I do not much care for the dance [around the Golden Calf]. Its expressive power in general is on no higher a level than the most primitive program music; and in its petrified mechanical

quality its 'beauty' seems hateful to me" (*Briefe*, p. 165). The closer Schönberg got to what might be construed as a musical representation of some "real" world, the more nervous he evidently became about lapsing into an older aesthetic mode.

45 "Everything I have written bears a certain inner resemblance to me" (*Briefe*, p. 154). Schönberg insists on the autobiographical element in response to Berg's inquiry about other depictions of Moses (for example, Strindberg's posthumous play *Moses*) that Schönberg might have had in mind as models. But Schönberg was equally insistent on the religious nature of the work, as when, shortly before his death, he wrote his disciple Josef Rufer that "the content and its treatment are purely religious-philosophical" (*Briefe*, p. 298). The latter remark was occasioned by what Schönberg viewed as the wrong kind of biographical approach—in particular, an entry in Grove's *Dictionary of Music* by Gerald Abraham, who had attempted to connect the conflict between the spiritual and the material in the opera with what he called "the inner conflicts of Schönberg's tortured and enigmatic mind" (Grove's *Dictionary of Music*, 4th ed. [London: Macmillan, 1940], VI [supplementary volume], 573).

46 For a comprehensive treatment of Schönberg's relation to Judaism and to the Jewish people, see Michael Mäckelmann, *Arnold Schönberg und das Judentum*, Hamburger Beiträge zur Musikwissenschaft, 28 (Hamburg: Karl Dieter Wagner, 1984).

47 For detailed comparisons of *Der biblische Weg* and *Moses und Aron*, see Mäckelmann, *Arnold Schönberg und das Judentum*, pp. 157–167, and also my own article, "Schönbergs *Der biblische Weg*, *Moses und Aron* und Probleme politischer Führung," in *Zeitgenossenschaft: Zur deutschsprachigen Literatur im 20. Jahrhundert*, ed. Paul Michael Lützeler, Herbert Lehnert, and Gerhild Scholz Williams (Frankfurt: Athenäum, 1987), pp. 61–76. Although *Der biblische Weg* has not yet been published in German, it is available in an Italian translation under the title *La via biblica*, in Schönberg, *Testi poetici e drammatici*, ed. Luigi Rognoni and trans. Emilio Castellani (Milan: Feltrinelli, 1967), pp. 77–150. I am grateful to the archive of the Arnold Schoenberg Institute at the University of Southern California for permission to examine Schönberg's autograph of the play.

48 Adorno briefly mentions the political setting in the following terms: "*Moses und Aron* was composed just before the outbreak of the Third Reich—probably as a defense against what was dawning" ("Sakrales Fragment," p. 460). Mäckelmann also suggests parallels between the political situation and the composition of the opera (*Arnold Schönberg und das Judentum*, pp. 140–148).

49 *Briefe*, p. 188.

50 "A Four-Point Program for Jewry," *Journal of the Arnold Schoenberg Institute* 3 (1979), 55.

51 Ibid., p. 50.

52 From "Brief über die jüdische Frage," reproduced in H. H. Stuckenschmidt, *Schönberg: Leben, Umwelt, Werk* (Zurich: Atlantis, 1974), p. 495.

53 "The Jewish Government in Exile," quoted in Alexander L. Ringer, "Arnold Schoenberg and the Politics of Jewish Survival," *Journal of the Arnold Schoenberg Institute* 3 (1979), 46. This handwritten document, which the institute allowed me to examine, raises questions about the composer's mental stability if one is to take him at his word. Is it possible that in his private papers he created fictions analogous to those within his theatrical works?

54 For a fine recent study that does take operas seriously for what they can tell us about their times, see Paul Robinson, *Opera and Ideas: From Mozart to Strauss* (New York: Harper and Row, 1985). Robinson, writing as an intellectual historian, presents Berlioz' *Les Troyens,* for example, as an embodiment of Hegelian historical process (pp. 103–154) and Verdi's *Don Carlos* as a critique of mid-nineteenth-century *Realpolitik* (pp. 155–209).

Here Comes Everybody
Scholarship and Black Theatre History

James V. Hatch

For more than a century, the study of Afro-American theatre history has been beset by five critical obstacles: the loss of primary sources in Africa and America; a severely circumscribed definition of theatre (as promulgated by most historians); a paucity of scholarly publication in Afro-American history; a disgraceful absence of theatre scholars who know both black and white theatre history; and an abundance of institutionalized racism. The sum of these obstacles results in a massive problem: Black American theatre history has not yet been assimilated into our mainstream bibliographies, directories, biographies, scholarly journals, and history texts.

A student who reads "American" in the title of a theatre text should expect more than European ethnics. Most texts and reference books ignore Native Americans, Hispanic Americans, and Asian Americans entirely; for Afro-Americans, they offer token entries or none. Examples abound: *American Theatre Companies* (1986; 2 vols., 1749–1887, and 1888–1930), edited by Weldon B. Durham, lists 165 companies—3 are black.[1] Allowing for editorial selection, the National Ethiopian Art Players, Gilpin Players, Pekin Stock Company, Alhambra Players, Lincoln Players of the Lincoln Theatre, and Krigwa Players Little Negro Theatre deserve mention. The handsomely illustrated, award-winning *Theatre in America: Two Hundred Years of Productions* by Mary C. Henderson is indexed to nearly 2,200 theatre artists, companies, and plays—15 are Blacks, and 6 of those are noted for their participation in white shows.[2] Among the dozens missing are the internationally acclaimed Shakespearean actor Ira Aldridge, the Ziegfeld Follies' star Bert Williams, Lorraine Hansberry and anyone from the cast of *A Raisin in the Sun,* Canada Lee from *Native Son,* and Lloyd Richards, head of the Yale Drama School. Henderson asserts, "After the 1920s, the black performer was an accepted part of the Broadway scene, and with the emergence of the black playwright in the 1950s, the place of all minorities in the American Theater has been assured."[3] Her history does not reveal it.

The Encyclopedia of the American Theatre, 1900–1975 (1980), edited by Edwin Bronner, refers only to *A Raisin in the Sun* and *The River Niger*.[4] From a possible 44 Obie awards presented to Blacks for the best off-Broadway work, the *Encyclopedia* lists 4. These omissions of black theatre history from mainstream texts are typical.

The roots of the problem are woven inextricably into America's social history and perpetuated by graduate programs in theatre departments. This continuing apartheid in an era when our scholars show increasing sophistication in national and multiethnic theatre history is unfair to students—and dishonest. This essay analyzes how this situation came to be and what can be done to remedy it.

Blk Love Song #1 (1969), a play by Kalamu Ya Salaam, begins with a black woman intoning, "Where is the seed of Africa? Where are the first men who walked the earth? Have they vanished?"[5] The chorus answers, "They are gone to America. They are gone to the New World."

Historians recover the past from artifacts—material and cultural. In Afro-America, Africanisms are the key cultural artifacts.[6] These first arrived in 1619, when a Dutch ship sold twenty slaves in Jamestown, Virginia.[7] Over the following two and a half centuries, millions of Africans (no accurate records were kept) continued to carry their speech, music, dance, and culture across the Middle Passage.[8] By the end of the Civil War, the African people—many of whose ancestors had lived here five and six generations—functioned in two cultures, African and American; but their Africanisms had become like the yams they had introduced from West Africa, so familiar and common that they now seemed indigenous to America. They had become invisible—that is, they were no longer acknowledged as African.

Africanisms should be distinguished from neo-Africanisms, which arrived in the mid-twentieth century. These were deliberate attempts by Afro-Americans to reintroduce African themes, dances, and rituals into the arts; they were a conscious import by black artists who had made their *hajj* to the homeland. Dancers Dunham and Primus reconstructed root and source dances for American audiences from the late thirties to the late forties, for example. The influence of neo-Africanisms is, however, a cultural overlay unlike that of indigenous Africanisms, which are the spine and the blood of Afro-American theatre and which the historian in search of artifacts must somehow trace back across four centuries to the African homeland.

The Greeks stand at the door of Western theatre history. Through artifacts—their plays, architecture, paintings, sculpture, vases, and other material from archaeological excavations—one may trace Greek theatre until its roots disappear into tribal mists. In like manner, the researcher in black theatre hopes to discover an African Epidaurus, but because of colonial politics this search within the parameters of a Greek paradigm has not validated African theatre as one worthy of investigation. For example, if one were to ask where the African Epidaurus was located, the reply might be in the land of the pharaohs at Abydos or Sakkara or Memphis. However, until recently, Egypt, the site of the most ancient monuments where religious ritual flourished, was excised politically from the African continent by Western historians who labeled the culture of the pharaohs not an African but a Semitic-Hamitic triumph. With Egypt and Arab North Africa skimmed off the top of the continent, the world's most ancient rituals disappeared from African history to become objects of Middle Eastern studies or a separate area study—Egyptology. Only in the late twentieth century have scholars again identified the "Negroid" features of the pharaohs of the Upper Nile with the people south of the Sahara.[9]

For Afro-Americans, a shared glory with the pharaohs is as legitimate as shared glory with the Greeks for Western Caucasians. Because the Memphite Dramas have not yet been tracked to Memphis, Tennessee, and found in Mother Zion's AME Easter services, historians must not assume that African culture did not survive the Middle Passage. When Afro-American culture is denied African roots, it is left to attach itself to European traditions which have afforded it little respect.

What primary sources are available to prove the contrary? What methodology should be employed? Because Afro-American theatre stems from roots on both sides of a hyphen, the hyphen must become a bridge. Africanisms that survived must be investigated—a difficult task which takes the historian into anthropology, sociology, psychology, and religion, and into unfamiliar cultures. Even then, when the genesis of African theatre has been defined, the leap across the Atlantic and across four hundred years remains.

Orlando Patterson has identified three main currents in the writing of black history: catastrophism, contributionism, and survivalism.[10] Catastrophist historians deny that any significant African culture survived the infamous Middle Passage. An example of the catastrophism school of history which dominated historical thinking is *White and Negro Spirituals, Their Life Span and Kinship* (1943) by George Pullen Jackson, who concludes:

I do not deny the possibility that there are, in American negro religious folk songs, certain African hang-overs. I would merely state that I haven't found any yet, nor do I know of any other who has found any. I have found what seems to be American negro racial emphases, nothing more. Others in the future may be more successful because more intent on finding the Ethiopian in the song-fuel heap. I wish them luck. That is their job. I have done mine.[11]

Jackson's tunnel vision was typical of a long line of cultural chauvinism. Afro-American theatre history suffered accordingly; fortunately, the catastrophism theory has been superseded.

A second group of scholars concentrated on the contributions of black musicians, inventors, artists, and athletes to the American mainstream. The work of these writers resonates with litanies of "the first Black": Ira Aldridge, the first black American actor to perform abroad; the African Grove, the first black theatre in America to produce Shakespeare; and so forth. While this approach is well intentioned, it places Afro-American culture at a disadvantage. For example, the talents of the nineteenth-century soprano Sisseretta Jones could be acclaimed only by dubbing her the Black Patti, a sobriquet derived by invidious comparison with the white singer Adelina Patti; on the other hand, Elvis Presley was never dubbed the white Chuck Berry. The third group, the survivalists, maintains that a considerable number of cultural, spiritual, and material artifacts did survive and that such artifacts have sustained Afro-Americans and influenced American life extensively. In recent years, survivalists have been able to document that African dance, song, ritual, and even language still flourish in Afro-America.

Many elements of African culture, crushed in North America, survived in Haiti, Jamaica, Surinam, Guyana, and the Bahia province of Brazil, where African slaves were allowed greater cultural expression. A religious drama, *Shango de Ima,* built on the Yoruba creation story and employing many Yoruba words, is still performed in Cuba.[12] Indeed, even in the continental United States words from Bantu, Mendi, Yoruba, and other African languages—including such words as "jazz," "yam," "ballyhoo," and "jukebox"—are present in American speech.[13]

Afro-American church rituals are the major source of Africanisms which have survived. The black church evolved from traditional African approaches to worship, but what were those original traditions? They are not easy to verify because the African kingdoms like the Benin, the Zulu, the Kikuyu, the Mendi, the Bantu, and others are as diverse as they are rich in art. In a humid climate hospitable to insects, the Africans committed their rituals not to paper or clay, but to practice, to habit, to oral history, to artifacts and notions which could be "read" by observers who understood these cultural signs.

When the journals and letters of early European explorers, missionaries, and entrepreneurs described African "performance," they offered unsympathetic accounts of savagery in the heart of darkness. When more sympathetic observers—such as Melville Herskovits, Lorenzo D. Turner, Leonard Goines, and Robert Farris Thompson—studied the cultures, the so-called savage African rituals suddenly became meaningful to "outsiders."

What defines ritual? For the purposes of this essay, Bruce McConachie's definition functions well: "ritual may be seen as the repetitious, formalized, and dramatically-structured communication of significant cultural meanings, effected through the involvement and catharsis of its participants, which functions to legitimate an image of a social order." The "dramatically-structured elements" may vary widely from ritual to ritual, but include music, song, call-response, liturgical chanting, dance, impersonation, incarnation, story—in sum, theatrical elements.[14] Rituals may also be divided into sacred and profane.

Within this generalized conception, the African religious ritual and Afro-American gospel tradition share three attributes: communally active participation (congregation/audience); collective and improvisational performance within the ritual; and shared belief that the ritual (ceremony/ performance) will legitimate realities that are individually and socially efficacious. These three attributes are found in the Afro-American church and later in their theatre, which may be contrasted with traditional European theatre, where the audience observes rather than participates in influencing the performer, where performance is "frozen" by stage direction and line recitation, and where entertainment is the major consciously shared purpose. The distinction between European and African traditions can be seen in the audience's relationship to the performance.

Thomas Pawley has set down some of the behavior patterns of black spectators: "shouting, jeering, hooting, laughter and an infinite number of non-linguistic vocal reactions indicative of approval or disapproval, enjoyment or dissatisfaction. Physical responses include beating on the seat, stamping on the floor, nudging or kicking companions, clapping or slapping hands (give me some skin), rocking back and forth, and, in extreme instances, leaping to one's feet in the manner of a sports crowd."[15]

Professor Pawley recounts a number of anecdotes from his thirty years in the black theatre; he notes that "swearing, especially if it involves the 'dozens' sexual references, both overt and covert, [and] sharp repartee will undoubtedly produce whoops of delight. Scenes of violence and physical conflict will also arouse the audience. . . . In a production of *The Slave,* one student yelled: 'Shoot him again to make sure he's dead.'" Pawley suggests that the response of black audiences has at least five traceable influences: the black church and the congregation's participation; the black nightclub experience; the black stage performances at theatres like the Apollo in Harlem and the Howard in Washington, D.C.; sports performances, particularly those based upon feats of black athletes competing with whites, such as Jackie Robinson and Joe Louis; and the origin of it all, the African audience tradition.

Regarding this last influence, Pawley quotes a *Washington Post* article concerning the performance in 1971 of a folk opera, *Moremi, the Hine of Ife,* by Duro Ladipo's theatre company. The audience was Nigerian: "Between explosions of laughter, spectators offered a constant stream of suggestions, instant criticism, and jokes of their own as Ladipo's company continued its performance. Surprisingly, the injection and other symptoms of the Yoruba affinity for anarchy did not seem to hamper the players who were able to build much of the byplay into their production."[16]

As the isolation of the Georgia Sea Islands preserved the Krio language of Sierra Leone in an Afro-American form called Gullah,[17] on the mainland the "rules" governing racial interaction preserved many Africanisms. Since black people had little reason or opportunity to attend white American theatre, the majority were unencumbered by Victorian audience traditions unless they aspired to the black bourgeoisie.

This cultural segregation has resulted today in a segregated theatre history, not always from overt racism, but from promulgating a narrow definition of theatre which has excluded Afro-American theatrical traditions, such as the black church's syncopated music, call-response between leader and congregation, spontaneous testimonies, and possession by the spirit. The historian must recognize that all these theatrical elements when employed for profit outside the house of God became elements of black secular theatre—ritual became commercial; performance became professional. From the Fisk University Jubilee Singers tours (1871) through late nineteenth century spectacles like Nate Salisbury's *Black America* (1895), where slave quarters and plantation life were recreated on stage as authentic environment for the spirituals, through the Hall Johnson Singers in *Green Pastures* (1932), to the professional voices in the Institutional Radio Choir in *The Gospel at Colonus* (1980), the church has been the path to professional careers in theatre.

In recent years, musicologists have begun to acknowledge that the rhythms of much American popular music (as distinct from European) have stemmed from Africa. Ragtime, jazz, blues, bebop, rhythm and blues, and even rock and roll would never have evolved without African amalgamation with European forms. That in the first half of the twentieth century cultural historians denied Africa now seems amazing until we recall the development of the music business. In popular music, exploitation of Africanisms made big bucks.

African dance, too, survived the Middle Passage and consequently was a formative influence on the theatre. Cultural historians Marshall and Jean Stearns have notated the African and Afro-American movements of feet, legs, hips, shoulders, arms, and hands, both past and contemporary.[18] Although the cultural bridges were sometimes fragile, they held. Black America danced with movements identifiably African, albeit greatly altered by Western forms. How were these Africanisms passed on? How did they come down to us? Cultural anthropologists Szwed, Abrahams, Kochman, Gwaltney, and Levine have documented two styles of passing the culture along to the next generation: the formal, visible, and voiced; and the informal, invisible, and silent.

First, the formal tradition. Fifteen years after the Civil War, seventy percent of black Americans could not read and write English.[19] Oral history with its attendant strengthening of memory remained the major source of family record. Examples of recall astounding in breadth and detail can be found in the slave narratives recorded by the abolitionists; in modern times, books like *All God's Dangers* (1974) set down by Theodore Rosengarten and Nell Irvin Painter's *The Narrative of Hosea Hudson* (1979) testify to the vitality of the oral tradition.

Although Blacks suffer from the same failure of memory and the same embroidery of glory as whites, formal oral history has preserved names and events and snatches of black performance for the theatre historian that otherwise would have been lost. Taped interviews with old entertainers identify and even partially recreate lost performances; for example, Leigh Whipper's memory of singing spirituals for fifty cents a performance in *Uncle Tom's Cabin* in 1895, or dancer Ida Forsyne Hubbard's recollections of Russia before World War I when she sang, *in Russian,* "I'm neither a soubrette / nor a chansonette / I'm neither English nor Parisian / I just speak Russian and wait for what comes to me."[20] Because so much of black performance occurred on an amateur level and in a casual setting, its events were seldom recorded in print.

More important than tape recordings to the historian in search of Africanisms is the informal, invisible tradition by which they have been passed on. Cultural archaeologist VèVè A. Clark,[21] in her study of Haitian popular theatre, examines ways to hear the "silences" in theatre history. Oral history embraces much more than an Uncle Remus telling tales to the "chillun"; it embraces silent signals locked within the voiced speech, as well as an aura of signals surrounding the voiced content of the speech. A historian must be sensitive to the informal content as well as that which is formally conveyed. The kinds of laughter, the placement of the voice in the throat, gestures of the hands, face, and feet, passed and received unconsciously—all provided direct transfusion of Africanisms from parent to child (see Zora Neale Hurston's folklore study, *Mules and Men*).[22] Other Africanisms may be passed along semiformally; for example, a child may sing a traditional song ("Steal Away") but never know it was a coded signal for slaves to run away. In like manner, a child may employ the term "yackity-yackity" without ever knowing it came from the Bantu *yakula-yakula*.

When a society is united by common bonds, these signs and signals carry emotions, ideas, and concepts both to an individual in the field and to an audience in the theatre. These signals have transmitted racial memory and, in many examples, specific bonding rituals: "signifying," "rapping," "toasting," and boasting appear formally on the black stage and less formally on the street.[23] To hear and enjoy these silences fully, one must either have grown up Black or have learned them through study. Otherwise, one sees only with the myopic vision that dominated American racial thought until the mid-twentieth century before the survivalism school of history uncovered evidence to the contrary.

Cultural ingenuousness on the part of historians complicates the task; even today, many theatre students believe that Afro-American theatre began with Lorraine Hansberry's *A Raisin in the Sun* (1959) and that whatever preceded amounted to little more than the stereotypes of minstrelsy. Hence, it is necessary to reexamine how a theatre scholar should approach racial caricatures.

To interpret the image, the historian must first recognize the origin and development of the evolving black character in the Western theatre.[24] Although the first African may not have stepped upon England's shores before 1554, the black image had entered English theatre earlier through two distinct images of kings: Balthasar and Lucifer. In the fourteenth century, the Christmas pageants presented the Magi bearing gifts to the Christ child; the kings represented the homage of the entire world and Balthasar symbolized the darker races. By the sixteenth century, the forces of darkness were appearing onstage in the guise of various black-faced devils and demons. In the seventeenth century, the English masques used black-faced figures much as the English aristocrats used black page boys—for novelty and display. In 1605, Inigo Jones designed Ben Jonson's *Masque of Blackness* for Queen Anne of Denmark.[25] The queen and her ladies blackened their faces, "a very loathsome sight." In the more serious mode of revenge tragedies, the Renaissance black king (then called a Moor or a blackamoor) became a captive and took bloody revenge upon his Christian captors. As the slave trade became the blue chip investment of its day, the tradition from Balthasar to *Oroonoko* faded away,[26] leaving the once-noble Othello as Friday, a wretch whose very face convicted him of sin, fit only to be a servant to the entrepreneur Robinson Crusoe.

A theatre historian should follow the development of this stereotype in America, focusing on our society's needs to capitalize on the distorted image: first, as an economic apology for slavery; second, as a moral scapegoat; third, as a psychological projection for suppressed appetites; and finally, as visible evidence of supposed black racial and cultural inferiority.[27] Our first indigenous black character to appear on the boards was a buffoon named Raccoon in *The Disappointment, or The Force of Credulity* (1767) by Andrew Barton.[28] Some scholars have maintained that Raccoon is not black, but Dutch or something else;[29] the point is moot, for other blackened creatures were in the offing, caricatures corrupting the diction, the thought, and the humanity of Afro-Americans.

A brief sampling of these stereotypes will suffice. First, diction. In a very early play, *The Candidates* (1770) by Robert Mumford, the black servant Ralpho asks his master for a new livery. The master gives him a cast-off suit of his own, and the white author has Ralpho express his enthusiasm over the secondhand livery: "Gadso! This figure of mine is not reconsiderable in its delurements and when I'm dressed out like a gentleman, the girls I'm a thinking, will find me desisible."[30]

This introduction of pre–Mrs. Malapropisms (1775) for comedy became a device that white authors placed in black mouths for 150 years. But the writers did not leave bad enough alone. As the number of slaves increased, so did the weight of white Christian guilt; consequently, whites further devalued the tattered black image onstage. By 1845, the diction of the servant had developed into near-gibberish. In *Fashion* by Anna Cora Mowatt, the opening scene shows Zeke examining his dashing new scarlet livery before the gaze of Millinette the French maid:

Zeke: Dere's a coat to take de eyes ob all Broadway! Oh! Missy, it am de fixins dat make de natural born gemman. A libery forever! Dere's da pair ob insuppressibles to stonish de colored population.

Millinette: Oh, oui, Monsieur Zeke. (Aside), I not comprend one word he say![31]

The corruption of black diction was linked to corruption of American common sense by racism. Long before *Uncle Tom's Cabin* (1852),[32] a popular scene for northern audiences had been the manumission of the slave. An early example appeared in *The Triumph of Love* (1795) by J. Murdock.[33] The master offered Sambo his freedom. After kissing the skirt of his master's coat, Sambo cried: "Oh marsa George, I feel how I never feel before. God bless you. (Cries.) I must go, or my heart burst. (Exits.)"

That a man who is offered his freedom takes it was only common sense to an American twenty years after the Declaration of Independence. Yet fifty years later, we had forgotten our common heritage. Here is the similar scene from the antiabolitionist play *The Guerrillas* (1862) by James MacCabe. Marse Arthur has just offered Jerry his freedom:

Jerry: Marse Arthur, youse jokin'.
Arthur: No, Jerry. I am serious. You are free.
Jerry: (Indignant) A free nigger? I don't want to be free. . . . What I want to be free for? (With feeling) Marse Arthur, I been in your family eber since I was born. If youse tired of old Jerry jis' take him out in de field and shoot him, don't set him free, please don't. . . .[34]

If the slaves loved the master, then all was forgiven; if the slaves were less than human, then God had ordained white dominance; if the slaves were happy, business as usual might continue. Theatre business and production mirrored the same oppression: whites routinely borrowed the music, the dance, and the culture of Blacks and appropriated the authorship with its spoils to themselves; whites excluded Blacks from their audiences; whites played the roles of Blacks onstage. Blacks created their own performances in their own spaces, but these self-segregated shows were not immune from white critics who, in describing black theatre performances, wrote from arrogance and ignorance. British comedian Charles Mathews' account of his visit to the African Grove Theatre in New York City provides a telling example.

The African Grove Theatre was founded in 1820 by William Henry Brown and a group of black actors for their own recreation. The African

Company became the first professional theatre for blacks. Begun as a social event in a garden, the Grove moved to a rented theatre space in lower Manhattan at Mercer and Bleecker streets, with a capacity of three or four hundred people. Newspapers of the time printed accounts of the theatre's successes, especially Shakespearean productions. The management "graciously made a partition at the back of their house for the accommodation of the whites." This move was a mistake: white rowdies caused so much disturbance that the police closed the theatre. At the African Grove, Ira Aldridge acted in his first plays before emigrating to Europe, where he became a star as a black tragedian.

In 1822, Charles Mathews, as described in his *Sketches of Mr. Mathews's Trip to America* (1824), attended a performance at the African Grove. When he returned to London, Mathews saw an excellent opportunity for parody and profit. He wrote:

> Mr. Mathews takes an opportunity of visiting the Niggers (or Negroes) Theatre. The black population being, in the national theatres, under certain restrictions have, to be quite at their ease, a theatre of their own. Here he sees a black tragedian (the Kentucky Roscius) perform the character of Hamlet and hears him deliver the soliloquy, "To be or not to be, dat is him question, whether him nobler in de mind to suffer or lift up him arms against one sea of hubble bubble and by opossum (oppose 'em) end em." At the word opossum the whole audience burst forth into one general cry of "opossum, opossum, opossum." On enquiring into the cause of this, Mr. Mathews was informed that "Opossum Up a Gum Tree" was the national air, or sort of "God Save the King" of Negroes. . . .[35]

Mathews' account invites speculation that he witnessed a performance of Ira Aldridge, since he billed himself as the African Roscius and often sang "Possum up a Gum Tree" between acts.[36] Mathews presents the actor as illiterate. Aldridge, as his European reviews plainly show, certainly would not have confounded buffoonery with *Hamlet*. But can a historian read between the lines to discover any historical truth in Mathews' buffoonery?

One can conjecture that a black audience at the African Grove in 1821 recognized the possum song, which Aldridge (and perhaps others) did sing between the acts of a tragedy, for it was the custom of many performers, white and black, to present comic interludes. If the audience did demand he sing the song because it was a favorite, that would also suggest that his audience attended the theatre regularly enough to recognize the performer and his material. While the Mathews account is extreme, it illustrates prejudice for profit and is typical of white nineteenth-century accounts of black performance, which must be read with a filter to remove the racism.

Paul Lawrence Dunbar's poem "We Wear the Mask" lamented the social mask which Blacks were forced to wear. But whites also wore the mask. In the forty years following Dan Emmett's minstrel show in 1842, hundreds of white men donned hog fat and burnt cork to make thousands of dollars by mimicking and distorting black music, black speech, black dance, and black culture, a tradition that lasted into the mid-twentieth century with Al Jolson, Eddie Cantor, George Jessel, and Amos and Andy.

In the words of the scholar Richard Moody, "The Negro minstrel show was the only genuinely indigenous form of American drama."[37] Because minstrelsy originally derived its materials from black plantation entertainments, a historian might ask if there is any truth about Afro-American culture to be uncovered in the hundreds of white minstrel sketches printed and performed. Are there ways to separate white distortion from black performance, because it was here that European and African sources first merged to become American theatre? Moody's observation demands a deeper inquiry than has been undertaken, one which may reveal the hidden and complex fate that lies behind the minstrel mask.[38]

Although it is now possible to understand how and why Afro-American theatre history became segregated from the mainstream, why it remains so is still unclear. To suggest causes and remedies, one must know the status of black theatre scholarship.

Bibliographies, dissertations, and histories came late to black theatre history. The first list of plays with Negro characters appeared in 1927,[39] but it was not until the 1970s that more carefully compiled bibliographies distinguished between black and white writers. In 1939, Hilda H. Lawson wrote *The Negro in American Drama,* the first dissertation in black theatre. A half century later, the total number of master's theses and doctoral dissertations numbered nearly two hundred and fifty. There is only one book-length history, written in 1967—*Black Drama, the Story of the American Negro in the Theatre* by Loften Mitchell—and it has a parochial New York emphasis. Until the 1960s, there were fewer than fifty plays published by Afro-Americans. To acquire a library containing every black theatre book in print would not be a costly investment.

American theatre history abounds in unexplored thesis and dissertation topics, in black theatre in particular. Almost nothing has been written about the hundreds of amateur and semiprofessional performances held in lodges, churches, schools, carnivals, and country fairs, for instance. The work of black professionals, particularly those from 1880 to 1930, remains sparsely documented. Studies of black artistic and technical theatre fraternities and unions and their relationships to white unions must be explored. Biographies of black performers presently number three dozen, and the majority of these are promotional. Little has been written about the black theatre and its circuits. During World War I, dozens of urban theatres were attended only by Blacks and hundreds of other theatres were segregated, usually with a "nigger heaven." Almost no scholarly work has been done on these segregated theatres, which operated through World War II. The fascinating task of tracing how black American music and dance influenced American mainstream musicals and then how, in turn, European forms influenced blacks must be researched.

The study of American theatre should become an integrated history, not a book with a chapter on Black performers. Style, music, dance, and lyrics of American musicals have both Black and white parents. The black parents' names are not familiar to most theatre historians, but they should be. Thus, a discussion of fin-de-siècle musicals should include those of Will Marion Cook, Rosamund Johnson, and Bert Williams in the same chapter with Victor Herbert, Oscar Hammerstein, and Reginald DeKoven. Then European and Afro-American traditions could be compared to show how the two forms influenced each other from ragtime to the jazz musicals of the twenties. These crossovers have continued for fifty years to the present day: *The Wiz* (1974), the wedding of black dance and music to the old Baum story, produced a new art, although the old-line critics did not easily surrender Judy Garland. Lee Breuer's production of *The Gospel at Colonus* (1980) made the Greek story dramatically exciting by using a black gospel church ritual.[40] These artful creations should be distinguished from the simple substituting of Blacks for whites, as in David Merrick's recasting of *Hello, Dolly!*

Graduate theatre departments bear the onus for the dearth of black theatre research.[41] Institutionalized racism is and will remain in the academic prison that confines young minds and talents to its cells. Neither the problem nor its solution is simple. Jobs and careers are at stake. A single black teacher on a white faculty may never encourage colleagues to read black theatre history or to direct a black play, for his or her special expertise is the primary job security for tenure.

This partisan marking of one's territory stems directly from the absence of Blacks who supervise research and teach in "white" areas of the curriculum. Although there are no current statistics available, conversations with Professors Winona Fletcher, Thomas Pawley, William R. Reardon, and

Errol Hill suggest that the number of black graduate students in theatre has declined, and the few who do study theatre write on black subjects since they do not expect to be invited to teach Greek drama.[42] White administrators do not require black graduates to write dissertations on multi-ethnic subjects; if they do, who is to evaluate that new material? How many graduate mentors suggest a black or a black/white subject to their white charges? How many suggest a white subject to a black candidate? What journal will publish the information when it has been written?

Theatre journal editors receive very few submissions concerning Afro-American theatre. Some theatre articles do appear in black literature journals, however. Originally these segregated organs appeared because mainstream periodicals did not treat black literature with seriousness; nowadays black journals perpetuate the separation through self-interest and hegemony, making it difficult to distinguish between a publication that focuses on a special interest from one that cultivates racial segregation.

So American theatre history remains a segregated and untruthful affair. It is here that the practitioners and the mentors must initiate changes. Students must be required to study ethnic theatre histories. Both white and black students preparing to teach should be able to teach all of American theatre history, without being ghettoized into their own race. Lillian Russell and Bert Williams, Alice Childress and Tennessee Williams, Ira Aldridge and Fannie Kemble should be known to all.

The past two decades have provided new research tools and texts, and some recent reference books include more black performance history than before. Directories like *The National Playwrights Directory* (1977) by Phyllis Johnson Kaye as well as the International Theatre Institute and the Theatre Communications Group annuals regularly list black companies.[43] Bibliographies are also more inclusive; Dr. Irving Brown in particular has made valiant efforts to include minorities in the *International Bibliography of Theatre*.[44] Among theatre history texts, *On with the Show!* by Robert C. Toll and *Living Theater* by Edwin Wilson and Alvin Goldfarb contain separate chapters on Blacks, which is better than none at all.[45] *Free, Adult, and Uncensored,* a history of the Federal Theatre Project by Lorraine Brown and John O'Connor, includes 3 black shows in a total of 16.[46] These studies are exceptions and barely a beginning.

One should not expect editors of compendia or encyclopedias to do original research; they turn to dissertations, to texts, to histories. If editors are not familiar with Fannin Belcher's seminal work, *The Place of the Negro in the Evolution of the American Theatre, 1776–1940* (New Haven: Yale University Press, 1940), they conclude that twelve black shows are sufficient to represent color in American drama. In all probability, most editors have passed through a graduate theatre school without a glance at black theatre history.

Thus, exclusion continues to be the rule. *American Women Dramatists of the Twentieth Century* (1982), compiled by Brenda Coven, lists 8 black women playwrights from a total of 168.[47] It is maddening for a scholar in black history to turn to Anthony Slide's *Selected Theatre Criticism* (1986), which compiles reviews of approximately 550 productions from 1900 to 1950 and notes only 12 "black" shows (3 written and produced by whites).[48] Anthologies of American plays sometimes print one black play, seldom two. Most importantly, the history book that treats all American theatre in an integrated fashion has yet to appear.

Who is to write these new, more comprehensive, more American books?—scholars trained in a comprehensively ethnic theatre history. And how are they to be trained?—in graduate schools. But who is to teach these new scholars when most present mentors know so little of ethnic histories? Let us learn. Professor Errol Hill of Dartmouth would never have written his revealing book *Shakespeare in Sable* had he not been familiar with Black *and* Shakespearean theatre; nor would Robert Toll have conceived his history of show business, *On with the Show!*, had he not first researched his book on minstrelsy, *Blacking Up*.[49] But more of this assimilated history is not likely to burst upon us until our theatre departments and graduate schools revise their curricula, assign dissertations to students regardless of race, train and hire teachers who know both black and white theatre history, and award books and studies that treat integrated subjects. All of this, assuming our best efforts, will require a generation of scholars.

The truth of American theatre history is and should be "Here Comes Everybody."

NOTES

1 Weldon B. Durham, ed., *American Theatre Companies*, 2 vols. (Westport, Conn.: Greenwood Press, 1986), II.

2 Mary C. Henderson, *Theatre in America: Two Hundred Years of Productions* (New York: Harry N. Abrams, 1986).

3 Ibid., p. 177.

4 Edwin Bronner, ed., *The Encyclopedia of the American Theatre, 1900–1975* (New York: A. S. Barnes, 1980).

5 Val Ferdinand [Kalamu Ya Salaam], *Blk Love Song #1,* in *Black Theatre USA,* ed. James V. Hatch and Ted Shine (New York: Free Press, 1974), p. 867.

6 For a discussion of Africanisms and neo-Africanisms, see James Hatch, "Speak to Me in Those Old Words, You Know, Those La-La Words, Those Tung-Tung Sounds (Some African Influences on the Afro-American Theatre)," *Yale/Theatre* (special issue on African theatre) 8:1 (1976), 25–34.

7 John Hope Franklin, *From Slavery to Freedom,* 3rd ed. (New York: Alfred A. Knopf, 1967), p. 71.

8 Philip D. Curtin, *The Atlantic Slave Trade: A Census* (Madison: University of Wisconsin Press, 1969).

9 Martin Bernal, *Black Athena: The Fabrications of Ancient Greece, 1785–1935* (New Brunswick, N.J.: Rutgers University Press, 1987). The most exciting recent scholarship has challenged the "Aryan" origins of classical Greece. Professor Bernal of Cornell University has presented convincing arguments that the roots of classical Greek civilization lie in Afroasiatic cultures and that nineteenth-century European cultural historians first obscured and finally erased these facts.

10 Orlando Patterson, "Rethinking Black History," *African Report* 17:9 (1972), 29–31.

11 George Pullen Jackson, *White and Negro Spirituals, Their Life Span and Kinship* (Locust Valley, N.Y.: J. J. Augustin Publisher, 1943), p. 293.

12 *Shango de Ima,* ed. Pepe Carril and trans. Susan Sherman (New York: Doubleday, 1970).

13 Winifred Kellersburger Vass, *The Bantu Speaking Heritage of the United States* (Los Angeles: Center of Afro-American Studies, University of California, 1979).

14 Bruce A. McConachie, "Towards a Postpositivist Theatre History," *Theatre Journal* 37 (1985), 474–475.

15 Thomas Pawley, "The Black Theatre Audience," *Players* (1971), 257–261.

16 Ibid., p. 261.

17 Lorenzo D. Turner, "African Survivals in the New World with Special Emphasis on the Arts," in *Africa Seen by American Negro Scholars,* ed. John A. Davis (New York: Dijon, 1958).

18 Marshall Stearns and Jean Stearns, *Jazz Dance, The Story of American Vernacular Dance* (New York: Macmillan, 1964).

19 Frederick G. Detweiler, *The Negro in the United States* (Chicago: University of Chicago Press, 1922), p. 61.

20 Interviews with Leigh Whipper and Ida Forsyne Hubbard (New York: Hatch-Billops Collection, 1972).

21 VèVè A. Clark, "The Archaeology of Black Theatre," *Black Scholar* 10 (1979), 43–56.

22 Zora Neale Hurston, *Mules and Men* (Philadelphia: Lippincott, 1935).

23 For a discussion of black speech and body rituals, see Lawrence W. Levine, *Black Culture and Black Consciousness* (New York: Oxford University Press,

1977); Roger D. Abrahams, *Deep Down in the Jungle* . . . (Chicago: Aldine Publishing, 1970); and Thomas Kochman, ed., *Rappin' and Stylin' Out* (Urbana: University of Illinois Press, 1972).

24 For a discussion of early black characters on the English stage, see Anthony Gerard Barthelemy, *Black Face Maligned Race* (Baton Rouge: Louisiana University Press, 1987); and G. K. Hunter. "Othello and Colour Prejudice," *Annual Shakespeare Lecture of the British Academy, 1967,* Proceedings of the British Academy, LIII (London: Oxford University Press, 1968).

25 Ben Jonson, *The Masque of Blackness* (London: University Wartburg Institute Journal, 1943).

26 Aphra Benn, *Oroonoko, or The Royal Slave, A True History* (London: Will. Canning, 1688), adapted for the stage by Thomas Southerne in 1694 (London: A. and C. Corbett, 1760).

27 To discuss Civil War plays or minstrelsy without analyzing the economic and psychological milieu is analogous to examining Joseph Conrad's *Heart of Darkness* purely as a spiritual odyssey of the soul.

28 Andrew Barton, *The Disappointment, or The Force of Credulity* (Philadelphia: Francis Shallus, 1767).

29 Introduction, in David Mays, ed., *The Disappointment, or The Force of Credulity by Andrew Barton, A Critical Edition of the First American Drama* (Gainesville: University of Florida Press, 1976), pp. 18–19.

30 Robert Mumford, *The Candidates,* in *Dramas from the American Theatre, 1762–1909,* ed. Richard Moody (New York: World Publishing, 1966), p. 15.

31 Anna Cora Mowatt, *Fashion* (London: Samuel French, 1850), p. 1.

32 George Aiken, adaptor, *Uncle Tom's Cabin,* in *Dramas from the American Theatre, 1762–1909,* ed. Richard Moody (Boston: Houghton Mifflin, 1966), pp. 360–396.

33 J. Murdock, *The Triumph of Love, or Happy Reconciliation* (Philadelphia: R. Folwell Publishers, 1795).

34 James D. MacCabe, Jr., *The Guerrillas* (Richmond: West and Johson, 1863), p. 83.

35 Charles Mathews, *Sketches of Mr. Mathews's Trip to America* (London: J. Limbird, 1824), p. 9.

36 Aldridge in his own memoir denied he played Hamlet at the African Grove Theatre, but Mathews may have seen him in another Shakespearean role. See the discussion in Herbert Marshall and Mildred Stock, *Ira Aldridge, The Negro Tragedian* (Carbondale: Southern Illinois University Press, 1968), pp. 40–44.

37 Moody, *Dramas,* p. 475.

38 Ralph Ellison's penetrating essays in *Shadow and Act* (London: Secker and Warburg, 1967), although rarely assigned to theatre students for the study of American minstrelsy, remain one of the most serious social and psychological analyses of that theatrical phenomenon.

39 Alain Locke and Montgomery Gregory, eds., *Plays of Negro Life* (New York: Harper and Brothers, 1927).

40 The first performance occurred at PS 122 on the Lower East Side in 1980. The Broadway production opened on March 24, 1988.

41 Exceptions should be noted: Professor William R. Reardon conducted several recruiting and scholarship programs for black Ph.D. candidates in the late sixties and early seventies. In recent years, New York University, Indiana University, University of California at Santa Barbara, and Ohio State University have graduated Afro-American scholars in theatre.

42 In November 1987, I held telephone conversations with Professors Winona Fletcher of Indiana University, Bloomington; Thomas Pawley of Lincoln University, Jefferson City, Missouri; William R. Reardon of the University of California, Santa Barbara; and Errol Hill of Dartmouth College, Hanover, New Hampshire. These theatre scholars, without recent statistical evidence to support their suppositions, were in unanimous agreement that the number of blacks in graduate theatre programs had dropped markedly in the 1980s.

43 Phyllis Johnson Kaye, ed., *The National Playwrights Directory* (New York: Drama Books Specialists, 1977).

44 Benito Ortolani, ed., *International Bibliography of Theatre: 1983* (Brooklyn: Theatre Research Data Center, Brooklyn College, City University of New York, 1986).

45 Robert C. Toll, *On with the Show!* (New York: Oxford University Press, 1976); Edwin Wilson and Alvin Goldfarb, *Living Theater: An Introduction to Theater History* (New York: McGraw-Hill, 1983).

46 Lorraine Brown and John O'Connor, *Free, Adult, and Uncensored, The Living History of the Federal Theatre Project* (Washington, D.C.: New Republic Books, 1978).

47 Brenda Coven, *American Women Dramatists of the Twentieth Century: A Bibliography* (Metuchen, N.J.: Scarecrow Press, 1982).

48 Anthony Slide, ed., *Selected Theatre Criticism*, vol. I, *1900–1920*; vol. II, *1921–1930*; vol. III, *1931–1950* (Metuchen, N.J.: Scarecrow Press, 1986).

49 Errol Hill, *Shakespeare in Sable, A History of Black Shakespearean Actors* (Amherst: University of Massachusetts Press, 1984); Robert C. Toll, *Blacking Up: The Minstrel Show in Nineteenth Century America* (New York: Oxford University Press, 1974).

Emphasizing the Avant-Garde
An Exploration in Theatre Historiography

Alan Woods

The history of the twentieth-century theatre, as it appears in most textbooks, is the history of a series of avant-garde movements. They emerge one after the other, as the century progresses, from realism and naturalism before the turn of the century through the most current deconstructive postmodernism. Each in turn spawns a manifesto or two, taking its brief moment of notoriety before sinking into apparent oblivion. Some elements of each movement linger on; but in general, faded avant-gardes quickly vanish before the relentless pressure of yet newer movements.

Although overstated for emphasis, this depiction of a standard twentieth-century pattern is not too far off the mark. Textbooks present the century as one of continuous experimentation, as theatre artists restlessly search out the new, constantly exploring as they seek to extend the range of their art, both in subject matter and in styles of presentation. Thus, Paul Kuritz, in *The Making of Theatre History,* provides excellent brief summaries of symbolism, futurism, dada and surrealism, expressionism, and constructivism,[1] while ignoring the popular theatre those movements rejected. It is easy, of course, to attack textbooks, which by their nature must generalize while being rigorously selective. The search for the new is present in virtually all areas of scholarly work: witness the many journals, for example, devoted to the documentation of the new, the experimental, the avant-garde. In the United States alone, *The Drama Review* and *Performing Arts Journal* document such phenomena, while no scholarly publication devotes such attention to the popular or commercial theatre.

The emphasis on the avant-garde runs throughout the century. Theatre historians are hardly the only ones perpetrating a bias for the new, as a glance at any weekly news magazine will confirm. Western society in general—and American society in particular—has long been captivated by the new and faintly contemptuous of the old. "New and improved" sells soap powder, but also can serve as an apt description of the major preoccupation of European and American societies in the twentieth century. While theatre historians cannot be faulted for reflecting the bias of their time, it should be possible to explore some of the effects those biases have on the way theatre is studied. Focusing on the new, the experimental, and the unusual has its benefits, but there are also clear dangers inherent in the practice that have been little examined or understood. Assumptions concerning the nature of theatrical art, along with the role and function of the historian and critic, are brought into sharp relief when one explores the ramifications of emphasizing the avant-garde at the expense of more conventional forms of theatre.

Stressing the new implies that history is synonymous with *progress*. Historical phenomena, it is assumed, will consistently and inevitably grow and develop in new directions. In this view, change follows a recurring pattern. Constantly pushing against the controlling and shaping force of tradition, a barrier which is often stultifying, change is an irresistible impulse. Despite the efforts of traditional forces to hold it back, progress is perceived as inevitable. It is almost always perceived as an improvement as well, reaching toward a perfection not previously gained. Charting that progress thus becomes the major task of the historian, who is charged with explicating new forms, with making patterns clear to those who otherwise are unable to discern contemporary events. Indeed, the very term "avant-garde," in its basic meaning, defines the process of progress: it is something ahead of its time, "in front of the line," constantly at the cutting edge of the search for the new.

That this neo-Darwinist view of historical process remains dominant must not obfuscate the fact that it is biased. Progress is neither inevitable nor, in terms of artistic movements, necessarily desirable. In some ways, the emphasis upon progress is detrimental. Achievements within traditional forms tend to be ignored, or glossed over, if they do not provide clear instances of "progression."

A further ramification of historians' focus on the new, and the assumption of the inevitability of progress, is the resultant emphasis upon the intention of the artist. If the intent is to be new, to stretch the limits of the art form, then often serious attention is paid, even if the resulting theatrical performance falls rather short of success. Thus, the marginally theatrical *serate* of the futurists and the playful events presented by dadaists receive attention, despite their lack of theatrical impact. Similarly, the happenings of the 1960s loom far larger in theatre history than one would expect, given their influence on theatre artists of the period. Stressing the artist's intention skirts dangerously close to the intentionalist fallacy, of course.

Literary bias also plays a role in the emphasis on avant-garde work. Much popular theatre lacks literary value (or even merit). Certainly traditional work, with its reliance on formulaic plots and characters, offers a less fertile field of exploration for the scholar than experiments seeking to expand both the vocabulary and the range of performance. It is hardly surprising that scholars prefer to spend time and effort on the work of Caryl Churchill rather than that of Michael Frayn, or on Sam Shepard instead of Neil Simon.

Events which are major phenomena by any objective standard receive little attention when only the new is stressed. An obvious example can be found in the incredible success of Agatha Christie's mystery-thriller *The Mousetrap*. Since its London opening in 1952, Christie's play has been seen by countless thousands of theatregoers, becoming the longest-running production in the history of English-language theatre. The play and its production, however, remain unanalyzed by scholars of theatre, who have not attempted to explain the unprecedented popularity of the piece. *The Mousetrap* was unable to reproduce its popularity when presented in the United States. Even so, the play clearly offers rich research material for the scholar willing to explore the reasons—many of them, one suspects, having little to do with theatrical matters—for its apparently unending appeal to the British audience.

The example could well be multiplied. Long-run productions in all major European and American theatre centers usually go unexplored, because they rarely represent avant-garde concerns. What such long-run productions as *Oh! Calcutta!* (New York), *Patate* (Paris), *Shear Madness* (Chicago and elsewhere in North America), or *The Drunkard* (Los Angeles) reveal about the nature of theatre in those cities and the role that those forms of theatre play for their audiences may be guessed, but has not been determined.

Emphasizing the avant-garde not only obscures specific productions which are not avant-garde, but also leads to the dismissal of traditional forms of theatrical performance and to the concomitant danger that the tradition may well be lost because it has never been recorded. The popular tradition rarely receives recognition, either because historians assume that something so popular must be well known and does not need documentation—why record the obvious?—or because some historians regard widely popular forms as unworthy of time and effort.

Theatrical history is full of examples of traditional forms left unrecorded. Why bother to record the details of tiring house facades in Elizabethan and Jacobean London, clearly visible to audiences at every performance? What need was there to keep an account of wandering performers during the tenth century A.D., or to describe the elements of the Athenian skene in the fifth century B.C.? All were obvious to the observer, so no pressing need was felt to keep accounts of them for the future.

History is equally silent where popular nonliterary forms are concerned. We possess exhaustive materials on the literary quarrels of the neoclassicists of the later seventeenth and early eighteenth centuries, but only tantalizing glimpses of contemporaneous popular theatrical forms. The frivolous and ephemeral entertainments of the *commedia dell'arte,* of the *boulevard* and *foire* theatres in France, of Hans Sachs in Germany—all were too trivial to merit being written down in their periods and are now known only in an incomplete and fragmented way, despite their enormous popularity.

The mistakes of past recorders of theatrical entertainment are patent to us in hindsight and frequently lamented. By stressing the new, however, twentieth-century historians repeat the omissions of previous ages. Just as traditional forms of the past are now lost, so will those performance styles which could now merit being termed "traditional" be lost unless they are recorded. The skills and performance dynamics of the entertainment form of vaudeville, for example, survive in the modern world only through a handful of performers, a few film records, and, of most importance, because a group of young performance artists in the early 1970s—the so-called new vaudevillians—consciously set out to preserve techniques and skills which had become superfluous for performers trained in psychological realism.

While some of the forms of vaudeville will presumably survive, other popular forms are less fortunate. Burlesque routines, music hall turns, some circus clowning—all exist primarily in somewhat artificial pastiches, often put together by survivors of the form aided by scholars. This was the case, in recent years, with such revues as *Sugar Babies* (burlesque), *Vagabond Stars* (Yiddish variety), and *The Vi-Ton-Ka Medicine Show* (medicine shows). While such entertainments help maintain the traditional forms, they frequently rely upon practitioners for performance style, and it is unclear if such pieces will survive their original artists. With no recording of the tradition, these forms can, and will, be lost.

The loss of traditional forms, paradoxically, reduces the impact of the experimental ones which are so thoroughly recorded. It is only in context that the avant-garde can be perceived as experimental: without Scribe and Robertson, Ibsen becomes musty and old-fashioned; without Rattigan, Pinter now seems highly conservative; Charles Ludlam's work appears merely sophomoric until placed against Neil Simon's polished comedies. The context within which the avant-garde takes place defines it and provides the limits beyond which it reaches. Without the framework of the traditional and popular forms, avant-garde work loses its reason for being.

Not all experimental work rejects the entertainment world from which it comes. Traditional entertainment forms provide the base from which avant-garde work springs in a positive sense as well. Beckett's tramps in *Waiting for Godot,* Weill's use of popular songs in *Mahagonny,* and much of Robert Wilson's visual imagery rest on elements of popular culture which may be virtually incomprehensible in the not-too-distant future, when the tradition they echo has died.

Without the context provided by popular theatrical forms, then, experimental work loses much of its point; the avant-garde can appear merely quirky and idiosyncratic. The reverse is not true, however: popular and traditional forms do not need experimentation to provide them with validity or to place the work in strong contrast. Rather, popular forms receive their validation from audiences. Box office success provides a sure measure of audience acceptance. Although such acceptance is readily apparent, far too little scholarly work has been done to examine the ways in which the audience accepts performances and what that implies. Audience acceptance provides another paradox: despite the fact that popular theatre is seen by millions of people (particularly in its cinematic and video transformations), the avant-garde forms seen by hundreds of people (at best) have received far more attention from historians.

Basic questions remain unanswered—and, indeed, some remain unasked. Only recently, for example, have useful efforts begun to explore how audiences connect with the theatrical work, or what impact the popular theatrical event has upon its audience. The works of such scholars as Sue-Ellen Case, Bruce McConachie, and Laurence Senelick examine audience response to specific forms of theatrical entertainment,[2] while Ronald Vince provides the beginnings of a theory of theatre historiography which insists on the importance of theatre's contextual framework.[3]

One element of the popular theatre has been explored, at least theoreti-cally: the use of popular theatre as evidence for areas of concern to its audi-ences. J. S. R. Goodlad, in a pioneering study, *A Sociology of Popular Drama*, provided the theoretical approach to popular drama which Rosemarie K. Bank later applied to nineteenth-century American melodrama.[4] Social and political contexts are now being considered in ways more sophisticated than Goodlad's early efforts by scholars such as Herbert Lindenberger and Steven Mullaney.[5]

A thorough exploration of the popular and traditional theatrical forms might begin, as well, to provide some concept of how the theatre functions within contemporary societies. Looking at the avant-garde and the experi-menters demonstrates one way in which the theatre functions, of course. The self-reflexive stance of the avant-garde, frequently centered on percep-tions of the art form itself, reveals a great deal about the theatre artist. Little research has been done on the function of theatrical entertainment in the larger society, however, and approaching the question through the popular forms might well be fruitful. An attempt to explain the popularity of *A Chorus Line* or *No Sex Please, We're British!* might inevitably lead into matters properly regarded as extratheatrical. Both productions enjoyed ex-tremely lengthy runs, suggesting that they successfully tapped an audience composed primarily of tourists or individuals distinct from the normal au-dience base for productions in New York and London. This implies social functions for such productions different from the norm. Again, the ways in which the popular theatre serves its audiences are unexplored, whether those audiences are the "regular" theatre audience or primarily tourists. In either case, the role of theatre most likely will be quite different from that of the avant-garde.

In short, the social function of the theatre tends to be overlooked when historians emphasize the art form itself, rather than the audience and the ways in which it uses the theatre. The societal aspects of theatrical enter-tainment are placed in sharp relief, it appears to me, when the popular forms receive the appropriate interest. This approach suggests examining theatre's sociological rather than purely artistic functions. The theatre, in this permutation, becomes the material for social research, rather than being an end for its own sake. Many theatre histories tend to ignore the-atre's social dimensions, keeping focus entirely on the art form itself. But the art form exists only in the context of its audience, so it seems only just to spend some research time on that audience and the larger society from which it comes. Such studies are now beginning to appear, as discussed above, although they remain in a distinct minority.

Popular forms of theatre also provide other research possibilities, more directly tied to areas of traditional concern to theatre scholars. The function of theatrical performance conventions, for example, remains little explored, possibly in part because, if one approaches performance from the avant-garde framework, conventions of performance exist primarily to be broken or redefined. It is of much greater import, from that perspective, to examine exactly how Pirandello shattered the illusion of the fourth wall than to explore how often the fourth wall's illusion was maintained by Pirandello's contemporaries (or even, as it turns out, by his immediate descendants).

In fact, performance conventions do offer rich research possibilities from a number of perspectives. Analyzing the means by which both audiences and artists agree willingly to suspend the disbelief which automatically accompanies theatrical performance can provide rich insights into both audience expectations and the confines within which the artists work. Despite the potential richness of the research, however, little has been done to explore either the ways in which conventions function or the ways in which conventions change over time, although many writers touch upon the use of theatrical conventions—Elizabeth Burns, Augusto Boal, and Richard Hornby, to mention three prominent theorists.[6]

Audiences at the present writing routinely accept, for example, the absence of house curtains in the theatre. When the audience enters the auditorium, it expects to see the setting fully visible onstage, often carefully lit to display various aspects of the design. The stage lights go out, typically, to signal the beginning of the performance; the return of illumination on the stage indicates that the play has begun.

As a convention, the absent curtain is relatively recent. Curtains were routinely used over the past century and a half to separate the world of the stage—the world of illusion—from the real world of the audience. The house curtain continued the illusion of the fourth wall, cutting off the world of the stage until the moment when the play actually began. The lifting (or, occasionally, opening) of the curtain signaled that the illusion had begun as the view through the picture frame of the proscenium arch appeared. Often the curtain revealed a beguiling and carefully arranged stage picture, usually welcomed by the audience's applause.

The shift in this particular convention has occurred during the past two decades, since the late 1960s. Several questions come to mind regarding curtain usage. Principal among them are: When did the change happen? Why? And how were audiences persuaded that this new way of beginning performances was acceptable?

GOOD ANALYSIS

When the change occurred cannot be answered; quite simply, none of the observers of theatrical events saw fit to record the change in convention or regarded it as important enough to remark upon. Nor is the exact date particularly important. Discovering the first production to discard the front curtain would be as futile as attempting to determine the hour and date of the beginning of the Renaissance.

If the date the change occurred cannot be pinpointed, why the change happened is equally vague, although of greater interest for its implications. The widespread use of thrust stages and theatres-in-the-round, all happening after 1948, must have had some influence. Those theatres did not use house curtains because, practically speaking, curtains were impossible. Hence, audiences began to be trained not to expect curtains. Expectations set up by informal summer theatres and various forms of alternative theatre, such as off- and off-off-Broadway, may have been another source for the disuse of the front curtain. If that is so, it points to another area little explored by scholars: the impact of practices stemming from purely pragmatic concerns on the traditional commercial theatre.

Equally important to the demise of the curtain convention may have been the practice of Bertolt Brecht and the theory of Epic Theatre expounded by both Brecht and Erwin Piscator. Their insistence that the means of theatrical production not be hidden, that audience members be able to see the rigging and the means of production (in part to demystify the event by making clear the source of theatrical magic), must have influenced the popular theatre, at least indirectly. Certainly, Brecht's ideas, filtered through commercial sensibilities, had reached Broadway as early as 1938, through Wilder's *Our Town,* with its Brechtian stage manager and constant reminder to the audience that what it was seeing was theatrical fiction, no matter how moving. That *Our Town* also dispensed with a front curtain makes a strong, if circumstantial, case for Brecht's influence.

The absence of the house curtain, therefore, should remind audiences that they are seeing a fictive event, and that everything they see in the performance area is illusory. To the degree that the convention has been accepted, it can be ignored as yet another extension and continuation of the willing suspension of disbelief. What was for the audiences of Brecht and Piscator (and Wilder as well) a distancing device, something which reminded them that they were in a theatre and not present at an actual event, has become yet another device in the arsenal of the commercial theatre, used to engender empathic responses. As an accepted part of the evening's entertainment, the absent curtain no longer makes a statement, and certainly no longer functions to create aesthetic distance. Audiences now have more time in which to contemplate the setting, to become more aware of the world of illusion being created on the stage.

The use of a front curtain dates only from the seventeenth century; its aesthetic function as a barrier between the audience and an illusionistic stage is even more recent. The convention of the front curtain is not, therefore, something fixed and immutable in the nature of theatre art. The change in the convention suggests, however, the avant-garde's influence on the traditional theatre. The convention of not having a curtain, familiarized through the avant-garde, has become standard, although now devoid of the significance that the lack of curtain—shattering an existent convention—once had. The new convention (no curtain) no doubt will in turn be broken by a new avant-garde and presumably will be replaced by a new conventional means of beginning performances, borrowed from the avant-garde.[7]

The process by which this particular convention was transformed from avant-garde, antiestablishment statement to mainstream convention has not been studied. Indeed, little is known in general about how such performance conventions shift from avant-garde to mainstream. Focusing on the avant-garde prevents those obvious shifts from reaching significance. Many other such unstudied conventions exist. The use (or nonuse) of masking the backstage and wing areas, direct address (or not) to the audience, and the time of performance are but three examples.

Despite the avant-garde's influence on the commercial theatre, experimentation has its own history and traditions, as C. D. Innes has reminded us.[8] If Innes is correct in seeing the avant-garde as important in its own right, not only for its dialectical relationship with the commercial theatre, then scholarly emphasis on the avant-garde removes these histories even more from an accurate picture of theatrical history as a whole. As a separate phenomenon, the avant-garde may indeed have its own rationale. With additional investigation, elements often regarded as demonstrating the influence of the avant-garde on the commercial stage may do no such thing. The fragmented vision of the expressionists may be reflected in the synecdochic settings Jo Mielziner provided after World War II for Williams and Miller, but it is equally possible that expressionism and selective realism have no connection whatsoever and that apparent visual similarities are the result of serendipity rather than causality.

Far too often causal connections have been assumed, rather than demonstrated, and far too often the assumption that the avant-garde always influences the traditional theatre has remained unchallenged. Regardless of the relationships between the avant-garde and the popular theatre, however, the fact remains that the popular theatre deserves study for its own sake and in its own right. The popular forms of theatre generally provide the base, both financially and in terms of audience support, on which the avant-garde depends. It seems an absurdity to ignore that base while stressing the exotic offshoots of experimentation.

Histories of theatrical practice must include the popular theatre. It provides the only form of theatrical entertainment for the vast majority of the audience. Without the popular theatre, there can be nothing for the avant-garde to be avant garde of. Understanding the popular theatre is fundamental to comprehending historical audiences, to perceiving the social functions of the theatre in various ages, and to knowing the context of avant-garde experimentation.

NOTES

1 Paul Kuritz, *The Making of Theatre History* (Englewood Cliffs, N.J.: Prentice-Hall, 1988), pp. 369–374.

2 Sue-Ellen Case, "Classic Drag: The Greek Creation of Female Parts," *Theatre Journal* 37 (1985), 317–328; Bruce A. McConachie and Daniel Friedman, eds., *Theatre for Working-Class Audiences in the United States, 1830–1980* (Westport, Conn.: Greenwood Press, 1985); Laurence Senelick, *British Music-Hall, 1840–1923* (Hamden, Conn.: Archon Books, 1981).

3 Ronald W. Vince, *Ancient and Medieval Theatre, A Historiographical Handbook* (Westport, Conn.: Greenwood Press, 1984); Vince, *Renaissance Theatre, A Historiographical Handbook* (Westport, Conn.: Greenwood Press, 1984).

4 J. S. R. Goodlad, *A Sociology of Popular Drama* (Totowa, N.J.: Rowman and Littlefield, 1972); Rosemarie K. Bank, "Melodrama as a Social Document: Social Factors in the American Frontier Play," *Theatre Studies* 22 (1975/1976), 42–49.

5 Herbert S. Lindenberger, *Opera: The Extravagant Art* (Ithaca: Cornell University Press, 1984); Steven Mullaney, *The Place of the Stage: License, Play and Power in Renaissance England* (Chicago: University of Chicago Press, 1987).

6 Elizabeth Burns, *Theatricality: A Study of Convention in the Theatre and in Social Life* (London: Longman, 1972); Augusto Boal, *Theater of the Oppressed,* trans. Charles A. McBride and Maria-Odilia Leal McBride (New York: Urizen Books, 1979); Richard Hornby, *Drama, Metadrama and Perception* (Lewisburg, Penn.: Bucknell University Press, 1986).

7 Indeed, the 1986 Broadway musical *Rags* employed the traditional curtain, to the highly vocal astonishment of two audience members seated near me at a preview performance. Young enough never to have seen a front curtain regularly used,

they found the curtain a startling way to, as one put it, "cut off the stage from the audience." *Rags* was not a success, so its use of the curtain may have simply been a symptom of the production's dated quality which contributed to its failure. It could also suggest that this particular convention may be returning.

8 C. D. Innes, *Holy Theatre: Ritual and the Avant Garde* (Cambridge and New York: Cambridge University Press, 1981).

Evidence and Documentation

Joseph Donohue

Notwithstanding the broad array of approaches to be found in contemporary scholarship and the contentious opposition of theorists of different camps, scholars appear to hold some widely shared convictions about how they do what they do. Probably the most fundamental of these convictions about general method is that, in order to produce sound scholarship, a scholar's obligations consist in providing the evidence necessary to substantiate an argument and in documenting that evidence clearly and with reasonable fullness. As a result, it is held to be incumbent on the working scholar to keep precise track of the ground that has been covered during research and, in writing, to provide enough signposts to allow a fellow scholar to retrace the path, or any segment of it, for purposes of verification or other, independent purposes.

So far as it goes, that view of the presentation of evidence and the function of documentation is a valid one. Yet it seems an excessively narrow pragmatism to suppose that the scholar need only be concerned with the proper gathering and labeling of evidence and not with the assumptions and values that effectively characterize such work. Of course, it has long been the case that scholars consider it a matter of lucid rhetoric, and of professional tact as well, to *place* their work in the exact yet amplitudinous contexts of what is known and unknown and of what must be reexamined and reevaluated. It is widely accepted also that good scholarship is good partly because, at least implicitly, it acknowledges its methods, describes its goals, and recognizes the perceived limits of its coverage and usefulness. All of these strategies contribute to a viable scholarly method, and most if not all works of theatre scholarship commonly rated high for their value and usefulness adhere to them.

And yet, at a time when the historiography of theatre studies is undergoing radical reassessment, even more appears to be required of us. It is necessary, we now find, to pause in the process of research and writing on the theatre to reflect on larger though seemingly less concrete issues. This proves an especially useful procedure when it comes to evaluating the place of evidence and documentation in the scholarly enterprise. Theatre history is still a young discipline, but it has begun to reach its maturity at a happy moment when pervasive attention is being given throughout humanistic scholarship to means and methods, to theory and practice. Theatre historians have arrived at a fortunate juncture, then; but it is not too much to say that, unless we thoroughly scrutinize these fundamental and far-reaching issues relating to the evidence we use and the tools and methods of its accumulation and identification, we risk producing a puerile, superficial, and ultimately useless scholarship. A comment of Bernard Shaw's offers by implication an apt example of the danger of what may be called the Unexamined Method. In the preface to *Major Barbara,* Shaw catalogues a long list of authors who, like him, have been concerned with a critique of society—"Voltaire, Rousseau, Bentham, Marx, Mill, Dickens, Carlyle, Ruskin, Butler, and Morris . . . , with Euripides, More, Montaigne, Molière, Beaumarchais, Swift, Goethe, Ibsen, Tolstoy, Jesus and the prophets all thrown in. . . ." In the very same sentence, Shaw professes that his current methods are of no use, and would not be if he were all the men he names, "as indeed in some sort I actually am," he adds, "standing as I do on all their shoulders."[1]

Shaw's care (one might alternatively call it ambition) to identify himself with his chief predecessors, while at the same time resolutely confronting a perceived crisis in method which he must address on his own, may serve as a useful model in framing questions about the nature and uses of evidence and documentation. At the same time, it must be understood that the present essay cannot undertake a thorough survey of either the kinds of evidence appropriate to theatre studies or the various means, methods, and materials of documentation in this field. The varying nature of evidence and the broad scope of documentation are exceedingly great, too much so for systematic treatment in anything less than a compendious guidebook—which, indeed, does not yet exist for theatre studies.[2] On the contrary, our concern here must be with the *a priori* necessity of scrutinizing the premises and assumptions underlying the discovery, generation, and use of evidence and its documentation. Not evidence and documentation themselves, but some ways of thinking about them constitute the present purpose.

But what are these entities that require such scrutiny? It is useful to begin by asking: What exactly is evidence? And what is documentation? In answer to the first question, a simple definition seems appropriate: any material, fact, or idea which establishes or corroborates the truth of a statement or allegation. Evidence can, of course, take almost any shape, depending on the subject matter and on the range of knowledge, industriousness, and inventiveness of the researcher. As for documentation, the *Britannica* provides a detailed and useful, yet ultimately limited, view:

[A] form of bibliographic control and organization that uses such tools as indexes, abstracts, and bibliographic essays, as well as the traditional methods of classification and cataloguing, to make information accessible. Its sphere also includes the creation of tools (*e.g.*, indexing and abstracting services); the development of media to contain information (*e.g.*, microforms and microphotography); and the development of organizational techniques (*e.g.*, KWIC [key word in context] and KWOC [key word out of context] indexing). In addition, documentation designates a special form of librarianship.[3]

This definition appears comprehensive and in addition lays important emphasis on accessibility of information, but it misses a crucial consideration. General information such as is contained in indexes, bibliographies, abstracts, and other reference tools becomes specific documentation only when imbedded in an argumentative structure which seeks to create new knowledge or revise our understanding of existing knowledge. The problem with the *Britannica* definition, then, is that it views documentation solely as the systematic presentation of information; it does not also acknowledge that the ultimate—indeed, the ordinary—use of such documentation is in the service of some particular truth. A catalogue of scene designs by a certain Baroque artist in a given theatre archive, for example, fulfills the *Britannica* definition of documentation, but the usefulness of that catalogue as documentation is not confined to its making accessible the holdings of the archive, important as such a service is. Its full usefulness becomes apparent only when, for example, the information it holds is used to document a study of that Baroque scene designer's work.

Of course, the conduct of scholarship may in some instances have as its first goal the creation of general documentation, such as indexes of promptbooks, bibliographies of plays, censuses of playbills, or biographies of performers—that is, categorically or otherwise systematically arranged listings, tabulations, or narratives intended to afford access to original documents or in some other way to the information the original documents contain. Some reference works are compendiums of sheer documentation, as in the instance of L. W. Conolly and J. P. Wearing's *English Drama and Theatre, 1800–1900: A Guide to Information Sources* (Detroit: Gale Research, 1978), which compiles and annotates a comprehensive series of bibliographical citations leading the student of the subject to contemporary and modern sources on history, criticism, individual authors, theatres, critics, and other aspects of the subject.

We may well ask: How do such works document their own claim to authority? The actual amount of formal documentation in *English Drama and Theatre, 1800–1900* is limited to a three-page introduction in which the compilers explain their approach ("extensive and representative coverage of primary and secondary materials important in the study of nineteenth-century English drama and theatre"), the format and arrangement of material, criteria for inclusion and exclusion of information, and so on. The compilers' claim to authority, then, is established almost exclusively through the usefulness of their work in practice. A similar example appears in the case of Philip H. Highfill, Kalman A. Burnim, and Edward A. Langhans, *A Biographical Dictionary of Actors, Actresses, Musicians, Dancers, Managers and Other Stage Personnel in London, 1660–1800* (12 vols. to date; Carbondale and Edwardsville: Southern Illinois University Press, 1973–). Not a single footnote appears to document statements of fact in the biographical entries, but, by way of a lucid narrative convention, a great deal of documentation is imbedded in the text itself, while introductory pages describing the types of sources used and the standards of factuality adhered to indicate the substantial authoritativeness of this reference work and, in fact, the extraordinary nature of the labor involved in creating it.

Indeed, some reference works are based so fundamentally on systematic analysis of subject matter that it is necessary for that analysis to be explicitly represented in some schematic form in the reference work itself. Such is the case with the recently inaugurated *International Bibliography of Theatre (IBT)*, edited by Benito Ortolani, co-sponsored by the American Society for Theatre Research and the International Association of Libraries and Museums of the Performing Arts, and published in cooperation with the International Federation for Theatre Research (Brooklyn: Theatre Research Data Center, Brooklyn College, CUNY, 1982–)—a large-scale cooperative effort of theatre historians to come to terms with the need for a basic bibliographical resource for research in theatre studies. In volume I (1982) there appears an extensive taxonomy, or classification system, for theatre studies which governs the content and format of the entries. In volume II (1983), partly in response to reactions from users and reviewers, a nine-page "Guide for Users" has been added, including the taxonomy (now described in terms of two basic classification systems: taxonomy of theatre and subject index) and providing descriptions of taxonomic and subject index terms and an analysis of a typical entry. The claim of such a work as the *IBT* to authoritative documentational status would indeed appear to exist in a larger magnitude from the ordinary reference work, since its usefulness hinges directly on the validity of its attempt at a comprehensive accounting for all the categories of knowledge in the field—a necessarily large claim which, despite some deficiencies inevitable in pioneer scholarship, it by and large justifies.

The term "documentation," then, refers essentially to making information accessible in ways appropriate to the subject matter. Only in a secondary sense does the term refer to the *apparatus* of documentation—for example, to taxonomies, lists of textual variants, footnotes, lists of works cited in a given article or book, appendices of additional materials, annotated bibliographies, and other adjuncts to the presentation of the scholarly argument itself. Documentation may well be presented on its own terms, then, as the *Britannica* definition indicates, or in some ancillary form appropriate to its function as part of an argument. Regardless of the form or format it takes, the ultimate question is always what the scholar who uses it does with it. That is, the question is finally one that has to do with interpretation—with history. The term "documentary history" may, in this context, seem somewhat oxymoronic; in fact, however, such a history differs from any other only by the extent to which it integrates substantial segments of primary documents into its argument or infers the structure of that argument from a perceived logical relationship of documents. Certainly, no work which forsakes argument for the presentation of "documentation" as such can make any valid claim as history. Evidence and documentation, then, are two closely connected entities, linked by the complementary services they render to scholarly inquiry and to the results of that inquiry in interpretive argument. It is useful to bear in mind the essential relationship and identical orientation of the two terms, lest we mistake the mere presentation of a piece of evidence or the mere provision of documentary apparatus as being all that evidence and documentation are about.

Having specified what, for general scholarly purposes, we may understand evidence and documentation to mean, we may now go on to identify some areas of the subject where scrutiny is at the present time especially important. No better example exists of a topic currently enjoying wide debate than the scholarly editing of dramatic text—or "script," to use a theatrical term increasingly employed by scholars and critics of the drama. One of the most highly respected textual critics and theorists of this century, W. W. Greg, writing in 1949, calls attention to "the tyranny of the copy-text," his term for a prejudice which he considered had vitiated much good editorial work in the generation before him. Greg's point is a precise technical one, but with important large-scale consequences. He acknowledges that standard modern editorial practice in determining "copy-text" (that is, selecting one of several existing texts to serve as the basis for a new critical edition) calls for choosing "whatever extant text may be supposed to represent most nearly what the author wrote and to follow it with the least possible alteration."

But Greg argues that the true theory or principle of copy-text requires a fundamental distinction between accidentals ("spelling, punctuation, word-division, and the like") and significant, or "substantive," readings. "It may happen," Greg observes, "that in a critical edition the text rightly chosen as copy may not by any means be the one that supplies most substantive readings in cases of variation." The copy-text should be relied on for accidentals, then, Greg argues, but this in itself is a narrow principle which should not govern the editor's choice among variant substantive readings from other relevant texts, a matter which belongs "to the general theory of textual criticism. . . ."[4] Thus, the upshot of Greg's critique is that too many editors have slavishly replicated the copy-texts on which their editions have been based because they have followed what they take to be the rules, but have ignored the higher claims of theory and its implications for method.

Greg is surely right to take fellow scholars to task for inflexibility and narrow-mindedness. Yet, for all his preeminence, Greg and the other editors of whom he speaks adversely have shared certain basic assumptions about authorial intention that cry out for reexamination. Whatever validity assumptions about authorial intention may have had in the traditional editing of literary texts, they have frequently come under attack in the last few years, especially in the case of dramatic authorship. As a result, certain principles governing the editing of a dramatic script now appear to have been clarified. First, it is understood that, in cases where more than one text of a given play is extant, it is a mistake simply to assume that one text (perhaps the latest one) represents the author's intentions more fully than any other. Instead, it seems to make much better sense to consider that each separate text may represent a different, independent "intentionality."

An example will illustrate the point. Steven Urkowitz takes this view of differing intentionalities in discussing the texts of Shakespeare's *King Lear*. He points out that editors have traditionally taken the quarto and folio texts of the play as *variant* texts, and so have drawn from them eclectically, using literary criteria, in order to establish a sort of master text—"what Shakespeare originally wrote"—a conflation that supposedly represents

Shakespeare's comprehensive intentions for the play.[5] Such an approach betrays a fundamental misconception of the nature of the evidence, Urkowitz argues. He points out that the quarto represents a relatively early text and production, whereas the folio text represents a revision by Shakespeare at a later date; the two texts thus emanate from two separate theatrical contexts and therefore represent two different "intentions," neither one *ipso facto* better than the other (though one might be judged so on literary or other grounds). Consequently, the conflated, or eclectic, text, however satisfyingly complete from a literary point of view (after all, what reader or audience could possibly want to do without some of Shakespeare's "best" writing?), represents neither a single composition by that dramatist nor a single production by his acting company, but only the result of a sort of expanded *Bartlett's Familiar Quotations* approach to Shakespeare's text.[6] Yet it is this kind of conflated text which has served as the basis for virtually all productions of *King Lear* through our own day, ever since Nahum Tate's Restoration adaptation of the play (itself another "intentionality" quite different from Shakespeare's) disappeared from the stage in the course of the nineteenth century.

Amazing as it may seem, then, it is safe to say that no modern audience has ever seen a production of Shakespeare's *King Lear* which corresponds textually to either of the productions seen by Shakespeare's own contemporaries. A fundamental principle of textual integrity, deduced from skeptical scrutiny of the prevailing theatrical circumstances under which Shakespeare lived and wrote and under which his plays were published, has thus emerged. A corollary principle of great importance also needs mention here, namely, that any cutting of a dramatic script imposes a certain interpretation—that is, an "intention"—on the text. Even if it is not so blatant as Laurence Olivier's in his film version of *Hamlet,* as announced in the initial voice-over, "This is the story of a man who could not make up his mind,"[7] an interpretation is discernible in any cutting (though some cuttings result in blurred or contradictory emphases). In the case of modern productions of *King Lear* and other plays with similar textual sources, we are still just beginning to discover that our productions, based as they almost inevitably are on cut versions of texts which are themselves conflated or otherwise eclectic, do not allow us to see Shakespeare with any kind of real integrity. Ironically, we are at the threshold of an era in which formerly notorious "bad" quartos are turning out to be good and interesting in their own way, and "good" quartos are proving to be even better.

Still another principle concerning the editing of dramatic text is now coming to be generally acknowledged, one long recognized by theatre practitioners and scholars but only recently embraced by literary editors, on whom theatre practitioners and scholars depend for editions of dramatic texts. This principle is that the composition of a play for performance is, normally, inherently a collaborative venture involving a range of theatrical practitioners, most notably actors, in addition to the playwright. D. F. McKenzie puts the point in the larger frame of reference of the theatrical occasion: "The relation of textual criticism to the realities of theatrical production has always been one of embarrassed impotence. The dramatic text is not only notoriously unstable, but, whatever the script, it is again never more than a pre-text for the theatrical occasion, and only a constituent part of it."[8]

Philip Gaskell has made the same point memorably in his discussion of the complex evolution of the text of Tom Stoppard's *Travesties,* from Stoppard's initial script, through rehearsal changes in the first production, further changes suggested by audience response and endorsed by the playwright, the playwright's own published reading text, and additional changes made in a second production by the same company (the Royal Shakespeare Company). As Gaskell explains:

> Stoppard said that the reading text of *Travesties* that was published between the first and second productions represents the play as he would like to have it performed by an ideal cast. But in the theatre, when he worked with an actual cast in developing the performance text of the second production, he helped to evolve a version which differed considerably from the published reading text. Stoppard not only accepted this performance version, but he actually preferred parts of it in the production. Yet he says that he is unlikely to incorporate these performance features in his published text. Should a future editor use them, or should he stick to Stoppard's published text?[9]

Although Gaskell is one of the least prescriptive of contemporary textual critics and bibliographers, one is tempted to formulate what, with deference to him, might be called Gaskell's Caveat, a cautionary reminder that should govern the research of all scholars, dramaturges, actors, theorists, and practitioners of theatre: *Ignorance of the text is no excuse.* It is a point that could be elaborated almost infinitely, with examples drawn from the various and often perplexing textual situations in the works of Georg Büchner, Henrik Ibsen, Oscar Wilde, William Butler Yeats, and Tennessee Williams, to name only five prominent instances.

Clearly, it is crucial to examine and be aware of the premises underlying one's scholarly method, whether that method involves evaluating evidence for the editing of texts or any other task. Dramatic textual scholarship has obviously come a long way from the days in which editors considered that they were performing a desirable service for their readership by presenting the last text seen through the press in the author's lifetime or by following some other dictum unreflective of the true and particular circumstances of textual generation and audience reception. Textual scholarship has come this distance through the healthy scrutiny of existing premises, assumptions, biases, and predilections, not by following "rules" which seem self-evident or which may be safely taken for granted. It is a custom that should be honored more in the observance than in the breach.

It is important, then, to cultivate the habit of subjecting evidence to a sustained and principled scrutiny, extending even to the scholar's own approaches to the task at hand. Doing so, often if not always, involves an attempt to set evidence in the widest possible artistic, social, cultural, critical, and theoretical contexts that circumstances and reasonable effort may allow. To infer a basic example from the previous discussion, an editor of Shakespeare's text must obviously be familiar with Elizabethan playhouse practice in order to understand how the stage directions in Elizabethan scripts are to be construed.

A similar familiarity with the cultural and social contexts of the play is called for in the person of, say, a dramaturge working on a production of *Twelfth Night*. Faced with an unfamiliar term in Feste's last-act comment, "And thus the whirligig of time brings in his revenges" (V.i.375–376), the dramaturge may take the simple expedient of consulting the *Oxford English Dictionary* and so discover in "whirligig" a wonderfully ironic reference to both a child's toy that is whirled, turned, or spun around and "an instrument of punishment formerly used, consisting of a large cage suspended so as to turn on a pivot." [10] If energetically pursued with the collaboration of the stage director, this is a discovery which might lead to such bold and effective staging as the imprisonment of Malvolio in a whirligig, in the scene (IV.ii) in which he is tormented by Feste masquerading as Sir Topas. It might also suggest the use of a child's top or other toy by, say, Sir Toby or Sir Andrew in some earlier scene. Feste's subsequent comment on the "whirligig of time" might thus take on an unusual richness that, through the imaginative use of stage properties, could be made meaningful to a modern audience. Of course, a booklet or program note prepared by the dramaturge of this hypothetical production could make such meanings accessible, but it remains likely that what is interesting to read in the moments before the lights go down may quickly be lost to memory without reinforcement in the production itself. Posters may characterize, program notes may entertain; but, no matter what ancillary help is made available to an audience, a play in production must be, as it were, self-documenting: it must establish lucid meanings and continuous conviction all by its own means and on its own terms.

Sometimes the resources for research are as familiar as published play texts or reference works, and their documentation consists in straight-forward bibliographical citation. The world of print—and prior to that the world of manuscript—is, of course, the scholar's traditional terrain. The advent of the digital computer, however, and even before that the emergence of such technologies as the microfilm camera and the resulting burgeoning of texts and other documents published in microform have changed the face of scholarship for good. If the great residue of primary documents is simultaneously the opportunity and the burden of the historian of the nineteenth-century theatre, the challenge facing everyone in the late twentieth century involves a vast shift in the nature of the tools of the trade themselves. Most especially with the development of the micro-computer, with its capacity for the speedy, efficient storage and processing of text and images (to say nothing of its capability for the organization and control of the physical environment, such as the lighting of a stage), the-atre scholarship has come to an important juncture in which large-scale changes are imminent. The imperative, already noted and illustrated above, to pay attention to premises and assumptions could not be more urgent than in the case of the computer.

We must begin by acknowledging that so much of what we now do, or hope to do, in the areas of compilation and classification of information and, finally, of interpretation of that information in order to create new knowledge involves the use of the computer. It is therefore crucial for us to pause and examine the underlying bases of what it is we do with these wonderful but often perplexing machines. One of the most outspoken commentators on the influence of computers in the world of learning, Joseph Weizenbaum, professor of computer science at MIT, has observed: "What the computer may do is to subtly modify the language in which the researcher thinks. I can see, in view of the manageability of certain kinds of information in a computer, as opposed to other kinds of ideas, that a scholar may slowly, imperceptibly alter his whole theoretical stance, in order to work with the computer. . . . The computer could change the whole flow of intellectual theory."[11] Weizenbaum's view of the conceptual hazards involved in using the computer for one's research has something in common with the old joke about looking under the streetlight for the dime one has lost elsewhere because the light is better there. The analogy is uncomfortably close in the case of one of the most important and promising uses of the computer, that of compiling databases of information for use in theatre history. Taking Weizenbaum's troubling prospect as reference, the issue might be phrased as follows: How does one construct a database of theatre history so as to take into account features of the subject that may not be amenable to description in a database?

Phrasing the question this way, of course, reveals an assumption, which most scholars may readily agree upon—that databases are very good for some things and not so good for others. We may scrutinize the issue more closely by posing an additional question of a more specific kind, one that might be thought typical of queries that are made of databases. It is, in fact, the sort of question I have posed for myself more than once in the process of designing a database for the study of the London theatre of the nineteenth century.[12] The question—actually a series of topically related questions—has to do with the well-known productions of Shakespeare mounted by Charles Kean at the Princess's Theatre in London in the 1850s. Behind these questions lies the purpose of attempting to estimate the impact and, beyond that, the significance of Kean's productions of Shakespeare for the history of nineteenth-century theatrical production.

Here are the questions: What other productions of Shakespeare were available to London playgoers during Charles Kean's tenure at the Princess's? Did any of them anticipate Kean's repertory? Did any repeat works Kean had already produced? How new were Kean's choices—specifically, with what relative frequency were the plays of Shakespeare that he produced available to London playgoers in the decade preceding Kean's tenure? What performers were seen in Kean's productions who were also seen acting in Shakespeare in the previous decade or in other productions in the same decade?

Now, this series of questions holds implicit a certain assumption about the benefit of a database. In this view, a database models a coherent gathering of a large number of facts representing states or conditions which are either true or false, depending on certain criteria—for example, a date of performance: *The Merchant of Venice* either was or was not performed at the Princess's during the 1852–1853 season. Computers can be programmed to hold large bodies of such facts in storage, accessible to query. In this way the computer becomes, however, a tyrannous truth machine whose very nature as a binary machine eliminates the possibility of a "both/and" case. No cognitive dissonance is allowed; it is present "in the computer" (as we conventionally put it), if at all, only as two terms construed as the true terms of a conflict of meaning—that is, as the *terms* of a conflict, not as a conflict itself. It seems inescapable, then, that computers are very good at implementing artifactual and logical modes of construing the world, but seemingly not good at all at dealing with experience of other kinds.

We must pause momentarily to consider what is meant by "artifactual" and "logical" modes. By "artifactual" I mean that the computer is good at implementing a reconstruction of theatrical activity which results from a scholar's analysis of the nature and function of an artifact and its relationship to other artifacts and to the original historical situation in which it emerged. A playbill, for example, is a highly useful artifact (see fig. 1), a kind of text which imparts to an audience certain information about the performance it will see, a text whose veracity is "proved" by that audience in comparing it to the performance itself. Subsequently, its veracity as evidence may be assumed by the scholar in the absence of contradictory information. (Other playbills for the same date could contradict it, however, as could the so-called indulgence slip, an erratum notice which begs the audience's indulgence for a substitution or cancellation; at least one instance has occurred in which a playbill, a newspaper advertisement, and a review all recorded the performance of a certain actress who in fact was indisposed, as an indulgence slip for that performance noted, and did not perform—a fact shamefacedly acknowledged afterward by the reviewer, who had decided he did not need to attend the performance he was obliged to review in order to write about it.)[13] Correlatively, a "logical" mode of construing the world is one in which the scholar may intuit or deduce certain relationships of data based on one-to-one, one-to-many, or many-to-many conditions. An actor, for example, will have only one birth date—at least, only one true one!—("one-to-one": one actor, one birth date), but may perform more than one role in a given performance ("one-to-many": one actor, many roles, or at least more than one); and several actors may do this doubling of roles in a given performance ("many-to-many": many actors, many doubled roles).[14]

Generally speaking, then, it may be assumed that databases deal with facts whose various relationships to other facts can be satisfactorily, though not necessarily definitively, construed in advance. (A good database should be susceptible of successively reconstrued relationships as the data are studied and become better understood.) A working knowledge of these relationships is necessary in order to design the structure of the database in the first place. The data structure—an articulation of the components of information and their basic relationships to one another—hence represents a series of logical relations of verified facts which are either constant or variable. The informational content of the database at any point thus assembles a picture of a reality composed of relations of variables and constants in a preconceived structure. The content may change from moment to moment, as data are input or updated, but the structure itself is a permanent feature of the world of the database.

So far, so good. We have, as it were, found the dime we were looking for, but we must now peer out from our well-lighted place under the streetlamp into the elusive and ambiguous shadows that surround us and acknowledge our inability to define their contours with any clarity. That is, we must frankly acknowledge that, to articulate a clear model of experience in the design of our database, we must exclude aspects of reality, modes of being, which cannot be construed by logical or instrumental analysis. For the truth is that, if we have been paying attention at all to the reactions to the increasing use of computers in the community of scholars, we know that critics, theoreticians, and others have for some time been leveling the charge of inadequacy at this model of factual comprehensiveness, this house of index cards. Placed in the context of theatre studies, their charge is, in plain language, that the computer database of theatrical history does not invoke any of the experiential contexts—artistic, social, cultural—that make the theatre profitable and interesting to study in the first place. That is, computers do not really help us to get at the real life of the form, the theatre itself, that the database purports to be about. More specifically even than this, the charge is that the informational model of the database of theatre history fails to provide an adequate representation of a world of process, a world in which imaginative creation, live performance, and instantaneous response are the essential features, and not facts.

Now, it must be immediately acknowledged that the database is indeed susceptible to this charge of failure to reify. Whatever it may be good for, it is not any good at all for that. Such a charge is made, however, by persons who resist coming to terms with the limitations (and the tremendous benefits as well) of binary structures. The database, of course, cannot reify an artistic experience. This is so simply because a database is composed of entity-based relationships of data which, by definition, cannot be construed directly as models of time, of temporal change. A database models time indirectly, by giving us facts about, for example, the changing repertory night after night. But these facts, like similar facts about new plays, new actors, and so on, constitute information about only the results of change; databases do not capture the process of change itself. Computers can be made to reflect the phenomena of human experience, but they do not, and cannot, encapsulate it.

There is, in fact, no way at all out of this dilemma over the alleged marginal status of facts in relation to the realities of artistic experience. A computer database is no substitute for experience. To think that a binary machine can somehow embody the process of time is to become a victim of chimeras. Only intellectual structures are embodied in computers, and the processes that go on inside them have to do only with the movement of electrons. A door must be open or shut (the English title of Alfred de Musset's play reminds us), and so it is with a gate, or circuit, in a memory chip.

Yet computer databases may be of tremendous assistance in our own human attempts to recapture and reassess the significant life of artistic forms and their contexts. What it all depends on, finally, is the formative intellectual power of the designer of the database and, in addition, the anticipated and real needs of its users. We must understand that the experience, for example, of the nineteenth-century playgoer is no more, and no less, accessible to us than, say, the experience of the nineteenth-century reader of novels, about whom so much reader-response theory has been formulated. In fact, it is helpful to emphasize the essential epistemological analogy between the theatre audience and the reader of novels (or plays, for that matter) and to point out that reader-response theory and audience-response theory have the same interest in the evanescent. That, of course, does not invalidate these enterprises; it only serves to characterize them. Computers, then, are very useful for what they do well—assisting us to do systematically and fully what we might otherwise do poorly or not at all. With Joseph Weizenbaum's cautions in mind, we should be prepared to use the power that computers afford for those purposes for which binary machines are significantly superior to human intellects in speed, accuracy, and comprehensive control (if not necessarily in storage capacity).

In order to make computers perform at their optimum capability, however, the theatre scholar must be aware of two very different principles. First, the modeling of intellectual structures for dealing with information must be based on a thorough analysis of the subject matter. This principle is the simple one of Skeptical Scrutiny. A database is a good one—that is, a serviceable one—to the extent that it reflects a pervasive sense of the logical and causative relationships of entities of data, at every level from micro to macro. An actress, for example, may have several names—a birth name, a professional name, and a married name, perhaps more than one, along with a title and possibly a sobriquet. A file of biographical information must somehow come to terms with these related facts, so that, for example, a computer query on the career of Ellen Tree connects her with the career of Mrs. Charles Kean—since they were, of course, the same person—while keeping the chronology of the two names clearly distinct.

The second principle, of a different sort, is that facts are inconclusive, muddled things by themselves; they take on coherence, meaning, and significance only in the act of interpretation. The analysis of subject matter that must precede the design and implementation of a database is thus itself an act, a comprehensive one, of interpretation. One looks at a playbill from the Victorian theatre and asks what kinds and categories of information are contained in it, but one must also ask what kind of audience was presumed to need or want to know all that information. Why, in comparison to the brief and summary character of the typical eighteenth-century bill, is this later text so dense, so packed with "facts"?[15] And why are certain seemingly important categories of information, such as the names of dramatists, almost never included in playbills, whereas, later in the century, they regularly turn up in programs? Answers to such questions must be forthcoming before the real significance of apparently straightforward data categories such as author, play title, genre, cast, and so on, can be confidently relied upon. One cannot postpone scrutiny of underlying meanings; the ghosts of values unassessed return to haunt the superficial analyst. It is a truth inadequately recognized that the mere setting down of the "facts of the matter" constitutes an interpretation, an evaluation, of the matter. To the extent that we do not control the pertinent facts of our inquiry by a pervasive understanding of them, they will come to control us. This principle, actually more of a caveat, may be called the Tyranny of the Commonplace. Indeed, these two principles have a force not confined to the design of a computer database; they should govern all theatre scholarship, no matter what ultimate form it may take.

There is a third principle, less easily articulated, but perhaps the most important of all. I call it the Insufficiency of Plenitude. By this I mean to point out that no amount of factual information, however seemingly comprehensive, can mask the inadequacy of argument or rhetorical purpose. Students of the theatre, especially the modern theatre, seem to be constantly confronting a multitude of facts, sometimes even an embarrassment of riches. And yet, no matter how much evidence lies at hand and no matter how well documented its presentation, it will fail in its establishing or supportive purpose without a lucid, conclusive argument. It will also fail without a well-sustained effort on the part of the author to link subject matter and audience (that is, the readership for scholarly writing) in some fresh and engaging way. "Who are my readers?" is a question we urge on

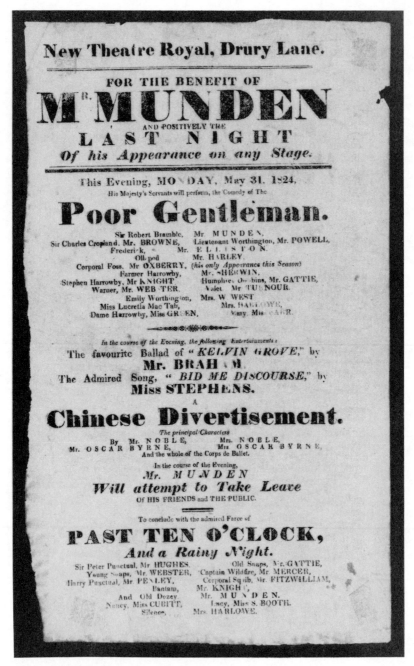

Fig. 1. Playbill, Munden's farewell benefit, Drury Lane Theatre, May 31, 1824. Author's collection.

our students, but one that perhaps we do not frequently enough direct toward ourselves. The bland, uncharacterized tone of some scholarly writing signals the failure of its authors to be clear simultaneously about their attitude toward their subject and their attitude toward their audience, neither of which it is ever safe to take for granted. In contrast, well-written scholarship has a consistent, positive tone that comes from assuming a coherent community of readers and users. And the most brilliant scholarship not only redefines its very subject and so alters the frontiers of knowledge in some critical way, but does so in such a manner as to bring the scholarly audience to redefine itself as well. The discovery and use of evidence and the implementation of documentation can be crucial factors in such broad, pervasive redefinitions of subject and audience.

Correlatively, there is a principle that should govern awareness of the relationship between facts and argument. There are, of course, degrees of trustworthiness of facts, and of sources generally, which must be acknowledged. Moreover, a subject may be very well defined by its sources in one aspect but not in another, and it is therefore important to indicate the gaps as well as the connections between sources. Even more fundamentally, it is crucial not to allow the implicit structure of an assemblage of facts to dictate the structure of the argument they are used to support. So the principle here is of the Primacy of Argument. Without adherence to such a principle, it would be all too easy to assume, for example, that a theatre for which a great deal of source material survives is inherently more important than one for which only fragmentary sources exist. A moment's thought should convince us that the survival of sources is subject to all the vagaries of life and is itself no guarantee of significance.

At the same time, the principle by which argument is primary is itself a tricky one. If not carefully scrutinized, it might lead us to believe that facts are important only insofar as they support the argument to which we have (perhaps prematurely) committed ourselves. Or it might bring us to distort some important values in the facts or sources available to us because we may tend to see them solely in terms of how they serve our present needs and interests. In dealing with facts and sources, we must be sure not to neglect their basic nature, which is a function of their origin and circumstances and which must be read, so to speak, in the language of their age. For instance, in the early days of commercial photography, in the late nineteenth century, theatrical photographers (such as Alfred Ellis, who had a studio in Baker Street, London) used stock backgrounds for photographing characters in scenes from plays. A scholar unaware of this fact who thought that the photographs were taken on the stage could misinterpret these background scenes as representing the actual scenery of the play, with catastrophic effects on the analysis of the mise-en-scène. Perusal of photography supply catalogues from the period, however, would turn up pages of stock backgrounds, effectively disabusing the ignorant scholar of this misunderstanding. Such a catalogue becomes, then, a grammar of photography in this period, which one neglects at one's peril.

It may indeed seem sometimes that no body of information, printed, graphic, or otherwise, may be confidently neglected by the theatre scholar, so broad is the field and so deeply are its connections embedded in the culture of the age. Conversely, it sometimes appears to be the case that source material turned up in one archive has only a vague or ambiguous connection with materials in other archives. Lack of cataloguing (for which no conscientious theatre archivist can be blamed, given the shortages of staff and funding and the insufficiency of time) is the besetting difficulty of theatre research. It requires sometimes near-heroic efforts to compare the holdings of one archive with those of another. In these circumstances, and for additional reasons as well, it is incumbent on the serious scholar to "pick the brain" of the archivist, taking legitimate advantage of knowledge seldom committed to paper or otherwise inaccessible to the peripatetic scholar.[16]

Ultimately, then, questions of scholarly evidence and documentation come down to what I perceive to be the author's fourfold obligation: to be faithful to the subject, true to sources, fair and frank with readers, and deferential to tradition. Fidelity to the subject requires, of course, a sustained skepticism much the opposite of blind trust, just as truthfulness to sources calls for an accuracy of treatment and a respect for the circumstances of origin much different from breezy confidence. Fairness and frankness to readers entails an almost instinctive sense of mutual give-and-take that rules out all pretentiousness, disingenuousness, or false modesty. A deference to scholarly tradition falls well this side of idolatry but eschews all arrogance, as well as the vulgarity of its verbal equivalent, jargon; it involves awareness that everyone's knowledge is partial, that age may bring wisdom almost as often as clogged arteries, and that today's deeper insight may prove tomorrow's meretricious trendiness. The burden of the entire obligatory list may perhaps be summarized as "consummate tact."

All in all, standing on the shoulders of those who have come before should be a pleasure, but must also remain a challenge, for any working scholar. As we comb an archive catalogue for unrecorded scene designs, take rehearsal notes on an actor's pronunciation of archaic words, or start a new file of data in the memory of our lap-top computer, it is useful to remember that time is always moving on even while we contemplate the past and its works, and our links with them. A sense of continuity and a sense of place seem equally desirable to maintain, along with a healthy consciousness of an ancient insight: "Practice is the basis of theory."[17] If we can manage to keep a sense of where we stand in the sometimes stormy process in which old knowledge is scrutinized, rejected, or revised and new knowledge created, we may more effectively seize the moment for useful scholarship of our own.

NOTES

1 Bernard Shaw, "Preface," *Major Barbara* (Baltimore: Penguin, 1959), p. 29.

2 For example, for literary studies, Margaret C. Patterson's *Literary Research Guide,* 2nd ed., 2nd. rev. printing (New York: Modern Language Association, 1984). No comparable guide for theatre studies exists; it is the most glaring lack facing the student and, indeed, the practicing scholar, and its absence indicates the struggle that theatre studies have undergone and are still undergoing to come into their own as a coherent, mature intellectual discipline.

3 *Encyclopaedia Britannica,* 15th ed., Macropaedia, s.v. "documentation."

4 W. W. Greg, "The Rationale of Copy-Text," English Institute, September 8, 1949, repr. in *A Mirror for Modern Scholars: Essays in Methods of Research in Literature,* ed. Lester A. Beaurline (New York: Odyssey, 1966), pp. 42, 46.

5 Jerome J. McGann, in *A Critique of Modern Textual Criticism* (Chicago: University of Chicago Press, 1983), discusses this issue in his introduction, pp. 3–5; see also esp. chapter 3, "The Ideology of Final Intentions," pp. 37 ff. McGann's purpose "to develop a fully elaborated argument for a socialized concept of authorship and textual authority" (p. 8) is particularly instructive for theatre scholars.

6 See Steven Urkowitz, *Shakespeare's Revision of "King Lear"* (Princeton: Princeton University Press, 1980). Urkowitz describes the benefits of close theatrical analysis for appreciating Shakespeare's composition and revision of his play: "To discover the play disguised in the script, one must learn and apply the secrets of plotting, tempo, and movement in the theater. Careful comparison of the Quarto and the Folio texts of *King Lear* offers abundant lessons in Shakespeare's own style of enriching the performance of his plays: surprises, quickenings of rhythms, and the repeated endowment of movement with meaning" (p. 148).

7 See Jack J. Jorgens, *Shakespeare on Film* (Bloomington: Indiana University Press, 1977), p. 209.

8 D. F. McKenzie, *Bibliography and the Sociology of Texts,* Panizzi Lectures, 1985 (London: British Library, 1986), pp. 40–41.

9 Philip Gaskell, *From Writer to Reader: Studies in Editorial Method* (Oxford: Clar-

endon, 1978), pp. 245–262; see also Gaskell's *A New Introduction to Bibliography,* repr. with corr. (Oxford: Clarendon, 1985).

10 *The Compact Edition of the Oxford English Dictionary: Complete Text Reproduced Micrographically,* 2 vols. (Oxford: Oxford University Press, 1971), s.v. "whirligig." The second meaning is apparently not generally noted in Shakespearean scholarship; see, for example, *Twelfth Night,* ed. J. M. Lothian and T. W. Craik, Arden edition (London: Methuen, 1975), V.i.375–376n. ("time's spinning-top" is the entire gloss), and C. T. Onions, *A Shakespeare Glossary,* where only the first meaning, narrowly defined as a "whipping top," is cited (2nd ed., rev.; Oxford: Clarendon, 1941).

11 "A Leading Computer Scientist Bemoans Our Love Affair with the Machine," *Chronicle of Higher Education,* February 6, 1985, p. 5. See also Joseph Weizenbaum, *Computer Power and Human Reason: From Judgment to Calculation* (San Francisco: W. H. Freeman, 1976).

12 "The London Stage 1800–1900: A Documentary Record and Calendar of Performances," under my general editorship and in association with my colleague James Ellis, bibliographical editor, is a long-term research program formed in 1972 which now has as its central project the design and creation of the London Stage 1800–1900 Database, a self-contained microcomputer implementation still under development.

13 This instance of documentary untruthfulness came to my attention in 1965, as I recall, in the course of research at the Folger Shakespeare Library. Evidently I failed to record its details or else buried them beyond retrieval. The reader may wish not to accept my memory of these facts as accurate or, in any case, may take this abject failure of documentation as a useful lesson: *Caveat discipulus.*

14 For a convenient introduction to database theory and practice, see C. J. Date, *Database: A Primer* (Reading, Mass.: Addison-Wesley, 1983). Other generally useful books on computing for humanities scholars are Susan Hockey, *A Guide to Computer Applications in the Humanities* (Baltimore: Johns Hopkins University Press, 1980); John V. Lombardi, *Computer Literacy: The Basic Concepts and Language* (Bloomington: Indiana University Press, 1983); and Robert L. Oakman, *Computer Methods for Literary Research,* rev. ed. (University of Georgia Press, 1984).

15 See, for example, two Drury Lane playbills for 1777 and 1838 reproduced as plates 24a and 24b in Michael R. Booth et al., *The Revels History of Drama in English,* vol. 6, 1750–1880 (London: Methuen, 1975).

16 See chapter 11, "Talking to People," in Thomas Mann, *A Guide to Library Research Methods* (New York: Oxford University Press, 1987), a broadly useful handbook. Theatre scholars should be aware of the existence of the Theatre Library Association, a professional organization of theatre librarians and working scholars which facilitates communication between these two groups and whose annual publication, *Performing Arts Resources,* now in its twelfth volume (ed.

Barbara Naomi Cohen-Stratyner; New York: Theatre Library Association, 1987), contains a number of aids, especially bibliographical, for the working scholar.

17 Gregory of Nanzianzus, *Orations*, 4.113, *Patrologia Graeca* (Paris, 1857, 1866), 35:649B, quoted in Jaroslav Pelikan, *Scholarship and Its Survival: Questions on the Idea of Graduate Education* (Princeton: Carnegie Foundation for the Advancement of Teaching, 1983), p. 49.

Performance Reconstruction
The Vital Link between Past and Future

Robert K. Sarlós

Without a living past, we have only an inert present and a
dead future.
— Carlos Fuentes, February 1988

. . . it is the task of the theatre historian to reconstruct past
styles of performance.
— A. M. Nagler, The Medieval Religious Stage

Imagination is not to be divorced from the facts: it is a way of
illuminating the facts.
— Alfred North Whitehead, 1929

I n an introductory speech to his poetry readings in the United States, Dylan Thomas described his omnivorous reading and dissection of other poets' work in pursuit of his craft. Apprentice painters roam museums and galleries, absorbing, sometimes sketching, their predecessors' work, to get under its skin, as it were. But what can theatre artists do to learn about such recent milestones in their profession as the Open Theatre, the Living Theatre's *Connection*, Tom O'Horgan's *Futz*, Elia Kazan's productions of Tennessee Williams—not to mention the Lunts, Brecht, Meyerhold, Copeau, the Group Theatre, and the thousands of artists, groups, and works that have gone before? They can read scripts and accounts of participants or eyewitnesses (including reviews), look at pictures, and occasionally hear or view a tape. But if theatre's essence lies in its transitoriness, it also lies in its presence—who can conjure *that* up, and how?

Theatre historians who labor, collecting and fitting together fragments of both the creative process and the performed artwork, can get close to that *dynamic sensory presence*. But they record the precious mosaics of their findings primarily in weighty tomes and obscure journals, with all too few illustrations. Even if they were not reluctant to compete with commercial and experimental theatre by staging museum pieces, logistics and fiscal and administrative factors would discourage them. Some have tried the impossible. A few have even succeeded in exciting spectators and stimulating artists.

The importance of applying theatre's past practice to its future became paramount in my thinking when, during the turbulent early 1950s in Hungary, I considered a career as a director and then as a dramaturge. Convinced that, to break new ground, practitioners must become familiar with the work of preceding artists, I was impressed by theatre history exhibits: scripts, stage properties, and costumes used by actors forever gone, along with playbills announcing their ephemeral presence on the boards and, especially, maquettes of theatres and stage settings that had once contained them. These empty replicas of milieu evoked the missing presence. My fascination with three-dimensional relics of theatre history changed into an obsession after listening to primitive recordings of great Hungarian actors— they sounded ludicrously declamatory on first hearing, only to chase chills down my spine after three or four repetitions. The exhibits I saw were, of course, accompanied by explanatory notes, and public airing of antique voices was inconceivable without commentary. Nevertheless, the historians' interpretation struck me as secondary to the availability of the original objects—fragments of the evanescent creative work. Artists often came to view the displays and listen to the tapes; they also consulted the predecessor of the current Hungarian Theatre Institute for information about previous productions of plays they were preparing for performance. My choice of theatre research as a profession thus sprang from the context of museum work, guided by the ideal that theatre artists and spectators would derive pleasure and profit from research culminating in displays and that the presentation of authentic primary sources in a proper context is the scholar's chief task.

Imagine my shock, then, on discovering in 1957 that, in contrast to European museums and collections, venerable American theatrical archives had given little thought to displays. Neither collections nor the historical works written by the scholars who primarily used them were of great concern to practicing artists. Nor did most scholars evince much interest in current theatre. Moreover, pictorial materials were organized without regard to potential users. Models of theatres and stage sets were rarely found. Existing ones were considered storage nuisances rather than exhibit items.

Historic costumes and props were acquired only by accident and kept as *curiosa*. There was a total absence of stage hardware.

Conditions have, of course, changed in thirty years: temporary exhibitions evoking various aspects of theatre history for the public are no longer a rarity in this country, and American curatorial and display techniques have outstripped their European counterparts. But the Lincoln Center's Library and Museum of Performing Arts still has no permanent exhibits, as any museum of natural history or fine arts does, and theatre historians are seldom invited to work alongside archivists and designers in mounting displays. The ingenious bicentennial exhibit at the Kennedy Center, "America on Stage—200 Years," was organized with only marginal involvement of scholars or artists. Consequently, some excellent items were exhibited with minimal, erroneous, or no identification.

If the use of theatrical artifacts to bridge the gap between past and current work receives only limited attention, clearly one cannot expect widespread acceptance of a more complex and less familiar, but—from the viewpoint of both artistic and scholarly activity—much more lively approach to theatre research: performance reconstruction. Yet one can hardly contemplate the regular and appropriate display of theatrical objects, or the linkage of past and current theatre practice, without soon concluding that spatial elements must be presented in an organic time flow to do justice to an art form that uses all four dimensions. To evoke various theatrical styles (of writing, design, and, especially, acting and staging) one must attempt to reconstruct not only the tangible environment, but also the ephemeral performance that occurred within it.

Despite my insistence on the primacy of authentic sources over their interpretation, it quickly becomes evident that, no matter how purist a posture the historian assumes, it is impossible to abjure interpretation. Anyone who reproduces original documents in print, or displays objects in a museum, is obliged to identify and authenticate them. Dates, places, users, and circumstances of known use need to be stated as accurately and clearly as available information permits, for the document or object to have more than sentimental value. Thus, a simple ground plan attributed to the Donaueschingen Passion was confusing and counterproductive until A. M. Nagler painstakingly proved that it matched production requirements of the Villingen version of the script. The notorious Swan Theatre drawing must still be treated skeptically, for we do not know whether the copyist or original draftsman is responsible for what seem distortions to us. A cheap theatrical dagger becomes worthy of display when, by linking it to a specific actor or production, one begins to elucidate a visual style, or when it helps explain some previously puzzling piece of business. What appeared even to trained eyes as box-sets in engravings of the LaGrange edition of Molière, or in opulent Galli-Bibiena prints, turned out, upon more thorough acquaintance with contemporary staging practices, to have been optical illusions.

In other words, one must ascertain as many facts as possible to sense and convey the context. Even though we cannot completely shed our individually and culturally determined points of view of history, the more information (whether in the form of facts or impressions) we possess, the more surely are we guided to that milieu that in reality is our goal: the performance from which documents, objects, and verbal and visual impressions derive and which they fragmentarily evoke.

Only through that milieu can style be perceived and identified. Style is comprehended in the bits of apparently disconnected information that filter down to us regarding the spatial arrangement, the color, or the texture of scenic elements; the breathing technique, vocal inflection, eye movement, or deportment of actors, and so forth. These fragments, then, require assembly by historians steeped in the period's aesthetic and material culture in order to "reconstruct past styles of performance" within the "limitations of what we may surmise."[1] Certainly, with accurate and lively descriptions of a performance in hand, the scholar weaving a narrative from available information will be able to set the imagination of trained readers in motion. But since we are dealing with spatial and temporal art—and given the historians' habitual translation of visual information into verbal form—it seems a logical step to proceed from conjectural reconstructions in *writing* to a demonstration of hypotheses by means of a *performance* reconstruction. No doubt, risks will multiply, but so will new questions that bring us closer to the style we seek. For it must be clear that thought processes during exigencies of production are usually quite different than in scholarly contemplation, despite the theatre historian's best attempt to assume the working artist's frame of mind.

Thus, I suggest a blending of the two modes of thinking: armed with data, the historian should approximately traverse the road followed by the original group of artists and create a dynamic, life-size, spatial and temporal (hence, four-dimensional) model. No matter that it cannot be an exact replica of the original work—it will bring all participants, including spectators, closer to a sensory realization of the style and atmosphere, the physical and emotional dynamics of a bygone era, than can mere reading.

The unavoidably incomplete nature of performance reconstruction intensifies the imaginative stimuli, extending them into auditory, tactile, and olfactory realms, with a force and urgency beyond the reach of written language.

The approach I advocate is not dissimilar to the one museums of anthropology and natural history routinely follow when converting hypotheses into three-dimensional life-size displays of human or animal habitats.[2] A caveat may be supplied for the specialist, but for the general public only outlines of the general agreement are indicated. Of course, by replacing immobile wax figures with live performers, one alters the technique of what Professor Takeshi Kurahashi, director of the Tsubouchi Memorial Theatre Museum of Tokyo's Waseda University, calls "museum in action"[3]—an idea not without precedent in either the general or the theatrical field. Historical villages or towns have been turned into museums in action; colonial Williamsburg might be the best-known example. Nor is one far from the truth to call an ossified Racine performance by the Comédie Française or a glacially moving Chekhov production of the Moscow Art Theatre a museum piece. They are examples of imperfect and inconsistent transmissions of a performance tradition.

Despite the condescension implied in the term "museum piece," what Shakespearean performer would not give an arm and a leg to be able to visit a theatre that, by means of ten or more generations of actors whose ancestors had worked alongside Burbage and Shakespeare (or Alleyn and Marlowe, for that matter), would present plays of that era in a meticulous, and ritually accurate, transmission of the original acting and staging style? To be sure, they would not have the slightest desire to duplicate what they had seen—but just to have seen it would be a boon. In Tokyo, anyone can see the Noh plays of Kannami (1333–1384), Zeami (1363–1444), and their contemporaries and immediate successors, performed by actors largely descended from those who first appeared in them, in the painstakingly transmitted, unaltered style of that era. (Limits of even such ritual transmission of aesthetic convention are reflected in current scholarly opinion that performance time today is twice as long as in Zeami's day—a change apparently made early in the Tokugawa Shogunate, in the seventeenth century.)

Recapturing the *spirit* of the Shakespearean staging tradition has been the aim of artists and scholars from William Poel and Frank Benson to Sir Tyrone Guthrie and Peter Brook. There is, of course, a world of difference—even beyond that of their respective historic periods—between rebuilding the Globe in Detroit or London and Brook's revivals of some twenty-five years ago. But they have in common the desire to find the original dynamic. That common thread remains, even if one argues that "third Globe"-ers are so intent on specific dimensions that they lose sight of the spirit,[4] or that Brook was seeking latter-day equivalents rather than reconstructions. I firmly believe it is within scholars' reach—sometimes working *as* artists, sometimes *with* them—to deepen the artist's and spectator's understanding of the Elizabethan and many another theatrical golden age.

Certainly, that potential has been demonstrated by renewed interest (both scholarly and artistic) in medieval religious theatre, in Baroque opera and ballet, and in various American nineteenth-century theatrical genres. In the first case, the initiatives taken by the Chichester Festival over sixty years ago were given new life by Glynne Wickham and others in the 1950s. Noah Greenberg's *Play of Daniel* on our shores broadened that impetus. Now medieval mysteries are performed with increasing frequency. Their academic study blossoms under the impact of the proven stageworthiness of ancient texts. Musicologists and dance historians are in part responsible for returning Monteverdi, Cimarosa, and early Mozart to the operatic repertoire; thanks to the continuing work of Shirley Wynne and Alan Curtis, and others who combine scholarship with performance, Lully, Rameau, and their contemporaries are not far behind.[5] Similarly, the extension of curiosity about historic Americana to architecture led to the discovery of hundreds of nineteenth-century theatre buildings (catalogued by the late Gene Chesley and posthumously published by John Frick and Carlton Ward),[6] many of which were returned to use. That resulted in the realization, by Michael Price of Goodspeed Opera House and others, that forgotten theatrical conventions can successfully be revived and flourish side by side with new works only remotely indebted to them.

The more modest experiments of the late Tom Lawrenson with early French Renaissance drama and Alan Woods with the plays of Cinthio, as well as my own and others' forays into the Stuart masque, have a more narrow appeal.[7] Yet the distinction between "pure" and "applied" research or, in these cases, between research into theatrical forms with indirect and immediate appeal is finally illusory. One reason is that applicability is rarely predictable; another, that seemingly inapplicable research contributes in the long run to the more evidently applicable kind. I believe the time has come to resurrect systematically and imaginatively works of art that at once represent significant forms or breakthroughs in theatre history and at the same time provide abundant documentation.

In rough chronological order, a list of such works might begin with the *Balet Comique de la Royne* (1581), the *Luzerner Osterspiel* (1583), and the *Oedipus Rex* that opened the Teatro Olimpico (1585). Deliberately omitting Tudor and Stuart England, where much effort has already been expended, I would continue with such monuments as *Le Cid,* one or another of Molière's comédies-ballets, Restoration and eighteenth-century plays for which a promptbook or other detailed information exists (though that tends to restrict the adventurer to Shakespeare adaptations when, for example, *Aureng-Zebe* and *The London Merchant* more nearly cry out for study). There should be reconstructions of Voltaire and Goethe productions for which the authors' notes are extant. Then we could move with greater assurance into the nineteenth century. Here the agenda would expand considerably: Victor Hugo, Macready, the Keans, Dingelstedt, Immermann, and Booth will keep many of us busy for years, not to mention the flood of material that becomes available in the period beginning with the Meininger, Antoine and Brahm, Stanislavsky and Lugné-Poë, Strindberg and Craig, Irving and Belasco. Stanislavsky's *Othello* and *The Three Sisters* may seem axiomatic exemplars, as are Reinhardt's *The Merchant of Venice,* his varied versions of *A Midsummer Night's Dream,* but the less obvious yet equally significant works of the Copeau-Dullin-Jouvet tradition, the Bauhaus, the Italian futurists, the Americans from Augustin Daly and Steele MacKaye to the Theatre Guild and Arthur Hopkins belong to this tentative list as much as Brecht's *Modellbücher* and Meyerhold's and Vakhtangov's experiments. (In the last few years, such reconstructions were attempted and videotaped as a sixteenth-century Florentine Carnival, a futurist extravaganza, and the 1931 Balinese dance recital that inspired Artaud.)

While individuals will disagree about particular works, lists are easily compiled. More difficult, but also more necessary, is groping toward a methodology. What follows is based primarily on my experience with *The Triumph of Peace,* about which I have now had the benefit of over ten years' hindsight.[8] However, it also entails results of the initial preparation for possible reconstruction of either the *Balet Comique* or the Luzern Passion with which my list began.

Four stages of reconstruction work can be distinguished, the first three closely paralleling work on any production while also significantly diverging from it. First, initial choice of the vehicle, involving preliminary research and interpretation; second, elaboration of the production concept, inextricably bound up with the assembly of the creative team and culmi-

nating in the rehearsal process; third, actual performance; fourth, evaluation and communication of results.

In the first stage, such basic questions must be faced as: What do we
want to learn, and how much need we know at the outset to get worth-
while, respectable results? Within what limitations must we work? Although one is not likely to answer any of these questions fully, the last one
is the trickiest and the one providing, at the same time, the greatest learning opportunities. For it is the unexpected hurdles inevitably encountered
in the process of crossing boundaries of theatrical styles that are at once
the bane of our existence and the underlying principle of the undertaking.
As recounted in *Theatre Survey,* we discovered that only three pairs of
wings, not the four used by Inigo Jones, could technically be accommo-
dated on the stage with which we had to work. We could not ask three
singers who were desperately holding onto unstable cloud machines and
doing their utmost to extend their vocal range simultaneously to throw
their connecting emblematic garlands to each other and strew rose petals
on the same cue as they began their trio. Twentieth-century VIPs, while
realizing a parallel in the sociopolitical aspects of the masque, simply could
not be drilled to acquire the dancing grace that came naturally to their
seventeenth-century counterparts. It was in these discoveries that our fundamental knowledge about the period's performing arts was gained. Such
specific problems, however, are often difficult to predict. What is of essence is to prepare team members to deal with them as they surface.

Nevertheless, preparation does begin with simple and specific questions:
When and where, for whom and by whom, was the work performed? Answers are not always easily forthcoming, but those arrived at start to define
the social and cultural milieu in which the style we seek to recapture flourished. In *The Triumph of Peace,* it was easy to determine that the performance took place in Inigo Jones' Banqueting Hall (which still stands,
though the lavish frescoes visible today are of later origin) on February 2,
1634, before Charles I, Henrietta Maria, and their court. It was organized
and performed by the four Inns of Court with the participation of professionals whose identity is not clear. James Shirley provided a script; William
Lawes and Simon Ives, music. Jones designed sets, costumes, and props.
The place, date, occasion, and the organizers' identities (headed by Bal-
thazar de Beaujoyeulx) behind the *Balet Comique* are similarly known, as is
the Lucerne factotum, Renward Cysat. As one gets nearer to actual production, questions, of course, will multiply. We knew some music and designs were missing for *Triumph,* so we either had to use contemporary elements from other shows or to create new ones in the spirit of the period.

We followed both approaches. Although prints for the *Balet Comique* give a good general impression, details of the perspective on the end-stage, the rigging of the garlands, and other elements of the ceiling (even details of the mansions in the foreground) are elusive. Likewise, the music appears sufficient, the dance patterns clear—yet almost certainly shortages and puzzles will manifest themselves during rehearsals. And, of course, we have no notations for the steps that fit into the patterns. Here Thoinot Arbeau's *L'Orchésographie* (1588) will serve a similar but more specific use in reconstructing dance steps, as did Italian emblem manuals in combination with Jones' sketchbooks in filling in missing design elements.

An interesting problem is raised by the different types of sources from Paris and from Lucerne: almost all the data we have for the *Balet Comique* are in print, self-consciously prepared for posterity. For the *Luzerner Osterspiel,* the records are working papers—Cysat seems to have been more concerned with recording his production's origins and processes than with its results. Consequently, we know more about his expenses, technical and personnel problems, and the logistics of recruiting, feeding, rehearsing his cast and crew. Beaujoyeulx painstakingly records the results—perhaps idealized not only for those in whose memory the event still lived, but for eternity.

It is difficult to say exactly where the first stage of preparation makes way for the second—elaboration of the production concept. Like any director, the historian engaged in reconstruction must exert maximum effort to understand the work in its context. But since a director's goal is a new work, not an approximate replica, the historian needs much more detail. Accurate meanings and historical inflections of textual phrases as well as period techniques for delivering such nuances are demanded. Props, scenery, and costumes must not only evoke the original spirit but function in the original manner—thus, they must be as accurate in detail as is humanly ascertainable and reproducible. This last phrase is crucial: it is not enough to learn how the pavane was danced, what kinds of canvas, glue, and pigment were used in making wings—it must be discovered whether physical preconditions for duplicating them can be created with relative efficiency and what the limiting factors are. Nevertheless, the knowledge of nuances of visual, aural, sensual values, social manners, and aesthetic tastes must be thorough in order to push for ideal solutions and to provide satisfactory compromises when faced with insurmountable obstacles.

Little needs to be said about the other half of the second stage—assembling the team. Clearly, personnel in charge must be much more steeped in historical understanding than relatively minor participants, yet one cannot sufficiently stress how important even the smallest description of period style can become. Therefore, all collaborators must enter the spirit of the enterprise, even those without prior training in period deportment, diction, and propriety. Fortunately, today increasing numbers of dancers and musicians are trained and equipped to replicate Renaissance and Baroque styles. Actors, even though not trained primarily to copy patterns of movement and diction, are often sufficiently knowledgeable and pliable. Scenic techniques and makeup are likely to cause the biggest problems. Whereas costume designers frequently demand objects that resemble those of the original period and are authentically built, scene designers are more often forced to superimpose authentic appearance on technologically more modern hardware. It will not be easy to persuade a carpenter or a scenic artist to use antiquated methods—though, again, historically motivated people can sometimes be found.

One puzzling question is: To what extent should historic information determine the conduct of rehearsals? It has been said that performers and technical staff must be conversant with everything ascertainable about the production they are reconstructing—but would duplication of original rehearsal methods and schedules help achieve performance style? I believe a more rigorous and more lengthy rehearsal period than that observed by the original cast and crew is called for. Our participants simply cannot possess certain sensibilities that came naturally to those in the era we seek to recapture; attitudes of Parisian courtiers, or of members of the Lucerne Brotherhood of the Crown of Thorns will be approximated by twentieth-century personnel only at the price of strenuous and concentrated work—no matter how much *fun* it also entails. For in rehearsing a performance reconstruction, one tends to apply a two-stage approach roughly parallel to that of a team working on *Marat/Sade*, where most roles require assumption first of the identity of a Charenton inmate, and only then of the character portrayed by the inmate. In Lucerne, where performers were naturally at the first of these stages, rehearsals were far fewer, less concentrated, and less intense than they will have to be today; but they were also spread over a longer period of time and entailed a greater proportion of home study and religious devotion.

Similar considerations apply to technical aspects of production. Constructing mansions, or rigging the ceiling decor at the Petit Bourbon, artisans no doubt followed familiar patterns unknown to us; yet creating the perspective on the end-stage was probably a first attempt to deal with a convention well known to us. Thus, our technicians will more easily solve the latter problems and encounter greater difficulty with the unusual tasks of mansion building and ceiling decoration. None of the purely technical (as opposed to stylistic) answers are likely to elude us for long once we decipher the fragmentary information available.

By the time the third stage—actual performance—is reached, the ensemble will be well tuned in period costumes, manners, and aesthetics; the presence of spectators, however, creates new tasks of acclimatization. Although no easier than those faced in regard to performers, these must be resolved more quickly. To integrate audiences into the historic ambience of *The Triumph of Peace,* we had planned to provide them appropriate costumes, free of charge; unfortunately, our efforts came to naught. Another device, the creation of a near-authentic seventeenth-century banquet as prelude to the performance—served up by costumed attendants and presided over by impersonated royalty—was quite effective. The meal was enhanced by accompanying entertainment in the form of madrigal singers, jugglers, and the like. Such an approach is not called for in all cases, nor is it always feasible. Other paratheatrical means may be substituted. To prepare spectators of the *Osterspiel* for its historic atmosphere, perhaps one could entice them to attend an elaborate and ornate solemn High Mass. Powerful elements of that devotional ceremony (antiphonal chant, organ and choir, the ringing of bells, celebrants and ministrants in sumptuous vestments, thuribles of incense, and so forth) will sensitize the public to witness the Passion, regardless of belief or disbelief. While lacking the hypnotic appeal of the Mass, a costumed town crier with drum and fife, making a singsong announcement of the performance in approximation of the medieval manner in which townspeople and out-of-town visitors were invited, would function as a simpler technique to the same end.

The primary means of instilling period spirit in spectators is, of course, the performance itself. In order to transport viewers and listeners not only into a past age but also across boundaries of a complex and quite foreign aesthetic, all conceivable theatrical and nontheatrical elements of make-believe should be employed. Noises, scents, and other stimuli external to the work itself, but characteristic and evocative of the place and time, should be courageously, imaginatively, and forcefully recreated and exploited—taking care that the work of art remains at the center of attention.

The fourth stage of the reconstruction—the evaluation of the work and communication of results—is certain to become the loneliest (and, in the short term, least rewarding) task facing the instigator. As a rule, theatre people done with a production want to forget it and go on to other things. The reconstruction is, however, incomplete until some conclusions have been drawn and communicated to the artists and scholars whom the project intended to benefit. After a brief respite, needed both for recovery from exhaustion and for gaining distance, it is necessary to address such considerations as follow. What answers to the original questions were, in fact, forthcoming? Did some questions have to be rephrased or entirely discarded? Were any new lines of inquiry or new puzzles discovered; by what types of further research ought their solution be attempted? To what extent was a period ambience created? Which techniques proved most effective? Can the degree of authenticity achieved by the performance be determined? What anachronisms presented themselves; what caused them? Were there conjectures that had seemed reasonable during preparation but which proved untenable in terms of performance dynamics? The scholar who initiated the venture may very well find other participants in the project unwilling to engage in such cerebration; outside observers may also be reluctant to comment.

Based on a written narrative of the original performance, ideally, the reconstruction will produce the kind of experience that, by means of consequent contemplation, leads to a new, more complete, and more enlightened narrative. Minimally, it ought to result in a sophisticated summing up of intuitive insights into sensual and emotional aspects of theatrical style, derived from the performance.

Work in Progress:
Reconstructing the *Luzerner Osterspiel*

Inspired by the process of thinking involved in the foregoing statement, and by discussions with colleagues that followed, in late 1984 I began preparations in earnest for a performance reconstruction of the Passion Play of Lucerne. What follows is an account of my thinking and activity during the first and second stage of that process, and preparations for the third. Perhaps it is worth reiterating that the procedure I proposed, the one I am reporting on, involves a blending of scholarly and artistic methods; that my goal as a scholar is to conjure up, to the limited extent possible, the evanescent creative process of the original team and the performance tradition ("the dynamic sensory presence") of the original work. To the extent such a project succeeds, it will excite spectators, stimulate artists, and enlighten scholars. But it will raise more questions than it will answer.

As early as 1943, M. Blakemore Evans declared Renward Cysat's 1583 production of the *Luzerner Osterspiel* "the one medieval Passion Play which could be reproduced today, without the slightest danger of serious error." [9] But despite the construction of two models of the square with performing and spectator spaces, and the staging of selected scenes by Oskar Eberle (1938), a post–World War II radio adaptation by Georg Thürer, and a recent performance of excerpts (1978), a full-scale modern production has not been attempted. Since Blakemore Evans' statement was made, research methodology in theatre and drama has greatly changed. On the one hand, we no longer promise not to make errors; but on the other, we have accepted the risk of making mistakes and mustered the courage necessary for attempting actual performance reconstructions. Thus, especially in view of the decades-long history of modern revivals of mystery cycles in England and North America, it is remarkable that interest in producing the *Luzerner Osterspiel* has not moved at a faster pace. After all, it is the theatre historian's natural choice. Even though the immense storehouse of texts and records left to posterity by Renward Cysat—city clerk, polyhistor, and true theatre man—does not originate exclusively from 1583, it does provide *the* most complete account of a medieval passion play's production.

Curiously, I was not alone in embarking on that awesome task. John E. Tailby, Germanist at the University of Leeds, had begun reconciling Cysat's famous stage plans and production notes; [10] Philippe de Bros, then artistic director of the Stadttheater Luzern, proposed to the City Council the Passion's performance in 1991 to celebrate the Swiss Confederation's 700th anniversary, and Christian Schieckel, scene designer at the Deutsches Theatermuseum in Munich, had been working on a large three-dimensional model, correcting inaccuracies of the earlier and smaller ones.

The Cysat manuscript collection, housed in the Zentralbibliothek Luzern, contains detailed and plentiful information on casting and other preparations, technical planning and expenses, rehearsal practices, audience accommodation, scenery, costumes, and props—almost all aspects a modern production would consider, including detailed ground plans for acting areas, and for actors' locations when not in action (see figs. 1 and 2).

The original place of the performance, moreover, the charming trapezoidal square of Lucerne, known as the Weinmarkt (once Fischmarkt), is for all practical purposes unchanged in its spatial configuration (see figs. 3 and 4), although Professor Tailby recently discovered evidence suggesting that the fountain that forms the square's focus may have been moved; he also contends that the spectators' main bleachers did not extend as far as usually assumed. [11]

In addition to the abundant information and the survival of the original

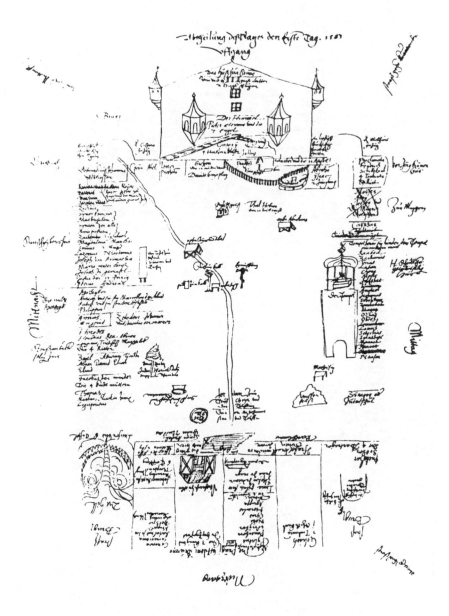

Fig. 1. *Renward Cysat's stage plan for the first day of the* Osterspiel *production of 1583 on the Fischmarkt (now Weinmarkt), Lucerne. Original in the Zentralbibliothek Luzern.*

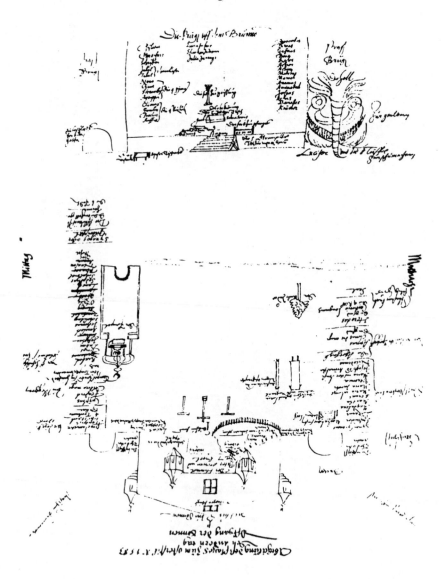

Fig. 2. *Cysat's arrangement of the mansions and stations on the second day.*
Zentralbibliothek Luzern.

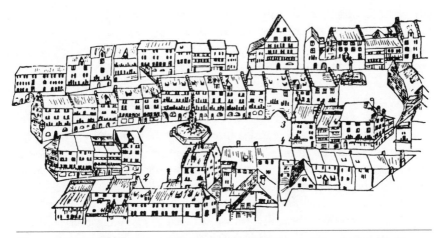

Fig. 3. The Fischmarkt (now Weinmarkt), according to Martin Martini's 1597 Stadtplan, *looking to the north. Numbers indicate main accesses to the square.* *Zentralbibliothek Luzern.*

Fig. 4. Recent postcard of the Weinmarkt; fountain in foreground, Hus zur Sunnen in back. Two of the access routes are visible.

performance space, my reasons for choosing this project over some others included the consideration that the *Osterspiel* is the culmination of a significant theatrical form and that my command of German is superior to my command of French or Italian.

Having chosen a vehicle (the main part of the first stage of performance reconstruction), I began the second: elaboration of the production concept and assembly of the team. It originally seemed that this phase was easily subdivisible into three tasks: interpreting the sources (most familiar to the historically oriented scholar); organization, including recruitment of collaborators; and overcoming historical taste differences (the conquest of culture shock) in arriving at a modern aesthetic. It soon became clear, however, that in addition to assembling willing collaborators (some with scholarly, others with practical theatre expertise), I also had to address a fourth category: fund raising and involvement in local (i.e., city and Kanton of Luzern) and federal Swiss politics. Moreover, after talking with both professional and amateur theatre people, as well as civic authorities, it developed that the road from interpreting sources to elaborating a production concept was to be much more complex than originally envisioned.

Foremost was the concern of reconciling historical authenticity with contemporary theatrical appeal—in other words, combining scholarly truthfulness to the historic text and theological context with a vivid contemporary artistic concept that would appeal to both collaborators and the public (including, but not limited to, live audiences). In the medieval religious view, mere attendance at, not to mention participation in, a passion play's performance was seen as an act of particularizing (i.e., personally partaking of) universal salvation. But in order to reach today's secular public, besides emphasizing the festive and aesthetic appeal of the spectacle itself, the performance would have to be guided by a distinctly twentieth-century production concept, without contravening the idea of religious salvation explicit in the text, or the Christian iconology implied by it.

The conclusion was unavoidable—that the production, like the Bible story itself, must find its communicable feelings, forms, images, and senses for today. This entails a careful elucidation of obscure textual and performance aspects without the intrusion of scholarly apparatus—that is, primarily in nonverbal form, by means of visual symbols, including gestures and movement of actors. Only in cases where theatrical means totally fail should adaptation, the cutting or modernization of performance elements, be considered. The difficult task of bridging the sixteenth century and the twentieth is somewhat eased by the fact that the story of the lowborn iconoclastic savior of humankind is not unlike other great dramas and myths. Although today's public may not be religious in the traditional sense, it is starved for myth and for thrilling, high-tension adventure, both of which are acutely present in Cysat's version of the Greatest Story Ever Told. It is, then, necessary and possible to inspire and resensitize the performers, and through them the spectators, to those internal ingredients. Hence the suggestion of a nonverbal overlay, conveying a radical spiritual reformer's clash both with established institutions and with personal apathy on a mass scale. A related concern was to minimize potential anti-Semitic readings of the Passion story, without falsifying text, context, and texture of the performance.

Organizational problems, too, became more complex by the minute. To begin with, it was necessary to secure more than the tolerance of Lucerne's citizens and authorities: their active support and participation was required. One certainly cannot occupy the Weinmarkt, obstruct traffic by erecting a platform around the fountain and bleachers for spectators, and mark off other acting areas for several weeks without the agreement of inhabitants and businesspeople who live and work on and off the square, or the city's building, fire, and police departments. Permits and contracts are required. Answers have to be given to such questions as: How are shops going to be made accessible? How will traffic be routed around rather than through the square? How many performances will there be, and how many rehearsals are needed in the square? Will business slack off or increase due to tourist interest?

No fewer questions arose on matters other than the physical considerations. Did I really envision an open-air spectacle in May, with a twelve-hour performance on each of two consecutive days? Would spectators sit still long enough? What would happen in case of rain? How would the casting of leading roles, the doubling of minor ones, the assembly of choral and instrumental groups, and the recruitment of a technical staff be accomplished? Who would be performing: professionals, amateurs, or a combination? Is it possible to entice living descendants of original performers to participate? Can even native Schwyzertütsch-speaking actors be counted on to pronounce, and audiences to understand, the sixteenth-century text? And how many will *care* in today's irreligious climate for a near-authentic replica of what was a spectacular display of Catholicism in a sea of engulfing Protestantism?

I was able to answer many, but not all, such questions during my first trip to Lucerne for research and persuasion in August 1985. I stated my conviction that many of the logistical problems would be dwarfed by the very significance of the undertaking and by the excitement generated among the public, once it recognized that. After all, this play at the pinnacle of medieval religious theatre is the most thoroughly documented one; it was produced by a brilliant polyhistor (a Swiss national hero with an as yet unrecognized stature not unlike that of Pestalozzi), whose numerous manuscripts survive and whose many other merits are yet unsung. I appealed to the citizens' pride in the historic beauty preserved in Lucerne that formed the perfect setting for this event; I spoke of the sixteenth-century union of highly developed arts (visual, musical, poetic, and theatrical) that fused into one. Perhaps the fact I spoke fluent German (though not Schwyzertütsch), that I had come from California to praise their cultural heritage, that there was a wild gleam in my eyes—and that I had brought color slides of computer-generated images of their Weinmarkt with the historic structures in part already, if only provisionally, built into the square—perhaps all that helped. For although I met with plenty of skepticism from citizens, scholars, civic leaders, and City Hall officials, I met with no antagonism. Questions were asked in order to get answers, not to try to stump me. As often as not, suggestions for solutions were made and names and addresses of possible collaborators were given. In this way, I succeeded in assembling a list of potential collaborators, some with scholarly expertise ranging from church and local history through linguistics to art history and musicology, others more experienced and skilled in performance-related areas.

Since, for both scholarly and public-relations reasons, the creation of a record seemed essential, I sought contact with film and TV people. Here, too, finances had to be reckoned with: filming/taping must not be allowed to become a liability—it should be turned into an asset, reducing, not multiplying, expenses. But how could we get commitments for recording that would cover at least some production costs and turn the event into one that brings income rather than loss to local business—on the Weinmarkt and in all of Lucerne? Fortunately, I also succeeded in interesting some people with skills and experience in video and others with connections to the tri-nation (West Germany, Austria, Switzerland) television conglomerate.

Clearly, three distinct but interconnected teams are required, each to deal with different yet intertwined aspects of the project: one organizational/administrative, one scholarly, and one artistic. These teams will operate simultaneously, each addressing distinct issues, but ones affecting decision making in the other realms. The organizational/administrative team will deal with logistics. For example, a schedule for the performance cannot be proposed on historical grounds; it needs to take into account current weather conditions (disruptive rains and cold spells preclude performance until the latter part of June) and the long-established, renowned Lucerne music festival, held in late August and early September. Other logistical issues range from fire prevention and traffic patterns, through participation of the Catholic church, the Tourist Bureau, the City Verein, and local merchants (particularly those located in the Weinmarkt), to fund raising, and arrangements for filming or videotaping the performance.

One area where logistics and production concept intersect is the length of the play and its historic performance duration of twice twelve hours: an apparent impossibility for modern spectators. But if one understands that medieval audiences did not sit politely still, but ate, drank, and socialized *in situ,* even left the stands to shop, take care of business, or answer calls of nature—as is acceptable during lengthy religious festivals or theatre performances to this day in many parts of the world—then instead of being faced with a "problem of audience accommodation," one is addressing performance style. For it is clear that the producer of a performance reconstruction cannot expect, any more than medieval producers of religious plays did, spectators to sit quietly through two full days of show time. It will have to be, as it had been, a folkfest: people eating, drinking, visiting, taking breaks for physical as well as mental needs. The presence of children also helped and will help make the atmosphere lively. One must, moreover, assume that churchgoers, friends, and relations of actors and other personnel connected with the production had to have known highlights and lowlights of the sacred spectacle they came to see. They knew which portions were packed with action, special effects, or music. Inspirational, devotional highpoints were also predictable. Presumably, too, local merchants of the sixteenth century were just as interested as their current counterparts in exploiting the opportunity provided by the gathering of out-of-town visitors and by the general festive air—whether by hawking their wares among the audience or by luring spectators to their shops and booths.

Although cognizant of the variety of tasks facing me (especially obtaining permission and support from both citizens and civic authorities, and raising funds in Switzerland and elsewhere), I nevertheless began by concentrating on the physical configuration of performing and spectator space. It quickly became clear that, prior to developing a modern working ground plan on which scenic units and blocking could be planned, the three-dimensional jigsaw puzzle presented by Cysat's historic ground plans and his conflicting notes had to be resolved. This involved ascertaining the actual positions occupied by bleachers for the spectators, the small platform erected over the fountain (*brügi*), and the stations where actors sat while waiting for their cues (*Höfe*; see figs. 5 and 6).

Because of my prior interest in stage models, I first thought to avail myself of that method of spatial problem solving. Then I remembered that a computer scientist colleague, Kenneth E. Joy, had experimented with computer models of stage sets, which made possible the simulation of sight lines, as well as allowing for the modification and rearrangements of various elements. Joy confirmed the feasibility of generating any element of the total picture in several versions (changing dimensions, proportions, and orientation) and integrating each into the overall model without disrupting the surroundings. Another programmable aspect was light variation: on the east/west-oriented Weinmarkt, original performances lasted from dawn to dusk on two consecutive days, so the changing daylight would have to be taken into account as much as the weather. As it happens, Joy specializes in algorithms capable of rendering images that express variations of reflected and refracted light, which in our model show up in terms of light and shade as well as in gradation of color. Thus, while in principle the results are not unlike the illustration accompanying John Golder's updating of the Théâtre du Marais reconstruction,[12] Joy's pictures are much more detailed, shaded, and illusionistic.

I proceeded to provide dimensions and photographs of the square as it exists today, which my computer scientist colleague used to generate a three-dimensional computer model.[13] That model includes all houses now standing in the Weinmarkt which, once established, remain unchanged; and the scenic elements, open to experimentation, which thus far amount to spectators' bleachers around three sides of the square, boxes (*Höfe*) for the actors, the elevated platform around the fountain's spire (*brügi*), and two bay windows (historic, not extant) on the house Zur Sunnen at one end of the square, between which Heaven was (and will be) located. Both types of elements were generated by writing explicit computer programs for each item. The laboriously generated houses are rendered as specific facades, with detailed particularized fronts and generic sides, roofs, and backs. Seats of the audience, supports for that seating, the position and varied configurations of the platform (raked, split level, etc.) have been accurately generated, while requiring only general dimensions. Unlike the houses, the latter elements will be altered according to requirements of primary sources on the one hand and current theatrical considerations on the other (see figs. 7 and 8). In creating the platform around the fountain,

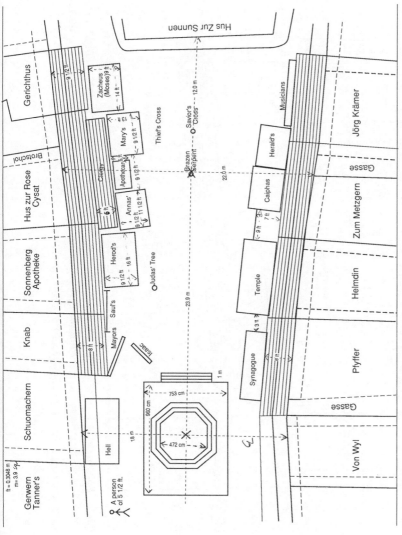

Fig. 5. Tentative ground plan of the Weinmarkt as set up for the first day. The platform is centered on the fountain—its relationship to Hell and the Synagogue is unsatisfactory; from the top row of the main bleachers behind the platform (not shown), the spectators can barely see actors near the lower end of the bleachers. The shaded area represents the bleachers nearest the houses; Höfe (i.e., actors' stations) are nearer the center of the square. Drawn by Annette Ke-Lee Chan.

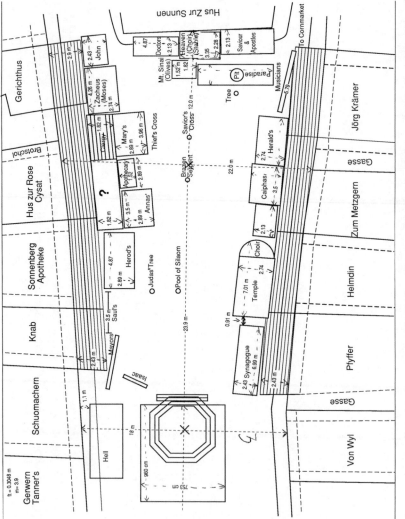

Fig. 6. The platform has been pushed back, its edge now flush with the fountain's basin, enlarging the acting area, improving the relationship to Hell and the Synagogue, and —by making the bleachers steeper —improving sight lines while reducing capacity. Drawn by Annette Ke-Lee Chan.

Fig. 7. Wide view of the computer model generated by Professor Joy, approximately from the roof of the Jörg Krämer house; the platform is centered on the fountain and raked; it is deeper than wide. The main bleachers have been reduced to reflect Professor Tailby's reasoning; some side bleachers, and actors' stations in front of them, are visible on both sides of the square.

Fig. 8. The computer model from the same perspective; the platform has been rotated, making it wider and shallower, thus increasing the ground-level acting area.

for instance, questions emerged. Was the platform centered on the fountain's spire, or was its front edge flush with the basin? Which dimension indicates width, which length? How high off the ground was the platform in front (i.e., toward the rest of the acting area)? Since it had to be three feet higher in back, did it slope, or did it have two levels (see figs. 9–12)? [14] How did the platform relate to various bleachers and scenic units?

Once the computer model is completed, any number of perspective views of the scene can be obtained by placing a "synthetic camera" at various positions around the square. These images are then examined for discrepancies or variations from the documented arrangement of scenic units, and alternate configurations of the model can be tested. The computer graphics' function is twofold, reflecting the dual nature of the entire enterprise. To the extent that they assist in reconciling contradictory information found in various manuscripts, in resolving alternate readings of unclear or ambiguous passages, or in testing conjectures intended to fill lacunae, they serve as a sophisticated tool in primary research—the historians' usual labor of unraveling what the sources do and do not reveal about a performance. The second function (which grows organically, and almost inseparably, from the first)—plotting the actual production on the basis of graphics provided by the earlier function and by Cysat's text, stage directions, and notes—will employ computer graphics in research more allied to the artistic processes of theatre. Therefore, this type of function will most likely find broader use by designers (especially of scenery and lights) and directors who wish to test products of their spatial imagination under simulated conditions and adapt them accordingly without the usual stress and expense involved (at a much later phase of the creative process) in manipulating actual personnel and equipment.

Because of the nature of our enterprise, these two functions are closely intertwined—separable only in those instances where Cysat's authenticated resolution of specific problems needs to be altered to suit modern logistical and aesthetic demands. We intend to keep such instances to a minimum.

The first task of the computer model, the generation of images accurately rendering the Weinmarkt as it appears today, will be followed by a variant, incorporating historic features no longer extant. The second immediate task involved "construction" of the platform stage (Cysat's *brügi*) and of the bleachers behind it as well as along the sides of the square. Not only must we deduce dimensions not specified by Cysat in order to ascertain the acting area available, we also need to arrive at optimum configuration of the scaffolding for purposes of economy and access to shops and residences during final rehearsals and performance. We have discovered,

Fig. 9. Close-up view of the platform from a different perspective. The spectator is assumed to be on the balcony of the so-called Pfyffer house.

Fig. 10. View of the platform from under the side bleachers. Any other view can be generated with relative ease.

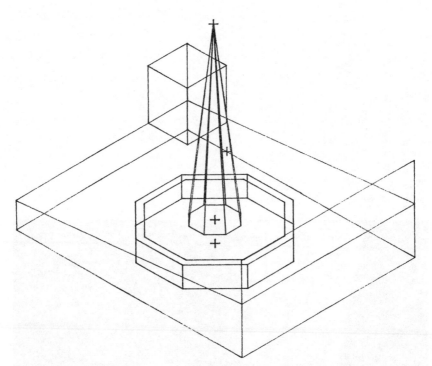

Fig. 11. View of the platform—centered on the fountain and raked—from the main bleachers. Generated and drawn by Professor Melvin R. Ramey with the CADKEY software package.

for instance, that Cysat's dimensions for the bleachers alongside the houses allowed unobstructed access to shops and also left upper-story windows with excellent sight lines. Last but not least, we have to deal with aesthetic requirements of staging. This will be the most difficult phase of computer work. It will, however, greatly ease the subsequent burden on the director when dealing with the extraordinarily numerous cast and musical and technical personnel in mounting a script over eleven thousand lines long— nearly three times the length of *Hamlet*—in an era lacking the leisurely pace of the sixteenth century and without the polyhistor Cysat's awe-inspiring combination of Renaissance talents and skills.

My work, preparing for the performance reconstruction of the *Luzerner Osterspiel,* continues on the basis of two principles. First, since the purpose of the project is to increase understanding of the theatrical dynamics of the

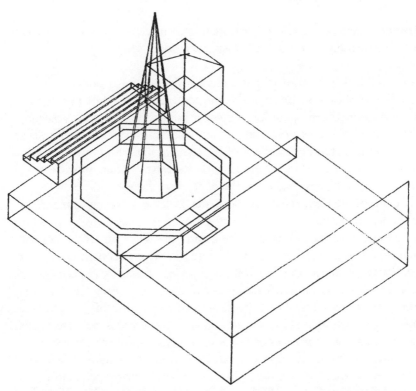

Fig. 12. View of the platform—flush with the basin, with two playing levels; front steps supplied, possible location of the sepulchre indicated—from the side bleachers. Generated and drawn by Professor Ramey with the CADKEY software package.

1583 production, such understanding cannot come from relating the play to its historic milieu alone; we must perceive its form and feeling in terms meaningful to us, by establishing as many contemporary parallels as possible. Second, while the performance reconstruction must take root in Lucerne, it must be supported by and be able to reach ever-broader communities. Beyond directly and indirectly participating citizens of the city, the project must involve and appeal to all those Swiss and other German-speaking people who cherish their cultural traditions. On another level, the reconstruction is aimed to address theatre scholars and practitioners and others with abiding interest in the European artistic heritage. Finally, the live performance and its visual record should be of interest to all who value rituals, festivals, and celebrations. A future modern version of the

Osterspiel, based on the reconstruction, might enrich the German repertory with a historically and spiritually inspired modern script.

To conclude: I have argued that a vigorous program of performance reconstruction should be undertaken in order to enhance vital links between past and future theatre practice, and at the same time to restore a balanced relationship between scholars and artists. The aim of such a program is an increased understanding of the aesthetic dynamics of significant forms and artistic breakthroughs in theatre history. Reconstructions must be accessible to theatre professionals and the general public alike.

A concentrated effort should be made to form working alliances between art museums and major performing arts collections in order to create more exhibitions dealing with theatre history. That would contribute not only to producing audiences more receptive to contemporary theatre, but also to preparing the ground for increased activity in performance reconstruction. Without relegating performance reconstructions to museums, serious thought should be given to the provision of theatre spaces both for performing arts collections and for arts museums, to foster thinking about and performances of historically significant theatre events.

Finally, a warning: the spirit of historicity must transcend theatre itself in order to be successful, and take into account the entire sociocultural milieu that determines the style we seek. Both in Europe and in the United States, the mood for such a form of research is improving. In and out of schools, at theatre festivals, attempts to produce more or less extensive replicas of theatrical and paratheatrical environments, such as fairs, are on the rise both numerically and in sophistication. Never before has there been a public with more eclectic tastes than there is in the last third of our century. In art museums and on concert programs, works created during greatly differing periods and according to a wide range of conventions are enjoyed side by side. The theatrical historian must in part justify this imaginative adventure by the principle that determines the composition of repertories of successful resident theatres all over Europe and occasionally in America: great works of any historic period belong to all our audiences, and we must better prepare ourselves for doing justice by them.

NOTES

1 A. M. Nagler, *The Medieval Religious Stage: Shapes and Phantoms* (New York: Yale University Press, 1976), p. ix.

2 Principles first articulated in "Creating Objects and Events: A Form of Theatre Research," *Theatre Research International* 5:1 (Winter 1979–1980).

3 Personal communication, spring 1984, Tokyo.

4 See my review of *The Third Globe: Symposium for the Reconstruction of the Globe Playhouse, Wayne State University, 1979*, ed. C. Walter Hodges et al., *Theatre Research International* 8:2 (Summer 1983), 160–161.

5 See, for example, Jutta Höpfel, "Innsbruck—heimliche Hauptstadt der alten Musik," *Tirol—immer einen Urlaub Wert* (Innsbruck: Heimatwerbung Tirol, 1982). This essay reports on performances and on workshops that led to them.

6 *Directory of Historic American Theatres* (Westport, Conn.: Greenwood Press, 1987).

7 See C. M. Fogarty and Tom Lawrenson, "The Lessons of the Reconstructed Performance," *Theatre Survey* 22:2 (November 1981), 141–160; Alan Woods, "Reporting Performance Research," *Theatre Survey* 22:2 (November 1981), 171–176.

8 See my "Valenciennes and Banqueting Hall: Theatre Research in Three and Four Dimensions," *Theatre Survey* 22:2 (November 1981), 161–170.

9 *The Passion Play of Lucerne: An Historical and Critical Introduction* (New York and London: MLA, 1943), p. ix; translated into German, 1961; complete text: *Das Luzerner Osterspiel*, 3 vols., ed. Heinz Wyss (Bern: Francke, 1967).

10 John E. Tailby, "Die luzerner Passionspielaufführung des Jahres 1583: Zur Deutung der Bühnenpläne Renward Cysats," in *The Theatre in the Middle Ages*, ed. Herman Braet et al. (Leuven: Leuven University Press, 1985).

11 Personal communication, July 1986, Bamberg.

12 "The Théâtre du Marais in 1644: A New Look at the Old Evidence concerning France's Second Public Theatre," *Theatre Survey* 25:2 (November 1984).

13 For a preliminary report, see my "Computer Modeling in the Reconstruction of the Passion Play," in *Le Théâtre et la Cité dans l'Europe Médiévale, Fifteenth-Century Studies*, v. 13, ed. Edelgaard E. DuBruck and William C. MacDonald (Stuttgart: Heinz, 1988).

14 Simultaneously with Joy's work, another colleague, Professor Melvin R. Ramey, assisted me with the CADKEY software package, creating perspective views of these two alternatives.

Actors' Biography and Mythmaking
The Example of Edmund Kean

Leigh Woods

> . . . *the actor's fear of his inadequacy as a person will prevent that inadequacy from being remedied. His success as an actor—his being loved as a character—will prevent him from acknowledging that he is afraid to be desired, loved, and judged as an actual individual with a life unrolling indefinitely in time. His success traps him in exhibitionism.*
> —*Bruce Wilshire,* Role Playing and Identity:
> The Limits of Theatre as Metaphor

Bruce Wilshire suggests that because an actor's most gratifying experience comes through his characterizations, he is thus prone to exercise the same "exhibitionism" in the conduct of his personal life.[1] Wilshire's image of the generic actor brings one to speculate on the repercussions of exhibitionism after an actor has died, since it might affect the ways in which his image is re-formed through the agency of biography. If exhibitionism figures as largely and inevitably in an actor's life as Wilshire suggests, due to the actor's social and psychological conditions, what, then, comprise the "limits of theatre as metaphor" in the writing of an actor's life?

I intend to explore this question by examining the biographies of Edmund Kean which have grown up over the last century and a half. Kean is an appropriate subject in this regard because of the conspicuous exhibitionism of his life away from the stage. Kean also serves as a model for the self-destructive artist, a prototype spawned and sanctified by his own Romantic period. This prototype was rendered popular in the years after Kean's death through a play by Alexandre Dumas, illustratively titled *Kean, ou Désordre et génie* (1836), and through another by Scribe and Legouvé about the life of the French actress Adrienne Lecouvreur (1849).

The Kean prototype may have arisen in the Romantic period, but its permutations and reverberations are still with us today. What was there in Kean's experience—or at least in the images of that experience which have survived him—which has proven so durable?

The Actor as Exhibitionist

Kean's early life conforms to Wilshire's invocation of "inadequacy as a person" as the root of an actor's tendency toward exhibitionism in his personal life. Born a bastard, passed as a child from one household to another, exposed at an early age to the corruption and vice of London street life, Kean gained a further sense of his inadequacy during a grinding career as an itinerant player for a decade before his triumphant appearance at Drury Lane as Shylock in January 1814. In Wilshire's hypothesis, the disparity between Kean's newly worshipful public, at the moment of his debut, and its previous indifference to him could hardly have been greater.

Such a circumstance offers ideal ground for the exhibitionism Wilshire locates in the lives of actors as a group, and his model is borne out in Kean's case by the unanimous opinions of the actor's earliest biographers, as well as the coterie of literary men who knew him and who set down their recollections of him after his death in 1833. Bryan Waller Procter saw his *Life of Edmund Kean* published in 1835 and translated into German the next year. From his knowledge of Kean, gleaned in personal contacts during his own career as a playwright and man-about-the-theatre, Procter writes that "in regard to the accounts given by Kean himself, (to say nothing of their differing *from each other*,) he was at once so fond of mystification, and so oblivious or careless of all truth relating to his childhood, that no reliance whatever can be placed upon them."[2]

Procter identifies a component in Kean's personality that drove the actor to alter, embroider, or invent details of his own early life for public consumption. This tendency created problems for Kean's biographers, who assume, collectively, an organic growth and development in his career as an artist. According to this formula, the germ of an actor's genius must lie within the details of his early life; developmental and evolutionary cause must, in this scheme, be adduced to explain later success. But where is the biographer to look for the source of talent and genius when the subject has persistently obscured or misrepresented the details of an apparently difficult and embarrassing childhood? In this sense, Kean as a man (to do violence to Wordsworth's phrase) sought to father his own image as a child, reinventing himself in a series of compulsive and inconsistent narratives. He was, in this, bringing something of this transformational skill as an actor to bear on himself as a subject, or even as a "character"; his biographers, then, were left to relay the stories of his they deemed particularly telling, colorful, or veracious.[3]

Colley Grattan was a contemporary of the actor and, like Procter, a writer and raconteur who knew Kean over a period of years. Grattan's estimate of the actor is typical: "In Kean's professional displays there was no evidence of study; in his personal conduct all appeared to result from it alone."[4] The man Grattan depicts either chose or was driven to exhibit his own life in such a way as to please and confound the audience he found in his offstage encounters. Marlon Brando early in his career was known similarly to embroider or to misrepresent the details of his birth and childhood, in Kean-like selective exhibitions of himself for public consumption.[5]

Indeterminacy as Obstacle and as Spur to Biography

The historical indeterminacy resulting from Kean's compulsive mythmaking has proved both frustrating and fascinating to his biographers over the years. The most scholarly among these, Harold Newcomb Hillebrand, writing on the centenary of Kean's death in 1933, concludes consistent with Procter that "the childhood of Edmund is well-nigh mythical." He commends Procter for his "constant willingness to confess insecurity [which] proves at the same time his good faith and the frailty of existing knowledge"; but then, in high academic form, he tries to clarify matters with answers that eluded Procter, while at the same time casting doubt on all kinds of evidence of Kean's life and career—including the actor's claim that he had attended Eton as a boy, where he did, in fact, later send his son Charles.[6]

Similar claims of having discovered or more sensibly interpreted various historical documents fill all Kean's biographies after Procter's. These quibbles, of course, partly result from Kean's own unreliability as a documentary source.[7] Viewed in one light, these authorial claims are familiar bookish debates among historians, each of whom seeks to legitimize his own work—and to justify a *new* version of Kean's life—by claiming the greatest care, attention, and discretion in discovering and interpreting primary sources. Taken in another light, though, the debate can be understood to have been generated by Kean himself in his refusal or inability during his life to render accurately the details of his earliest experience. Kean stands, in this, at once as his own seditious autobiographer, whenever his dubious accounts have crept into his biographies (as his attendance at Eton did into Hawkins, for example), and also as a sort of guerrilla historian as, post mortem, he prods his biographers to find some elusive secret to his art which they hope must lie seductively in an undiscovered or hastily read document.

At the same time, then, that Kean has obscured and complicated his biographers' work, he has also prompted new biographies long after his death, through his simple failure to disclose details which, in his biographers' eyes at least, seem crucial. Hence, Kean's presence in his biographies is more determinate than are many of the anecdotes used to encapsulate him and more pervasive, too, in its insidiousness.

Among Kean's biographers, Procter, Doran, Hillebrand, Playfair, and FitzSimons all begin their accounts of the actor with lengthy discussions of his uncertain parentage and, perhaps consequentially, uncertain birthdate.[8] One reason for such uniformity of interest and approach lies, I think, in these biographers' attempts to ground their narratives in a scrupulous facticity. This collective attempt might seem perverse, in the light of the paucity of hard facts surrounding Kean's childhood. But, by making their concessions to uncertainty early, they legitimate the conjectural elements which they have inherited or which they generate themselves later in their books. In this fashion, the unfolding of Kean's life, in the biographical narratives, is made to seem less hypothetical as it progresses.

On the one hand, the indeterminability of Kean's origins sets his acting, captured through extensive eyewitness accounts, in stark and dramatic contrast. Kean the actor in his biographical incarnations moves out of the shadows and, fittingly though figuratively, into the light when he mounts the London stage for his first triumphal performances and, later, his more pathetic ones. But, on the other hand, just as Kean's early life is left always partly indeterminate, so, too, is the "cause" for his acting. Thus, even as the several biographers' initial pages feed a sharpened sense of the adult actor at his work, they also cloak his acting in the veil of uncertain origin.

By feeling it incumbent to address the matter of Kean's biological origin, by setting this for themselves as their initial challenge, and then by failing to meet it, these biographers inspire an image of Kean's acting existing outside of any knowable cause or human agency. They mystify it. Their tendency in this is, of course, quite consistent with Romantic notions of art as remote from quotidian concerns, but it is quite striking in the durability it has shown through the work of Kean's three twentieth-century biographers, including the scholarly Hillebrand. The relative historical indeterminacy of Kean's childhood, although exacerbated by certain causes peculiar to that actor, is likely to be recapitulated in the lives of many actors—and other people—whose fame as adults often generates questions concerning their childhood which defy answers based on any factually reliable source.

Gossip

Only Procter among the full-length biographers knew Kean personally. In compiling his narrative of Kean, he trusted heavily in letters and testimony from the actor's estranged wife, Mary Chambers Kean. I am not the first to call the objectivity of such testimony into question. Just as testimony in divorce trials is often jaundiced, it is likely that Mary Kean's retrospective views of her husband are tainted and self-serving. On the other hand, this is largely what makes them so interesting, to both the biographer and the casual observer. The Winston diaries, used extensively by Disher, FitzSimons, and Playfair, are rendered dubious for similar reasons. Their author was employed by the management of the Drury Lane theatre where Kean worked and so was apt to put Kean's fractiousness and irresponsibility into the worst light. Winston was a company man, and Kean was not. As Playfair has noted in his 1983 version of Kean's life, Winston's most vivid tales of the actor's drinking and whoring are repeated at second and third hand,[9] conveying the sense that Winston took it upon himself to act as a repository for any Kean gossip that came his way.

One senses in Winston's accounts of Kean, and from those offered up by the actor's gentleman cronies—Lord Byron, Colley Grattan, and Leman Rede—the closeness of the London theatrical community and the love of people connected with the theatre for sensational tales of actors. In Kean's case, such fascination and vicarious thrill seeking were compounded by the actor's posturing away from the stage: a pet lion he reportedly kept, his late-night breakneck horse rides, his attendance at (and occasional participation in) illegal boxing matches, his founding of the sinister-sounding Wolves Club, and his alter ego as Alanienouidet, complete with full Huron

Indian war dress and paint! These stories, and others, stand quite aside from (or as adjunct to) those featuring his notorious alcoholism and philandering.

His flamboyant exploits in various public settings may testify to Kean's instinct for self-promotion—and, in a professional context, self-preservation—as well as to some inclination to exhibitionism and self-destruction. A lesson he seems to have learned in the early-modern days of mass journalism was that any publicity served his interests as an actor better than none. The gossip Kean helped to engender lined his own pockets, and it kept them lined for many years after he had passed his prime, even as it fed his audiences' voracious interest in tracking some of the most conspicuous qualities of his characters into the details of his personal life. This phenomenon is still with us, in the sensationalism of the gossip columnists and tabloids, and in their symbiotic relationship to the entertainment industry.

To judge the matter specifically from the chronicles of Kean, gossip seems oddly to appropriate a greater authority to itself once it is written down. And the more often it is written, the greater the weight of the authority it assumes. This circumstance figures in the biographies of Kean when accounts that have the feel of the anecdotal are passed along from one biographer to the next, because they have been given credence previously by those who knew Kean, because they conform to certain accepted images of the actor, or simply because they are good stories. The biographers are literary men, first and foremost, and so trade in the written word. Their profession inclines them to trust in the accounts of writers like themselves, particularly when the accounts inspire imaginative response in them. They tend to authenticate the reliability of their predecessors, minor quibbles aside, because their own credibility depends upon it. In fact, by raising minor quibbles, they imply and concede a fundamental legitimacy to their predecessors which, in turn, feeds their own (see note 7).

An example of the handing down of problematical accounts, legitimized by frequent repetition, lies in Procter's story which has Kean as a boy staying at the house of one Mrs. Clarke, a refined woman who adopted him for a time. While there, he was insulted by a guest to the house, whereupon, according to Procter, he stalked out in a childish rage, stayed away for three weeks, and was found finally "on a dunghill, in a state of exhaustion, ragged and foot-sore, and altogether in squalid disorder." [10] This is a colorful account, and in Procter's hands particularly telling in the inclusion of the picturesque and presumably malodorous dunghill. F. W. Hawkins, writing some thirty-four years after Procter, has it that Kean was found on a "dust-heap near Mrs. Clarke's house, rugged, squalid, and footsore."[11] It seems odd that Hawkins would borrow Procter's "ragged . . . footsore . . . squalid" and not his dunghill as well. Is this an instance of Victorian refinement and self-censorship? A proud attempt at originality? The discovery of some new source? It is impossible to say. But in a narrative sense, Hawkins' alteration makes Kean sound old before his time as well as outcast, as he is in Procter. The implications of the story change, even as most of its details stay the same.

J. Fitzgerald Molloy, writing nineteen years after Hawkins, focuses more on Kean's reconciliation with the solicitous Mrs. Clarke than he does on the boy's disappearance. Perhaps this is because, in Molloy's version, Kean had been missing for only *one* week when he was found, or because he had only been located near the "door" of a stable. The actor-to-be then showed a softer side, in Molloy's account, when "at last he opened his dark eyes, and his lips were seen to move. . . . 'Am I in heaven in my bed of roses?'"[12] In this version, Kean is rendered more sensitive, refined, and articulate than he was in either of the previous biographies.

Forty-five years after Molloy, Hillebrand includes as his first appendix an anonymous and undated account which may have served as the model for the story of Kean's boyish pride.[13] Then again, it may not have. This story, reported by Hillebrand to have been written "in a feminine hand," refers throughout to an anonymous "friend" of the writer as the source for several tales of Kean as a boy, though it never identifies Mrs. Clarke by name. This version has Kean discovered after only a week (as Molloy would have it), asleep on a dunghill (as Procter would have it), and includes Kean's dreamy question about his "bed of roses" (again consistent with Molloy's version). Quite aside from the fact that this account dwells entirely in the realm of the second and third hand, it was written at least thirty years after the events it describes, and so may have been subject both to the fitfulness of memory—if it came from Mrs. Clarke at all—and to the improvements of imagination. It is odd, too, that the last of Kean's nineteenth-century biographers, Molloy, should have remained most faithful to the written account supplied by Hillebrand's appendix. Where, we wonder, had Procter and Hawkins gotten their information on this point, and might it have been more authoritative than Hillebrand's appendix?

In any case, the story works well in the telling, and it stands clearly within the matrix of the several biographers' *a priori* assumptions about Kean's deprived childhood. It also involves dialogue, at least in the versions of Molloy and Hillebrand, and this lends it both the illusion of authenticity and the flavor of the theatre. One might suppose that had Procter and Hawkins worked from the same source(s?) as Molloy and Hillebrand, they, too, would have included the mutable Kean's delirious reference to his "bed of roses."

Mythmaking as Impetus to New and Better Myths

As a problem in historical method, what marks the document treating Kean's boyhood fractiousness in Hillebrand's appendix as the source of the story—much less as authentic and reliable? In its various versions, rather, the tale reminds one of the camp game in which a simple sentence is passed in a circle from mouth to mouth, in whispers, until it emerges finally from the person sitting next to its original teller, but in a form entirely altered from its original version.

A similar instance of the embellishments wrought in biography through the combined agencies of succession and imagination is found in the several versions of Kean's journey to Drury Lane prior to his epochal London debut as Shylock. Procter has Kean preparing, deliberately, "for the awful evening. His stock of 'properties' was very scanty. He tied up his wig and collar, however, and an old pair of black silk stockings, in a pocket handkerchief, thrust them into his great coat pocket, (his coat with 'the great capes,') and trudged through the snow to Drury Lane."[14] Hawkins then enlarges on the actor's preparations for the theatre by supplying some very specific atmospheric detail: "Snatching up a small bundle containing the few necessaries with which he was bound to provide himself, he kissed his wife and infant son, and hurriedly left the house. 'I wish,' he muttered, 'that I was going to be shot.' With his well-worn boots soaked with the thickly encumbered slush, he slunk in at the stage door as if desirous of escaping observation. . . ."[15] Molloy's version of the same event reads: "Towards six o'clock he wrapped himself in his rough coat of many capes, and with Shylock's costume in a bundle under his arm, left his garret, his wife's tremulous words of encouragement and hope ringing in his ears as he took his way through the silent, snow-covered streets to Drury Lane."[16] Hillebrand, in so many other matters the most rigorous and exacting historian among the biographers, avoids putting himself vicariously in Kean's shoes, but instead waxes dramatic on the ominous weather surrounding the debut: "The weather that evening is said to have been bad—the air filled with a smoky drizzle and the ground foul with the slush of melting snow. It should, of course, be bad; the great stage manager of fate could hardly overlook so appropriate a setting."[17]

"The great stage manager of fate"? Remarkable are the ways in which scholarly dispassion can be overborne by the scholar's sense of narrative immanence. The biographers share a sense of the significance of the debut, and each of them except Procter (the only one who might have been present that night) fabricates details of an atmosphere which he can know only at third hand. Their excitement as storytellers simply overtakes them, as it does at various other points in their several books. In such moments, they achieve a narrative excitement and specificity, but these are qualities born of their own enthusiasms and imaginations rather than of the facts, whatever these may have been.

It is noteworthy, too, that four among Kean's early memorialists wrote plays at some points in their careers. Procter, in fact, adopted the pen name of "Barry Cornwall" when he authored plays in the 1820s. Colley Grattan wrote only one play, but that was the disastrous *Ben Nazir,* which represented one of Kean's most humiliating failures when he appeared in it once in 1827, without having learned his lines. Leman Rede, whose brief biographical sketch of Kean actually predates Procter's biography, enjoyed some renown as a playwright in the 1830s. John Doran wrote a play called *The Wandering Jew* while a young man, before he became a theatre historian.

On the one hand, the standing of these men within the London theatre gave them access to Kean, which they were to draw upon later to construct their various portraits of him. Had they not been playwrights, they might not have seen Kean at such close quarters. On the other hand, though, it is dangerous to assume that their proximity to Kean in itself guarantees the reliability of their accounts. None of them achieved anything close to Kean's reputation or income from the stage. Playwriting in London during the first half of the nineteenth century was a singularly unrewarding pursuit. It was damned by critics and literary men for its requisite of pandering to the tastes of unlearned masses, unprotected by statute from plagiarism and outright theft, and, except for a very small group of men, woefully underpaid. Furthermore, educated opinion of the time held that the theatre had fallen to such a low estate that it had become a corrupt and degraded institution; Procter, Grattan, Rede, and Doran, as men who generated the major parts of their livelihoods away from the theatre, would have been susceptible to this view.

One wonders how this influenced their views of Kean, in his standing as a popular artist. Grattan's comparison of Kean to Byron and Napoleon is illuminating:

> What Byron was to Bonaparte, Kean most assuredly was to Byron . . . after all, which was most a stage-player of the three? Was not the political world the great theatre of Napoleon's deeds—the social world of Byron's doings? Did not both act a part from first to last? and was not Kean more an actor in the broad gaze of London life than on the narrow boards of Drury Lane? The generic signs of genius were common to them all; and they were undoubtedly of the same species of mind. . . . Reckless, restless, adventurous, intemperate; brain-fevered by success, desperate in reverse . . . Napoleon in Egypt, Byron in Greece, Kean in Canada [among the Hurons],—each at the head of his wild and half-savage tribe . . . each, on their several stages, acting the self-same part—straining for the world's applause, not labouring for their own delight. . . .[18]

Kean's popular success counts against him, in Grattan's estimate; perhaps this helps to explain why the actor's memorialists among the playwrights were so fascinated to see him fail on the stage, described his failures in such meticulous detail, and passed this tone and fixation along to more recent biographers. Partly, at least, they seem jealous of his success, characterizing it as a kind of failure or seeking out elements of failure within it.

Another factor which might have prejudiced playwrights as a professional group against Kean lay in the actor's habit of improvising his lines. From his earliest days, when he had played often and on short notice in the English provinces, Kean grew accustomed to inventing lines of his own or to substituting some from another play when his memory proved faulty. He also grew skilled at improvisation in wordless pantomime from his frequent playing of the Harlequin—a character he claimed to have hated, but whose techniques could serve him, nonetheless, when all else failed. In the period of his decline, Kean, ravaged by drink and disease though still eager to please, reverted to his early experience: unfortunately for him, he was enacting material less amenable to improvisation and before the London audience, too, which was much more discriminating. The living playwrights whose work he treated in such a cavalier way cannot have appreciated him for it. Nor would active playwrights have greeted with much enthusiasm the shape which Kean's repertoire assumed, dominated as time went on by Shakespeare and other English classics. Like Garrick, the progenitor of a revolutionary acting style, Kean, paradoxically, was not very prominent as an actor in new plays; he did not, in this connection, feed the freshness and vitality of the British theatre by nurturing aspiring playwrights.

It is understandable, then, that Kean's contemporary memorialists among the playwrights might have embraced the more sensational anecdotes and implications about the actor that came their way: first, in an authorly desire to shape and tailor his experience to their own imaginative visions of his irresponsibility; second, in their resentment of an actor whose interests did not serve their own; and third, in simple rivalry with a noted actor—indeed, *the* noted actor—whose act, in a sense, they were trying to top.

Excusing the Actor

Perhaps the early frequency of variously "theatricalized" treatments of Kean explains the resort of more recent biographers to vivid, though objectively insupportable, views of his life. Giles Playfair's first version of Kean's life contends, for instance, that at the age of fifteen the adolescent Kean possessed a perspective far in advance of his years when he "looked back on his childhood as an old man does on crowded years that have gone before." Playfair later elaborates this image of Kean's precocity, or premature aging, when he describes the actor near death, possessing "about him an air of mystery and other-earthliness which usually belongs only to men who have reached a great age."[19] In Playfair's view, although the actor had erred, his suffering for such error was more than proportionate.

Playfair may have taken his cue in this from Procter, who had Kean on his deathbed showing his son Charles, with paternal solicitude, "how Garrick and [Spranger] Barry had acted Lear. . . . And then he would give in his own fashion, that tenderest of all tender passages: 'Pray do not mock me,' &c., where Lear, awakening from his madness, recognizes at last his true Cordelia. Nothing could exceed the effect of this, recited as it was under such circumstances. This, it may be said, was the last act of the actor's life."[20] Hawkins, too, may have planted the imaginative seed in Playfair for Kean's premature aging and the disproportionate suffering that caused it when he wrote of an appearance by the actor as King Lear in 1828:

The one favourite objection of one or two critics to this representation of the old monarch—viz., that his passion was too robust for the attendant infirmity of age and failing intellect—was rendered dumb. . . . His Lear that night [March 17] was as grand, as imaginative, and poetical, as heart-subduing as the most expectant could wish; and in the last scene, where the waning strength of the actor seemed to identify him completely with the gradual yielding up of the old king's breath—how noble, and sublime, and touching was that performance.[21]

In the instances just quoted, the need to identify Kean with his Lear engenders a misleading image of the actor's characterization. Kean played only three times (all in 1823) in the original version of Shakespeare's play which has Lear die at its conclusion. At all other times, he appeared in Nahum Tate's durable alteration, which lets the old king live on at the end in retirement.[22] Kean's suffering finds a recurrent biographical analogue in the model of Shakespeare's King Lear even when this was not, in the main, the Lear that he acted through the major part of his career. Nor was his Lear ever as well received or critically acclaimed as his Hamlet, Richard III, or Shylock among his Shakespearean roles. In the biographies of Procter, Hawkins, and Playfair, however, Lear is made to bulk larger in Kean's repertoire than it actually did and, more strangely still, to improve in its playing even as the actor's other characterizations deteriorate. Real life and the theatre are rendered indistinguishable in such accounts of Kean's suffering, but at the expense of accuracy.

Kean's marriage, too, comes in for theatricalized treatment by Playfair and FitzSimons, who amplify its tragic possibilities as a means of mitigating the actor's responsibility for his adultery. Playfair opines of Kean's engagement to Mary Chambers, an actress in his touring company, that "from the beginning they never stood a chance of getting on together, for only a very deep affection and understanding could have justified their marriage."[23] FitzSimons is even more speculative (and to be fair, uncharacteristically so), in contending: "Ever since their marriage, Mary had been aware of his need for other women and, although this disgusted her, she had come to accept it. She had never been a satisfactory partner sexually; she could not shed her gentility with her clothes. . . . The marriage had never been a happy one."[24] FitzSimons and Playfair might claim, in this, to have been working directly from Mary Kean's correspondence (as Procter had done), to have been moving counter to Victorian prudery and reticence in sexual matters, or to have been liberated by perspectives offered in Freudian psychology. Examined more closely, though, their assumptions about Kean's married life are quite astonishing in the utter confidence with which they are advanced—as if the biographers had traveled backward in time together to hover under the Keans' marriage bed!

"Kean as victim," either of circumstances or of others, is the scenario which emerges most frequently from accounts of the actor over the years. We have looked previously at Hillebrand's invocation of the "great stage manager of fate" who had brought foul weather on the evening of Kean's formal debut; he depicts the actor up against it again during his first performances after the sensational Cox versus Kean adultery trial of 1825. Hillebrand here captures a Kean who, during

> each of those interminable nights through which, like a condemned man on a scaffold, he had postured before a congregation of yelling fiends had drained from him the vital essence of self-respect; he ate his heart in unceasing resentment against the cruel injustice of man to man. Aching with a hundred wounds he turned to anything that would assuage his pain—to drink, women, and the flattery of sycophants.[25]

Curious here is Hillebrand's eagerness to stress and specify Kean's suffering as grounds for exculpating the actor's most self-destructive behavior. In fact, every one of Kean's biographers and memorialists has found some irresistible grounds by which to absolve the actor from ultimate responsibility for the unhappy turns in his life. FitzSimons takes up the nineteenth-century tendency to excuse Kean's indiscretions by referring to the circumstances of his birth, in contending that the actor's "dissipated way of life was, perhaps, a manifestation of an hereditary urge toward self-destruction. His father had committed suicide and his maternal great-grandfather, Henry Carey, had also taken his own life." But FitzSimons conflates this evolutionary explanation of Kean's behavior with a more modern one, which excuses Kean's actions by arguing that a "study of Kean has led me to believe that much of his eccentric behavior could have been caused by his medical condition."[26] This interpretation is more *au courant* than the ones involving hereditary curses, but merely testifies again to the biographers' collective need to pardon Kean for the way in which he led his life and, so, to compensate him—and us—for the brilliance of his acting.

Procter, in this connection as in so many others, sounded a theme which would later find variations consistent with changing values. In his concluding remarks on the life of Kean, Procter wrote:

> If his faults be retorted upon us, we may reply that his unchecked childhood was of itself sufficient to extenuate many errors; that years

of penury and suffering should also be taken into the account, in his favour; and that the sudden and almost unparalleled fortune that met him, and lifted him, in a moment, from obscurity and want to the very summit of prosperity and fame, was such as scarcely any man, with the common weakness of humanity, could have encountered without rendering himself liable to some little reproach.[27]

Procter's sense of Kean's fate lies embedded in the phenomenon of success and it brings us back to Bruce Wilshire's contention, cited at the opening, that the generic actor's public success can lead him into a wilderness of exhibitionism.

Some Pitfalls and Potentials in Actors' Biography

In a way, Wilshire falls prey to the "limits of theatre as metaphor" he himself invokes in his subtitle. On one hand, the image of the self-destructive actor has proven extremely durable, in theory as well as biography, up to our own time. A brief list from the last half century would include as some of its more conspicuous examples John Barrymore, Errol Flynn, Marilyn Monroe, Elvis Presley, and Richard Burton. But, on the other hand, such models in the Kean mold, in the ways their experience is recreated, continue to render performers' skill as ineluctable, mystical, the function of public caprice and of personal endowment rather than of intelligence or of application. The performers I have named consistently generate views of their lives which conflate their stage and film characters with themselves and which, in this, offer a literal and simplistic explanation of what actors do when they act. It may be, of course, that the actual endeavor of acting is mostly prosaic and mundane, but this, somehow, is not what audiences want to see, hear, and read. So, we are continually put in mind of something very like William Hazlitt's generic description of actors, written in 1817, with Edmund Kean in mind:

> With respect to the extravagance of actors, as a traditional character, it is not to be wondered at. They live from hand to mouth: they plunge from want to luxury; they have no means of making money *breed,* and all professions that do not live by turning money into money, or have not the certainty of accumulating it in the end by parsimony, spend it. Uncertain of the future, they make sure of the present moment. This

is not unwise. Chilled with poverty, steeped in contempt, they sometimes pass into the pinnacle of public favour; yet even there they cannot calculate on the continuance of success, but are "like the giddy
sailor on the mast, ready with every blast to topple down into the fatal
bowels of the deep!"[28]

These are some of the ways, then, that Edmund Kean stands in actors'
biography as a prototype, one with which we are dealing still and will, I
think, recurrently, for some time to come. This prototype testifies at least
partly to a metaphor for the actor which blurs and distorts the outlines of
Kean's own life; partly, too, it owes to Kean's skill in creating a sort of
characterization of the doomed actor which lives on long after his stage
roles have receded in human memory. He immersed himself in a sense of
doom pervasive enough that, even when he forgot his lines in *Ben Nazir,*
Colley Grattan, the wounded playwright, could feel only pity: "When he
saw me he hung down his head, and waved his hand, and uttered some
expressions of deep sorrow, and even remorse. 'I have ruined a fine play
and myself; I cannot look you in the face—' were the first words that I
caught. I said something in return as cheering and consolatory as I could. I
may say that all sense of my own disappointment was forgotten in the
compassion I felt for him."[29] Nor was Grattan oblivious to Kean's tendency to posture in his private life.

But the actor's exhibitionism, in Wilshire's model, was so consummate
that it succeeded spectacularly even when he failed miserably on the stage—
in fact, partly *because* he had failed on the stage. Although it would be
difficult, now, to say authoritatively how this exhibitionism served him in
his acting, it is certain that it has influenced the succession of his biographers as they have spun out their various versions of his life.

Kean made of himself a fascinating character; he left it for others to
write that character down. His biographers have been happy in their various ways to rewrite his character for him, updating it to suit their own
fancies and the tastes of their times—something as Dumas *père* did in his
play on Kean in 1836, or as Jean-Paul Sartre did in his reworking of Dumas'
play in 1954, or as Raymund FitzSimons, one of Kean's most recent biographers, has done in a dramatized version of the actor's life, starring Ben
Kingsley, in 1983.

Consistent with Paul Ricoeur's invocation of a sort of magic lying in the
"rule of metaphor,"[30] one might speculate on whether the integrity of
actors' biography lies most nearly in storytelling, and in retrospective play-
making. Does there exist a disposition in the writers of actors' lives to

make of them "plays," after a fashion, which generate their own dramatic imperatives parallel to, but in some ways distinct from, the particular experience of the biographical subjects? Does an actor's biographer tend to exclude the more prosaic or ambiguous details of the subject's life out of narrative and dramatic expediency? Do narrative impulses join with dramatic ones and then tend, generally, to usurp more purely scholarly or strictly memorial ones?

If they do, such a tandem might elaborate the power conceded the narrative in historical discourse by Hayden White.[31] Not only does the biographical narrative furnish a way of selecting and organizing fact, consistent with the narrator's preexistent values; but it can, finally, absorb fact, amoebalike, and reconstitute it in order to transcend it. It can, in this, tilt the narrative mode into a dramatic one, suiting its form to its subject, and can then alternate itself rapidly and imperceptibly between the two, according to the biographer's interest and emphasis. This pattern has surely been much in evidence in the sequence of biographies featuring the "life" of Edmund Kean.

NOTES

1 Bruce Wilshire, *Role Playing and Identity: The Limits of Theatre as Metaphor* (Bloomington: Indiana University Press, 1982), p. 272.

2 Bryan Waller Procter, *The Life of Edmund Kean* (London: Edward Moxon, 1835), I, 3–4.

3 The major biographical account of Kean before Procter's is found in Leman Rede's articles in *New Monthly Magazine and Literary Journal* (1834), part 1, 434–443, and part 2, 51–62. Thomas Colley Grattan included a chapter on Kean in the second volume of his memoir, *Beaten Paths and Those Who Trod Them*, 2nd ed. (London: Chapman and Hull, 1862), pp. 175–221; and John Doran has a lengthy section on the actor in the second volume of his *Annals of the English Stage* (New York: W. J. Middleton, 1865), pp. 377–414. In the same year, John W. Francis, M.D., recalled Kean's American visits in *Old New York* (1865; rpt. New York: Benjamin Blom, 1971), pp. 218–238. The full-length biographies of Kean, after Procter's, include F. W. Hawkins, *The Life of Edmund Kean* (London: Tinsley Brothers, 1869); J. Fitzgerald Molloy, *The Life and Adventures of Edmund Kean* (London: Ward and Downey, 1888); Harold Newcomb Hillebrand, *Edmund Kean* (New York: Columbia University Press, 1933); Giles Playfair, *Kean* (New York: E. P. Dutton, 1939; reprinted with slight revisions, 1950); and Playfair's *The Flash of Lightning: A Portrait of Edmund Kean* (London: William Kimber, 1983); and Raymund FitzSimons, *Edmund Kean:*

Fire from Heaven (London: Hamish Hamilton, 1976). There is also a fictional-ized biography of the actor by Maurice Willson Disher, *Mad Genius: A Biogra-phy of Edmund Kean with Particular Reference to the Women Who Made and Un-made Him* (London: Hutchinson, 1950). If readers agree with my conclusions about the affinity between fiction and Kean biography, they may not find Disher's book so very fanciful in comparison to the various biographies.

4 Grattan, *Beaten Paths,* II, 175.

5 Joe Morella and Edward Z. Epstein, *Brando: The Unauthorized Biography* (New York: Crown Publishers, 1973), p. 16; Bob Thomas, *Brando: Portrait of the Rebel as Artist* (London: W. H. Allen, 1973), p. 26.

6 Hillebrand, *Edmund Kean,* pp. 11, 18, 24.

7 F. W. Hawkins, writing in 1869, claims to have availed himself "of some original sources of information [never identified] which have fallen into my hands" (*Life,* p. ix). J. Fitzgerald Molloy, in 1888, points to his having been "greatly helped by notes found amongst papers of the late Mr. John Forster [Dickens' biographer], who, as Charles Lamb states, was at work upon the tragedian's life," and he refers as well to his having gotten portraits and playbills "together with some original letters" out of Kean's correspondence from Henry Irving (*Life and Adventures,* pp. v–vi). It is interesting here that Molloy legitimizes his new sources by the unimpeachability of their holders, rather than by their in-trinsic veracity or reliability. Giles Playfair, writing first on Kean in 1939, reports having "happened on some family papers, now in the strong-room of Charles Kean's firm of solicitors . . . obviously intended as material for a biography" (*Kean,* p. vi). Even Maurice Willson Disher, writing in his fictionalized biogra-phy in 1950, claims to have marshaled "abundant justification for it, old and new. The earliest biographies have been used as well as Hazlitt's critiques and entries from the journals of Byron. . . . New material is provided by the diaries of James Winston, front-of-the-house manager of Drury Lane" (*Mad Genius,* pp. 11–12). Raymund FitzSimons, writing in 1976, claims that his biography of Kean "contains new facts and new interpretations of events in his life" and that his will be the first *biography* to have made systematic use of the Winston diaries (*Edmund Kean,* p. xi). Most recently, Giles Playfair, in his third and presumably last version of Kean's life in 1983, takes pride in claiming that the Winston dia-ries have not affected "in any essential sense my [previous] view of Edmund Kean" and then exultantly corrects FitzSimons' reading of small details from those diaries (*Flash of Lightning,* pp. 13, 180).

8 Procter, *Life,* I, 4–7; Doran, *Annals,* II, 378; Hillebrand, *Edmund Kean,* pp. 1–3; Playfair, *Kean,* pp. v–vi; Playfair, *Flash of Lightning,* p. 15; FitzSimons, *Ed-mund Kean,* p. 1. Among Kean's biographers, F. W. Hawkins specifies both par-entage and birth, perhaps as part of his effort to redeem Kean's memory "from the stains and dirt which envy, hatred, and all uncharitableness have cast upon it" (*Life,* I, x); Molloy is similarly decisive, perhaps in his search for a novel-istically felicitous style. His opening sentence reads, "Towards four o'clock one

bleak and bitter morning in the month of March, 1787, Miss Tidswell, a player engaged at Drury Lane, was wakened by the sound of loud rapping at the street door of the house in which she dwelt . . ." (*Life and Adventures*, I, 1). "Month of March," in particular, has a nice ring to it.

9 Playfair, *Flash of Lightning*, p. 12.
10 Procter, *Life*, I, 32.
11 Hawkins, *Life*, I, 36.
12 Molloy, *Life and Adventures*, I, 31.
13 Hillebrand, *Edmund Kean*, pp. 351–358.
14 Procter, *Life*, II, 34–35.
15 Hawkins, *Life*, I, 125.
16 Molloy, *Life and Adventures*, I, 136.
17 Hillebrand, *Edmund Kean*, p. 108.
18 Grattan, *Beaten Paths*, II, 195–196.
19 Playfair, *Kean*, pp. 22, 309.
20 Procter, *Life*, II, 244–245.
21 Hawkins, *Life*, II, 319–320.
22 Hillebrand, *Edmund Kean*, pp. 233–234; FitzSimons, *Edmund Kean*, p. 171.
23 Playfair, *Kean*, p. 49.
24 FitzSimons, *Edmund Kean*, p. 156.
25 Hillebrand, *Edmund Kean*, p. 255.
26 FitzSimons, *Edmund Kean*, pp. 18, xii.
27 Procter, *Life*, II, 248.
28 William Hazlitt, *Hazlitt on Theatre*, ed. William Archer and Robert Lowe (1895; rpt. New York: Hill and Wang, n.d.), p. 140.
29 Grattan, *Beaten Paths*, II, 219.
30 Paul Ricoeur, *The Rule of Metaphor: Multi-Disciplinary Studies on the Creation of Meaning in Language*, trans. Robert Czerny (Toronto: University of Toronto Press, 1977). Illustrative of Ricoeur's thought on the subject is his contention that "metaphor is that strategy of discourse by which language divests itself of its function of direct description in order to reach the mythic level where its function of discovery is set free" (p. 247).
31 See the bibliography in this volume for the list of titles through which White's thinking on historical narrative has unfolded.

Autobiography and Theatre History

Thomas Postlewait

Precious little historical evidence exists on the public or private lives of individual theatre performers before the Renaissance. A few names and anecdotes survive in the classical and early medieval records (Thespis, Quintus Roscius, Aesopus, Vitalis). During the medieval age, various references to *scenici* (players), *mimi* (mimes), and *histriones* (actors) are documented, but these records do not offer descriptive lives of the actors. For several reasons, including their marginal status in society, performers did not warrant detailed personal attention. Nor, apparently, did they themselves provide self-descriptions in the form of letters, commentaries, or memoirs. The idea of doing so, even if they could write, probably did not occur to performers then, given their status, the place of theatre in medieval culture, and the religious and political conditions.

By the Renaissance, however, theatre people began to achieve a more notable place within society. The surviving records, besides naming individual clerics, clerks, guild members, and other "amateurs" (including a few women) who acted in the religious drama, identify the growing number of professional troupes and players in secular drama. Though their move toward respectability was often closer to a rake's than a pilgrim's progress (especially in the imagination of the public), performers began to take on a new professional status not only as members of a social and economic group but as individuals. Italian actors emerged from the *commedia dell'arte* tradition of comic types to become known individually. Then, in the seventeenth century, for example, Tiberio Fiorillo, the famous "Scaramouche" of the Italian Company in Paris, became an international star. A similar process of emerging identification and fame for actors occurred in England: Will Kemp, Richard Tarlton, Robert Armin, Richard Burbage, Edward Alleyn.[1] Some performers had their portraits painted; a few even accumulated sufficient wealth to purchase estates, an early sign that performers had begun to establish themselves in modern society.

The proliferation of legal records and commentary on performers was part of the general European growth of historical consciousness. Individuals, including theatre people, began not only to perceive but to distinguish their identity in the mirror of history—a history of self-discovery, self-distinction, and self-questioning. Of course, the printing press (along with the spread of vernacular education) offered the essential means for this new documentation, but the major religious, humanistic, capitalistic, and scientific transformations of Western culture provided the underlying causes. These major changes contributed to the growth of cities, the centralization of audiences, the secularization of culture, the building of permanent theatres, and the commercialization of entertainment. At the same time, the royal systems of power and patronage, from the Florence of the Medici to the Paris of Louis XIV, enhanced the lives and importance of theatre artists who were commissioned to demonstrate and celebrate—by means of festivals, masques, intermezzi, operas, and plays—the royal and aristocratic hold on power and wealth. All of these activities, aspects of the movable feast of Renaissance prodigality, though often pulling the theatre in opposing directions of patronage and commercialism, nonetheless situated theatre people increasingly at the center of the expansion of professional culture.

We can thus chart from the sixteenth century forward a process by which a multitude of performers, singers, designers, and managers entered the historical, if not always the social, registers. Soon theatre people achieved sufficient importance to warrant, or at least call forth, not only published commentaries on their professional activities but also reports on their offstage lives—often written by others, but in time by the theatre artists themselves. In the seventeenth century, for actors and actresses alike, the commentary that inscribed the performer in his or her time—and subsequently in our historical reconstructions—was usually anecdotal, contractual, or procedural, much of it recorded unsystematically. By the eighteenth century, though, the publishing world provided information in abundance on and by performers. Newspapers, journals, pamphlets, and books fed the public's new appetite for production reviews, gossip, encomia, satire, and slander on the performers' public and private activities. Although this interest in actors' lives on and off the stage was often salacious and the writing sometimes slanderous, the demand for publications became plentiful. Perhaps most significantly, the popular "memoir" (either an autobiography or a biography) was soon not only a common but a necessary adjunct to the role of theatre in society.

When Colley Cibber, for example, published his delightful *Apology* in

1740 (three more editions followed during his lifetime), he identified a special reason for the growing interest in actors, especially in accounts of their private lives:

> A Man who has pass'd above Forty Years of his Life upon a Theatre, where he has never appear'd to be Himself, may have naturally excited the Curiosity of his Spectators to know what he really was when in no body's Shape but his own; and whether he, who by his Profession had so long been ridiculing his Benefactors, might not, when the Coat of his Profession was off, deserve to be laugh'd at himself; or from his being often seen in the most flagrant and immoral Characters, whether he might not see as great a Rogue when he look'd into the Glass himself as when he held it to others.[2]

Cibber's division of the actor into public and private selves, in part a rhetorical device of enticement, was essentially a response to the contemporary critique of the stage. Traditionally, this criticism had been cast in moral strains but during his lifetime was being increasingly reformulated in social and psychological terms. Although acknowledging the moral issues, Cibber also appealed to the public's growing fascination with the nature of personal life in the theatre profession.

The case of David Garrick is illustrative, for, as the bibliographer Robert W. Lowe notes, "showers were written about everything he did."[3] This great interest in Garrick resulted from his being the most famous actor of his era; but more significantly the fame itself, for Garrick or any other actor, served to focus attention on acting as an emblem of a potential (though not necessary) split between not only character and performer but art and life.

This concern for the complex relation between intrinsic and extrinsic identity (previously dramatized, of course, by Shakespeare and other Renaissance playwrights as a condition of willed deception, mistaken identity, or the protean possibilities of role playing) had concentrated itself in the eighteenth century on a perceived gap between public behavior and private selfhood, between the artifice of social manners and the integrity of personal sentiment. In these terms, an accomplished actor such as Garrick served as a representative figure, a public and private individual to be investigated. Both his art, which seemingly overcame the distance between external performance techniques and internal vital passion (by means of native sensibility), and his life, which closed the social gap between an actor and a gentleman (by means of moral sensibility), offered reassuring evidence that the problem of a split identity was eminently solvable.[4]

Yet despite the widespread cult of sensibility, which can be seen as a cultural attempt to sanction private feelings as a measure of public ethos, the problematic relation between inner and outer identity continued to concern many observers. It was to be expected, then, that actors' lives as well as acting techniques served as touchstones for these concerns. Indeed, the great *philosophe* Denis Diderot, in *Paradox of the Actor,* represented the actor's split identity as a philosophical issue for the age. He took up a theatrical debate on the topic of technique versus emotion to illustrate a cultural condition, the problem of sincerity, of true selfhood and expression.[5]

This same problem was also finding expression in two narrative genres that achieved maturity in the eighteenth century: the novel and autobiography (e.g., Fielding's *Tom Jones* and Rousseau's *Confessions*). Of course, Rousseau's achievement was to transform autobiography into a quintessential form for representing the dynamic tension between public and private identities, for demonstrating, that is, the art of self-dramatization. Surprisingly, there has been little study of the cultural relations between the increase in interest in the lives of actors and the growth of autobiography, even though during the eighteenth century (and ever since) acting and autobiographies alike have offered culturally significant modes for representing and dramatizing the dialectical relation between appearances and reality, falsehood and truth, surface and depth, social roles and psychological being, performance and audience. Thus, Garrick the actor and Rousseau the autobiographer can be seen as quintessential figures (and rhetorical figurations) of the era. Diderot's deliberation on the paradox of the impersonal actor served as the timely complement to the growth of theatre autobiographies and biographies during this period. Romanticism accelerated then reformulated these concerns and modes of expression.

Since the eighteenth century, the publication of theatrical autobiographies has increased in number, concurrent with the enormous growth of performance in its various forms and appeals. An expansive "public appetite for gossip" provided, as Fanny Kemble acknowledges on the first page of *Record of a Girlhood,* sufficient cause and justification for publishing "gossip about myself." Even before the twentieth century, the supply and demand for such "gossip" had become an industry, matching the growth of the entertainment industry. Today autobiographies, memoirs, reminiscences, recollections, self-edited diaries, self-collected letters with connecting commentaries, dictated memories (often prepared by a collaborator or ghost writer), articles and publicity handouts provided for newspapers and magazines, and television interviews (which increasingly are used by performers as a substitute for or supplement to self-written reports)—all pour out in enormous quantities to a public that cannot get enough information about actors and other performers, our secular saints and sinners. Since the medieval age, performers have gone from historical nonentities to the idols of the marketplace. In the process, the lives of the saints have been swept away by the lives of the actors—a cultural transformation of theatre, social and moral values, and the idea of identity itself.

For the theatre historian and biographer, this supply of information is an apparent godsend. In English alone, discounting unpublished letters and diaries, there are several thousand theatrical autobiographies (my general term here for published self-reports in various forms that reveal aspects of a career in the performing acts). Their value is immeasurable, for they give us, in historical abundance, the direct report, the inside story on events, personalities, and organizations.

But how direct? And how reliable and forthcoming are they? Though possibly derived from diaries, appointment books, or scrapbooks of press cuttings, theatre autobiographies are often notable more for their well-rehearsed anecdotes than for their accuracy on productions, people, and places. Typically, they are episodic, chatty, and, of course, self-aggrandizing. Their defining character, and often their charm, depends upon the self-serving performance of the autobiographer, a masquerade moved from stage to page. This characteristic trait of playing to the audience is hardly a fault—unless one demands introspection and cultural interpretation from all autobiographies—but it does present special problems for the theatre historian and biographer.

For instance, Philip Highfill, Jr., one of the editors of *A Biographical Dictionary of Actors, Actresses, Musicians, Dancers, Managers, and Other Stage Personnel in London, 1660–1800,* has identified "the problem of anecdotal evidence" as the primary factor that threatens the scholarly methodology and integrity of the *Dictionary.* Though he argues that anecdotes cannot simply be dismissed, for some are "eminently believable," he nevertheless gives a general warning: "credibility is seldom certain." The theatre historian and biographer, though understandably fascinated by a good story, must question this evidence most carefully.[6]

It is true that many theatre autobiographies, despite their anecdotal embellishments, supply us with valuable information. Also, some of them, such as those by Fanny Kemble, Joseph Jefferson, and Ethel Waters, provide evocative pictures of theatrical and social culture. Yet even the most matter-of-fact memoir is not without narrative qualities. Of course, the autobiographies that we tend to prize most are those that often beguile us with their literary skills of character drawing, scene setting, and storytelling. They reveal the creative and recreative imagination at work. For this reason, Leslie Stephen argues that "an autobiography, alone of all books, may be more valuable in proportion to the amount of misrepresentation which it contains."[7] A historian, less interested in literary achievement, might well protest, but the fact still remains that all autobiographies represent the historical in narrative terms.

No doubt it is often possible for theatre historians to identify factual errors and unreliable anecdotes. Yet after we have corrected specific data, we still are faced with the formal aspects of autobiographies—their style, voice, plotting, characterization, typology, themes, and genre—that define them, at least in part, as literary texts. No neat distinction between history and fiction is possible because autobiography and the novel have developed as sibling forms, especially since the eighteenth century. For instance, Mary Wells' autobiography, *Memoirs of the Life of Mrs. Sumbel, Late Wells* (3 vols.; London: C. Chapple, 1811), with its "checquered passage" of "our heroine" through adventures, distresses, intimacies, persecutions, seductions, criminal prosecutions, and imprisonment, realizes all of the defining traits of the picaresque novel.[8] Mrs. Wells, as a narrative character, comes close to being the theatrical reincarnation of Moll Flanders. Her autobiography, like the famous *Narrative of the Life of Mrs. Charlotte Charke* (1755), provided the audience of her time with a familiar narrative version of the adventures of an outcast woman. Whether true or false, it is an intriguing story, written under conditions of economic duress to attract a paying audience.

Less sensational autobiographies, though apparently more reliable, still draw upon a full range of narrative devices. For example, Fanny Kemble's series of multivolume and quite popular autobiographies were written and received as scrupulous reports on her activities and the social conditions of her age, yet these volumes reveal numerous traits and conventions of eighteenth- and nineteenth-century novels. Indeed, a study of her writing style and sensibility, as affected by her reading habits and tastes, would be valuable. Kemble was assiduously well read, so all of her works show signs of various literary influences from the novelists, poets, and essayists of England, France, and Germany. Her writings invite, but so far have not received, a careful literary analysis. Her epistolary mode of self-representation gives the autobiographies a documentary quality, but even her earliest letters reveal a calculated literary style, a creative shaping of narrative voice. We need to ask to what extent these autobiographies exist not only as historical records but as epistolary fictions. Consider her first autobiography,

Record of a Girlhood, written in 1879, but dealing with her life in the 1820s and 1830s. Among its literary influences, can we not find signs of Charles Dickens' novels, especially *Dombey and Sons* and *Bleak House,* as in the re-curring theme of financial devastation from a Chancery law case; the evoca-tive, sometimes sentimental picture of relations between children and par-ents; the heartfelt yet slightly patronizing attitude toward working people; and her self-presentation as a Victorian heroine of self-sacrifice? Of course, much of what she wrote was true to her social and psychological life as a woman in Victorian culture, but her manner of writing was in large mea-sure self-consciously literary. So, too, was her purpose.

Although most performers have not developed their literary sensibility in the manner of Fanny Kemble, they have still been influenced by the novel when they came to write their autobiographies. In fact, we might well argue that the less aware a writer is of literary models and styles, the more that writer will necessarily take up and be controlled by the domi-nant modes and models of the age. This literary influence on autobiogra-phers comes in part from popular novels, but also, especially since the nineteenth century, from stage memoirs, which conventionalized many lit-erary features and thereby became models for how to write an autobiogra-phy. More recently, both film and television have provided narrative ver-sions of actors' lives that influence the subject matter and writing style of memoirs. So, just as Mary Wells' memoir reveals many of the features of the picaresque novel, a modern autobiography may well be dominated by the narrative themes, conventions, and stylistic techniques that commonly appear in popular novels, films, television stories, newspapers, magazines, and recently published autobiographies by performers.

Moreover, most theatre autobiographies, like most vocational auto-biographies and novels, tend to represent the development of the author's career as a coherent, unified, and teleological process, even though the ear-lier self, when recalled clearly, may well be a stranger, as Elizabeth Robins acknowledged when, fifty years after the fact, she wrote about her first year in London:

> I write about those days at a great distance—not only in terms of time. I cannot feel very close to that young woman who went about with my name so long ago. In the interval, I have thought about the person she then was much less than I have thought about other people as they were. She is often strange to me, sometimes antipathetic, now and then incredible, but for the self-conviction that stares me in the face from the scribbled page [of saved diaries]. There, too, I am often

at odds with her. She records scenes and feelings I have clean forgotten; she leaves out some that in my memory stand fast forever. And the omissions, that I have now in mind, are not those prompted by discretion. They are mere failure to recognise values.[9]

Those changing values, even more than passing decades, are often so substantial as to make consistency of personality in life, if not autobiography, impossible.

This problem of presenting oneself in a narrative is also complicated by literary techniques of characterization. Specifically, an autobiography, in its rhetorical and formal features (if not always in its author's conscious intentions), establishes and mediates the relationship between the writer and the desired readers by means of the narrative "I." This figure of selfhood, however historical it is supposed to be, is divided in narrative terms into three different personae: the author, the character (whom Robins calls the "other Me"), and the narrator (or implied author). The author is outside the text and after the events, making decisions about what to report. The character is the figure within the text who gets reported (or created). And the narrator is the rhetorical voice that defines the report's stylistic tone and attitude (toward character and audience). The three personae are interrelated but not interchangeable.

The character, even though a version of the writer, is a created identity, a representative figure of the author's idea of self. By means of not only available documents but also calculated hindsight, faulty memory, and self-deception, the author selects the significant and crucial events that point toward the person (or personality) the author has become—or, more exactly, the person the author desires the reader to see and value. The life is given a direction and meaning, culminating in the present self, but this causal order is retrospectively imposed through an act of reasoning (and rationalizing) backward. As Noel Coward warns in his own autobiography: "it is a tricky business tracing the development of a character along the avenues of reminiscence."[10] An idea of selfhood is achieved; an idea of achievement is given selfhood.

Beyond these aspects of the double identity of author and character, there is the third persona: the narrator who exists as a voice, a style, an attitude that mediates between character and author as well as character and reader. This voice or "delivery" makes manifest not only the main character in the autobiography but all the other characters who are there to serve the primary function of revealing—or concealing—aspects of the protagonist. A strong narrator or narrative voice, such as Joseph Jefferson's or Sarah Bernhardt's, can create, by means of a unified style, an apparent resolution of the opposition between author and character. But this rhetorical success in creating and sustaining a stylistic process of literary figuration, while pleasing to the literary critic, should be troubling to the theatre historian. To the degree that a theatre autobiography triumphs in overcoming the separation of these three personae, it creates major problems in historical reliability.

Besides these literary aspects of narrator, character, and author, there are generic traits of topic, theme, scene, and plot in autobiography that define and shape what gets reported. In fact, no writer can avoid following at least some common traits. Some autobiographers seldom deviate from stereotypical conventions. Of course, history provides the basic conditions for personal experiences, attitudes, and values. But autobiography calls forth conventional modes of expression, which at one point or another tend to take on a life of their own, whether or not the writer actually had the experiences.

Perhaps the generic demands are most evident in the formal order of the plot itself. Autobiography has often followed a pattern of narrative development from childhood through journey to crisis, conversion, and confession.[11] Theatre autobiographies have some of these features, but they are usually more committed to vocational narration than to introspection and self-judgment. The public's judgment sanctions the performer's life. Still, the conventional patterns are regularly apparent: a life of innocence (or enclosure), paradise lost (or confinement escaped), struggle, journey and quest, discovery and appreciation by others (which, in turn, often leads somewhat later to a moment of self-assessment), success, public glory (usually at the price of personal hardship), and abundant recompense, as viewed retrospectively.[12] This basic plot is vague enough to accommodate many different versions of events at each stage of the life. Yet, by means of this distribution, the particular actions embedded in the general narrative serve to illustrate its common meanings (which can range from the melodramatic to the mythic).

Thus, despite the guidance of memories and documents, what one recalls and identifies as one's own experiences may be instead culturally shared, recurring narratives. For example, childhood memories, which appear as distanced experiences, are commonly recollected not only fitfully but conventionally. In the words of Ethel Barrymore: "One may write about the child one was with the same freedom that a novelist creates a character. There is no fear of egotism, for the portrait is one of faint colors, and the incidents that crowd in on any small life are incidents of childhood rather than of a particular child." [13] These incidents, while no doubt grounded in the basic conditions of the way one was raised, quite often are shaped by literary conventions. For example, when we consider how childhood regularly gets represented in nineteenth-century poetry and fiction, it is hardly surprising that many performers writing during and just after this period evoke childhood in either a Wordsworthian (Lillah McCarthy, Lillie Langtry, Johnston Forbes-Robertson) or a Dickensian (Constance Collier, Elsa Lanchester) mode. Some, such as Ellen Terry, give us both modes.

Beyond childhood, the memories may be less formulaic, but still the autobiographies (and the biographies based upon them) quite often chart a life story according to standard plot conventions. Within these standard "chapters" or "stages" of a life, theatre autobiographies commonly develop additional standard topics, including the emotional reports of first appearances and opening-night anticipations, the comic stories of stage mishaps and pranks, the descriptions of professional camaraderie, the demonstrations on how performers care for one another, the series of anecdotal tributes to character actors (and to actors as characters), the traveler's tall tale (usually taller the further abroad one goes), the moral exemplum on economic frugality or the confession of financial prodigality, the name-dropping catalogues of the famous, the commentaries (often vague) and the anecdotes (usually unreliable) on acting methods, and the chronicles of hardships faced and overcome (often matched by a sad, sympathetic fable of another performer who has been defeated by age, misfortune, or personal vice).

Of course, no single autobiography presents all of these composite traits. All autobiographies have their own specific stylistic and historical qualities. The form and content of these works vary from period to period, writer to writer. Indeed, we read them, sometimes avidly, for their specificity, their historical picture of a time and place. Obviously, then, formal patterns in autobiographies need to be considered within the context of historical conditions. Performers, working together in the theatre and sharing similar cultural experiences and values, reveal (and conceal) many of the same attitudes, experiences, and beliefs. The difficulty for the theatre historian is to figure out how the historical and literary factors (the social and artistic cultures) intermix to create an autobiographical mode of expression.

In the final analysis, historical and fictional discourses cannot be separated from their institutional, social, and cultural functions. Therefore, just as we investigate the conditions, aims, and values of theatre, we need to ask, period by period, what are the generic, social, financial, vocational, and moral functions of autobiographies. For example, what, in Foucault's terms, are the possible "rules of formation" in a particular period that called forth certain narratives to the exclusion of others? What modes of self-representation tended to recur? What ideas of the performer and the theatre did these works attempt to meet or displace? What ideologies operated, explicitly and implicitly? Were there any discernible patterns in form, theme, characterization, and style? In turn, were there key matters that the writer excluded, falsified, denied, or failed to perceive?

The social context for an autobiography always shapes the writer's discourse. It also shapes the audience's response. We need to consider, therefore, not only the writer's idea of the audience's expectations, as foreseen in the writing process, but also the reader's ideas of the actor and the theatre that contribute to the ways the work was read (and is read by us). For each period, what was the rhetorical contract between the writer's report of personal information and the reader's trust, between calculated self-revelation and reader sympathy? Supposedly the contract of autobiography is based on truth, but is this really the operating principle for writer and readers?

From the viewpoint of reception, we need to keep in mind that theatre autobiographies, like all autobiographies, have at least two audiences: the members of one's intimate circles, including those of family and profession, and the general public. The writer tries to shape the story of a life to inform, please, convince, counter, and control both audiences. But sometimes, in serving one audience, the writer may not satisfy the other. So decisions have to be made throughout not only on what can or cannot (should or should not) be said but on how things are said.[14] The historian needs to evaluate the writer's intentions in terms of both audiences—and also to see that each of these audiences can often be divided into subgroups.[15]

Also influencing each autobiographer are those personal friends, enemies, family members, lovers, employers, advisors, and critics whom one may or may not name and discuss out of a sense of pride, respect, obligation, discretion, intimacy, dislike, fear, regret, or shame. Their presence or absence in an autobiography may be misleading, if not purposefully deceptive. Finally, beyond these many faces of the audience, there is also that faceless one: the future, which is another name for the abiding memory of the readers and historians for whom one also presents the life story, not only as a stay against mortality but as an attempt to establish one's place in the judgments of theatre history.

Perhaps even more to the point, the performer's autobiography, besides being a record of accomplishment, is an appeal like all performance for recognition, for approval, for love. The loving, even desiring, gaze of the spectator and reader constitutes the performer's existential as well as professional mission to be recognized (not necessarily known, which is often the fearful condition of incompleteness or emptiness that performance may help overcome or avoid). Given this need for recognition, as the form of self-identification, the task in writing becomes far more complex and important than just communicating to an audience the truth behind or beneath appearances. The dilemma, at least at the level of the modern mythology of fame, is the desire to be valued as a masked being, a performing self, and yet still to be loved despite this self-displacing (and sometimes self-denying) need for performance. Whatever the performer's impulse in autobiography to reveal the secret or unmasked self, there is also a strong need to maintain the achieved self, which is the basis of fame and love.

Quite apparently, then, theatre autobiographies cannot be read as straightforward historical documents. But we should not assume that because they have narrative qualities they lack historical truths. Autobiographies require interpretation, not just neat dissection into true and false categories. The theatre historian, in search of the performer "in Nobody's Shape but His Own," may well find not only that no clear separation can be established between face and mask, presence and absence, private and public personality, life and art, but also that even these dualisms are too neat because they split identity, documents, and historical conditions in ways that are reductive. Our task is to understand how and why historical meanings are embedded in narrative forms, not to ignore, deny, or dismiss such formal qualities. Indeed, at the levels of sense, structure, and temporality, history is narrative, as Paul Ricoeur argues: "The form of life to which narrative discourse belongs is our historical condition itself."[16] By way of illustration, I want to look at some distinctive features of certain autobiographies by actresses. In order to focus my comments, I consider autobiographies by English and American women performers of the late nineteenth and early twentieth centuries. What follows, I must insist, is not a summary of women's lives in the theatre, nor a poetics of actresses' autobiographies.

Actresses' autobiographies of this period, though apparently similar in many ways to those written by men, reveal some definitive, if not always exclusive, features that recur enough to invite consideration as special attributes. Why this is so and how it operates should be discernible, at least in general ways, when we consider women's history. No doubt, men and women of the same culture share many similar experiences and values. Since the Renaissance, actors and actresses have increasingly become part of a shared community. But throughout history, women's lives, under varying conditions of patriarchy, have developed differently from men's in psychological, social, vocational, and biological terms. The resulting distinctions are not easy matters to categorize and analyze—whatever their bases in ideologies of gender—but they still shape all aspects of women's (and men's) lives. Surely, then, these differences must also affect the writing of autobiography.[17]

Most actresses, for instance, report the development of their careers in terms of such recurring general topics as ties with and breaks from family, dependency on men, moral honor and rectitude (which mainly means sexual identity, practices, and values), defenses and demonstrations of their roles as mothers, wives, sisters, or unmarried women, and alternating moods of hope and discouragement. More specifically, these topics get developed in certain narrative moments, such as, for example, the crucial meeting—the encounter that provides the opportunity or catalyst for success. Narrative requires turning points: in women's autobiographies these moments, often a meeting with a grand man of the theatre, are usually fortuitous and unexpected, as if these actresses depended upon luck, grace, and the goodwill of others rather than their own determination. Yet, in most cases, these women were persevering, even tenacious, in their careers, however much they may have masked their ambition. They had to be strong-willed or they would not have succeeded in a very competitive and often cruel profession. Still, as they report matters, their own ambitions and contributions are seldom acknowledged.

If we are to believe Marie Wilton, for example, it never once occurred to her to become a theatre manager until her brother-in-law suggested the idea and then provided the money. In similar manner, Ethel Barrymore, seemingly helpless in launching her London career, depended upon the intervention of Henry Irving, a benevolent deus ex machina as she reported matters; Lillah McCarthy, her career at a crossroads, walked in the door to meet Bernard Shaw just when he was looking for someone to play Ann Whitefield in *Man and Superman;* and Elizabeth Robins, almost ready to accept a terrible contract, was counseled away from potential disaster by Oscar Wilde and Herbert Beerbohm Tree. In fact, Robins spent over a hundred pages of her autobiography, *Both Sides of the Curtain,* to dramatize, with self-irony, her various meetings with these and other grand men, as she tried to find a way to get on the stage in London. (Another irony, as she expressed it, was that two women, Mrs. Kendal and

Genevieve Ward, were the ones who provided the first London role, not any of the great men.)

This recurring trait of the crucial meeting, though having a basis in the operating conditions of the theatre, should put us on guard because of its conventionality. As reported, it may hide as much as its reveals about an actress' career, her sense of self, and the nature of distributive power. Here, for example, is a seemingly irresistible moment for readers and biographers: Ellen Terry's dramatization of how she returned to the stage, after spending six years in domestic solitude with Edward Godwin, the father of her two children, Edith and Gordon Craig.

> Oh, blissful quiet days! How soon they came to an end! Already the shadow of financial trouble fell across my peace. Yet still I never thought of returning to the stage. One day I was driving in a narrow lane, when the wheel of the pony-cart came off. I was standing there, thinking what I should do next, when a whole crowd of horsemen in "pink" came leaping over the hedge into the lane. One of them stopped and asked if he could do anything. Then he looked hard at me and exclaimed: "Good God! it's Nelly."
> The man was Charles Reade [the playwright].
> "Where have you been all these years?" he said.
> "I have been having a very happy time," I answered.
> "Well, you've had it long enough. Come back to the stage!"
> "No, never!"
> "You're a fool! You ought to come back."
> Suddenly I remembered the bailiff in the house a few miles away, and I said laughingly: "Well, perhaps I would think of it if some one would give me forty pounds a week!"
> "Done!" said Charles Reade. "I'll give you that, and more, if you'll come and play Philippa Chester in *The Wandering Heir*." [18]

What could be more of a Victorian melodrama, right down to the bailiff in the house and the sudden rescuer? Yet the many biographers of Ellen Terry have repeated it, only occasionally admitting even parenthetically that it might not be true or that it might serve purposes other than direct reporting.

Edy Craig warned that her mother romanticized the period of retreat, but it was Gordon Craig, in his angry, unreliable little book *Ellen Terry and Her Secret Self,* who came closest to interpreting the theatrical, if not the factual, import of this little drama. Craig treated it as a melodramatic version of paradise lost: the tempter seduced Ellen from her husband.

Reade, "like some ludicrous Mephistopheles," tempted her back to the stage. Reade's triumphant "Done!" is, in Craig's opinion, "almost like the words of Faust—one expects to see a flash of red light."[19] This version (with its probable origins in Craig's memory of Irving's production of *Faust*) may not be the melodrama that Ellen Terry intended, but surely Craig was right to see that she had created, right down to her famous exclamation marks, a highly theatrical (and possibly obfuscating) explanation for her return to the stage. It hid the fact, for example, that she had already made at least one visit (and likely others) to London before this, thus reestablishing her theatre contacts. Given the financial and emotional problems she was having with Godwin, she may well have determined to take charge of her life.

At the very least, whatever her ambivalence and possible guilt about abandoning her domestic role, she wanted to contribute to her children's welfare. How else but the stage? She felt the pull of her professional life, the desire to be welcomed back into the theatre community. She does not admit this directly, but she concludes the chapter on "the simple life" of retirement with a revealing anecdote, a story about a circus goat that pined away in rustic retreat, desiring "the lights of the circus, the lively conversation and the applause of the crowd." Although provided with "the free run of the garden," the goat was ungrateful; only when it returned to the ring was it happy: "You can't force a goat any more than you can force a child to live the simple life." Or, for that matter, any more than you can force Ellen Terry—once she had determined to return to the stage.

Of course, chance and good fortune attend many lives in the theatre; serendipity does play its role for men and women alike. But what stands out in the actresses' autobiographies is the way the crucial meeting gets enhanced and elaborated not just as an anecdote but as a regular generic trait that gives power to men and dependency to women. A version of sexual and social subordination gets expressed, in the voice of gratitude, as a story of need, rescue, and feminine respect for male authority. But is this report simply a matter-of-fact description of the actress' experiences, personal feelings, and sense of self? Or is something calculated and perhaps misleading being described? Even after we give fair consideration to the social and economic history that indeed gave men the controlling power in the theatre, we still must consider the possibility that these actresses may be hiding their own contributions to the development of their careers. But why? If their reports are misleading and unreliable, what is the purpose, besides a good anecdote?

Part of the answer can be found in another pervasive feature of actresses' autobiographies: the presentation of oneself as a divided being, a public and private person. Of course, as noted above, the split between mask and face is an abiding aspect of the historical and aesthetic conditions for performers since the Renaissance. Their autobiographies, then, are supposed to be their mode of revelation, their way of taking off the coat of the profession, as Cibber says. But even a behind-the-scenes look at the profession is selective.

To be expected, much about private life goes unmentioned in late Victorian and early-modern autobiographies. For men and women alike, a code of separate spheres became pervasive in social conduct and writing. Most men of the era usually treated private matters as irrelevant to a report on public life. The career is the essential thing: the source of identity, the achievement of independent character and willpower. The public life defined male identity. Reports on private life—the family home, the good wife and children, the fishing trip, the mountain hike—served primarily to humanize the character of the public man, whose sense of professional mission and determination provided the crucial narrative.

Women likewise obscured private matters. Yet for women autobiographers, including performers, this separation of public from private life proved to be difficult in both life and writing. For actresses, this division between public and private selves was especially troublesome because of their high visibility before a public that desired to look behind the scenes at their supposedly unconventional activities. Women professionals, few in number, did not feel that private life was irrelevant to public life, but for various reasons they were quite reticent about discussing the details of their private lives. Yet they faced a dilemma: if they did not discuss their private affairs, the assumption was that they had something (usually sexual) to hide. But to provide details made them vulnerable to attacks, misunderstandings, and demands for more information. Moreover, from society's viewpoint, the private realm was supposed to be a woman's natural abode. To step beyond it into a profession was an act of both abandonment and invasion. The line between private and public thus became charged with significance. Isadora Duncan may overstate the case, but she surely speaks for many women autobiographers: "No woman has ever told the whole truth of her life. The autobiographies of most famous women are a series of accounts of the outward existence, of petty details and anecdotes which give no realization of their real life. For the great moments of joy or agony they remain strangely silent."[20]

Apparently, when writing an autobiography, professional women find it difficult to articulate—or perhaps even to locate—the problems they face in the conflicts between their public and private lives. In an essay that looks at autobiographies by women in politics, Patricia Meyer Spacks describes these women (e.g., Emma Goldman, Eleanor Roosevelt, Golda Meir) as "selves in hiding," a concept that also can be applied to most actresses before the contemporary era.

In her analysis of how these women presented themselves in their autobiographies, Spacks identifies several common features: (1) the accounts key on work, love, and friendship; (2) the women "all won not only fame but notoriety, each the object of bitter attack for her public achievements"; (3) "they reveal through the structure, language, and detail of their narratives, a painful fact: the identity of public performance may cause its female possessor to experience intensely, or at any rate to reveal emphatically, pre-existent uncertainties of personal identity"; (4) though none of the writers "openly prides herself on 'goodness,' yet all hint at a dominating wish to define themselves as 'good,' mainly in the sense of 'altruistic' behavior"; (5) they experience a curious tension between celebrating a version of self-achievement and representing themselves as selfless and unwillful; (6) "the subordination or loss of self in the cause for something larger than oneself—this theme repeatedly organizes women's autobiographies"; (7) "instead of using the cause ultimately to enlarge the sense of self, these women seem to diminish self."[21] The autobiography thus becomes a series of omissions and denials—a process of marginalizing self in the very process of putting forward a surrogate self or protagonist in the autobiography. Paradoxically, the writing of an autobiography becomes a mode of self-denial.

In varying degrees, these features can also be found in most autobiographies by actresses. Moreover, in the theatre profession a special issue comes to the fore—namely, the sexuality of the actress. Her public identity and her private life are affected, qualified, and conditioned by the ways society perceives (that is, imagines) her sexual appeal and sexual behavior. To a great extent, then, she perceives herself, her place in the profession, and her place in society in terms of explicit sexual definitions. Consequently, the dilemmas between public and private life that the actress faces (in common with all professional women) are intensified, and often circumscribed, by sexual issues.

Because theatre was one of the first professions open to women, actresses were among the first women to write vocational autobiographies (e.g., Charlotte Charke's memoir, George Anne Bellamy's apology). To be expected, these autobiographies reflected, often in a distorted manner, the sexual issues and definitions that pertained to actresses' lives—or, more to the point, pertained to the public's fascination with actresses' private lives. These early works created a sensation because of the suspect sexual status of an actress socially and morally.

An example of this abiding fascination with actresses as sexual beings can be found in Robert W. Lowe's highly respected *A Bibliographical Account of English Theatrical Literature* (1888). In his headnotes for the listings on Elizabeth Barry and Anne Bracegirdle, he cannot avoid making this issue paramount. On Barry: "Her private character was of the worst. Tom Brown says, 'Should you lie with her all night, she would not know you next morning, unless you had another five pounds at her service.'" And on Bracegirdle: "A brilliant actress, whose chastity seems to have surprised her contemporaries, and exercised the minds of more recent historians. Good Genest [the Reverend John Genest, the theatre historian] quaintly remarks that she was 'perhaps a woman of a cold constitution.' Congreve was one of her admirers, and some of the indecent poetry of the period asserted that he married her."[22] The women are damned if they have sexual affairs, damned if they don't. The life of an actress, as told by men, becomes a series of sexual anecdotes; who cares if the stories are based on truth? No wonder, then, that actresses as autobiographers have attempted to fight against this malicious commentary, which historians are sure to carry forward (as Lowe demonstrates).

Ever since the eighteenth century, actresses, when writing their autobiographies, have had to decide how to discuss (or avoid discussing) sexual issues. Even in the twentieth century, actresses have found that they must confront, usually defensively, three interrelated issues that pertain to their place in the profession: their sexuality, their suspect morality, and their ambition or assertiveness. Often in the Victorian and Edwardian ages a rhetoric of denial was used to meet the sexual topic. Rose Eytinge, an American actress, proclaims that "I never suffered any of those perils and temptations which, we are told, beset the paths of girls who adopt the stage as a profession." Ada Reeve, one of the Gaiety Girls, insists that "there was little immorality among the much-maligned Chorus Ladies." Even though she acknowledges receiving diamond bracelets, necklaces, and "yes! even a diamond tiara," there "never was any question of a 'payment in kind.'" Constance Collier, also a Gaiety Girl, makes a similar defense: "Each one of those girls seemed to have some obligation to fulfil—a sister to take care of or some pensioner to keep. They had wonderful manners; they did not smoke or drink or swear. No wonder that so many of them, at that time, married into the aristocracy—it was as if Nature were fortifying herself and using the blood and strength of these magnificent plebeians to build a finer race."[23] This kind of obligatory denial, whether true or false, seems to be both a generic and a historical feature of the autobiographies. Today, of course, sexual life is usually acknowledged, with an equally generic and historical obligation, but this is only the other side of the same coin: the commerce in actresses' sexuality, whether denied, veiled, or revealed.

Certain methods and patterns have evolved in autobiographies for countering, displacing, obscuring, or ignoring the sexual issue. For example, as part of the theme of altruism, mentioned by Spacks, actresses have usually insisted that they are good mothers, good wives, good sisters, good colleagues. They are "useful," Ellen Terry's favorite word for herself; they are attentive; they are caring, loving, and generous. Whatever the nature of their domestic affairs, they feel a need to spell out their commitment to duty and discipline, to hard work and self-control. The onus of their professionalism has required a moral rhetoric of decency and goodness, even when their behavior has been above reproach. Consequently, actresses have attempted to prove that their careers, instead of being corrupting, provide a healthy environment for family and women in general. In Lillah McCarthy's words: "No other art makes such demands upon self-control; and I believe that no other art develops character as well, at all events in a woman."[24] To note the pervasive emphasis on goodness is not to deny the reports, but we should also ask why this insistence is necessary and what other matters it displaces.

Of course, doubts and guilt do find expression, sometimes obliquely, as in the case of Gertrude Lawrence's seemingly lighthearted anecdote about a statement her teenage daughter Pamela made to a reporter: "She gave the journalist a good story—about how her mother really disliked her work and would prefer to stay at home and live a quiet, retired life away from the stage, of which she was tired."[25] Might we not conjecture that a daughter's wish surfaced in the autobiography as an unresolved conflict between private and public life for the mother?

In accord with the good woman theme, the autobiographies generally lack insistence upon ambition and self-determination, as we saw in the reports on crucial meetings with men. In fact, self-interest in the form of ambition is seldom acknowledged. When admitted, it is balanced, often within a page or two, by an example of self-sacrifice, duty, service, or womanly passivity. Thus, on the one hand, actresses often have attempted in their autobiographies and their lives to avoid being contained by other people's sexual and social definitions of them; but, on the other hand, they have underplayed or denied their own assertive selfhood. More to the point, they have characterized themselves (quite sincerely much of the time, but not without some possible calculation) as existing in relation to—in service to, in fulfillment of—another person or idea or purpose. That "other" can be a husband, a lover, a director, children, God, stage roles, the public, or another woman. Yet this other is almost never history, the era, the spirit of the times, the culture, the arts—as it is commonly for strong-willed men who see themselves as the expression and embodiment of these large forces. (In this sense, for self-possessed men there is no other, just the extensions of self, mirrored in people's responses to them.)

In women's autobiographies in general this relation to the other is a recurring pattern: Margaret Cavendish and the duke of Newcastle, Beatrice Webb and Sidney Webb, Hilda Doolittle and Sigmund Freud, Lillian Hellman and Dashiell Hammett, Simone de Beauvoir and Jean-Paul Sartre. So, too, in the theatre: Mr. and Mrs. Charles Calvert, Ellen Terry and Henry Irving, W. H. and Madge Kendal, Eva Moore and Harry Esmond, Constance and Frank Benson, Mabel and Wilfred Pickles, Isadora Duncan and Gordon Craig, Elsa Lanchester and Charles Laughton. Eva Moore titled separate chapters in her autobiography "Harry, the Man," "Harry, the Playwright," and "Harry, the Actor." She printed many letters to him, few to herself. Marie Wilton and Squire Bancroft even wrote their autobiographies together, alternating section by section, page by page, even though she was the one who successfully transformed and managed the Prince of Wales Theatre. Any suggestion that the woman is more important than the man is almost always avoided, as Madge Kendal insisted: "My husband never was my leading man. I was always his leading lady."[26]

Historically, then, this emphasis upon the other expresses the conditions under which women have lived, their relation to men's social values, prejudices, and controls. It also may express the women's communal values and sensibilities that manifest themselves, both because of and in spite of social conditions. And, as I have implied, these recurring motifs and themes may get reported not only to put forward an acceptable version of the actress as woman (mother, wife, sister, friend) but also to hide or deny aspects of self that the actress, as professional woman and private person, feels cannot be reported without negative consequences.

Whatever the case, the issue is not simply that actresses subordinate themselves to others, in order to be valued and valuable. Of course, the approval that comes from a loving mate, a dependent child, or an adoring public is a common and primary process for all of us in establishing our self-identity. But more than this, these actresses, though they have been self-willed women who have achieved much on their own terms, go out of their way, with a few exceptions, to offer a life story that credits to others key aspects of their strength, their purpose, their identity. Granted, they may also complain about what Gertrude Lawrence calls the "patriarchal age." And they may attack male egotism, as Wells, Terry, and Waters do. But this disapproval reinforces their descriptions of their own selflessness.

This investiture of the other, a process of authorizing a split self, should not simply be mistaken, however, for subservience. Self-displacement is not necessarily self-effacement. As Mary G. Mason points out: "This recognition of another consciousness—and I emphasize recognition rather than deference—this grounding of identity through relation to the chosen other, seems . . . to enable women to write openly about themselves." [27] Sometimes, perhaps; but whatever the case, whether it be a sign of acquiescence or liberation, this process of splitting identity—not only between self and other but between public and private identities—appears to be not just a common trait but an abiding condition of most women's autobiographies.

The task for the theatre historian is to understand why these various divisions, displacements, and denials of self occur. Sometimes these autobiographies express in various degrees of reliability the actual conditions and values of the actresses. But often, for whatever reasons, the versions of self are misleading and incomplete, thus requiring a select judgment if not skepticism from the theatre historian. At least for the period under consideration, these autobiographies are models of how to maintain a public mask even when writing in the private voice. In the process, however, aspects of both public and private life go unreported—and many reported matters are suspect.

In other words, individually the autobiographies can be quite unreliable. As historical documents, they often fail to describe accurately what happened in the public career and private life of the actress; as narratives, they fail to articulate fully the social significance and personal consciousness of a professional woman in the theatre. Accordingly, theatre historians are regularly frustrated and misled by what is reported; literary critics are disappointed by the apparent lack of self-examination. Yet collectively—in their literary, rhetorical, and social figurations of identity— these autobiographies may indeed be profoundly valuable documents, expressing, however obliquely, complex truths about actresses' lives—on and off the stage.

NOTES

1 Gerald Eades Bentley points out that theatre scholars have identified "more than a thousand players . . . by name" for the period between 1590 and 1642 in England (*The Profession of Player in Shakespeare's Time, 1590–1642* [Princeton, N.J.: Princeton University Press, 1984], p. 4).

2 Colley Cibber, *An Apology for the Life of Mr. Colley Cibber, Written by Himself,* 2 vols., new ed. with notes and supplement by Robert W. Lowe (London: John C. Nimmo, 1889), I, 4–5.

3 Robert W. Lowe, *A Bibliographical Account of English Theatrical Literature* (London: John C. Nimmo, 1888), p. 136. Lowe points out that there were publications on "almost every notable occurrence in his career." Gerald M. Berkowitz confirms this in *David Garrick, A Reference Guide* (Boston: G. K. Hall, 1980). The first seventy-nine pages of this annotated bibliography cover hundreds of writings on and by Garrick during his lifetime.

4 From this perspective, the commentary on Garrick's apparent "natural" acting style is significant less as a measure of realism on the stage (perhaps a misleading issue) and more as a manifestation of the cultural concern for the split sensibility.

5 For three valuable studies on various historical, theoretical, and paradigmatic aspects of eighteenth-century acting, see Leigh Wood's *Garrick Claims the Stage: Acting as Social Emblem in Eighteenth-Century England* (Westport, Conn.: Greenwood Press, 1984); William Worthen's *The Idea of the Actor* (Princeton: Princeton University Press, 1984); and Joseph Roach's *The Player's Passion: Studies in the Science of Acting* (Newark: University of Delaware Press, 1985).

6 Philip Highfill, Jr., "A Peep behind the Curtain: Mass Theatrical Biography," in George Winchester Stone, Jr., and Philip H. Highfill, Jr., *In Search of Restoration and Eighteenth-Century Theatrical Biography* (Los Angeles: William Andrews Clark Memorial Library, University of California, Los Angeles, 1976), pp. 53–58. Needless to say, the perfect illustration that documentation on performers increased decisively after the Renaissance is the scholarly project of compiling a fourteen-volume biographical dictionary on theatre people in London between 1660 and 1800.

7 Leslie Stephen, *Hours in a Library,* 3 vols. (London: Smith, Elder, 1892), III, 237.

8 See, for example, the "seven chief qualities distinguishing the picaresque novel," in William Flint Thrall, Addison Hibbard, and C. Hugh Homan, *A Handbook to Literature,* rev. ed. (New York: Odyssey Press, 1960). All seven traits, from

type of character and narrative voice to episodic plotting and themes of petty criminality, fit Mrs. Wells' autobiography exactly.

9 Elizabeth Robins, *Both Sides of the Curtain* (London: William Heinemann, 1940), p. 18.

10 Noel Coward, *Present Indicative* (Garden City, N.Y.: Doubleday, Doran, 1937), p. 3.

11 For a study of the generic conventions of autobiographies, see Susanna Egan, *Patterns of Experience in Autobiography* (Chapel Hill: University of North Carolina Press, 1984). Egan argues that the generic "stages of the written life" are lost paradise, journey or quest, conversion, and confession. These narrative patterns, related to childhood, youth, maturity, and old age, become verbal constructions: "all of them are fictions" (p. 5). This is also the conclusion that Linda H. Peterson reaches in her recent book, *Victorian Autobiography: The Tradition of Self-Interpretation* (New Haven: Yale University Press, 1986): "autobiography, apparently the most personal and individual of literary genres, is in fact a highly conventional, even prescriptive form, and . . . its generic conventions shape our way of thinking about the most private aspects of our lives" (p. 2). Avrom Fleishman notes in *Figures of Autobiography: The Language of Self-Writing in Victorian and Modern England* (Berkeley: University of California Press, 1983) that these common topoi, which derive from Saint Augustine, have continued to shape modern secular autobiographies. We should note, however, that women's autobiographies do not conform exactly to the confessional model; nor do they usually take on the mode of the egotistical sublime of Rousseau or Wordsworth. In Estelle Jelinek's words, men's experiences are "described in heroic or exceptional terms: alienation, initiation, manhood, apotheosis, transformation, guilt, identity crisis, and symbolic journeys." Women's experiences are less heroic as reported: "heartbreak, anger, loneliness, motherhood, humility, confusion, and self-abnegation" (*Women's Autobiography* [Bloomington: Indiana University Press, 1980], p. 5). While clearly sharing some of these traits, autobiographies by actors and actresses do not quite fit within either of these summaries.

12 An alternative plot that recurs is the didactic tale of the disappointed or lost life: the crucial turn is not toward success but toward failure. The narrative features hardships; the theme focuses on moral turpitude. The fault may be located in self, others, or the theatre profession, which corrupts an innocent or weak soul.

13 Ethel Barrymore, *Memories: An Autobiography* (New York: Harper and Row, 1955), pp. 7–8.

14 We need more studies on both audiences, especially on the general public. Who were the intended audiences in different periods? What were their sociological and economic traits? Were any of them dominated by women? If so, what does this signify, if anything? Also, what about the means of publishing: publisher, cost, distribution? What are the records on library readers, a major factor in readership since the nineteenth century? Was the autobiography extracted or

serialized in a popular journal before being published as a book? These and other questions need to be asked as part of the historical investigation of theatre autobiographies and their meanings.

15 It would seem appropriate, for example, when reading Ethel Waters' *His Eye Is on the Sparrow* (London: W. H. Allen, 1951), with its powerful descriptions of being a black performer in white America, to gauge her shifting aims as she directs her comments to (or at) blacks, whites, men, and women. The public audience for whom she writes seems to vary, depending upon the point she is making. By featuring her own struggle, she demonstrates, sometimes defiantly to whites and men, that though black women are continually victimized, she refuses to be a victim. She also seems to invite black readers, especially black women, to identify with her, to enjoy her defiant, shocking narrative of hardships faced and overcome. Her sense of self in relation to different audiences (including white women, whom she sometimes pointedly sets at a distance from herself) shapes the historical record, which is a narrative of triumph against great odds (hence the teleological function of the conclusion: her success on Broadway in a "white" play, *The Member of the Wedding*).

16 Paul Ricoeur, "The Narrative Function," in *Hermeneutics and the Human Sciences,* ed. and trans. John B. Thompson (Cambridge: Cambridge University Press; Paris: Editions de la Maison des Sciences de l'Homme, 1981), p. 288. See also *Time and Narrative,* 3 vols., trans. Kathleen Blamey and David Pellauer (Chicago: University of Chicago Press, 1984–1988).

17 In considering the topic of actresses' autobiographies, I want to identify *in a preliminary manner* some of their special traits, in terms of both historical import and literary form. This is not to say that a cultural law of feminine difference controls and limits women's writing. Nor am I suggesting that biology is destiny. However, it is undeniable that gender practices and assumptions shape psychological and social identity for men as well as women in all cultures. We should expect, then, to find gender factors in the writing of autobiography. At the very least, we should be able to identify some defining traits that occur in autobiographies by actresses, without having to claim that all of these traits are to be found exclusively in women's writing or only in the period under consideration. Recurring patterns, not laws, are sought. The interpretation of these patterns is our challenge and responsibility—a task not to be ignored by male historians, however difficult it may be to undertake and complete fairly.

18 Ellen Terry, *The Story of My Life* (London: Hutchinson, 1908), pp. 82–83.

19 Gordon Craig, *Ellen Terry and Her Secret Self* (London: Sampson, Low, Marston, 1931), p. 34.

20 Isadora Duncan, *My Life* (New York: Boni and Liveright, 1927 [1928]), p. 3. Duncan's statement serves as both a commentary on previous autobiographies and a manifesto of liberation in her own case. Yet despite her Whitmanesque openness to all sensual experience, including sex, Duncan, too, passes over some of the "great moments of joy or agony" in *My Life*. A comparison of her

autobiography and Francis Steegmuller's edition of her letters to Gordon Craig, *Your Isadora* (New York: Random House, 1974, pp. 146–151), reveals some striking omissions in what gets reported (e.g., the events surrounding her pregnancy, including her deep depression, apparent suicide attempt, and dependency upon another woman, Kathleen Bruce, who came to stay with her after receiving pleading letters). In *My Life*, Duncan claims, however, that Bruce's appearance was "a happy surprise" (pp. 191–197).

21 Patricia Meyer Spacks, "Selves in Hiding," in *Women's Autobiography: Essays in Criticism*, ed. and intro. Estelle C. Jelinek (Bloomington: Indiana University Press, 1980), pp. 112–132.

22 Lowe, *A Bibliographical Account*, pp. 14, 29.

23 Rose Eytinge, *The Memories of Rose Eytinge* (New York: Frederick A. Stokes, 1905), pp. 7–8; Ada Reeve, *Take It for a Fact* (London: Heinemann, 1954), p. 74; Constance Collier, *Harlequinade, The Story of My Life*, preface by Noel Coward (London: John Lane, The Bodley Head, 1929), p. 48.

24 Lillah McCarthy, *Myself and My Friends, with an Aside by Bernard Shaw* (London: Thorton Butterworth, 1933), p. 29.

25 Gertrude Lawrence, *A Star Danced* (Garden City, N.Y.: Doubleday, Doran, 1945), p. 200.

26 Madge Kendal, *Dame Madge Kendal, By Herself* (London: Murray, 1933), p. 70. The autobiography was written after her husband died. But the title is misleading, for it is not a record of a woman living "by herself," except in the sad, self-pitying sense. She had come to feel that the whole world had unfairly abandoned and misunderstood her.

27 Mary G. Mason, "The Other Voice: Autobiographies of Woman Writers," in *Autobiography: Essays Theoretical and Critical*, ed. James Olney (Princeton, N.J.: Princeton University Press, 1980), p. 210.

Historiography
A Select Bibliography

Thomas Postlewait

T his three-part bibliography offers a select listing of essays and books that consider the issues, problems, methodologies, and theories of historiography. It is limited to publications in English during the last twenty years. For the most part, the bibliography supplements the sources cited in the separate essays in this collection. No attempt has been made here to compile a comprehensive listing of writings on historiography; instead a cross section of representative works is offered. These publications—as well as their bibliographies—should point the reader to additional writings on historiography and the philosophy of history. For example, see Martin Klein, Lester Stephens, and the journal *History and Theory* for extensive bibliographies.

Needless to say, by limiting this catalogue to publications of the last twenty years, I have not listed major works in historiography, from Hegel, Weber, Dilthey, Croce, and Wöllflin to Bloch, Poulet, Becker, Cassirer, and Dvořák. Moreover, even in the case of more recent writers who have contributed to the practice and philosophy of history, such as Northrop Frye, Kenneth Burke, Erwin Panofsky, Hannah Arendt, Isaiah Berlin, Fernand Braudel, Claude Lévi-Strauss, Clifford Geertz, and Michel Foucault, the listings are suggestive, not all-inclusive. My aim, therefore, is to provide a preliminary guide to current work in historiography and to suggest the range of issues and approaches open to theatre historians. This bibliography is a starting place for investigating historiography in several fields of study, but a good researcher should move beyond it rapidly.

The first section focuses primarily on theatre historiography, with a few limited items on dance, opera, and musicology. Though I fully agree with Joseph Roach that there exists today a "needlessly parochial separation of theatre history, dance history, and musicology into discrete fields," this bibliography does not close the gap. Clearly, a comprehensive bibliography on the historiography of these interrelated fields is greatly needed. In the case of theatre history, the works by R. W. Vince should be consulted for a valuable overview of the twentieth-century approaches to the study of the separate eras, from the classical age to the eighteenth century.

The line between dramatic and theatre studies is hard to draw, but for the most part this bibliography does not list studies that focus on the historiography of drama. Thus, some valuable works that consider aspects of theatre historiography, at least implicitly, are missing, especially those that feature a particular period (e.g., the Renaissance studies of Stephen Greenblatt), those that mainly present dramatic analysis (the drama theory of Bernard Beckerman), those that basically focus on theatrical codes and structures (the semiotics of Keir Elam), and those that express a contemporary perspective (the writings of Herbert Blau). Nor have I attempted to list the many studies of the Renaissance stage (but see Michael Shapiro's bibliography). Theatre historiography, not dramatic study (or even theatre history), is the issue here.

The second section of the bibliography focuses mainly on historiographical studies of the methodology, critical theory, and philosophy of art history and literary history (all genres), with additional listings on aesthetics, art and archaeology, the sociology of art, popular culture, and theories of biography and autobiography. In general, then, this section provides selected listings in the cultural history of the arts, but the listings for the historiography of general cultural studies, as defined by sociology and anthropology, are in section 3.

The third section covers writings on the theory of history as a discipline, general historiography, intellectual history, history and the social sciences, history and anthropology, history and archaeology, history and science, psychohistory, and the philosophy of history. This section is necessarily selective because the number of writings on historiography in these various fields is enormous. The works listed are representative. Their own bibliographies, in turn, provide many additional items for investigation.

In a limited number of cases, certain writers are listed in more than one part of the bibliography because of the range of their writings (e.g., Raymond Williams, Herbert Lindenberger, Hayden White, Kenneth Burke, Roland Barthes). Otherwise, authors can be found in the section that covers their major area of specialization.

Each section lists a few bibliographies that itemize writings on historiography, but no attempt has been made to provide a survey of the growing number of field bibliographies. Nor have I listed the representative journals—such as *New Literary History, Representations, Signs, Humanities in Society, Journal of the History of Ideas, Literature and History, Art History, biography, Clio, Past and Present, Journal of Interdisciplinary History,* and *American Historical Review*—that publish frequently on historiography. The one exception to this general exclusion of journals is *History and Theory,* which has become the paramount journal on historiography. Unfortunately, most theatre historians are not familiar with this journal or many of the essays and books listed here. Perhaps this bibliography—and this collection of essays—will spark the interest of more historians and their students in the historical methodologies, critical problems, and theoretical issues that apply to the study, writing, and teaching of history.

Theatre History: Methodology, Terminology, and Theory

Allen, Ralph, et al. "Research in Theatre History." *Educational Theatre Journal* 19 (1967), 260–263.

Arnott, James. "An Introduction to Theatrical Scholarship." *Theatre Quarterly* 39 (Spring–Summer 1981), 29–42.

Bailey, Claudia Jean. *A Guide to Reference and Bibliography for Theatre Research,* 2nd ed. Columbus: Ohio State University Libraries Publications, 1983.

Bank, Rosemarie K., and Harold Nichols. *The Status of Theatre Research, 1984.* Commission on Theatre Research. Landham, Md.: University Press of America, 1986.

Barba, Eugenio. "Theatre Anthropology." *The Drama Review* 26:2 (Summer 1982), 5–32.

Beckerman, Bernard. "Review of T. J. King's *Shakespearean Staging, 1599–1642.*" *Renaissance Drama,* n.s. 4 (1971), 237–244.

Booth, Michael. "Theatre History and the Literary Critic." *Yearbook of English Studies* 9 (1979), 15–27.

Brandon, James R., and Elizabeth Wichmann, eds. *Asian Theatre: A Study Guide and Annotated Bibliography.* Washington, D.C.: American Theatre Association, 1980.

Brockett, Oscar. "Appendix." In *History of the Theatre,* 5th ed. (Boston: Allyn and Bacon, 1986).

———. "The Humanities: Theatre History." *Southern Speech Communication Journal* 41 (Winter 1976), 142–150.

———. "Research in Theatre History." *Educational Theatre Journal* 19 (June 1967), 267–275.

———. "Some Reflections on Research in Theatre History." *Educational Theatre Journal* 17 (May 1965), 111–117.

Buckland, Theresa. "Definitions of Folk Dance: Some Explorations." *Folk Dance Journal* 4:4 (1983), 315–332.

Carlson, Marvin. "Contemporary Concerns in the Semiotics of Theatre." *Semiotica* 48:3/4 (1984), 281–291.

———. "Local Semiosis and Theatrical Interpretation." *Semiotica,* forthcoming.

———. "Semiotics and Theatre Historiography: Problems and Opportunities." *Literary Research,* forthcoming.

———. "The Theatre Event and Filmic Documentation." *Degrés* (1986).

———. *Theories of the Theatre: A Historical and Critical Survey from the Greeks to the Present.* Ithaca: Cornell University Press, 1984.

Case, Sue-Ellen. *Feminism and Theatre.* New York: Methuen, 1988.

Cheshire, David. *Theatre: History, Criticism, and Reference.* London: Clive Bingley, 1967.

Davidson, Clifford. *Drama and Art: An Introduction to the Use of Evidence from the Visual Arts for the Study of Early Drama*. Kalamazoo: Medieval Institute, Western Michigan University, 1977.

Dietrich, Julia C. "Folk Drama Scholarship: The State of the Art." *Research Opportunities in Renaissance Drama* 19 (1976), 15–32.

Dietrich, Margret, ed. *Regie in Dokumentation, Forschung und Lehre*. Salzburg: Otto Muller, 1975. Includes some essays in English.

Donohue, Joseph. "Introduction [on theatre historiography]." In *The Stage in the 18th Century*, ed. J. D. Browning. New York: Garland Publishing, 1981.

———. "Theatre Scholarship and Technology: A Look at the Future of the Discipline." *Theatre Survey* 22 (November 1981), 133–139.

Donohue, Joseph, and James Ellis. "The London Stage 1800–1900: Project in Progress." *Theatre Quarterly* 29 (Spring 1978), 59–62.

Duvignaud, Jean. "The Theatre in Society: Society in Theatre." In *Sociology of Literature and Drama*, ed. Elizabeth and Tom Burns. Harmondsworth, England: Penguin, 1973.

Edwards, Christopher, and Ian Herbert. "Computer Databases for the Performing Arts: Tandem and International Bibliography of Theatre." *Theatre Notebook* 39 (1985), 149–152.

Ellis, James. "A Taxonomy of the Theatre: Simon Trussler's A Classification for the Performing Arts." *Theatre Research International* 1 : 3 (1976), 216–222.

Fischer-Lichte, Erika. "The Performance as an 'Interpretant' of the Drama." *Semiotica* 64 : 3/4 (1987), 197–212.

———. "The Theatrical Code." In *Multimedial Communication*, vol. 2, *Theatre Semiotics*, ed. Ernest W. B. Hess-Luttich. Tübingen: Gunter Narr, 1983.

Forbes, Fred R., Jr. *Dance: An Annotated Bibliography, 1965–1982*. New York: Garland Publishing, 1986.

George, David E. R. "A Question of Method: Ibsen's Reception in Germany." In *Transformations in Modern European Drama*, ed. Ian Donaldson. Atlantic Highlands, N.J.: Humanities Press, 1983.

Gillespie, Patti, and Kenneth Cameron. *Western Theatre: Revolution and Revival*. New York: Macmillan, 1984.

Hauptfleisch, Temple. "Theatre Research: Some Thoughts on a New Disciple." *Theatreforum* 5 : 1 (May 1984), 66–79.

Hays, Michael. "Theatre History and Practice: An Alternative View of the Drama." *New German Technique* 12 (1977), 85–97.

Headley, Robert. "Theatre Preservation Bibliography." *Marquee* 15 : 4 (1983), 39–40.

Herbert, Ian. "Computer Databases for Theatre Studies." *New Theatre Quarterly* 6 (May 1986), 175–180.

Hernadi, Paul. "Re-presenting the Past: A Note on Narrative Historiography and Historical Drama." *History and Theory* 15 (1976), 45–51.

Highfill, Philip H., Jr., Kalman A. Burnim, and Edward A. Langhans. "Preface." In *A Biographical Dictionary of Actors, Actresses, Musicians, Dancers, Managers, and Other Stage Personnel in London, 1660–1800.* Carbondale: Southern Illinois University Press, 1973–.

Holoman, D. Kern, and Claude V. Palisca, eds. *Musicology in the 1980's.* New York: Da Capo, 1982.

Hornby, Richard. "The Ph.D in Theatre: A Vanishing Degree?" *Theatre News* 16:3 (Spring 1984), 16.

Howard, Diana. *Directory of Theatre Research and Information Resources in the United Kingdom.* 2nd revised ed. London: Society for Theatre Research, 1986.

Hume, Robert H. "English Drama and Theatre 1660–1800: New Directions in Research." *Theatre Survey* 23 (1982), 71–100.

———. "Studies in English Drama 1660–1800." *Philological Quarterly* 55 (1976), 451–487; 56 (1977), 438–469; 57 (1978), 437–472.

Hyslop, Gabrielle. "Researching the Acting of French Melodrama, 1800–1830." *Nineteenth Century Theatre* 15:2 (Winter 1987), 85–113.

International Bibliography of Theatre 1982–Present, ed. Benito Ortolani. Brooklyn: Brooklyn College, City University of New York, Theatre Research Data Center, 1985–.

Joseph, Bertram. "The Ph.D. Program in Drama." *Educational Theatre Journal* 19 (1967), 166–173.

Kealiinohomuku, Joann W., ed. *Dance History Research: Perspectives from Related Arts and Disciplines.* New York: CORD, 1970.

Kerman, Joseph. *Contemplating Music: Challenges to Musicology.* Cambridge: Harvard University Press, 1985.

Larson, Orville. "Exhibition Catalogues: Critical Resources for Research in Theatre Art." *Educational Theatre Journal* 28 (October 1976), 389–397.

Lavin, G. A. "The Elizabethan Theatre and the Inductive Method." In *The Elizabethan Theatre II,* ed. David Galloway. Hamden, Conn.: Archon Books, 1970.

Lindenberger, Herbert. *Historical Drama: The Relation of Literature and Reality.* Chicago: University of Chicago Press, 1975.

———. *Opera: The Extravagant Art.* Ithaca: Cornell University Press, 1984.

Longfield, Robert. "Researching Theatres . . . and Theatre History." *Marquee* 14:1 (1982), 12.

MacAloon, John J., ed. *Rite, Drama, Festival, Spectacle: Rehearsals toward a Theory of Cultural Performances.* Philadelphia: Institute for the Study of Human Issues, 1984.

McConachie, Bruce A. "Towards a Postpositivist Theatre History." *Theatre Journal* 37 (1985), 465–486.

Marco, Guy A. *Opera: A Research and Information Guide.* New York: Garland, 1984.

Marinis, Marco de. "A Faithful Betrayal of Performance: Notes on the Use of Video in Theatre." *New Theatre Quarterly* 1:4 (November 1985), 383–389.

———. "Theatrical Comprehension: A Socio-Semiotic Approach." *Theater* 15:1 (Winter 1983), 12–17.

Marshall, Thomas. "The First Quarter Century of ASTR." *Theatre Survey* 22 (November 1981), 117–124.

Meisel, Martin. *Realizations: Narrative, Pictorial, and Theatrical Arts in Nineteenth-Century England*. Princeton, N.J.: Princeton University Press, 1983.

Meserve, Walter J. "The State of Research in American Theatre History." *Theatre Survey* 22 (November 1981), 125–131.

Orgel, Stephen. "The Authentic Shakespeare." *Representations* 21 (Winter 1988), 1–26.

———. "Shakespeare Imagines a Theater." *Poetics Today* 5:3 (1984), 549–561.

———. "What Is a Text?" *Research Opportunities in Renaissance Drama* 24 (1981), 3–6.

Pavis, Patrice. *Languages of the Stage: Essays in the Semiology of Theatre*. New York: Performing Arts Journal Publications, 1982.

———. "Socio-Criticism," trans. Helen Knode. *Theatre* 15 (Winter 1983), 8–11.

———. "Theatre Analysis: Some Questions and a Questionnaire." *New Theatre Quarterly* 1:2 (May 1985), 208–212.

Performing Arts Resources. 1974–present.

Pistonik, Vesna. "Towards a Redefinition of Dramatic Genre and Stage History." *Modern Drama* 28:4 (December 1985), 677–687.

Pladott, Dinnah. "The Dynamics of the Sign Systems in the Theatre." In *Multimedia Communication*, vol. 2, *Theatre Semiotics*. Tübingen: Gunter Narr, 1982.

Postlewait, Thomas. "The Concept of Periodization in Theatre History." *Theatre Journal* 40:3 (October 1988), 299–318.

———. "Introduction." In *Prophet of the New Drama: William Archer and the Ibsen Campaign*. Westport, Conn.: Greenwood Press, 1986.

———. "Review Essay: The International Bibliography of Theatre: 1982." *Theatre History Studies* 6 (1986), 200–210.

———. "Review Essay: The International Bibliography of Theatre, 1983." *Theatre History Studies* 7 (1987), 176–182.

Reynolds, L. D., and N. G. Wilson. *Scribes and Scholars: A Guide to the Transmission of Greek and Latin Literature*. 2nd ed. Oxford: Clarendon Press, 1974.

Ritchie, Stanley. "Authentic Reconstruction of Musical Performance: History and Influence." *The Drama Review* 28:3 (Fall 1984), 67–73.

Roach, Joseph. "Preface." In *The Player's Passion: Studies in the Science of Acting*. Newark: University of Delaware Press, 1985.

Sarlós, Robert K. "A. M. Nagler and Theatre History in America." *Theatre Research International* 9:1 (Spring 1984), 1–6.

———. "Creating Objects and Events: A Form of Theatre Research." *Theatre Research International* 5:1 (Winter 1979–1980), 83–88.

————. "From Historical Research to Modern Production: A Stuart Masque." In *Regie in Dokumentation, Forschung und Lehre,* ed. Margret Dietrich. Salzburg: O. Muller, 1975.

————. "Performance Reconstruction: The Vital Link." *The Drama Review* 28:3/T103 (Fall 1984), 3–8.

Schechner, Richard. *Between Theatre and Anthropology.* Philadelphia: University of Pennsylvania Press, 1985.

————. "Drama, Script, Theatre, and Performance." *Drama Review* 17:3 (September 1973), 5–36.

————. *Essays on Performance Theory, 1970–1976.* New York: Drama Book Specialists, 1977.

Schechner, Richard, and Mady Schuman, eds. *Ritual, Play and Performance: Readings in the Social Sciences/Theatre.* New York: Seabury Press, 1976.

Schmitt, Natalie Crohn. "Recording the Theatre in Photographs." *Educational Theatre Journal* 28 (October 1976), 376–388.

Senelick, Laurence. "Popular Entertainment and Recent Scholarship." *Nineteenth Century Theatre* 15:2 (Winter 1987), 141–155.

Shapiro, Michael. "Annotated Bibliography on Original Staging in Elizabethan Plays." *Research Opportunities in Renaissance Drama* 24 (1981), 23–49.

Sheingorn, Pamela. "On Using Medieval Art in the Study of Medieval Drama: An Introduction to Methodology." *Research Opportunities in Renaissance Drama* 22 (1979), 101–109.

Staggenburg, Robert G. "The Postmodern Episteme and the Theatre Historian." *Theatre Survey,* forthcoming.

States, Bert O. *Great Reckonings in Little Rooms: On the Phenomenology of Theatre.* Berkeley: University of California Press, 1985.

Stone, George Winchester, Jr., and Philip H. Highfill, Jr. *In Search of Restoration and Eighteenth-Century Theatrical Biography.* Los Angeles: William Andrews Clark Memorial Library, University of California, Los Angeles, 1976.

Styan, J. L. *Drama, Stage, and Audience.* Cambridge: Cambridge University Press, 1975.

Swaminathan, Saraswati. "Performing Arts: Documentation, Preservation, Retrieval." *Sangeet Natak: Journal of the Performing Arts* (New Delhi) 70 (October–December 1983), 32–37.

Taplin, Oliver. *The Stagecraft of Aeschylus.* Oxford: Clarendon Press, 1977.

Trapido, Joel, with Edward A. Langhans and James R. Brandon, eds. *An International Dictionary of Theatre Language.* Westport, Conn.: Greenwood Press, 1985.

Trussler, Simon. "Towards a Classification for the Performing Arts." *Theatre Quarterly* 2:6 (April–June 1972), 84–87.

Tyrell, John, and Rosemary Wise. *A Guide to International Congress Reports in Musicology, 1900–1975.* New York: Garland, 1979.

Vince, Ronald W. *Ancient and Medieval Theatre, A Historiographical Handbook.* Westport, Conn.: Greenwood Press, 1984.

———. "Comparative Theatre Historiography." *Essays in Theatre* 1 (1983), 64–72.

———. *Neoclassical Theatre, A Historiographical Handbook.* Westport, Conn.: Greenwood Press, 1988.

———. *Renaissance Theatre, A Historiographical Handbook.* Westport, Conn.: Greenwood Press, 1984.

Weales, Gerald. "Theatre Literature and Criticism." *Educational Theatre Journal* 19 (1967), 301–307.

Williams, Raymond. *Drama in Performance,* rev. ed. London: Penguin, 1968.

Williams, Simon. "Opera Redux: New and Old Directions in Opera Scholarship." *Nineteenth Century Theatre* 16:1 (June 1988), 50–63.

Wilson, Garff B. "Consider Theatrical Biographies." *Yale Theatre Review* 5 (1973), 139–145.

Woods, Alan, ed. *The Historiography of Theatre History.* Supplement to *Theatre Studies* 21 (1974–1975).

———. "The McDowell Research Classification System for the Cataloguing of Scene and Costume Designs." In *Stage Design: Papers from the Fifteenth International Congress of SIMBAS,* ed. Ginnine Cocuzza and Barbara Naomi Cohen-Stratyner. New York: Theatre Library Association, 1983.

———. "Reconstruction of Historical Performances for Modern Production: Performance Research at the OSU 'Theatre Research Institute.'" In *Acts of the Ninth International Congress of the Libraries and Museums of the Performing Arts,* ed. Per Pio and Eva Steinaa. Copenhagen: Royal Library, 1976.

———. "Reporting Performance Research." *Theatre Survey* 22 (November 1981), 171–176.

———. "Theatre Reconstruction: Tentative Steps toward a Methodology." *Theatre Survey* 12 (1971), 46–57.

Wynne, Shirley. "Reconstruction of Dance from 1700." In *Dance History Research: Perspectives from Related Arts and Disciplines,* ed. Joann W. Kealiinohomuku. New York: CORD, 1970.

Zarrilli, Phillip B. "Toward a Definition of Performance Studies." *Theatre Journal* 38:3/4 (October–December 1986), 372–376, 493–496.

Art, Literary, and Cultural History: Methodology, Criticism, and Theory

Aagaard-Mogensen, Lars, ed. *Culture and Art.* Atlantic Highlands, N.J.: Humanities Press, 1976.

Aaron, Daniel, ed. *Studies in Biography.* Cambridge, Mass.: Harvard University Press, 1978.

Ackerman, James S. "Toward a New Social Theory of Art." *New Literary History* 4 (Winter 1973), 315–330.

Ackerman, James S., and Rhys Carpenter. *Art and Archaeology.* Englewood Cliffs, N.J.: Prentice-Hall, 1963.

Adorno, Theodor W. *Aesthetic Theory.* Boston: Routledge and Kegan Paul, 1984.

———. *Introduction to the Sociology of Music,* trans. E. B. Ashton. New York: Seabury Press, 1976.

Albrecht, M. C. "Art as an Institution." *American Sociological Review* 33:3 (1968), 383–397.

Albrecht, M. C., J. H. Barnett, and M. Griff, eds. *The Sociology of Art and Literature.* London: Duckworth, 1970.

Alpers, Svetlana. *The Art of Describing: Dutch Art in the Seventeenth Century.* Chicago: University of Chicago Press, 1983.

———. "Describe or Narrate? A Problem in Realistic Representation." *New Literary History* 8 (1976), 16–41.

———. "Is Art History?" *Daedalus* 106 (Summer 1977), 1–13.

———. "Style Is What You Make It: The Visual Arts Once Again." In *The Concept of Style,* ed. Berel Lang. Philadelphia: University of Pennsylvania Press, 1979.

Altick, R. D. *Lives and Letters: A History of Literary Biography in England and America.* New York: Knopf, 1965.

Anderson, Judith H. *Biographical Truth: The Representation of Historical Persons in Tudor-Stuart Writing.* New Haven: Yale University Press, 1984.

Antal, Frederick. "Remarks on the Method of Art History." *Burlington Magazine* 91 (1949), 49–52, 73–75.

Arntzen, Etta, and Robert Rainwater. *Guide to the Literature of Art History.* Chicago: American Library Association, 1979.

Attridge, Derek, et al., eds. *Poststructuralism and the Question of History.* Cambridge: Cambridge University Press, 1987.

Auerbach, Erich. "Vico and Aesthetic Historism." In *Scenes from the Drama of European Literature,* foreword by Paolo Velesio. Minneapolis: University of Minnesota Press, 1984.

Baldwin, Michael, Charles Harrison, and Mel Ramsden. "Art History, Art Criticism, and Explanation." *Art History* 4:4 (1981), 432–456.

Banfield, Ann. "Where Epistemology, Style, and Grammar Meet Literary History." *New Literary History* 9:3 (Spring 1978), 415–454.

Baron, Samuel H., and Carl Pletsch. eds. *Introspection in Biography, The Biographer's Quest for Self-Awareness.* Hillside, N.J.: Analytic Press, 1985.

Barrett, Michele, et al. *Ideology and Cultural Production.* London: Croom Helm, 1979.

Barthes, Roland. "History or Literature." In *On Racine,* trans. Richard Howard. New York: Performing Arts Journal Publications, 1983; Hill and Wang 1964.

————. *Image, Music, Text,* trans. Stephen Heath. New York: Hill and Wang, 1977.

Baxandall, Lee and S. Morawski, eds. *Marx and Engels on Literature and Art.* St. Louis: Telos Press, 1973.

Baxandall, Michael. "The Language of Art History." *New Literary History* 8 (Spring 1977), 452–466.

————. *Painting and Experience in Fifteenth Century Italy: A Primer in the Social History of Style.* New York: Oxford University Press, 1972.

————. *Patterns of Intention: On the Historical Explanation of Pictures.* New Haven: Yale University Press, 1986.

Belting, Hans. *The End of the History of Art?,* trans. Christopher Wood. Chicago: University of Chicago Press, 1987.

Benjamin, Walter. "Edward Fuchs, Collector and Historian." In *One-Way Street and Other Writings,* trans. Edmund Jephcott and Kingsley Shorter; intro. Susan Sontag. London: NLB, 1979.

————. "Theses on the Philosophy of History." In *Illuminations,* ed. Hannah Arendt, trans. Harry Zohn. New York: Schocken, 1969.

Bennett, Tony. *Formalism and Marxism.* London: Methuen, 1979.

Bercovitch, Sacvan, ed. *Reconstructing American Literary History.* Cambridge, Mass.: Harvard University Press, 1986.

Bigsby, C. W. E., ed. *Approaches to Popular Culture.* London: Arnold, 1976.

Blassingame, John W. "Black Autobiographies as Histories and Literature." *Black Scholar* 5 (1973–1974), 2–9.

Bloom, Harold. *The Anxiety of Influence: A Theory of Poetry.* New Haven: Yale University Press, 1973.

————. *Poetry and Repression.* New Haven: Yale University Press, 1976.

Braudy, Leo. *Narrative Form in History and Fiction.* Princeton: Princeton University Press, 1970.

Brazier, Paul. *Art History in Education: An Annotated Bibliography,* intro. Anthony Dyson; foreword Peter Murray. London: Heineman Educational for the Institute of Education, University of London, 1985.

Bremner, Robert, ed. *Essays on History and Literature.* Columbus: Ohio State University Press, 1966.

Bromwich, David. "The Uses of Biography." *Yale Review* 73 (1984), 161–176.

Broude, Norma, and Mary D. Garrard, eds. *Feminism and Art History, Questioning the Litany.* New York: Harper and Row, 1982.

Brown, Marshall. "The Classic Is the Baroque: On the Principle of Wölfflin's Art History." *Critical Inquiry* 9:2 (December 1982), 379–404.

Bruns, Gerald L. *Inventions: Writing, Textuality and Understanding in Literary History.* New Haven: Yale University Press, 1982.

Bruss, Elizabeth W. *Autobiographical Acts: The Changing Situation of a Literary Genre.* Baltimore: Johns Hopkins University Press, 1976.

Burke, Kenneth. "Dramatism." In *The International Encyclopedia of the Social Sciences*, ed. David L. Sills. New York: Macmillan and Frye Press, 1968.

———. *A Grammar of Motives*. Berkeley: University of California Press, 1945.

Burns, Tom and Elizabeth, eds. *Sociology of Literature and Drama*. Baltimore: Penguin, 1973.

Cadenhead, I. E., Jr., ed. *Literature and History*. Tulsa: University of Tulsa Press, 1970.

Cherry, D. "Feminist Interventions: Feminist Imperatives." *Art History* 5:4 (1982), 501–507.

Clark, T. J. *The Absolute Bourgeois: Artists and Politics in France, 1848–1851*. Princeton: Princeton University Press, 1982.

———. "The Conditions of Artistic Creation." *Times Literary Supplement*, May 1974, 562.

Clifford, James Lowry. *From Puzzles to Portraits: Problems of a Literary Biographer*. Chapel Hill: University of North Carolina Press, 1970.

Cohen, Ralph, ed. *New Directions in Literary History*. Baltimore: Johns Hopkins University Press, 1977.

Cohen, Walter, and Peter Hohendahl. "Marxist Literary Critics: Problems and Proposals." *Humanities in Society* 6:2/3 (Spring–Summer 1983), 161–177.

Colie, R. L. "Johan Huizinga and the Task of Cultural History." *American Historical Review* 64 (1964), 607–630.

Creedy, Jean, ed. *The Social Context of Art*. London: Tavistock, 1970.

Culler, Jonathan. "Literary History, Allegory, and Semiology." *New Literary History* 7 (Winter 1976), 259–270.

———. *The Pursuit of Signs*. Ithaca: Cornell University Press, 1981.

Damon, Phillip, ed. *Literary Criticism and Historical Understanding*. New York: Columbia University Press, 1967.

Deinhard, Hanna. *Meaning and Expression: Towards a Sociology of Art*. Boston: Beacon Press, 1970.

De Man, Paul. "Autobiography as De-facement." *MLN* 94 (1979), 919–930.

———. "Literary History and Literary Modernity." *Daedalus* 99 (1970), 384–404.

Derrida, Jacques. *The Ear of the Other: Otobiography, Transference, Translation*, ed. Christie McDonald; trans. Peggy Kamuf. New York: Schocken Books, 1985.

———. "Genesis and Structure and Phenomenology." In *Writing and Difference*, trans. Alan Bass. Chicago: University of Chicago Press, 1978.

———. "The Law of Genre." *Critical Inquiry* 7 (1980), 55–82.

———. *Margins of Philosophy*, trans. Alan Bass. Chicago: University of Chicago Press, 1982.

———. *Of Grammatology*, trans. Gayatri C. Spivak. Baltimore: Johns Hopkins University Press, 1976.

Desmond, William. "Hegel, Art, and History." In *History and Systems: Hegel's Philosophy of History*, ed. Robert L. Perkins. Albany: SUNY Press, 1984.

Dickie, George. *Art and the Aesthetic: An Institutional Analysis*. Ithaca: Cornell University Press, 1974.

Doumato, Lamia. "The Literature of Women in Art." *Oxford Art Journal* 3 (1980).

Duvignaud, Jean. *The Sociology of Art*, trans. Timothy Wilson. New York: Harper and Row, 1972 [1967].

Eagleton, Terry. *Walter Benjamin, or Towards a Revolutionary Criticism*. London: NLB, 1981.

Eakin, Paul John. *Fictions in Autobiography: Studies in the Art of Self Invention*. Princeton: Princeton University Press, 1985.

Eco, Umberto. *Semiotics and the Philosophy of Language*. Bloomington: Indiana University Press, 1984.

Edel, Leon. *Writing Lives: Principia Biographica*. London: W. W. Norton, 1984.

Edel, Leon, et al. *Telling Lives, The Biographer's Art*, ed. Marc Pachter. Washington, D.C.: New Republic Books, 1979.

Egan, Susanna. *Patterns of Experience in Autobiography*. Chapel Hill: University of North Carolina Press, 1984.

Ellmann, Richard. *Golden Codgers: Biographical Speculations*. London: Oxford University Press, 1973.

Empson, William. *Using Biography*. Cambridge, Mass.: Harvard University Press, 1984.

Finch, Margaret. *Style in Art History: An Introduction to Theories of Style and Sequence*. London: Metuchen, 1974.

Foster, Kurt W. "Aby Warburg's History of Art: Collective Memory and the Social Mediation of Images." *Daedalus* 105 (1976), 169–176.

———. "Critical History of Art, or Transfiguration of Values?" *New Literary History* 3 (Spring 1972), 459–470.

Fowler, Alastair. *Kinds of Literature, An Introduction to the Theory of Genres and Modes*. Cambridge: Harvard University Press, 1982.

Frankl, Paul. *The Principles of Architectural History: The Four Phases of Architectural Style, 1420–1900*, trans. and ed. James F. O'Gorman; foreword James S. Ackerman. Cambridge: Harvard University Press, 1968.

Friedson, Anthony M., ed. *New Directions in Biography*. Honolulu: University of Hawaii Press, 1981.

Frow, John. *Marxism and Literary History*. Cambridge: Harvard University Press, 1986.

Frye, Northrop. "Literary History." *New Literary History*. 12:2 (Winter 1981), 219–225.

Gates, Henry Louis, Jr., ed. *"Race," Writing, and Difference*. Chicago: University of Chicago Press, 1987.

Gay, Peter. *Art and Act: On Causes in History—Manet, Gropius, Mondrian*. New York: Harper and Row, 1976.

Geertz, Clifford. "Art as a Cultural System." *Modern Language Notes* 91 (1976), 1473–1499.

Goldmann, Lucien. *Essays on Method in the Sociology of Literature,* trans. and ed. William Q. Boelhower. St. Louis: Telos Press, 1980.

———. *Towards a Sociology of the Novel.* London: Tavistock, 1975.

Gombrich, E. H. *Aby Warburg, An Intellectual Biography.* London: Warburg Institute, 1970; Chicago: University of Chicago Press, 1986.

———. *Art History and the Social Sciences: The Romances Lecture for 1973.* Oxford: Clarendon Press, 1975.

———. "Evolution in the Arts." *British Journal of Aesthetics* 4 : 3 (July 1964), 263–270.

———. "The Father of Art History [Hegel]." In *Tributes, Interpreters of Our Cultural Tradition.* Ithaca: Cornell University Press, 1984.

———. *Ideals and Idols: Essays on Values in History and in Art.* Oxford: Phaidon Press, 1979.

———. *In Search of Cultural History.* Oxford: Clarendon Press, 1969.

———. *Meditations on a Hobby Horse.* London: Phaidon, 1963.

———. *Norm and Form: Studies in the Art of the Renaissance.* London: Phaidon Press, 1966.

———. "A Plea for Pluralism." *American Art Journal* 3 (Spring 1971), 83–87.

———. *Reflections on the History of Art,* ed. Richard Woodfield. Berkeley: University of California Press, 1987.

———. "The Renaissance: Period or Movement?" In Arthur G. Dickens et al., *Background to the English Renaissance: Introductory Lectures.* London: Gray-Mills, 1974.

———. *The Sense of Order.* Ithaca: Cornell University Press, 1978.

———. "Style." In *International Encyclopedia of the Social Sciences,* ed. David L. Sills. New York: Macmillan and Free Press, 1968.

———. *Tributes: Interpreters of Our Cultural Tradition.* Oxford: Phaidon, 1984.

Grabar, Oleg. "On the Universality of the History of Art." *Art Journal* 42 : 4 (Winter, 1982), 281–283.

Graff, Gerald. *Professing Literature, An Institutional History.* Chicago: University of Chicago Press, 1987.

Greenberg, Clement. *The Collected Essays and Criticism,* 4 vols., ed. John Obrian. Chicago: University of Chicago Press, 1986.

Guillén, Claudio. "Literary Change and Multiple Duration." *Comparative Literature Studies* 12 (1977), 100–118.

———. *Literature as System: Essays toward the Theory of Literary History.* Princeton, N.J.: Princeton University Press, 1971.

Gumbrecht, Hans Ulrich. "History of Literature—Fragment of a Vanished Totality?" *New Literary History* 16 (Spring 1985), 467–479.

Hadjinicolaou, Nicos. *Art History and Class Struggle,* trans. Louise Asmal. London: Pluto Press, 1978.

Hall, Jacquelyn Dowd. "Second Thoughts: On Writing a Feminist Biography." *Feminist Studies* 13:1 (Spring 1987), 19–37.

Harding, Sandra, ed. *Feminism and Methodology*. Bloomington: Indiana University Press, 1987.

Hartman, Geoffrey H. "The Culture of Criticism." *PMLA* 99 (May 1984), 371–397.

———. "History-Writing as Answerable Style." In *The Fate of Reading and Other Essays*. Chicago: University of Chicago Press, 1975.

———. "Toward Literary History." *Daedalus* 99 (1970), 355–383.

Haskall, Francis. *Past and Present in Art and Taste: Selected Essays*. New Haven: Yale University Press, 1986.

Hauser, Arnold. *The Philosophy of Art History*. New York: Alfred Knopf, 1958; Evanston, Ill.: Northwestern University Press, 1985.

———. *The Social History of Art*, 2 vols., trans. Stanley Godman with the author. New York: A. Knopf, 1951.

———. *The Sociology of Art*, trans. Kenneth J. Northcott. Chicago: University of Chicago Press, 1982.

Hernadi, Paul. "Clio's Cousins: Historiography as Translation, Fiction, and Criticism." *New Literary History* 7:2 (1976), 248–257.

———. "The Erotics of Retrospection: Historytelling, Audience Response, and the Strategies of Desire." *New Literary History* 12:2 (1981), 243–252.

Hess, Thomas B., and Elizabeth B. Baker, eds. *Art and Sexual Politics*. New York: Macmillan, 1973.

Hirsch, E. D., Jr. *The Aims of Interpretation*. Chicago: University of Chicago Press, 1976.

———. "Three Dimensions of Hermeneutics." *New Literary History* 3 (Winter 1972), 245–261.

———. *Validity in Interpretation*. New Haven: Yale University Press, 1967.

Hohendahl, Peter U. "Beyond Reception Aesthetics," trans. Philip Brewster. *New German Critique* 28 (Winter 1983), 108–146.

———. *The Institution of Criticism*. Ithaca: Cornell University Press, 1982.

Holly, Michael Ann. *Panofsky and the Foundations of Art History*. Ithaca: Cornell University Press, 1984.

Holroyd, Michael. "History and Biography." *Salmagundi* 46 (1979), 13–26.

Hood, William. "In Defense of Art History: A Response to Brunilde Ridgway." *Art Bulletin* 58 (1986), 480–481.

Hughes, Peter. "Narrative, Scene, and the Fictions of History." In *Contemporary Approaches to Narrative*, ed. Anthony Mortimer. Tübingen: Narr, 1984.

Huizinga, Johan. "The Task of Cultural History." In *Men and Ideas*, trans. James S. Holmes and Hans van Marle. Princeton, N.J.: Princeton University Press, 1984.

Jameson, Fredric. "Figural Relativism, or The Poetics of Historiography." *Diacritics* 6:1 (Winter 1976), 2–9.

———. "From Criticism to History." *New Literary History* 12 (Winter 1981), 367–375.

————. *Marxism and Form*. Princeton, N.J.: Princeton University Press, 1972.

————. "Marxism and Historicism." *New Literary History* 11 (Autumn 1979), 41–73.

Janson, H. W. "Criteria of Periodization in the History of European Art." In *Sixteen Studies*. New York: Harry H. Abrams, 1974.

Jauss, Hans Robert. *Aesthetic Experience and Literary Hermeneutics,* trans. Michael Shaw. Minneapolis: University of Minnesota Press, 1982.

————. *Toward an Aesthetic of Reception*, trans. Timothy Bahti. Minneapolis: University of Minnesota Press, 1982.

Jelinek, Estelle C., ed. *Women's Autobiography, Essays in Criticism*. Bloomington: Indiana University Press, 1980.

Kamerman, Jack B., and Rosanne Martorella. *Performers and Performances: The Social Organization of Artistic Work*. New York: Praeger; South Hadley, Mass.: Bergin and Garvey, 1983.

Kermode, Frank. *A Sense of an Ending*. New York: Oxford University Press, 1967.

Kleinbauer, W. Eugene, ed. *Modern Perspectives in Western Art History: An Anthology of Twentieth-Century Writings on the Visual Arts*. New York: Holt, Rinehart, and Winston, 1971.

Kroeber, Karl. "The Evolution of Literary Study, 1883–1983." *PMLA* 99:3 (May 1984), 326–339.

Kubler, George. *The Shape of Time: Remarks on the History of Things*. New Haven: Yale University Press, 1962.

————. "Style and the Representation of Historical Time." *Annals of the New York Academy of Sciences* 138 (1967), 849–855.

————. "Toward a Reductive Theory of Visual Style." In *The Concept of Style,* rev. ed., ed. Berel Lang. Ithaca: Cornell University Press, 1987.

Kuhns, Richard. *Psychoanalytic Theory of Art, A Philosophy of Art on Developmental Principles*. New York: Columbia University Press, 1983.

Lang, Berel. *Philosophy and the Art of Writing: Studies in Philosophical and Literary Style*. Lewisburg, Penn.: Bucknell University Press, 1982.

Lang, Berel, ed. *The Concept of Style,* rev. and expanded ed. Ithaca: Cornell University Press, 1987.

Lentricchia, Frank. *After the New Criticism*. Chicago: University of Chicago Press, 1980.

————. *Criticism and Social Change*. Chicago: University of Chicago Press, 1983.

————. "The Historicity of Frye's *Anatomy*." *Salmagundi* 40 (1978), 97–121.

————. "Reading History with Kenneth Burke." In *Representing Kenneth Burke,* Selected papers from the English Institute, ed. Hayden White and Margaret Brose. Baltimore: Johns Hopkins University Press, 1982.

Levin, Harry. "Semantics of Culture." *Daedalus* 94 (Winter 1965), 1–13.

Lindenberger, Herbert. "Toward a New History in Literary Study." *Profession 84.* New York: MLA, 1984, 16–23.

Lodge, David. "Historicism and Literary History: Mapping the Modern Period." *New Literary History* 10 : 3 (Spring 1979), 547–555.

Lodge, K. R. "The Language of Art History." *Art History* 2 : 1 (1979), 73–84.

Lotman, Y. M., and B. A. Uspensky. "On the Semiotic Mechanism of Culture." *New Literary History* 9 : 2 (Winter 1978), 211–232.

McCorkel, Christine. "Sense and Sensibility: An Epistemological Approach to the Philosophy of Art History." *Journal of Aesthetics and Art Criticism* 34 (Fall 1975), 35–50.

McGann, Jerome J. *The Beauty of Inflections: Literary Investigations in Historical Method and Theory*. New York: Oxford University Press, 1985.

———. *A Critique of Modern Textual Criticism*. Chicago: University of Chicago Press, 1983.

———, ed. *Historical Studies and Literary Criticism*. Madison: University of Wisconsin Press, 1985.

———. *The Romantic Ideology*. Chicago: University of Chicago Press, 1983.

———. *Social Values and Poetic Acts: The Historical Judgment of Literary Work*. Cambridge: Harvard University Press, 1988.

———. "The Text, the Poem, and the Problem of Historical Method." *New Literary History* 12 (1981), 269–288.

Macherey, Pierre. *A Theory of Literary Production*, trans. Geoffrey Wall. London: Routledge and Kegan Paul, 1978.

Manning, Frank E. *The Celebration of Society: Perspectives on Contemporary Cultural Performance*. Bowling Green, Ohio: Bowling Green Popular Press, 1983.

Miller, J. Hillis. "Narrative and History." *ELH* 41 (1974), 455–473.

Morson, Gary Saul, ed. *Literature and History, Theoretical Problems and Russian Case Studies*. Stanford: Stanford University Press, 1986.

Nadel, Ira Bruce. *Biography: Fiction, Fact, and Form*. New York: St. Martin's Press, 1984.

Nochlin, Linda. "Why Have There Been No Great Women Artists?" *Art News* 169 : 9 (January 1971), 22–39, 67–71; reprinted in *Art and Sexual Politics: Women's Liberation, Women Artists, and Art History*, ed. Thomas B. Hess and Elizabeth C. Baker. New York: Macmillan, 1973.

Novarr, David. *The Lines of Life: Theories of Biography 1880–1970*. West Lafayette, Ind.: Purdue University Press, 1986.

Olney, James, ed. *Autobiography: Essays Theoretical and Critical*. Princeton: Princeton University Press, 1980.

———. *Metaphors of Self, The Meaning of Autobiography*. Princeton: Princeton University Press, 1972.

Orenstein, Gloria Feman. "Art History." *Signs* 1 (Winter 1975), 505–525.

Panofsky, Erwin. *Idea: A Concept in Art Theory*, trans. Joseph J. S. Peake. Columbia: University of South Carolina Press, 1968.

———. *Meaning in the Visual Arts: Papers in and on Art History*. Garden City: Doubleday, 1955; rpt. Chicago: University of Chicago Press, 1982.

Parker, Roszika, and Griselda Pollock. *Old Mistresses: Women, Art and Iconology.*
London: Routledge and Kegan Paul, 1981.

Passmore, John. "History of Art and History of Literature: A Commentary."
New Literary History 3 (1974), 575–587.

Pechter, Edward. "The New Historicism and Its Discontexts: Politicizing
Renaissance Drama." *PMLA* 102:3 (May 1987), 292–303.

Pierce, C. S. "The Logic of Drawing History from Ancient Documents."
Collected Papers, vol. 7, chapter 3, ed. A. W. Burks. Cambridge, Mass.: Harvard
University Press, 1958.

Podro, Michael. *The Critical Historians of Art.* New Haven: Yale University Press,
1982.

———. "Hegel's Dinner Guests and the History of Art." *New Lugano Review*
(Spring 1977), 19–25.

Preziosi, Donald. "Constru(ct)ing the Origins of Art." *Art Journal* 42:4 (1982),
320–325.

Rampersad, Arnold. "Biography, Autobiography, and Afro-American Culture."
Yale Review 73 (1983), 1–16.

Rees, A. L., and Frances Borzello, eds. *The New Art History.* London: Camden
Press, 1986.

Reiss, Timothy J. *The Discourse of Modernism.* Ithaca: Cornell University Press,
1982.

Ridgway, Brunilde Sismonda. "The State of Research in Ancient Art." *Art
Bulletin* 58 (1986), 8–23.

Roberts, David D. *Benedetto Croce and the Uses of Historicism.* Berkeley: University
of California Press, 1987.

Rosand, David. "Art History and Criticism: The Past as Present." *New Literary
History* 5 (Spring 1974), 435–445.

Ryan, Michael. *Marxism and Deconstruction: A Critical Articulation.* Baltimore:
Johns Hopkins University Press, 1982.

Salerno, Luigi. "Historiography." *Encyclopedia of World Art* 7 (1963), 507–534.

Schabert, Ina. "Fictional Biography, Factual Biography and Their
Contaminations." *biography* 5:1 (Winter 1982), 1–16.

Schulz, Leonard, and Walter Wetzels, eds. *Literature and History.* Lanham, Md.:
University Press of America, 1983.

Shils, Edward. *Tradition.* Chicago: University of Chicago Press, 1981.

Showalter, Elaine, ed. *The New Feminist Criticism: Essays on Women, Literature,
and Theory.* London: Virago, 1986.

Silbermann, A. "Introductory Definitions of the Sociology of Art." *International
Social Science Journal* 20:4 (1968), 567–588.

Smith, Sidonie. *A Poetics of Women's Autobiography.* Bloomington: Indiana
University Press, 1987.

Spacks, Patricia M. "Women's Stories, Women's Selves." *Hudson Review* 30 (1977),
29–46.

Spengemann, William C. *The Forms of Autobiography: Episodes in the History of a Literary Genre*. New Haven: Yale University Press, 1980. See bibliographical essay, pp. 170–245.

Stanton, Domna C., ed. *The Female Autograph*. New York: New York Literary Forum, 1984.

Starobinski, Jean. "The Meaning of Literary History." *New Literary History* 7 (Autumn 1975), 83–88.

Steinberg, Leo. "Objectivity and the Shrinking Self." *Daedalus* 98 (Summer 1969), 824–836.

Summers, David. "Conventions in the History of Art." *New Literary History* 13 (1981), 103–125.

———. "The 'Visual Arts' and the Problem of Art Historical Description." *Art Journal* 42:4 (1982), 301–310.

Sypher, Wylie, ed. *Art History: An Anthology of Modern Criticism*. New York: Vintage, 1963.

Taylor, Donald S. "Literary Criticism and Historical Inference." *Clio* 5 (1976) 345–370.

Toliver, Harold. *The Past That Poets Make*. Cambridge: Harvard University Press, 1981.

Turner, Victor. *Dramas, Fields, and Metaphors: Symbolic Action in Human Society*. Ithaca: Cornell University Press, 1974.

———. *From Ritual to Theatre: The Human Seriousness of Play*. New York: Performing Arts Journal Publications, 1982.

Turner, Victor, and Edward M. Bruner, eds. *The Anthropology of Experience*, epilogue by Clifford Geertz. Urbana: University of Illinois Press, 1986.

Vanderbilt, Kermit. *American Literature and the Academy: The Roots, Growth, and Maturity of a Profession*. Philadelphia: University of Pennsylvania Press, 1987.

Wallis, Mieczyslaw. "The History of Art as the History of Semantic Structures." In *Arts and Signs*. Bloomington: Indiana University Press, 1975.

Weimann, Robert. *Structure and Society in Literary History: Studies in the History and Theory of Historical Criticism*, exp. ed. Charlottesville: University Press of Virginia, 1984.

Weintraub, Karl J. "Autobiography and Historical Consciousness." *Critical Inquiry* 1:4 (1975), 821–848.

———. *The Value of the Individual: Self and Circumstance in Autobiography*. Chicago: University of Chicago Press, 1978.

Wellek, René. "The Concept of Evolution in Literary History." In *Concepts of Criticism*. New Haven: Yale University Press, 1963.

———. *The Disciplines of Criticism*, ed. Peter Demetz, Thomas Greene, and Lowry Nelson, Jr. New Haven: Yale University Press, 1968.

———. "English Literary Historiography during the Nineteenth Century." In *Discriminations: Further Concepts of Criticism*. New Haven: Yale University Press, 1970.

————. *A History of Modern Criticism, 1750–1950*. 6 vols. New York: Cambridge University Press, 1965–1986.

Wellek, René, and Austin Warren. *Theory of Literature*. 3rd ed. New York: Harcourt, Brace, and World, 1956.

Werckmeister, O. K. "Marx on Ideology and Art." *New Literary History* 4:3 (Spring 1973), 501–520.

————. "Radical Art History." *Art Journal* 42:4 (Winter 1982), 284–291.

White, Hayden. "Literary History: The Point of It All." *New Literary History* 2 (1970–1971), 173–186.

————. "The Problem of Change in Literary History." *New Literary History* 7:1 (Autumn 1975), 97–111.

Whittemore, Reed. *Pure Lives: The Early Biographies*. Baltimore: Johns Hopkins University Press, 1988.

Williams, Raymond. *Culture and Society 1780/1950*. New York: Harper and Row, 1958.

————. *Keywords*. London: Fontana, 1976.

————. *Marxism and Literature*. Oxford: Oxford University Press, 1977.

————. *The Sociology of Culture*. New York: Schocken Books, 1981.

Wolff, Janet. *Aesthetics and the Sociology of Art*. London: George Allen and Unwin, 1983.

————. *The Social Production of Art*. London: Macmillan, 1981.

Wollheim, Richard. *Art and Its Objects, with Six Supplemental Essays,* 2nd ed. Cambridge: Cambridge University Press, 1980.

Zerner, H. "Alois Riegl: Art, Value, and Historicism." *Daedalus* 105:1 (Winter 1976), 177–188.

General Historiography: Methodology, Criticism, and Theory

Abrams, Philip. *Historical Sociology*. Ithaca: Cornell University Press, 1982.

Albin, Mel, ed. *New Directions in Psychohistory: The Adelphi Papers in Honor of Erik H. Erikson*. Lexington, Mass.: Lexington Books, 1980.

Anderson, Perry. *Arguments within English Marxism*. London: New Left Books, 1980.

Ankersmit, F. R. *Narrative Logic: A Semantic Analysis of Historian's Language*. The Hague: Martinus Nijhoff, 1983.

Apel, Karl-Otto. *Understanding and Explanation,* trans. Georgia Warnke. Cambridge, Mass.: MIT Press, 1984.

Arendt, Hannah. "The Concept of History." In *Between Past and Future*. New York: Viking Press, 1981.

Aron, Raymond. *History, Truth, Liberty,* ed. Franciszek Draus; memoir by Edward Shils. Chicago: University of Chicago Press, 1985.

———. *Introduction to the Philosophy of History*. Ithaca: Cornell University Press, 1978.

Atkinson, R. F. *Knowledge and Explanation in History*. Ithaca: Cornell University Press, 1978.

Bann, Stephen. *The Clothing of Clio: A Study of the Representation of History in Nineteenth-Century Britain and France*. Cambridge: Cambridge University Press, 1984.

———. "Towards a Critical Historiography: Recent Work in Philosophy of History." *Philosophy* 56 (1981), 365–385.

Barnard, F. M. "Accounting for Actions: Causality and Teleology." *History and Theory* 20 : 3 (1981), 291–312.

———. "Natural Growth and Purposive Development: Vico and Herder." *History and Theory* 18 : 1 (1979), 16–36.

Barnes, Barry. *T. S. Kuhn and Social Science*. New York: Columbia University Press, 1982.

Barraclough, Geoffrey. *Main Trends in History*. New York: Holmes and Meier, 1978.

Barthes, Roland. "Historical Discourse." In *Introduction to Structuralism*, ed. Michael Lane. New York: Basic Books, 1970.

———. *Michelet*, trans. Richard Howard. New York: Hill and Wang, 1987.

Barzun, Jacques. *Clio and the Doctors: Psycho-history, Quanto-history and History*. Chicago: University of Chicago Press, 1974.

Bauman, Richard. *Story, Performance, and Event: Contextual Studies of Oral Narrative*. Cambridge: Cambridge University Press, 1986.

Becker, Carl. "What Are Historical Facts?" In *Ideas in History*, 2 vols., ed. Ronald H. Nash. New York: Dutton, 1969.

Beer, Samuel H., et al. "New Trends in Historiography." *Daedalus* 98 (1969), 891–976.

Berger, Peter, and Hansfried Kellner. *Sociology Reinterpreted, An Essay on Method and Vocation*. Garden City, N.Y.: Doubleday and Anchor Books, 1981.

Berkhofer, Robert F. "Clio and the Culture Concept: Some Impressions of a Changing Relationship in American Historiography." In *The Idea of Culture in the Social Sciences*, ed. Louis Schneider and Charles M. Bonjean. Cambridge: Cambridge University Press, 1973.

Berlin, Isaiah. *Against the Current: Essays in the History of Ideas*. New York: Viking Press, 1980.

———. *Concepts and Categories: Philosophical Essays*, ed. Henry Hardy; intro. Bernard Williams. New York: Viking Press, 1979.

———. *Four Essays on Liberty*. London: Oxford University Press, 1969.

———. *Historical Inevitability*. London: Oxford University Press, 1954.

———. *Vico and Herder: Two Studies in the History of Ideas*. New York: Viking Press, 1976.

Blackburn, Robin, ed. *Ideology in Social Science*. London: Fontana, 1972.

Bloch, Marc. *The Historian's Craft*, trans. Peter Putnam; intro. Joseph R. Strayer. New York: Alfred Knopf, 1953.

Bourdieu, Pierre. *Outline of a Theory of Practice*, trans. Richard Nice. Cambridge: Cambridge University Press, 1977 (1972).

Braudel, Fernand. *Afterthoughts on Material Civilization and Capitalism*, trans. Patricia M. Ranum. Baltimore: Johns Hopkins University Press, 1977.

———. "Foreword." In T. Stoianovich, *French Historical Method*. Ithaca: Cornell University Press, 1976.

———. *On History*, trans. Sarah Matthews. Chicago: University of Chicago Press, 1980.

Breisach, Ernst. *Historiography, Ancient, Medieval and Modern*. Chicago: University of Chicago Press, 1983 (extensive bibliography).

Brown, Richard Harvey, and Stanford M. Lyman, eds. *Structure, Consciousness, and History*. Cambridge: Cambridge University Press, 1978.

Burke, Kenneth. *Attitudes toward History*, 3rd ed. Berkeley: University of California Press, 1984.

Burke, Peter. *Popular Culture in Early Modern Europe*. London: T. Smith, 1978.

———. *Sociology and History*. London: G. Allen and Unwin, 1980.

———. *Vico*. New York: Oxford University Press, 1985.

Callinicas, Alex. *Making History: Agency, Structure and Change in Social Theory*. Ithaca: Cornell University Press, 1987.

Canary, R. H., and H. Kozicki, eds. *The Writing of History: Literary Form and Historical Understanding*. Madison: University of Wisconsin Press, 1978.

Carr, David. *Phenomenology and the Problem of History*. Evanston: Northwestern University Press, 1974.

———. *Time, Narrative, and History*. Bloomington: Indiana University Press, 1986.

Carr, David, et al., eds. *Philosophy of History and Contemporary Historiography*. Ottawa: Ottawa University Press, 1982.

Carrard, Philippe. "Writing the Past: Le Roy Ladurie and the Voice of the New History." *Studies in Twentieth Century Literature* 10:1 (Fall 1985), 9–30.

Carroll, Berenice, ed. *Liberating Women's History*. Urbana: University of Illinois Press, 1976.

Certeau, Michel de. *The Writing of History*, trans. Tom Conley. New York: Columbia University Press, 1988.

Clifford, James, and George E. Marcus, eds. *Writing Culture, The Poetics and Politics of Ethnography*. Berkeley: University of California Press, 1986.

Cohen, G. A. *Karl Marx's Theory of History: A Defence*. Oxford: Oxford University Press, 1978.

Cohen, Jon S. "The Achievements of Economic History: The Marxist School." *Journal of Economic History* 38:1 (March 1978), 29–57.

Cohen, Sande. *Historical Culture: On the Recording of an Academic Discipline.* Berkeley: University of California Press, 1986.

———. "Structuralism and the Writing of Intellectual History." *History and Theory* 17 (1978), 175–206.

Conceptual Frameworks in Women's History. Bronxville, N.Y.: Sarah Lawrence Publications, 1976.

Danto, Arthur C. *Analytical Philosophy of History.* Cambridge: Cambridge University Press, 1965.

Davis, Natalie Zemon. "The Possibilities of the Past." *Journal of Interdisciplinary History* 12 : 2 (1981), 267–275.

———. "'Women's History' in Transition: The European Case." *Feminist Studies* 3 : 3/4 (Winter 1975/1976), 83–103.

Delzell, Charles E., ed. *The Future of History.* Nashville: Vanderbilt University Press, 1976.

Douglas, Mary. *Cultural Bias.* London: Royal Anthropological Institute of Great Britain and Ireland, 1978.

———. *How Institutions Think.* Syracuse, N.Y.: Syracuse University Press, 1986.

———. *Implicit Meanings.* Boston: Routledge and Kegan Paul, 1975.

———. *Natural Symbols: Explorations in Cosmology,* 2nd ed. London: Barrie and Jenkins, 1973.

Dray, William. *Laws and Explanation in History.* London: Oxford University Press, 1957.

———. "On the Nature and Role of Narrative in Historiography." *History and Theory* 10 : 2 (1971), 153–171.

———. *Perspectives on History.* New York: Harper and Row, 1966.

———. *Philosophical Analysis and History.* New York: Harper and Row, 1966.

———. *Philosophy of History.* Englewood Cliffs, N.J.: Prentice-Hall, 1964.

Dumoulin, J., and D. Moisi, eds. *The Historian between the Ethnologist and the Futurologist.* Paris/The Hague: Mouton, 1973.

Elias, Norbert. *The Civilizing Process,* 2 vols., trans. Edmund Jephcott. 1, *The History of Manners;* 2, *Power and Civility.* New York: Pantheon Books, 1982.

———. "Introduction: Sociology and History." In *The Court Society,* trans. Edmund Jephcott. New York: Pantheon Books, 1983.

———. *What Is Sociology?,* trans. Stephen Mennell and Grace Morrissey; foreword by Reinhard Bendix. New York: Columbia University Press, 1978.

Elton, G. R. *The Practice of History.* London: Methuen, 1967.

Erikson, Erik H. *Life History and the Historical Moment.* New York: Norton, 1975.

Evans-Pritchard, E. E. *Anthropology and History.* Cambridge: Cambridge University Press, 1961.

Fain, Haskell. *Between Philosophy and History.* Princeton: Princeton University Press, 1970.

Febvre, Lucien. *A New Kind of History,* ed. Peter Burke. London: Routledge and Kegan Paul, 1973.

Ferro, Marc. *The Use and Abuse of History, or How the Past Is Taught.* Boston: Routledge and Kegan Paul, 1984.

Finley, M. I. *Ancient History: Evidence and Models.* New York: Viking Press, 1986.

———. "'Progress' in Historiography." *Daedalus* 106 (Summer 1977), 124–142.

———. *The Use and Abuse of History.* New York: Viking Press, 1975.

Fischer, David Hackett. *Historians' Fallacies: Toward a Logic of Historical Thought.* New York: Harper and Row, 1970.

Fleischer, Helmut. *Marxism and History,* trans. Eric Mosbacher. New York: Harper, 1973.

Fogel, Robert W., and G. R. Elton. *Which Road to the Past?: Two Views of History.* New Haven: Yale University Press, 1983.

Forster, Robert. "Achievements of the Annales School." *Journal of Economic History* 38:1 (March 1978), 58–76.

Foucault, Michel. *The Archaeology of Knowledge,* trans. A. M. Sheridan Smith. New York: Harper and Row, 1976.

———. "History, Discourse and Discontinuity," trans. Anthony M. Nazzaro. *Salmagundi* 20 (Summer–Fall 1972), 225–248.

———. *Language, Counter-Memory, Practice,* ed. Donald F. Bouchard; trans. Donald F. Bouchard and Sherry Simon. Ithaca: Cornell University Press, 1977.

———. "Nietzsche, Genealogy, History." In *Language, Counter-Memory, Practice,* ed. Donald F. Bouchard. Ithaca: Cornell University Press, 1977.

———. *The Order of Things: An Archaeology of the Human Sciences.* New York: Pantheon Books, 1970.

———. "Orders of Discourse." *Social Science Information* 10 (1971), 7–30.

———. "Politics and the Study of Discourse." *Ideology and Consciousness* 3 (Spring 1978), 7–26.

Freeman, David. "Psychoanalytic Narration and the Problem of Historical Knowledge." *Psychoanalysis and Contemporary Thought* 8 (1985), 133–182.

Friedlander, Saul. *History and Psychoanalysis, An Inquiry into the Possibilities and Limits of Psychohistory,* trans. Susan Suleiman. New York: Holmes and Meier, 1978.

Funke, Gerhard. "Phenomenology and History." In *Phenomenology and the Social Sciences,* ed. Maurice Natanson. Evanston, Ill.: Northwestern University Press, 1973.

Furet, François. *In the Workshop of History,* trans. Jonathan Mandelbaum. Chicago: University of Chicago Press, 1984 [Paris, 1982].

Gadamer, Hans G. "The Problem of Historical Consciousness." In *Interpretative Social Science: A Reader,* ed. P. Rabinow and W. Sullivan. Berkeley: University of California Press, 1979.

———. *Truth and Historicity.* The Hague: M. Nijhoff, 1972.

———. *Truth and Method,* 2nd ed., trans. and ed. Garrett Barden and John Cumming. New York: Continuum, 1982.

Gallie, W. B. *Philosophy and the Historical Understanding,* 2nd ed. New York: Schocken, 1968.

Gardiner, Patrick, ed. *The Philosophy of History.* Oxford: Oxford University Press, 1974.

Garfinkel, Harold. *Studies in Ethnomethodology.* Cambridge, England: Polity Press, 1985.

Gay, Peter. *Freud for Historians.* New York: Oxford University Press, 1986.

———. *Style in History.* New York: Basic Books, 1974.

Gay, Peter, and Gerald J. Cavanaugh, eds. *Historians at Work.* 4 vols. New York: Harper and Row, 1972–1975.

Geertz, Clifford. *The Interpretation of Cultures: Selected Essays.* New York: Basic Books, 1973.

———. *Local Knowledge, Further Essays in Interpretative Anthropology.* New York: Basic Books, 1983.

———. *Works and Lives: The Anthropologist as Author.* Palo Alto: Stanford University Press, 1988.

Gellner, Ernest. *Thought and Change.* London: Weidenfeld and Nicolson, 1964.

Giddens, Anthony. *The Constitution of Society: Introduction to the Theory of Structuration.* Berkeley: University of California Press, 1984.

Giddens, Anthony, and Jonathan H. Turner, eds. *Social Theory Today.* Stanford: Stanford University Press, 1987.

Gilbert, Felix. *History: Choice and Commitment.* Cambridge, Mass.: Harvard University Press, 1977.

———. "Intellectual History: Its Aims and Methods." *Daedalus* 100 (Winter 1971), 80–97.

Gilbert, Felix, and Stephen Graubard, eds. *Historical Studies Today.* New York: W. W. Norton, 1972.

Gillespie, Michael Allen. *Hegel, Heidegger and the Ground of History.* Chicago: University of Chicago Press, 1984.

Ginzburg, Carlo. "Morelli, Freud, and Sherlock Holmes: Clues and Scientific Method." *History Workshop* 9 (1980), 5–36.

Godelier, Maurice. "Intrastructures, Societies, and History." *Current Anthropology* 19:4 (1978), 763–771.

———. *Perspectives In Marxist Anthropology,* trans. Robert Brain. New York: Cambridge University Press, 1977.

Goldstein, Jan. "Foucault among the Sociologists: The 'Disciplines' and the History of the Professions." *History and Theory* 23:1 (1984), 170–192.

Goldstein, L. J. *Historical Knowing.* Austin: University of Texas Press, 1976.

Goodman, Nelson. *Ways of Worldmaking.* Indianapolis: Hackett Publishing, 1978.

Gorman, J. L. *The Expression of Historical Knowledge.* Edinburgh: University of Edinburgh Press, 1982.

Habermas, Jürgen. *Communication and the Evolution of Society,* trans. and intro. Thomas McCarthy. Boston: Beacon, 1979.

———. "History and Evolution." *Telos* 39 (1979), 5–44.

———. *Knowledge and Human Interests,* 2nd ed., trans. Jeremy J. Shapiro. London: Heinemann, 1978.

———. *The Theory of Communicative Action,* trans. Thomas McCarthy. Boston: Beacon Press, 1984.

Haidu, Peter. "Semiotics and History." *Semiotica* 40:3–4 (1982), 187–228.

Hamerow, Theodore S. *Reflections on History and Historians.* Madison: University of Wisconsin Press, 1987.

Handlin, Oscar. *Truth in History.* Cambridge, Mass.: Belknap Press, 1979.

Harris, Marvin. *Cultural Materialism: The Struggle for a Science of Culture.* New York: Random House, 1979.

———. *The Rise of Anthropological Theory: A History of Theories of Culture.* New York: Crowell, 1968.

Hartsock, Nancy. *Money, Sex and Power: Toward a Feminist Historical Materialism.* New York: Longman, 1983.

Heller, Agnes. *A Theory of History.* London: Routledge and Kegan Paul, 1982.

Henige, David. *Oral Historiography.* London: Longman, 1982.

Hexter, J. H. *Doing History.* Bloomington: Indiana University Press, 1971.

———. "Fernand Braudel and the *Monde Braudelien.*" *Journal of Modern History* 44:4 (December 1972), 480–541.

———. *The History Primer.* New York: Basic Books, 1971.

———. *On Historians.* Cambridge, Mass.: Harvard University Press, 1979.

———. *Reappraisals in History,* 2nd ed. Chicago: University of Chicago Press, 1979.

Higham, John, and Paul K. Conkin, eds. *New Directions in American Intellectual History.* Baltimore: Johns Hopkins University Press, 1979.

Hirst, Paul Q. *Marxism and Historical Writing.* London: Routledge and Kegan Paul, 1985.

———. *Social Evolution and Sociological Categories.* New York: Holmes and Meier, 1976.

History and Theory. 1961–present. See bibliographies of works in the philosophy of history in *Beihefte* 1, 3, 7, 10, 12, 13, 18.

Hobsbawm, Eric. "From Social History to the History of Society." In *Historical Studies Today,* ed. Felix Gilbert & Stephen R. Graubard. New York: Norton, 1971.

———. "Karl Marx's Contribution to Historiography." In *Ideology in Social Science,* ed. Robin Blackburn. London: Fontana, 1972.

———. "Marx and History." *New Left Review* 143 (1984), 39–50.

———. "The Revival of Narrative: Some Comments." *Past and Present* 86 (February 1980), 3–8.

———. "The Social Function of the Past." *Past and Present* 55 (1972), 3–17.

Hodder, Ian. *Reading the Past: Current Approaches to Interpretation in Archaeology.* New York: Cambridge University Press, 1987.

Hollinger, D. A. "T. S. Kuhn's Theory of Science and Its Implications for History." *American Historical Review* 78 (1973), 370–393.

Hoy, David Couzens. "History, Historicity, and Historiography in *Being and Time*." In *Heidegger and Modern Philosophy,* ed. Michael Murray. New Haven: Yale University Press, 1978.

Hughes, John, et al., eds. *Classical Disputes In Sociology.* London: Allen and Unwin, 1987.

Hughes, Stuart H. *History as Art and as Science.* New York: Harper and Row, 1964.

Hutton, Patrick H. "The History of Mentalities: The New Map of Cultural History." *History and Theory* 20 : 3 (1981), 237–259.

Iggers, Georg G. *The German Conception of History,* rev. ed. Middletown, Conn.: Wesleyan University Press, 1983.

———. *New Directions in European Historiography,* rev. ed. Middletown, Conn.: Wesleyan University Press, 1984.

Jaeger, Hans. "Generations in History: Reflections on a Controversial Concept." *History and Theory* 24 : 3 (1985), 273–292.

Kammen, Michael, ed. *The Past before Us.* Ithaca: Cornell University Press, 1980.

Kaplan, Steven L., ed. *Understanding Popular Culture.* Berlin: Mouton, 1984.

Kellner, Hans. "Disorderly Conduct: Braudel's Mediterranean Satire." *History and Theory* 18 (1979), 197–222.

———. "Time Out: The Discontinuity of Historical Consciousness." *History and Theory* 14 : 3 (1975), 275–296.

Kelly, Joan. *Women, History, and Theory: The Essays of Joan Kelly.* Chicago: University of Chicago Press, 1984.

Kinser, Samuel. "Annalistic Paradigm? The Geohistorical Structure of Fernand Braudel." *American Historical Review* 86 (1981), 63–105.

———. "Capitalism Enshrined: Braudel's Triptych of Modern Economic History." *Journal of Modern History* 53 (1981), 673–682.

Klein, Martin. "Bibliography of Writings on Historiography and the Philosophy of History." In *Generalization in the Writing of History,* ed. Louis Gottschalk. Chicago: University of Chicago Press, 1963.

Koselleck, Reinhart. *Futures Past, on the Semantics of Historical Time,* trans. Keith Tribe. Cambridge: MIT Press, 1985.

Kracauer, Siegfried. *History: The Last Things before the Last.* New York: Oxford University Press, 1969.

———. "Time and History." *History and Theory* 5 (1966), Beiheft 6, 65–78.

Kramnick, Isaac. "Reflections on Revolution: Definition and Explanation in Recent Scholarship." *History and Theory* 11 : 1 (1972), 26–63.

Kroeber, Alfred L., and Clyde Kluckhohn. *Culture: A Critical Review of Concepts and Definitions.* Cambridge, Mass.: The Museum, 1952.

Kuhn, Thomas. *The Essential Tension: Selected Studies in Scientific Tradition and Change.* Chicago: University of Chicago Press, 1977.

———. *The Structure of Scientific Revolutions,* 2nd ed. Chicago: University of Chicago Press, 1970.

Kuzminski, Adrian. "Defending Historical Realism." *History and Theory* 18 (1979), 316–349.

———. "Names, Descriptions, and Pictures." *Review of Metaphysics* 32 (1979), 453–470.

———. "Showing and Saying: Wittgenstein's Mystical Realism." *Yale Review* 68 (1979), 453–470.

LaCapra, Dominick. *History and Criticism.* Ithaca: Cornell University Press, 1985.

———. "History and Psychoanalysis." *Critical Inquiry* 13 : 2 (Winter 1987), 222–251.

———. *Rethinking Intellectual History.* Ithaca: Cornell University Press, 1983.

LaCapra, Dominick, and Steven L. Kaplan, eds. *Modern European Intellectual History.* Ithaca: Cornell University Press, 1982.

Landers, David S., and Charles Tilly. *History as Social Science.* Englewood Cliffs, N.J.: Prentice-Hall, 1971.

Lefebvre, Henri. *The Sociology of Marx,* trans. Norbert Guterman. New York: Columbia University Press, 1982.

Le Goff, Jacques, and Pierre Nova, eds. *Constructing the Past: Essays in Historical Methodology,* intro. Colin Lucas. Cambridge: Cambridge University Press, 1985.

Lerner, Gerda. *The Majority Finds Its Past: Placing Women in History.* New York: Oxford University Press, 1979.

———. *Teaching Women's History.* Washington, D.C.: American Historical Association, 1981.

Le Roy Ladurie, Emmanual. "The Historian and the Computer." In *The Territory of the Historian,* trans. Ben Reynolds and Sian Reynolds. Chicago: University of Chicago Press, 1979.

———. *The Mind and Method of the Historian,* trans. Sian Reynolds and Ben Reynolds. Chicago: University of Chicago Press, 1981.

———. "Recent Historical 'Discoveries.'" *Daedalus* 106 (Fall 1977), 141–155.

Levine, Joseph M. *Humanism and History: Origins of Modern English Historiography.* Ithaca: Cornell University Press, 1987.

Lévi-Strauss, Claude. *The Savage Mind.* London: George Weidenfeld and Nicolson Ltd., 1966.

Lipset, Seymour Martin, and Richard Hofstadter, eds. *Sociology and History: Methods.* New York: Basic Books, 1968.

Lloyd, Christopher. *Explanation in Social History.* Oxford: Basil Blackwell, 1986. See extensive bibliography.

Loewenberg, Peter. *Decoding the Past: The Psychohistorical Approach.* New York: A. Knopf, 1983.

Lukács, Georg. *History and Class Consciousness,* trans. Rodney Livingstone. London: Merlin Press, 1971.

Lukacs, John. *Historical Consciousness or the Remembered Past.* New York: Harper and Row, 1968.

McCullagh, C. Behan. "Colligation and Classification in History." *History and Theory* 17 (1978), 267–284.

———. *Justifying Historical Descriptions*. Cambridge: Cambridge University Press, 1984.

MacFarlane, Alan. "History, Anthropology and the Study of Communities." *Social History* 5 (1977), 631–652.

MacIntyre, M. B. "Recent Australian Feminist Historiography." *History Workshop* 5 (1978), 98–110.

McLennan, Gregor. "History and Theory: Contemporary Debates and Directions." *Literature and History* 10 : 2 (Autumn, 1984), 139–164.

———. *Marxism and the Methodologies of History*. London: Verso/NLB, 1981.

MacNeish, Richard S. *The Science of Archaeology?*. North Scituate, Mass.: Duxbury Press, 1978.

Mandelbaum, Maurice. *The Anatomy of Historical Knowledge*. Baltimore: Johns Hopkins University Press, 1977.

Marías, Julián. *Generations: A Historical Method*, trans. Harold C. Raley. University, Ala.: University of Alabama Press, 1970.

Marrou, Henri I. *The Meaning of History*, trans. Robert J. Olsen. Baltimore: Helicon, 1966 [Paris, 1954].

Martin, Biddy. "Feminism, Criticism, and Foucault." *New German Critique* 27 (Fall 1982), 3–30.

Martin, Rex. *Historical Explanation: Re-enactment and Practical Inference*. Ithaca: Cornell University Press, 1977.

Mayhew, Bruce H. "Causality, Historical Particularism and Other Errors in Sociological Discourse." *Journal for the Theory of Social Behaviour* 13 (1983), 285–300.

Meier, August, and Elliott Rudwick. *Black History and the History Profession, 1915–1980*. Urbana: University of Illinois Press, 1986.

Meyerhoff, Hans, ed. *The Philosophy of History in Our Time*. New York: Anchor Books, 1959.

Miller, James. *History and Human Existence: From Marx to Merleau-Ponty*. Berkeley: University of California Press, 1979.

Mink, Louis O. "Everyman His or Her Own Annalist." *Critical Inquiry* 7 : 4 (Summer 1981), 777–783.

———. *Historical Understanding*, ed. Brian Fay, Eugene O. Golob, and Richard T. Vann. Ithaca: Cornell University Press, 1987.

———. "History and Fiction as Modes of Comprehension." *New Literary History* 1 (1970), 541–558.

———. *Mind, History, and Dialectic*. Bloomington: Indiana University Press, 1969.

———. "Narrative Form as a Cognitive Instrument." In *The Writing of History: Literary Form and Historical Understanding*, ed. R. H. Canary and H. Kozicki. Madison: University of Wisconsin Press, 1978.

———. "Philosophical Analysis and Historical Understanding." *Review of Metaphysics* 21:4 (June 1968), 667–698.

———. "Review Essay: *Historians' Fallacies* by David H. Fischer." *History and Theory* 10 (1971), 106–122.

Momigliano, Arnaldo. *Essays in Ancient and Modern Historiography*. Middletown, Conn.: Wesleyan University Press, 1977.

———. *Studies in Historiography*. New York: Harper and Row, 1966.

Morris, Wesley. *Towards a New Historicism*. Princeton: Princeton University Press, 1972.

Munz, Peter. *Our Knowledge of the Growth of Knowledge: Popper or Wittgenstein?*. London: Routledge and Kegan Paul, 1985.

———. *The Shapes of Time: A New Look at the Philosophy of History*. Middletown: Wesleyan University Press, 1977.

Murphey, Murray. *Our Knowledge of the Historical Past*. Indianapolis: Bobbs-Merrill, 1973.

Nadel, George H., ed. *History and Theory: Studies in the Philosophy of History*. New York: Harper and Row, 1965.

Nagel, Ernest. *Principles of the Theory of Probability*. Chicago: University of Chicago Press, 1982.

Nisbet, Robert A. *Social Change and History: Aspects of the Western Theory of Development*. New York: Oxford University Press, 1964.

Oakeshott, Michael. *On History and Other Essays*. Totowa, N.J.: Barnes and Noble, 1983.

Olafson, Frederick A. *The Dialectic of Action: A Philosophical Interpretation of History and the Humanities*. Chicago: University of Chicago Press, 1979.

Palmer, Richard E. *Hermeneutics: Interpretation Theory in Schleiermacher, Dilthey, Heidegger, and Gadamer*. Evanston: Northwestern University Press, 1969.

Parker, Christopher J. W. "Academic History: Paradigms and Dialectic." *Literature and History* 5:2 (Autumn 1979), 165–182.

Parker, Harold T., and Georg G. Iggers, eds. *International Handbook of Historical Studies*. Westport, Conn.: Greenwood, 1979.

Pepper, Stephen C. *World Hypotheses: A Study in Evidence*. Berkeley: University of California Press, 1966.

Perelman, Chaim. *The New Rhetoric and the Humanities: Essays on Rhetoric and its Applications,* intro. Harold Zyskind. Dordrecht, Holland: D. Reidel, 1979.

———. *The Realm of Rhetoric,* trans. William Kluback; intro. Carroll C. Arnold. Notre Dame: University of Notre Dame Press, 1982.

Perelman, Chaim, and L. Olbrechts-Tyteca. *The New Rhetoric: A Treatise on Argumentation,* trans. John Wilkerson and Purcell Weaver. Notre Dame: University of Notre Dame Press, 1969.

Polkinghorne, Donald. *Methodology for the Human Sciences: Systems of Inquiry*. Albany: State University of New York Press, 1983.

Pomper, Philip. *The Structure of Mind in History: Five Major Figures in Psychohistory.* New York: Columbia University Press, 1985.

Popper, Karl. *Objective Knowledge, An Evolutionary Approach.* Oxford: Oxford University Press, 1972.

Porter, Dale H. *The Emergence of the Past.* Chicago: University of Chicago Press, 1981.

Putnam, Hilary. *Reason, Truth, and History.* Cambridge: Cambridge University Press, 1981.

Rabb, T. K., and R. I. Rotberg, eds. *The New History: The 1980s and Beyond.* Princeton: Princeton University Press, 1982.

Rabinow, Paul, and William M. Sullivan, eds. *Interpretive Social Science: A Reader.* Berkeley: University of California Press, 1979.

Ricoeur, Paul. *The Contribution of French Historiography to the Theory of History.* Oxford: Clarendon Press, 1980.

———. "Explanation and Understanding: On Some Remarkable Connections among the Theory of the Text, Theory of Action, and Theory of History." In *The Philosophy of Paul Ricoeur,* ed. C. E. Reagan and D. Stewart. Boston: Beacon Press, 1978.

———. "History and Hermeneutics," trans. David Pellaner. *Journal of Philosophy* 73 (1976), 683–695.

———. *History and Truth,* trans. C. A. Kelbey. Evanston, Ill.: Northwestern University Press, 1965.

———. *The Reality of the Historical Past.* Milwaukee: Marquette University Press, 1984.

———. *Time and Narrative,* 3 vols., trans. Kathleen McLaughlin and David Pellauer. Chicago: University of Chicago Press, 1984–1988.

Rorty, Richard, J. B. Schneewind, and Quentin Skinner, eds. *Philosophy in History: Essays on the Historiography of Philosophy.* New York: Cambridge University Press, 1984.

Rossi, Alice. "Feminist History in Perspective: Sociological Contributions to Biographic Analysis." In *A Sampler of Women's Studies,* ed. Dorothy Gies McGuigan. Ann Arbor: University of Michigan Press, 1973.

Sahlins, Marshall. *Culture and Practical Reason.* Chicago: University of Chicago Press, 1976.

———. *Historical Metaphors and Mythical Realities.* Ann Arbor: University of Michigan Press, 1981.

Sartre, Jean-Paul. "Replies to Structuralism," trans. Robert D-Amico. *Telos* 6 (Fall 1971), 110–116.

———. *Search for a Method,* trans. Hazel E. Barnes. New York: A. Knopf, 1963.

Schmidt, Alfred. *History and Structure: An Essay on Hegelian-Marxist and Structuralist Theories of History,* trans. Jeffrey Herf. Cambridge, Mass.: MIT Press, 1981.

Seldon, Anthony, and Joanna Pappworth. *By Word of Mouth: "Elite" Oral History.* London: Methuen, 1983.

Shafer, Robert Jones. *A Guide to Historical Method,* 3rd ed. Homewood, Ill.: Dorsey, 1980.

Shaw, W. H. *Marx's Theory of History.* London: Hutchinson, 1978.

Shweder, Richard A., and Robert A. Levine, eds. *Culture Theory: Essays on Mind, Self and Emotion.* Cambridge: Cambridge University Press, 1984.

Skinner, Quentin. "Hermeneutics and the Role of History." *New Literary History* 7 (Autumn 1975), 209–232.

———. "The Limits of Historical Explanation." *Philosophy* 41 (1966), 199–215.

———. "Meaning and Understanding in the History of Ideas." *History and Theory* 8 (1969), 3–53.

Smith, Cyril Stanley. *From Art to Science: Seventy-two Objects Illustrating the Nature of Discovery.* Cambridge, Mass.: MIT Press, 1980.

———. *A Search for Structure: Selected Essays on Science, Art, and History.* Cambridge, Mass.: MIT Press, 1981.

Spence, Donald. *Narrative Truth and Historical Truth: Meaning and Interpretation in Psychoanalysis.* New York: Norton, 1982.

Stalnaker, Robert C. "Events, Periods, and Institutions in Historians' Language." *History and Theory* 6 (1967), 159–179.

Stannard, David E. *Shrinking History, On Freud and the Failure of Psychohistory.* New York: Oxford University Press, 1980.

Starn, Randolph. "Historians and 'Crisis.'" *Past and Present* 52 (August 1971), 3–22.

Stephens, Lester D. *Historiography.* Metuchen, N.J.: Scarecrow Press, 1975. Contains an annotated bibliography which itemizes additional works not listed here.

———. *Probing the Past: A Guide to the Study and Teaching of History.* Boston: Allyn and Bacon, 1974.

Stern, Fritz, ed. *The Varieties of History: From Voltaire to the Present.* Cleveland: World Publishing, 1956.

Stinchcombe, Arthur L. *Theoretical Methods in Social History.* New York: Academic Press, 1978.

Stoianovich, Traian. *French Historical Method: The Annales Paradigm.* Ithaca: Cornell University Press, 1976.

Stone, Lawrence. *The Past and the Present.* Boston: Routledge and Kegan Paul, 1981.

———. "Prosopography." *Daedalus* 100 (Winter 1971), 46–79.

———. "The Revival of Narrative: Reflections on a New Old History." *Past and Present* 85 (1979), 3–24.

Struever, Nancy S. "Historiography and Linguistics." In *International Handbook of Historical Studies,* ed. H. T. Parker and G. Iggers. Westport, Conn.: Greenwood Press, 1979.

————. *The Language of History in the Renaissance: Rhetoric and Historical Consciousness in Florentine Humanism.* Princeton: Princeton University Press, 1970.

————. "The Study of Language and the Study of History." *Journal of Interdisciplinary History* 4 (1974), 401–415.

————. "Topics in History." *History and Theory* 19 : 4, Beiheft 19 (1980), 66–79.

Suppe, Frederick, ed. *The Structure of Scientific Theories.* Urbana: University of Illinois Press, 1977.

Susman, Warren. *Culture as History: The Transformation of American Society in the Twentieth Century.* New York: Pantheon Books, 1984.

Taylor, Robert M., Jr., and Ralph J. Crandall, eds. *Generations and Change: Genealogical Perspectives in Social History.* Macon, Ga.: Mercer University Press, 1986.

Thompson, E. P. *The Poverty of Theory.* London: Merlin, 1978.

Tilly, Charles. *As Sociology Meets History.* New York: Academic Press, 1981.

Topolski, Jerzy. "Conditions of Truth in Historical Narratives." *History and Theory* 20 (1981), 47–60.

————. *Methodology of History,* trans. Olgierd Wojtasiewicz. Boston and Warsaw: D. Reidel Publishing, 1976.

Turner, Roy. *Ethnomethodology.* Harmondsworth: Penguin, 1974.

Vaughn, Stephen, ed. *The Vital Past: Writings on the Uses of History.* Athens: University of Georgia Press, 1984.

Veyne, Paul. *Writing History: Essay on Epistemology,* trans. Mina Moore-Rinvolucri. Middletown, Conn.: Wesleyan University Press, 1984 [Paris, 1971].

Vilar, Pierre. "Constructing Marxist History." In *Constructing the Past,* ed. Jacques Le Goff and Pierre Nora; trans. Ian Patterson. Cambridge: Cambridge University Press; Paris: Editions de la maison des sciences de l'homme, 1985.

————. "Marxist History, A History in the Making: Towards a Dialogue with Althusser." *New Left Review* 80 (July–August 1973), 64–106.

Voegelin, Eric. *Order and History,* 5 vols. Baton Rouge: Louisiana State University Press, 1957–1987.

Walsh, W. H. "Truth and Fact in History Reconsidered." *History and Theory* 16 : 4 (1977), 53–71.

Walters, Ronald G. "Signs of the Times: Clifford Geertz and Historians." *Social Research* 47 (1980), 537–556.

Wedgwood, C. V. *The Sense of the Past: Thirteen Studies in the Theory and Practice of History.* New York: Collier Books, 1967 (reissue, under new title, of *Truth and Opinion,* 1960).

Wehler, Hans-Ulrich. "Psychoanalysis and History." *Social Research* 47 (1980), 519–536.

Weingartner, Rudolph H. "Some Philosophic Comments on Cultural History." *History and Theory* 7 (1968), 38–59.

White, Hayden. *The Content of the Form: Narrative Discourse and Historical Representation*. Baltimore: Johns Hopkins University Press, 1987.

———. "The Discourse of History." *Humanities in Society* 2 : 1 (Winter 1979), 1–16.

———. *Metahistory: The Historical Imagination in Nineteenth-Century Europe*. Baltimore: Johns Hopkins University Press, 1973.

———. "The Narrativization of Real Events," *Critical Inquiry* 7 : 4 (Summer 1981), 793–798.

———. "The Tasks of Intellectual History." *Monist* 53 : 4 (October 1969), 606–630.

———. *Tropics of Discourse: Essays in Cultural Criticism*. Baltimore: Johns Hopkins University Press, 1978.

White, Morton. *Foundations of Historical Knowledge*. New York: Harper and Row, 1965.

Wilden, Anthony. *System and Structure*. London: Tavistock, 1972.

Williams, Brooke. "History in Relation to Semiotic." In *Frontiers in Semiotics,* ed. John Deely, Brooke Williams, and Felicia E. Kruse. Bloomington: Indiana University Press, 1986.

———. "What Has History to Do with Semiotic?" *Semiotica* 54:3/4 (1985), 267–333.

Williams, Raymond. "The Uses of Cultural Theory." *New Left Review* 158 (July–August 1986), 19–31.

Winks, Robin W. *The Historian as Detective*. New York: Harper and Row, 1968.

Winner, Irene P., and Thomas G. Winner. "The Semiotics of Cultured Texts." *Semiotica* 18 (1976), 101–156.

Wright, G. H. von. *Explanation and Understanding*. Ithaca: Cornell University Press, 1971.

———. *Freedom and Determination*. Amsterdam: North-Holland, 1980.

Wuthnow, Robert. *Meaning and Moral Order: Explorations in Cultural Analysis*. Berkeley: University of California Press, 1987.

Wuthnow, Robert, et al. *Cultural Analysis: The Work of Peter L. Berger, Mary Douglas, Michel Foucault and Jürgen Habermas*. Boston: Routledge and Kegan Paul, 1984.

Notes on Contributors

MARVIN CARLSON is the Sidney E. Cohn Professor of Theatre Studies and Distinguished Professor of Theatre and Comparative Literature at the Graduate Center of the City University of New York. He is the author of books and articles on European theatre history and on theatrical theory, including *Theories of the Theatre* (1984) and the forthcoming *Places of Performance: A Semiotic Study of Theatre Architecture,* both from Cornell University Press.

TRACY C. DAVIS, assistant professor in the Department of Drama, University of Calgary (Alberta), trained as a performer before undertaking graduate study at the University of Warrick, where she completed a doctoral dissertation on English popular and critical response to Ibsen. She has been a Webster Fellow in the Humanities, SSHRC Canada Research Fellow, and Queen's National Scholar at Queen's University (Ontario). Active in the English and Canadian women's movements, she has integrated scholarly inquiries with feminist political convictions. While preparing a book on the employment of women in the Victorian theatre, she has published articles in *New Theatre Quarterly, Theatre Notebook, Essays in Theatre, American Journal of Semiotics, Nineteenth Century Theatre Research,* and *Modern Drama.*

JOSEPH DONOHUE, professor of English at the University of Massachusetts, edits the journal *Nineteenth Century Theatre* and is general editor of "The London Stage 1800–1900: A Documentary Record and Calendar of Performances." Author of *Dramatic Character in the English Romantic Age* (Princeton, 1965) and author or editor of other studies of the late eighteenth- and nineteenth-century English theatre, he is currently completing, with Ruth Berggren, an illustrated reconstructive edition of *The Importance of Being Earnest,* to be published by Southern Illinois University Press. He is a past president of the American Society for Theatre Research and currently a member of the Executive Committee and a vice-president of the International Federation for Theatre Research.

ERIKA FISCHER-LICHTE teaches General and Comparative Literature, Drama, and Theatre at Bayreuth University. Among her publications are *Bedeutung— Probleme einer semiotischen Hermeneutik und Ästhetik* (Munich: Beck, 1979), *Semiotik des Theatres,* 3 vols. (Tübingen: Narr, 1983), books on Kleist's *Prinz von Homburg* as well as on Schiller's *Don Carlos* (Frankfurt: Diesterweg, 1985 and 1987), and approximately fifty articles on various subjects. She is the editor of *Das Drama und seine Inszenierung* (Tübingen: Niemeyer, 1985) and of *Theatre: Familiar and Foreign* (forthcoming).

JAMES V. HATCH, professor of English at the City College of New York, is co-founder of the Hatch-Billops Collection, the archives of Afro-American cultural history. He is author and editor of *Black Theatre USA* (Free Press, 1974), *Black Playwrights 1832–1977* (Bowker, 1977), and co-author of *The Roots of Black Drama*, forthcoming from Wayne State University Press in 1989. A National Endowment for the Humanities fellow, he is currently writing a biography of the black poet and playwright Owen Dodson.

HERBERT LINDENBERGER is Avalon Professor of Humanities at Stanford University, where he founded the program in Comparative Literature in 1969. His books include *On Wordsworth's "Prelude"* (Princeton University Press, 1963), *Georg Büchner* (Southern Illinois University Press, 1964), *Historical Drama: The Relation of Literature and Reality* (University of Chicago Press, 1975), *Saul's Fall: A Critical Fiction* (Johns Hopkins University Press, 1979), and *Opera: The Extravagant Art* (Cornell University Press, 1984). He is currently finishing a group of essays on the interrelations of value, history, and institutions.

BRUCE A. MCCONACHIE directs the American Studies program and teaches in the Theatre Department at the College of William and Mary. He is the co-editor of *Theatre for Working-Class Audiences in the United States, 1830–1980* (Greenwood Press, 1985) and has published on topics related to theatre historiography and American theatre history in *Theatre Journal, Studies in Popular Culture, Theatre Survey, American Music,* and other journals.

THOMAS POSTLEWAIT, associate professor in the Department of Theatre and Drama at Indiana University, is author of *Prophet of the New Drama: William Archer and the Ibsen Campaign* (Greenwood Press, 1986), editor of *William Archer on Ibsen: The Major Essays* (Greenwood Press, 1984), and co-editor (with James Paradis) of *Victorian Science and Victorian Values: Literary Perspectives* (New York Academy of Science and Rutgers University Press, 1981, 1985). Current projects include a book in progress on the concept of periodization in cultural history and an edition of the Bernard Shaw–William Archer letters and theatre reviews.

JOSEPH R. ROACH, professor of Theatre and English at Northwestern University, directs the interdisciplinary Ph.D. in Theatre and Drama. His book *Player's Passion: Studies in the Science of Acting* (University of Delaware Press) won the Barnard Hewitt Award for 1985. He is currently at work on a study of the idea of performance in the eighteenth century.

ROBERT K. SARLÓS, Ph.D., Yale University, teaches Theatre History and directs the doctoral program in Theatre at the University of California, Davis. His publications, exhibits, and lectures range in subject from Elizabethan theatre through Baroque scenic techniques to American theatre and Hungarian drama, emphasizing varied methods of research, documentation, and teaching. His book *Jig Cook and the Provincetown Players: Theatre in Ferment* (University of Massachusetts Press) received the Barnard Hewitt Award in 1983.

R. W. VINCE, who holds degrees from McMaster, Rice, and Northwestern universities, is professor of English at McMaster University, where he teaches Theatre History and Dramatic Literature. He is interested in the methods of theatre historians and has published three books on theatre historiography, *Ancient and Medieval Theatre* (Greenwood Press, 1984), *Renaissance Theatre* (Greenwood Press, 1984), and *Neoclassical Theatre* (Greenwood Press, 1988). He is editor of a forthcoming *Companion to the Medieval Theatre* and is currently working on the historiography of the colonial theatres of the Americas.

ALAN WOODS is the director of the Jerome Lawrence and Robert E. Lee Theatre Research Institute at Ohio State University, where he is also an associate professor of Theatre and director of Graduate Studies. He is a former editor of *Theatre Journal* and has published widely on topics related to American theatre history. He was trained at Columbia University and the University of Southern California and is currently working on a study of theatrical conventions.

LEIGH WOODS is the head of Theatre Studies at the University of Michigan. He wrote *Garrick Claims the Stage* (Greenwood Press) and has had articles in *Shakespeare Quarterly, Scandinavian Review, Theatre Survey, Themes in Drama,* and *Theatre Journal*. A professional actor as well, he has appeared in more than seventy productions, most recently in Stoppard's *Every Good Boy Deserves Favor* and Delbanco's *Wolf* at the University of Michigan's Project Theatre.

Index

Absolutism, 122, 129, 130, 131, 138

Acting: books and manuals, 20–21, 23, 24, 26–27, 29, 30, 89, 100, 104, 110–111, 112, 206; career, 61–62, 64, 70–71, 254, 256–257, 260, 263; characterization, 26–28, 30, 74, 88–90, 107; conventions, 23, 29–35, 100; emotional representation, 23–25, 26, 27, 28, 30, 34, 111, 112, 250–252; exhibitionism, x, 230, 231–232, 235, 243, 244; lines of business, 86, 88–90; movement, 19, 20, 24, 27, 28, 29, 31, 32, 74, 100, 102, 113, 115, 201; problem of self-identity in, 250–252, 254–256, 263–268; as a profession, 61–62, 69, 70–71, 76, 86, 248, 249, 250, 266; style, 21, 74, 99–116; teachers of, 21, 65, 89, 111. *See also* Autobiography, of actresses; Human body; Opera; Popular theatre; Theatre; Virtuosity

Adamson, W., 43, 44

Addison, J., 105

African Grove Theatre, 151, 157–159

Africanisms, 149, 150, 151–159

African theatre, 150, 151, 153

Afro-American culture: religious life of, 151–152, 153; transmission, 150, 154–159. *See also* Racism; Slavery

Afro-American theatre, x, 148–165

Aldridge, I., 148, 151, 158

Alhambra Players, 148

"Alienation effect," 30, 31, 173

American Society for Theatre Research, 7, 180

American Studies, 37–38

American Theatre Companies, 148

American Women Dramatists of the Twentieth Century, 162

Amos and Andy, 159

Amussen, S. E., 63

Andreini family, 70

Andromaque, 129

Anecdote (as evidence), 4, 6, 103, 233, 234–238, 240, 248, 252, 257, 262, 263

Annales tradition, 63

Anthropology, x, 60, 63, 99, 133, 150, 152, 154, 202

Antoine, A., 204

Arbeau, T., 206

Archaeology, 8, 15, 65

Aristocracy. *See* Social class

Aristotle, 3, 4, 9, 45, 66, 67, 74

Arnott, J., 1, 11

Artaud, A., 30, 31, 33

Art history, x, 60, 63, 67, 216

The Art of Speaking, 111, 112

Aschengreen, F., 60

Association for Canadian Theatre History, 7

Athenaeus, 2

Attitudes toward History, 48

Audience (theatre): behavior, 152–153; communal, 71–72; development, 94–97; identification, 30, 46–55; imitation, 19, 23–25; reception, 64, 65, 66, 73, 82–97, 170–171, 172; response, 64–65, 82–97; surrogation, 99–116. *See also* Empathy; Rhetoric

Aukin, L., 72

Aureng-Zebe, 204

Auster, A., 62

Autobiography: of actresses, 259–269;